A Casebook of Psychotherapy Integration

A Casebook
of Psychotherapy
Integration

EDITED BY
George Stricker and Jerry Gold

AMERICAN PSYCHOLOGICAL ASSOCIATION
WASHINGTON, DC

BP53

Published by
American Psychological Association
750 First Street, NE
Washington, DC 20002
www.apa.org

To order
APA Order Department
P.O. Box 92984
Washington, DC 20090-2984
Tel: (800) 374-2721; Direct: (202) 336-5510
Fax: (202) 336-5502; TDD/TTY: (202) 336-6123
Online: www.apa.org/books/
E-mail: order@apa.org

In the U.K., Europe, Africa, and the Middle East, copies may be ordered from
American Psychological Association
3 Henrietta Street
Covent Garden, London
WC2E 8LU England

Typeset in Goudy by Stephen D. McDougal, Mechanicsville, MD

Printer: Bookmart Press, North Bergen, NJ
Cover Designer: Berg Design, Albany, NY
Technical/Production Editor: Harriet Kaplan

The opinions and statements published are the responsibility of the authors, and such opinions and statements do not necessarily represent the policies of the American Psychological Association.

Library of Congress Cataloging-in-Publication Data

A casebook of psychotherapy integration / edited by George Stricker, and Jerry Gold. — 1st ed.
    p. cm.
  Includes index.
  ISBN 1-59147-405-1
  1. Eclectic psychotherapy. I.Stricker, George. II. Gold, Jerold R.

  RC489.E24C33 2006
  616.89'14—dc22   2005029126

British Library Cataloguing-in-Publication Data
A CIP record is available from the British Library.

Printed in the United States of America
First Edition

7/31/07

CONTENTS

CONTRIBUTORS

David M. Allen, Department of Psychiatry, University of Tennessee
Health Science Center, Memphis

Jack C. Anchin, Department of Psychology, University at Buffalo, The
State University of New York

Bernard D. Beitman, Department of Psychiatry, University of Missouri—
Columbia

Matteo Bertoni, Pacific Graduate School of Psychology, Palo Alto, CA

Larry E. Beutler, National Center on the Psychology of Terrorism, Palo
Alto, CA; Pacific Graduate School, Palo Alto, CA; Stanford
University School of Medicine, Stanford, CA; Naval Postgraduate
School, Monterey, CA

Arthur C. Bohart, Department of Psychology, California State University
Dominguez Hills; Saybrook Graduate School and Research Center,
San Francisco, CA

Robert C. Chope, Department of Counseling, College of Health and
Human Services, San Francisco State University, San Francisco, CA

Andrés J. Consoli, Department of Counseling, College of, Health and
Human Services, San Francisco State University, San Francisco, CA

Barry L. Duncan, Institute for the Study of Therapeutic Change,
Ft. Lauderdale, FL

Diana Fosha, Director and Founder, The AEDP Institute, New York, NY

Jerry Gold, The Derner Institute, Adelphi University, Garden City, NY

Marvin R. Goldfried, Department of Psychology, State University of New
York, Stony Brook

Glenn E. Good, Department of Educational, School, and Counseling
Psychology, University of Missouri—Columbia

T. Mark Harwood, Department of Psychology, Humboldt State
University, Arcata, CA

Arnold A. Lazarus, Rutgers Universit, New Brunswick, NJ; Lazarus Institute, Princeton, NJ

Jay L. Lebow, Family Institute at Northwestern and Department of Psychology, Northwestern University, Evanston, IL

James P. McCullough Jr., Department of Psychology, Virginia Commonwealth University, Richmond

Louise McCutcheon, ORYGEN Research Centre and the Department of Psychiatry, University of Melbourne, Victoria, Australia

Stanley B. Messer, Graduate School of Applied and Professional Psychology, Rutgers, The State University of New Jersey, Piscataway

Scott D. Miller, Institute for the Study of Therapeutic Change, Chicago, IL

William C. Nichols, Athens, GA

Anthony Ryle, Maudsley and South London NHS Trust, Co-ordinated Psychological Treatments Service, Munroe Clinic, Guy's Hospital, London, England

Angela M. Soth, Department of Educational, School, and Counseling Psychology, University of Missouri—Columbia

Jacqueline A. Sparks, Department of Human Development and Family Studies, University of Rhode Island, Kingston

George Stricker, The American School of Professional Psychology, Argosy University, Arlington, VA

Jimena Thomann, Pacific Graduate School of Psychology, Palo Alto, CA

Paul L. Wachtel, City College and Graduate Center, City University of New York, NY

Jeanne C. Watson, Ontario Institute for Studies in Education, University of Ontario, Toronto, Ontario, Canada

Barry E. Wolfe, Center for Training in Psychotherapy Integration, Rockville, MD

Danny Yeung, The AEDP Institute, New York, NY

A Casebook of Psychotherapy Integration

1

INTRODUCTION: AN OVERVIEW OF PSYCHOTHERAPY INTEGRATION

JERRY GOLD AND GEORGE STRICKER

The profession of psychotherapy has a relatively brief formal history. Though some writers (cf. Frank, 1961) have pointed out that every society at all points in human history has identified a group of persons whose role involved the alleviation of psychological suffering, that activity has "belonged" formally to psychotherapists for only 100 years or so. During that period of time, psychotherapists have been eager to incorporate theories, methods, ideas, and procedures that originated in other sciences and disciplines. In fact, it would be difficult to find an academic field that in some way has not had some impact on thinking and writing about psychotherapy and its practice.

However, within the discipline of psychotherapy itself, our history is marked by deep division and segregation of theories and methods. Psychotherapists of one orientation or another have been loath to learn from their clinical colleagues. Our collective behavior seems to have been governed by a powerful xenophobic fear and loathing that caused immediate and reflexive dismissal of approaches to psychotherapy that were different than one's own. When psychotherapists of one orientation did in fact take notice of the work of another school of psychotherapy, they typically did so with disdain and hostility. The clinical and research literatures were compiled primarily with reports meant to demonstrate that the writer's preferred brand of psychotherapy clinically outperformed all others, or that the author's theory was the best in terms of theoretical accuracy and sophistication. In fact, Luborsky et al. (1999) found that the allegiance of the investigator correlated with the results of psychotherapy outcome studies.

Of course, there always have been some enlightened exceptions to this majority position. Even early in the history of the field, certain psychotherapists were eager to learn from their colleagues. The contributions of these pioneers are reviewed in this chapter.

Today, in a manner that also parallels the contemporary political and sociological conditions in this country, the age of official segregation of the schools of psychotherapy largely has ended. Many if not most psychotherapists identify themselves as integrative or eclectic in orientation (Santoro, Kister, Karpiak, & Norcross, 2004); every year there are many publications whose explicit goal is to discuss and to describe the integration of different therapies; and the discipline supports a journal (*Journal of Psychotherapy Integration*) and professional organization (Society for the Exploration of Psychotherapy Integration) that have as their explicit goals the advancement of this approach to theory building, research, and practice.

The age of psychotherapeutic turf wars has ended. Are we now at a point where the sectarian preferences and prejudices that for many decades separated psychotherapists of varying orientations have completely been resolved? Probably not, and it might be most accurate to say that the attitude of "Mine is better than yours" has been replaced by the milder, more hopeful, and more humane saying, "Good fences make good neighbors." What does this mean? Psychotherapists still are trained primarily in one or two modalities and seem to refer back to those "home" theories and methods, even when they cross the fence into the next yard to ask advice of a neighbor and to borrow some tools (Stricker & Gold, 1996). One tries to co-exist peacefully with one's neighbors even when disagreements exist and, over time, people who live and work in proximity to one another may consciously or unwittingly learn from one another. Some neighbors are enthusiastic about this, and others just go along for the ride. On the old television show, *All in the Family*, the bigoted Archie Bunker and his liberal son-in-law Mike "the Meathead" eventually worked out a relationship that included grudging respect, affection, and the ability to learn from each other.

Why has interest in psychotherapy integration flourished over the last few decades? How did this new receptivity emerge in this previously contentious world? Several answers to this question have been suggested, identifying factors within the discipline of psychotherapy and in the wider sociocultural, political, and economic context in which psychotherapy exists.

A review of the factors within the field of psychotherapy (Norcross & Newman, 1992) has identified eight factors that have promoted increased efforts at integrating various therapies:

1. The ever increasing number of schools of psychotherapy.
2. The lack of unequivocal scientific support for superior efficacy of any single psychotherapy.
3. The failure of any theory to completely explain and predict pathology, or personality and behavioral change.
4. The rapid growth in the varieties and importance of short-term, focused psychotherapies.
5. Greater communication between clinicians and scholars that has resulted in increased willingness and opportunity for experimentation.
6. The effects of the grim realities of third-party support for long-term psychotherapies.
7. Identification of common factors in all psychotherapies that are related to outcome.
8. Growth of professional organizations, conferences, and journals that are dedicated to the exploration of psychotherapy integration.

Others (e.g., Gold, 1993) have pointed out that the formerly privileged and embattled status of psychotherapy as a general endeavor within the mental health professions has been challenged severely; the emergence of effective psychopharmacology has led to an intellectual shift toward biological explanations of psychopathology, and to the economic and clinical intrusions of managed care. This adversity encouraged psychotherapists to leave behind their sectarian differences and to learn from one another, perhaps for the first time.

Other more positive changes may have been responsible for the recent and rapid rise of interest in integrative therapies. Most of the original sectarian versions of psychotherapy (such as behavior therapy, client-centered therapy, and psychoanalysis) were created several generations ago. The founders and their immediate successors are gone, and the succeeding generations may have learned to be less sectarian and therefore more confident and comfortable about crossing boundaries and in using "heretical" ideas from outside any particular orientation than were earlier clinicians who were part of the process of creating a new therapeutic approach.

Finally, many psychotherapists who entered the field in the last 3 decades of the 20th century had been influenced profoundly by the social upheaval and change that had colored American and Western European life. The civil rights movement, conflict over the war in Vietnam, and the gay rights and women's rights movements all contributed to the breaking down of barriers between people and to the development of larger and more inclusive systems of thinking. Psychotherapists participated in, and sometimes led, these struggles and brought these hard-won gains back to their practices, their classrooms, and their writing and theorizing.

A BRIEF HISTORY OF PSYCHOTHERAPY INTEGRATION

Most of the early work in psychotherapy integration was derived from clinical practice and often was based on a single or a few case reports. These explorations of integration were often attempts to introduce ideas and techniques from one psychotherapeutic model (e.g., psychodynamic psychotherapy) into the framework of another model of psychotherapy (e.g., behavior therapy). These attempts were relatively narrow in scope, and they typically did not connect with a more sophisticated theoretical view of patients, of personality and psychopathology, or of psychotherapeutic change. As exploration in this area matured, however, psychotherapy integration, in its most complex and sophisticated forms, moved beyond its limited clinical derivations and offered new insights into the fields of personology and psychopathology.

The first attempt to synthesize ideas from various therapeutic models, and the contribution most often cited as the initial precursor to contemporary psychotherapy integration, was French's (1933) call to the psychoanalytic world regarding the need for analytic theory and practice that accounted for the findings of Pavlov in the area of classical conditioning. A second seminal contribution, and perhaps the first truly integrative article ever published, was Rosenzweig's (1936) formulation of the common factors hypothesis, namely, that the many varieties of psychotherapy share a limited number of essential effective ingredients. Rosenzweig's article is frequently cited even today in the psychotherapy integration literature. He is considered to be the founder of the *common factors* approach to psychotherapy integration (Duncan, 2002), which posits that all psychotherapies include similar, in not identical, interventions and processes that lead to change and differ most in the ways those interventions and processes are named.

During the 1940s and 1950s, several efforts at integrating then-current versions of psychoanalytic theory and learning theory were proposed. Many of these efforts were courageous and original but had little lasting impact on the field. However, one pioneering approach to integration has exerted a lasting impact on thinking about psychopathology and psychotherapy. John Dollard and Neal Miller (1950), in their book *Personality and Psychotherapy*, integrated central psychoanalytic ideas about unconscious motivation and conflict with concepts drawn from the learning theories of Clark Hull, Kenneth Spence, Edward Tolman, and O. Hobart Mowrer. Although many traditional psychoanalysts and learning theorists ignored or dismissed the book at the time of its publication, some in both communities who were open to contributions from other theories and from empirical research found inspiration in Dollard and Miller's unique synthesis. For example, Wachtel (1977) cited the book in his groundbreaking integration of psychoanalysis and behavior therapy, which arguably remains the single most important work in the contemporary psychotherapy integration literature.

Another highly influential work, one that was most notable for its introduction of the concept of the "corrective emotional experience," was the book *Psychoanalytic Therapy*, written by Franz Alexander and the aforementioned Thomas French (Alexander & French, 1946). The book, a rethinking of psychoanalysis, was not specifically integrative, but it introduced a theory that has affected the thinking of many integrative clinicians. Alexander and French produced one of first studies of the possibility of psychotherapeutic change arising from a multiplicity of interactive and technical factors. At the heart of this volume is a description of the clinical effects of the *corrective emotional experience*, which was defined as an interactive event between therapist and patient in which the attitudes, emotions, and behavior of the therapist were assumed to powerfully and immediately modify unconscious assumptions and perceptions derived from the patient's early development and interpersonal history. This idea and the prescriptive perspective on interventions to which it led expanded the clinician's role from the exclusive provision of insight via interpretation to include also behavioral interaction and the provision of new experience as valid therapeutic endeavors. This work also was scorned and attacked by conventionally minded analysts; nonetheless, it has served as an inspiration to psychodynamically oriented psychotherapists who wish to expand their therapeutic repertoire.

Work in this vein continued through the 1950s, 1960s, and 1970s with an increasing number of articles and books appearing in which some kind of methodological integration was proposed or described. For example, Marks and Gelder (1966) compared and found similarities between then-current versions of behavior therapy and psychoanalysis. Alexander (1963) and Beier (1966) argued that the therapist's influence on the patient could be understood within the perspective of conditioning theories, especially with regard to the reinforcement value of the therapist's responsiveness and approval. More specifically, Beier described the subtle and powerful ways through which unconscious processes and conflicts are subject to shaping and to extinction within the verbal, emotional, and interpersonal interaction of psychotherapy; he detailed an integrative therapy that he described as a synthesis of Freud and Skinner. Bergin (1968) explored the possibility of integrating behavior therapy and client-centered therapy and demonstrated that the usefulness of systematic desensitization could be improved by applying that method within the context of a warm, empathic, and *prizing* (a term used in person-centered theory and an update of the concept of unconditional positive regard) psychotherapeutic relationship. Feather and Rhodes (1972) wrote about an integrative approach that they labeled *psychodynamic behavior therapy* This creative treatment involved using behavioral techniques, such as systematic desensitization, to uncover and to resolve unconscious conflicts.

These contributions remain interesting and useful to theoretical and clinical research even today. However, they reflect the distance that existed between the clinically oriented emerging field that would become known as *psychotherapy integration* and the more theoretical and empirically driven fields of personality theory and psychopathology. Authors such as those just cited, and their like-minded colleagues, said little that was new about existing theories of personality and seemed to accept the status quo in such matters. A new era in the dialogue between personology and psychotherapy integration, and a new mode of psychotherapy integration, was ushered in by the publication of Wachtel's (1977) landmark book, *Psychoanalysis and Behavior Therapy: Toward an Integration*. This book remains the single most influential and widely cited work in modern psychotherapy integration. It is the prototype of the most complex and sophisticated form of psychotherapy integration, namely *theoretical integration*. Wachtel's integrative, psychodynamic psychotherapy was derived from his unique personality theory, which he called *cyclical psychodynamics*. This book, and the hugely positive response that it generated, opened the floodgates in the field of psychotherapy integration.

During the 1980s, many prominent psychotherapy scholars and clinicians explored the technical, theoretical, and philosophical possibilities of integrating therapies in a newly invigorated and enthusiastic way (Arkowitz & Messer, 1984). The Society for the Exploration of Psychotherapy Integration was founded in the early 1980s and began to publish the *Journal of Psychotherapy Integration* in 1991. Moreover, two thorough handbooks on psychotherapy integration, which included many of the most important integrative therapies then available, were published in the early 1990s (Norcross & Goldfried, 1992; Stricker & Gold, 1993). These handbooks demonstrated that integrative thinking had progressed beyond an exclusive focus on the synthesis of psychoanalytic and behavioral models. Current integrative therapies combine cognitive, humanistic, experiential, and family systems models with each other and with sophisticated psychoanalytic, behavioral, and humanistic components of treatment in ever more complex permutations. It was during this last decade of the 20th century that psychotherapy integration truly came of age (Arkowitz, 1991).

MODES OF PSYCHOTHERAPY INTEGRATION

Usage of the term *psychotherapy integration* is relatively recent, having become a commonly accepted descriptor after the organization of the Society for the Exploration of Psychotherapy Integration in 1983. *Psychotherapy integration* refers to the search for, and study of, the ways in which the various schools or models of psychotherapy can inform, enrich, and ultimately be combined, rather than to a specific theory or method of psychotherapy.

A consensus has been reached among authors who have contributed to the psychotherapy integration literature about a classification system for identifying the various approaches, or "modes," of contemporary psychotherapy integration (Gold, 1996; Stricker & Gold, 2003). These modes define general ways in which theory and technique can be and are integrated. The four modes of integration are known as *technical eclecticism, the common factors approach, theoretical integration,* and *assimilative integration*. Each integrative psychotherapy can be considered an example of one of these modes, and the process of psychotherapy integration makes use of these modes as well.

Technical Eclecticism

Technical eclecticism is the most clinical and technically oriented form of psychotherapy integration and involves the least attention to the integration of concepts and theories. It is closely related to what generally is called *eclectic psychotherapy* and can be approached in a very disciplined and coherent manner as well as in a more idiosyncratic form. In it, a broad and comprehensive assessment of the patient leads to the selection of clinical strategies and techniques from two or more therapies, which may then be applied sequentially or in combination. Technically eclectic assessment (such as the assessment of the BASIC ID described by Lazarus, 2002) identifies problems to be intervened in and describes the interconnections between different problems; strengths; and the cognitive, behavioral, emotional, and interpersonal characteristics of the patient. Techniques are chosen on the basis of the best clinical match to the needs of the patient, as guided by clinical knowledge and by research findings. Significant versions of technically eclectic psychotherapy are multimodal therapy (Lazarus, 1992, 2002) and prescriptive psychotherapy (Beutler, Alomohamed, Moleiro, & Romanelli, 2002). *Multimodal therapy* might best be described as a broad-spectrum behavior therapy, and that in fact was Lazarus's original name for his system. This psychotherapy evolved as Lazarus became disenchanted with the limits of then-traditional behavior therapy and is based on the supplementation of behavioral interventions with cognitive, imagery-based, and experiential interventions. Prescriptive psychotherapy (Beutler et al., 2002) is a flexible and empirically driven system in which the therapist attempts to use the research literature and clinical knowledge to match patient characteristics and the focal problems that are of immediate clinical concern with the most efficacious interventions. This therapy does not limit the schools of therapy from which it draws its techniques, aiming at the broadest application of techniques to problems.

Common Factors Approach

Common factors integration starts from the identification of specific effective ingredients of any group of therapies. As noted above, this viewpoint is based on Rosenzweig's (1936) seminal discovery that all therapies share certain change processes, irrespective of their allegiance to particular methods and theories. Frank's (1961) cross-cultural studies of various systems of healing led him to much the same conclusion, namely, that all systems of psychological healing share certain common, effective ingredients, such as socially sanctioned rituals, the provision of hope, and the shaping of an outlook on life that offers encouragement to the patient. This work remains a central touchstone of the common factors approach as well.

The integrative therapies that result from this process are structured around the goal of maximizing the patient's exposure to the unique combination of therapeutic factors that best ameliorate his or her problems. Those therapists who organize their work within an integrative common factors approach therefore aim to identify which of the several known common factors is most important in the treatment of each individual. After the most clinically significant common factors are selected, the therapist reviews the spectrum of techniques and psychotherapeutic interactions to locate those that have been found to promote and contain those factors. Garfield's (2000) common factors–based integrative therapy, which relies on insight, exposure, the provision of new experience, and the provision of hope through the therapeutic relationship, is one well-known form of common factors integration.

Theoretical Integration

Theoretical integration is the acme of integrative efforts, and it is also the most complex, sophisticated, and difficult. Theoretically integrated systems of psychotherapy result from the synthesis of aspects of various personality theories, the amalgamation of models of personality and psychopathology, and the use, in a conceptually guided way, of the mechanisms of psychological change and the techniques that produce such change from two or more traditional systems. These original integrative theories explain behavior, psychological experience, and interpersonal relationships in multidirectional and interactional terms in the context of the mutual influence of environmental, motivational, cognitive, and affective variables.

Interventions and techniques in such psychotherapies are drawn from each of the component theories. These psychotherapies also use original techniques in addition to those incorporated from the traditional therapeutic schools that are the bases of this new approach. Superficially, therapies that are technically eclectic may be identical in terms of the selection of interventions with therapies that are based on theoretical integration. However, at the theoretical level deeper distinctions emerge, including the divergence of the belief systems that guide the choice of clinical strategies and techniques on the part of the respective therapists. Theoretical integration greatly expands the vision and understanding of the therapist. It goes beyond technical eclecticism in clinical practice by increasing the number and type of intrapsychic and behavioral variables that can be targeted therapeutically. Subtle interactions among various levels and spheres of behavior; interpersonal interactions; and motivational, cognitive, and affective internal states and processes can be evaluated and intervened in from several complementary therapeutic perspectives. This expanded conceptual framework allows problems at one level or in one sphere of psychological life to be addressed in formerly incompatible ways. That is, the therapist might intervene in a problem in affect tolerance not only to help the patient to be more comfortable emotionally but also to promote change in motivation or to rid the patient of a way of thinking about emotion that maintains powerful unconscious feelings. Wachtel's cyclical psychodynamic theory (1977) and its integrative therapy was the first fully developed form of theoretical integration. Wachtel developed a psychodynamically based model of personality, psychopathology, and change that acknowledges and uses reinforcement and social learning principles and that allows the therapist to use interventions from behavioral, cognitive, systems, and experiential therapies (Wachtel, 1997). Other important examples of theoretical integration include Ryle's (1990) cognitive–analytic therapy, Allen's (1993) unified psychotherapy, and Fensterheim's (1993) behavioral psychotherapy.

Assimilative Integration

The fourth and most recently described mode of psychotherapy integration is assimilative integration. Assimilative integration occurs when the therapist maintains a central theoretical position but incorporates (assimilates) techniques drawn from other orientations. It has been the focus of much recent interest; a recent issue of the *Journal of Psychotherapy Integration* (Gold & Messer, 2001) was devoted to this topic.

Messer (1992) was the first to discuss the concept of assimilation within the context of psychotherapy integration. Messer attempted to place human behavior in general, and the actions and interactions that occur specifically in psychotherapy, in a common contextual framework by arguing that all actions are defined and contained by the interpersonal, historical, and physical context in which those acts occur. He went on to suggest that because any therapeutic intervention is an interpersonal action (and a highly complex one at that), those interventions must be defined, and perhaps even created, by the larger context of the therapy.

Assimilative integration (Messer, 1992; Stricker & Gold, 2002) is a derivative of both theoretical integration and technical eclecticism. Certain theoretically integrative approaches may be regarded as assimilative because they incorporate new techniques into the existing context of therapy (i.e., the therapist's dominant or "home" theory). When techniques are applied clinically within a theoretical context that differs from the context in which they were developed, the meaning, impact, and use of those interventions are modified in powerful ways. When these interventions (such as the use of a gestalt exercise within the context of psychodynamic therapy) are assimilated into a different theoretical orientation, their nature is altered by this new context and by the new integrative intentions and purposes of the therapist. Thus, a behavioral method such as systematic desensitization will mean something entirely different to a patient whose ongoing therapeutic experience has been largely defined by experientially oriented exploration than that intervention would mean to a patient in traditional behavior therapy. One such model of assimilative integration is the psychodynamically based integrative therapy that we have developed and described (Gold & Stricker, 2001; Stricker & Gold, 1996). In this approach, therapy proceeds according to standard psychodynamic guidelines, but methods from other therapies are used when called for, and they may indirectly advance certain psychodynamic goals as well as address the target concern effectively.

PLAN AND PURPOSE OF THE CASEBOOK

This volume is meant for students and practitioners of psychotherapy who are interested in obtaining a glimpse of the work of experienced psychotherapists who have pioneered progress in psychotherapy integration. The contributors are leaders in this particular field; their work is broadly known and widely cited. We believe that this casebook will be extremely useful as a supplementary text in basic and advanced courses in general psychotherapeutic technique as well as in graduate courses in psychology, social work, and counseling that address the topic of psychotherapy integration. We also hope that it will be useful to experienced psychotherapists who are searching for ways to expand their practice.

We have selected cases that represent the four established modes of psychotherapy integration described above as well as several that do not fit easily into that framework of categorization. Technical eclecticism is represented by Lazarus's (chap. 2) description of multimodal therapy and by the case conducted within the framework of systematic treatment selection and prescriptive therapy (Beutler, Harwood, Bertoni, & Thomann, chap. 3). Chapter 4, by Beitman, Soth, and Good, is reflective of common factors integration. Assimilative integration is represented by Stricker's (chap. 5) depiction of assimilative psychodynamic psychotherapy integration and by Wolfe's (chap. 6) description of treating an individual with a public speaking phobia. The final mode, theoretical integration, is illustrated by the eight cases included in chapters 7 through 14. Chapters 15 through 21 include cases that are on the cutting edge of psychotherapy integration and do not easily fit into the framework of the four modes. These include cases that exemplify integration of individual and couples or family therapy, three cases that are typical of a trend toward using the patient's perspective as a guide to integration, and two cases that explore the use of a philosophical perspective on integration. In the final chapter, we attempt a "meta-integration" of the various positions in the hope of pointing the way toward future trends and progress.

THE FUTURE OF PSYCHOTHERAPY INTEGRATION

It should be apparent that psychotherapy integration has moved from the fringes of psychotherapeutic activity and thinking to a much more prominent and central place. This is evident not only in the formal realms of professional and academic life, where journals are published, books are written, and psychotherapies are studied, but also in the more informal interactions that go on among practitioners. Psychotherapists of various persuasions and orientations seem to get along better these days; they talk more freely about approaches other than their own and seem to be more willing to experiment with new methods and with integrative perspectives.

At the same time, much more work remains to be done. Future progress in psychotherapy integration may be stalled or even be made impossible by overly strict demands for rigor and regularity in psychotherapy that emphasize conformity to manuals and guidelines at the expense of clinical experimentation and innovation. Pressure both within the profession of psychotherapy and from without (from government, insurance companies, and the public) for empirical support for the effectiveness of psychotherapy and for manuals that standardize psychotherapeutic practice are particularly relevant here. Although empirical support for psychotherapy is to be valued and pursued, many advances occur in the consulting room of individual therapists who cannot submit their work to large-scale research investigations.

Similarly, the essence of manualized psychotherapy (which is aimed at ensuring uniformity) runs counter to the spirit and practice of psychotherapy integration. In many ways, the term *psychotherapy integration* is synonymous with *psychotherapeutic creativity and originality*, and it is difficult to see how creativity can be accounted for and operationalized in a set of instructions, such as in a manual. Moreover, moving beyond the issue of originality per se, it is uncertain how manuals can address what is perhaps the key clinical question in psychotherapy integration: How do we identify and respond to the moment in which an integrative shift is useful, advantageous, and perhaps necessary? These moments can be described in general terms, but they arise clinically at specific moments with specific people who happen to be therapists and patients. It is nearly impossible for us to contemplate how to write an instruction book that says, "Integrate here."

Most advances in psychotherapy integration have been made by theoreticians and clinicians. Progress in the empirical evaluation of integrative psychotherapies has been slow and limited in scope, though some preliminary research support does exist for certain integrative models, such as prescriptive psychotherapy, dialectical behavior therapy, and cognitive–analytic therapy (Stricker & Gold, 2003). More and better research is needed to meet this challenge.

An intriguing and potentially important strand in the psychotherapy integration literature is concerned with integration that is initiated by the patient and with the therapist's ability to identify, accept, and make use of patients' insight into their own therapy and change. A radical set of publications (Bohart & Tallman, 1999; Duncan & Miller, 2000; Gold, 1994, 2000; Rennie, 2000) has turned the whole integrative enterprise inside out and has generated a fair amount of attention and contention. This development bears watching in the future.

Finally, the popularity and proliferation of integrative therapies may cause an ironic and unwanted problem, one that the psychotherapy integration movement in fact has meant to help alleviate. By 1990 there were more than 400 identifiable forms of psychotherapy in the English language literature alone (Gold, 1996). Integrative psychotherapists seem to be as adept at creating new forms of psychotherapy as are their nonintegrative colleagues. It is important to keep in mind that *psychotherapy integration* refers to a process, not to a product (Stricker, 1994). Otherwise, in our attempt to integrate, will we create even more separation and divergence in the field? The answer remains hidden in the future.

REFERENCES

Alexander, F. (1963). Psychotherapy in the light of learning theory. *American Journal of Psychiatry, 120,* 440–448.

Alexander, F., & French, T. (1946). *Psychoanalytic therapy.* New York: Ronald Press.

Allen, D. M. (1993). Unified psychotherapy. In G. Stricker & J. R. Gold (Eds.), *Comprehensive handbook of psychotherapy integration* (pp. 125–138). New York: Plenum Press.

Arkowitz, H. (1991). Introductory statement: Psychotherapy integration comes of age. *Journal of Psychotherapy Integration, 1,* 1–4.

Arkowitz, H., & Messer, S. (Eds.). (1984). *Psychoanalytic therapy and behavioral therapy: Is integration possible?* New York: Plenum Press.

Beier, E. G. (1966). *The silent language of psychotherapy.* Chicago: Aldine.

Bergin, A. E. (1968). Technique for improving desensitization via warmth, empathy, and emotional re-experiencing of hierarchy events. In R. Rubin & C. M. Franks (Eds.), *Advances in behavior therapy* (pp. 20–33). New York: Academic Press.

Beutler, L. E., Alomohamed, S., Moleiro, C., & Romanelli, R. (2002). Systematic treatment selection and prescriptive therapy. In F. W. Kaslow (Ed. in Chief) & J. Lebow (Vol. Ed.), *Comprehensive handbook of psychotherapy: Vol. 4. Integrative/eclectic* (pp. 255–272). New York: Wiley.

Bohart, A. C., & Tallman, K. (1999). *How clients make therapy work.* Washington, DC: American Psychological Association.

Dollard, J., & Miller, N. E. (1950). *Personality and psychotherapy.* New York: McGraw-Hill.

Duncan, B. L. (2002). The legacy of Saul Rosenzweig. *Journal of Psychotherapy Integration, 12,* 32–57.

Duncan, B. L., & Miller, S. D. (2000). The client's theory of change: Consulting the client in the integrative change process. *Journal of Psychotherapy Integration*, *10*, 169–188.

Feather, B. W., & Rhodes, J. W. (1972). Psychodynamic behavior therapy: I. Theory and rationale. *Archives of General Psychiatry*, *26*, 496–502.

Fensterheim, H. (1993). Behavioral psychotherapy. In G. Stricker & J. R. Gold (Eds.), *Comprehensive handbook of psychotherapy integration* (pp. 73–86). New York: Plenum Press.

Frank, J. (1961). *Persuasion and healing*. Baltimore: Johns Hopkins.

French, T. M. (1933). Interrelations between psychoanalysis and the experimental work of Pavlov. *American Journal of Psychiatry*, *89*, 1165–1203.

Garfield, S. (2000). Eclecticism and integration: A personal retrospective view. *Journal of Psychotherapy Integration*, *10*, 341–356.

Gold, J. R. (1993). The sociohistorical context of psychotherapy integration. In G. Stricker & J. R. Gold (Eds.), *Comprehensive handbook of psychotherapy integration* (pp. 3–8). New York: Plenum Press.

Gold, J. (1994). When the patient does the integrating: Lessons for theory and practice. *Journal of Psychotherapy Integration*, *4*, 133–154.

Gold, J. (1996). *Key concepts in psychotherapy integration*. New York: Plenum Press.

Gold, J. (2000). The psychodynamics of the patient's activity. *Journal of Psychotherapy Integration*, *10*, 207–220.

Gold, J., & Messer, S. B. (Eds.). (2001). *Journal of Psychotherapy Integration*, *11*(1).

Gold, J., & Stricker, G. (2001). Relational psychoanalysis as a foundation for assimilative integration. *Journal of Psychotherapy Integration*, *11*, 47–63.

Lazarus, A. A. (1992). Multimodal therapy: Technical eclecticism with minimal integration. In J. C. Norcross & M. R. Goldfried (Eds.), *Handbook of psychotherapy integration* (pp. 231 –263). New York: Basic Books.

Lazarus, A. A. (2002). The multimodal assessment treatment method. In F. W. Kaslow (Ed. in Chief) & J. Lebow (Vol. Ed.), *Comprehensive handbook of psychotherapy: Vol. 4. Integrative/eclectic* (pp. 241–254). New York: Wiley.

Luborsky, L., Diguer, L., Seligman, D. A., Rosenthal, R., Krause, E. D., Johnson, S., et al. (1999). The researcher's own therapy allegiances: A "wild card" in comparisons of treatment efficacy. *Clinical Psychology: Science and Practice*, *6*, 95–106.

Marks, I. M., & Gelder, M. G. (1966). Common ground between behavior therapy and psychodynamic methods. *British Journal of Medical Psychology*, *39*, 11–23.

Messer, S. (1992). A critical examination of belief structures in integrative and eclectic psychotherapy. In J. C. Norcross & M. R. Goldfried (Eds.), *Handbook of psychotherapy integration* (pp. 130–168). New York: Basic Books.

Norcross, J. C., & Goldfried, M. R. (Eds.). (1992). *Handbook of psychotherapy integration*. New York: Basic Books.

Norcross, J. C., & Newman, C. (1992). Psychotherapy integration: Setting the context. In J. C. Norcross & M. R. Goldfried (Eds.), *Handbook of psychotherapy integration* (pp. 3–46). New York: Basic Books.

Rennie, D. L. (2000). Aspects of the client's conscious control of the psychotherapeutic process. *Journal of Psychotherapy Integration, 10*, 151–168.

Rosenzweig, S. (1936). Some implicit common factors in diverse methods of psychotherapy. *American Journal of Orthopsychiatry, 6*, 412–415.

Ryle, A. (1990). *Cognitive–analytic therapy: Active participation in change.* Chichester, England: Wiley.

Santoro, S. O., Kister, K. M., Karpiak, C. P., & Norcross, J. C. (2004, April). *Clinical psychologists in the 2000s: A national study.* Paper presented at the annual meeting of the Eastern Psychological Association, Washington, DC.

Stricker, G. (1994). Reflections on psychotherapy integration. *Clinical Psychology: Science and Practice, 1*, 3–12.

Stricker, G., & Gold, J. R. (Eds.). (1993). *Comprehensive handbook of psychotherapy integration.* New York: Plenum Press.

Stricker, G., & Gold, J. (1996). An assimilative model for psychodynamically oriented integrative psychotherapy. *Clinical Psychology: Science and Practice, 3*, 47–58.

Stricker, G., & Gold, J. (2002). An assimilative approach to integrative psychodynamic psychotherapy. In F. W. Kaslow (Ed. in Chief) & J. Lebow (Vol. Ed.), *Comprehensive handbook of psychotherapy: Vol. 4. Integrative/eclectic* (pp. 295–316). New York: Wiley.

Stricker, G., & Gold, J. (2003). Integrative psychotherapies. In A. Gurman & S. Messer (Eds.), *Essential psychotherapies* (pp. 317–349). New York: Guilford Press.

Wachtel, P. L. (1977). *Psychoanalysis and behavior therapy: Toward an integration.* New York: Basic Books.

Wachtel, P. L. (1997). *Psychoanalysis, behavior therapy, and the representational world.* Washington, DC: American Psychological Association.

2

MULTIMODAL THERAPY: A SEVEN-POINT INTEGRATION

ARNOLD A. LAZARUS

The integrative approach described in this chapter is the upshot of various factors. First came my initial exposure to several different orientations, mainly the writings of Alfred Adler, Sigmund Freud, Carl Rogers, and Harry Stack Sullivan. This left me eager to acquire additional information. I set off on a journey in search of answers to the following question: What information is necessary to function as a truly effective, efficient, and successful clinician?

I attended numerous study groups, seminars, workshops, and institutes that enabled me to learn from gestalt therapists, bioenergetic analysts, hypnotherapists, family and group therapists, sex therapists, conditioning therapists, Ericksonian therapists, reality therapists, and rational–emotive therapists, among others. It became evident that patients would often receive what the purveyors of each specific school or orientation provided, whether or not that was what they needed.

Obviously, no single approach has all the answers, but each orientation offers some worthwhile methods and notions. Is it possible to band together the most salient components of the various approaches? The conflicting theories espoused by the protagonists in these differing domains proved confusing until I read London's (1963) book, which included this statement: "However interesting, plausible, and appealing a theory may be, it is techniques, not theories, that are actually used on people. Study of the effects of psychotherapy, therefore, is always the study of the effectiveness of techniques" (p. 33).

Inspired by this thought, I commenced to gather effective techniques from many orientations without subscribing to the theories that spawned them (Lazarus, 1967). I argued that to combine aspects of different theories in the hope of creating more robust methods would only create a mélange of diverse and incompatible notions, whereas technical (not theoretical) eclecticism would permit one to import and apply a broad range of potent strategies. Subsequently, I wrote at length about the pros of technical eclecticism and the cons of theoretical integration (see, e.g., Lazarus, 1995, 1996; Lazarus & Beutler, 1993).

The use of disembodied techniques without any theory to guide the therapist would result in a mishmash of methods haphazardly administered. The theoretical substrate that directs my treatment trajectory is *social and cognitive learning theory* (e.g., Bandura, 1977, 1986; Rotter, 1954), because its tenets are open to confirmation or refutation. Instead of postulating putative complexes and unconscious forces, social learning theory rests on testable developmental factors (e.g., modeling, observational and enactive learning, the acquisition of expectancies, operant and respondent conditioning, and various self-regulatory mechanisms). It must be emphasized again that my standpoint remains consistently within the orbit of social–cognitive learning theory; although I draw on effective methods from any orientation, I do not meld divergent theories.

The approach I have termed *multimodal therapy* (MMT; see, e.g., Lazarus, 1997, 2005) evolved from a series of follow-up studies. Most forms of therapy are *trimodal*—they emphasize the need to assess and address problems relating to affect, behavior, and cognition. The multimodal approach underscores seven interactive modalities. In addition to evaluating affect, behavior, and cognition, MMT emphasizes the need to examine sensory responses, mental images, interpersonal factors, and biological considerations, thus yielding a seven-point perspective from which to operate. Using the mnemonic acronym BASIC ID (taken from the initial letters of the foregoing modalities: behavior, affect, sensation, imagery, cognition, interpersonal relationships, and drugs and biological factors), MMT examines the discrete and interactive impact of these seven dimensions. Further follow-ups have suggested that more lasting and durable results ensue when significant problems are addressed across BASIC ID (Lazarus, 2005).

Here are two final points in this brief overview:

1. Whenever feasible, MMT uses empirically supported methods and techniques.

2. MMT is not another form of conversational therapy that takes place entirely within the confines of an office. As in most behavioral approaches, in vivo excursions are often a part of the treatment, but the practitioners of MMT also deliberately draw on external resources to facilitate progress and elicit relevant help from a diverse range of people. Thus, multimodal clinicians transcend the BASIC ID and its social learning foundation. For example, some seemingly enormous life problems have been rapidly resolved by putting clients in touch with a competent accountant, a landscaper, a specialist physician, an architect, or a master plumber. The case presented in this chapter describes the enormous benefits that accrued from the help of a powerful attorney. There is a clear limit to how much one can do with talk, insight, cognitive restructuring, and behavioral interventions (see Lazarus & Zur, 2002).

CASE MATERIAL

The following case study demonstrates the applicability of MMT and BASIC ID.

Demographic and Clinical Information

Harriet Peters, an attractive, soft-spoken 50-year-old homemaker, was referred to me for therapy by a psychopharmacologist who described her as "anxious and depressed" and added that she had a "somatization disorder." He prescribed Paxil and Xanax, which she added to the cache of painkillers, anticholinergics, and other drugs her internist had prescribed. Her sons, ages 27 and 25, held "good jobs" and were married; the "elder boy had a 2-year-old daughter."

Harriet had been married to Jack, aged 54, for 29 years. He had recently become a corporate CEO. Jack, an only child, was raised in an affluent household. His father was a successful attorney and his mother was a stockbroker. Harriet, the oldest of three, had a more modest background. Her parents both taught music in different high schools, and her father worked at a local hardware store on weekends to supplement their income. There were no significant untoward events in Harriet's personal history. In her description, "We are a close-knit family to this day." Harriet met Jack at the end of her junior year in college, and it was considered quite a coup when she married the highly eligible young man. Jack obtained his master of business administration and gained employment at a large corporation where he became the CEO after 28 years. Harriet also completed college but chose to be a full-time homemaker after the birth of her first child.

The first 10 years of the marriage were "very good" according to Harriet, but when Jack became an upper level manager, she said,

> he turned into a workaholic. When our boys were about 8 and 6, I almost became a single parent. Jack went overseas on frequent business trips, and even when he was in town, he had to attend conferences and meetings and was often incommunicado.

Harriet often begged Jack to spend more time with her and the boys, and his standard retort was that she needed to get her priorities straight. Whereas their sex life had been very active for the first 10 to 12 years of marriage, it became less so as Jack devoted an increasing amount of time and energy to his job, and after he was appointed to the position of CEO it almost became nonexistent. Jack blamed this on the fact that Harriet was so frequently indisposed. She was diagnosed with fibrositis, irritable bowel syndrome, and migraine headaches. Harriet explained,

> I used to be pretty healthy, but for the past 4 or 5 years I have suffered from chronic pain. Something always hurts. If it's not my back and neck, it's my gut, or my head. When they all kick in together I'm a complete wreck.

Case Formulation

After the initial interview, Harriet was handed the Multimodal Life History Inventory (Lazarus & Lazarus, 1991) and was asked to complete it at home. After I perused the completed questionnaire, the following issues stood out:

- *Behavior*: Some minor compulsivity (e.g., too fastidious about housework). Avoids confrontations. Overapologetic. Has recently stopped playing the piano.
- *Affect*: Anxiety. Depression. Disappointment. Feelings of inferiority and personal failure.
- *Sensation*: Chronic pain (lower back, abdomen, neck and shoulders, head). Tension. Muscle spasms.
- *Imagery*: Nightmares (usually centered on being lost or pursued by hostile attackers). Unfavorable self-image. Romantic fantasies.
- *Cognition*: Rather perfectionistic. Self-blame. "It is important to please other people." "It is wrong to complain. Grin and bear it."
- *Interpersonal*: Often reticent. Seldom expresses anger. Too compliant. Often puts others' needs before her own. Unfulfilling marriage. Virtually no sex life. Has withdrawn from most of her friends.

- *Drugs–biology*: Under the care of an internist and psychopharmacologist who have prescribed various medications. Needs to improve her eating habits. Insufficient exercise.

Clinical Interactions and Interventions

One of my first recommendations was that it would probably be helpful if I could meet her husband, whose perspective may shed additional light on the matter. I also suggested that perhaps a little later, the two of them might also benefit from some couple sessions. Harriet retorted, "Jack won't give you the time of day!" She said that he was totally contemptuous of psychiatrists and psychologists and made the most insulting and disparaging remarks about all mental health practitioners. Harriet had not informed Jack that she had seen a psychiatrist and was taking Paxil, and she had no intentions of telling him that she was seeing me. "That will only irritate him even more," she said, "and he would become even more contemptuous of me. It would just give him a license to call me crazy." She mentioned that she was paying for her therapy out of a private account that Jack did not know about.

I dropped the subject for the time being and went to work on Harriet's tension (relaxation exercises, positive imagery projections, diaphragmatic breathing). Because she seemed able to conjure up the most vivid images, I urged her to practice positive coping images several times a day. I also addressed her unassertiveness; explored her rights and entitlements; encouraged her to challenge her self-abnegation; and persuaded her to spend more time with her friends, join a yoga class, and take up walking or some other form of exercise.

Although the aforementioned target areas exemplified the initial treatment framework, the sessions also delved into various revelations and recollections and examined the impact of diverse interrelated issues and events in her life. We met weekly, with occasional phone calls and e-mail communications between sessions. Because she was an avid reader, I gave her two of my self-help books (Lazarus, 2001; Lazarus & Lazarus, 1997), and we discussed many of the points therein during our sessions. Harriet's level of overcompliance became the main focus of the assertiveness training. One of her mantras became, "Stop apologizing. Contradict and challenge."

She had great difficulty in learning to stand up for herself. Nevertheless, about 2 months into the therapy there was clear evidence that Harriet was making progress. She reported feeling less depressed, less enervated, more enthusiastic, and more self-accepting, and she had joined both a tennis club and a book club. She was seeing her friends and spending time with her granddaughter, and she was playing the piano again. In multimodal terms, the modalities that had been the main focus of therapeutic attention were the dimensions of behavior, sensation, imagery, cognition, and interpersonal relationships.

On her own initiative, she decided to join a gym, get a personal trainer, and have a massage two or three times a week. Her headaches, bowel disturbances, and other physical afflictions had abated, which she attributed to her fitness regimen. Harriet met with her psychopharmacologist once every 4 or 5 weeks. He would assess her progress and titrate her medication, and usually he and I would then have a brief phone conversation. (Harriet had given us written permission to discuss her.) I was pleased that she had discontinued taking Xanax after the first month of therapy, but when the psychiatrist mentioned to me that Harriet could start reducing her intake of the Paxil, I asked him to keep her on it a while longer. I explained that I was about to explore her marriage, and I sensed that some rocky territory lay ahead. He agreed to my request.

During the course of our conversations, Harriet expressed a central cognition, or what some call a *schema*: "I have not been a very good wife." Consequently, we explored the subject of marriage in general and her own marriage in particular. I gave her Fay's (1998) *Making It as a Couple*. She already had my book *Marital Myths Revisited* (Lazarus, 2001).

I began to suspect that Jack had probably been sexually involved with several women during the course of their marriage. I kept this opinion to myself. The timing of this type of revelation is crucial, and I sensed that Harriet was not ready to face this issue. I resorted to an imaginary excursion by asking Harriet to picture, as clearly as possible, the trajectory of her marriage from its inception to its present state of affairs (pun intended). In essence she admitted, reluctantly at first, that most of the positive aspects had waned. I believe I managed to disabuse her of the notion that this was because she had been a bad wife. Subsequently, I asked her to picture the marriage henceforth and to tell me what she envisaged and anticipated as the months and the years rolled by. She had great difficulty with this time-projection technique and said she drew a blank, whereupon I inquired, trying to sound casual, if she thought that divorce may be in the cards. For the first time since we had met, she became angry and accusatory. "What are you saying?" she snapped. "Are you suggesting that Jack and I should split up?" I replied, somewhat defensively, "I'm merely trying to cover all the bases. I want to be sure that you will be ready to handle anything that may come down the pike." I was pleased that she was now able to challenge and confront me.

Any further discussions of divorce were deferred, but as Harriet continued discussing her marriage over the next several weeks, I grew progressively more and more convinced that Jack's interests and affections lay elsewhere. Harriet alluded to various lapses and contradictions. For example, Jack was due to return from an overseas business trip on a Monday, but one of Harriet's friends said she had glimpsed him getting into an elevator at a local hotel on Sunday. When she mentioned this to Jack, she claims that he barked that her "nutty friend" was obviously mistaken. When she found a brand-new bottle of expensive perfume in the glove compartment of Jack's car, he claimed that he had bought it for her but had forgotten to give it to her. She remarked, "That's the first time he ever bought perfume for me." I did not pursue it.

Jack soon evinced other behaviors that led me to suspect that he wanted to be found out. For example, he left an American Express receipt for $3,000 from a jewelry store in London on the dining room table. When Harriet confronted him (this was additional evidence of her newfound assertive behavior), he professed to have laid out the money as a gift for a business associate. A woman had been responsible for enabling him to secure a multimillion-dollar deal, and he claimed that his company would reimburse him. "It's purely and simply a business expense," he insisted.

A couple of weeks later, Harriet stated that in retrospect, she had long begun to feel that her marriage was doomed, but that it was too scary for her to fully admit it and that is why she was unable to look into the future as I had previously requested. She also felt that her self-deception and denial and its attendant pressures lay behind many of her somatic problems. I began to prepare Harriet to face the ordeals of a likely divorce. I drew on mental imagery techniques in the hope of enabling her to foresee a better quality of life without Jack. I introduced role-playing and behavior rehearsal techniques to ensure that she would not be browbeaten or intimidated by Jack.

Being perhaps overly optimistic, I suggested that if I could meet with Jack, there was an outside chance that the marriage could still be saved. Harriet surprised me by stating, "I'm not so sure I want it to be saved." I then commented, "Well, perhaps I could facilitate a more amicable divorce process." I again broached the idea of calling her husband. "Go ahead," she said, "I no longer care what he will say to me about my seeing a psychologist, so be my guest, but remember that you are proceeding at your own peril." We agreed that I would call him at home rather than at his office. Because Harriet never knew when Jack would be home, she offered to call me when an opportune moment arose. About 5 days later she called me around 9 p.m. and said, "Jack's home now. Good luck!"

I called their house and Jack answered. I apologized for intruding on his time, gave my name, identified myself as a clinical psychologist and said that Harriet was seeing me in therapy. I wondered if he'd be good enough to meet with me at a mutually convenient time. I stated, "I have known your wife for a few months under somewhat artificial conditions, so there would undoubtedly be much helpful information you could provide after knowing her for almost 3 decades." I don't have a verbatim record of his comments, but they went more or less as follows:

> As far as I'm concerned all you shrinks are even crazier than the losers who waste their time and money on you. I'm a very busy man and I sure as hell won't waste my precious time talking to the likes of you.

He then hung up.

Prior to the foregoing, the idea of arranging a clinical meeting with her two sons and daughters-in-law had also occurred to me. However, I was completely taken aback by the speed with which matters proceeded. Harriet was served with divorce papers within 2 weeks of my brief phone call.

When Jack excoriated Harriet for secretly "crying on some stupid shrink's shoulder," she informed him that she was neither blind nor stupid. She told him that she was well aware of his extramarital exploits, of the fact that his love of money meant more to him than his sons, and that in retrospect their marriage should have ended about 20 years ago. She was disconcerted but not distraught. We agreed that the mainstay of the therapy would now focus primarily on getting through the divorce, which Harriet said would undoubtedly be nasty.

In essence, Jack had control of virtually all their finances, and he had concealed most of their assets. He had retained two highly accomplished but unscrupulous attorneys to represent him. One of them (I'll call him "Benjie Joseph") had the reputation of "being capable of squeezing blood out of a stone—the nemesis of widows and children." I had never met him or seen him. Harriet's lawyer (I'll call him "Charlie Abbott") a man I knew fairly well, was intelligent, fair-minded, and well meaning, but probably no match for Mr. Joseph and his associate.

Given Harriet's vivid imagery capacities, I borrowed and adapted a technique from neurolinguistic programming, which can be empowering for some people. As an exercise, several times a day, she would form a clear picture of Jack and then imagine him shrinking in size, smaller and smaller, until he was the size of a tiny bug or an ant on which she would step. Harriet enjoyed doing this exercise and reported that it made her feel "cleansed and free inside."

Jack, who was reputed to be worth millions, had offered Harriet a $100,000 divorce settlement, and Abbott had advised her to take it. With Harriet's permission, I called him to discuss the matter, pointing out that Harriet had been Jack's loyal and faithful wife for 3 decades; had raised their two sons; and had helped Jack climb the corporate ladder by running interference, entertaining clients, and taking care of all his creature comforts. It soon became apparent to me that Abbott was afraid to go up against Benjie Joseph. He was clearly shortchanging Harriet. I was literally losing sleep over this matter.

The day before she was due to appear in court, I had an idea. Several years ago I had treated a renowned lawyer (let's call him "James B. Kanner") and his wife for marital difficulties. Fortunately, because of (or in spite of) my ministrations, their tribulations soon vanished, and I acquired a powerful and grateful admirer. Kanner was a leading attorney whose celebrated cases made headline news many times a year. A standing joke was that his middle initial stood for "barracuda." His clients were mainly huge corporations, banks, government agencies, and entertainment icons. When he and his wife were back on track, he said to me, "Arnie, I owe you one. Let me know if I can ever do something in return." I said that he had paid my fees and owed me nothing. Nevertheless, I now mulled over whether to call him for advice regarding Harriet's situation. Would he be insulted to be asked about a case that might be considered trivial compared with his usual work?

I decided we had nothing to lose, so I called him and he got back to me several hours later. With great deference I outlined Harriet's situation and characterized it as a scenario wherein the kindhearted damsel was about to be pilloried by the evil monster. He listened to my account, and when I mentioned that Benjie Joseph was the opposing attorney, in his deeply resonant voice he slowly uttered four words: "I hate Benjie Joseph." He inquired who was representing Harriet, and when I said Charlie Abbott, he chuckled and said something like, "Charlie's a sweet guy but Benjie Joseph will devour him. Why don't I call Abbott and politely tell him to take a hike?" He then told me that Harriet should go to his office the first thing the next morning to sign some papers. "Tell her to ask for Janice, and to identify herself as 'Arnie's friend.' I'll be in the courthouse on another matter, but I'll find out in which room the Peters trial will be heard, and I'll be there." I explained that "the damsel" was impecunious, but Jimmy said that he would represent her pro bono or levy a small contingency fee just for the fun of going up against Benjie Joseph and to be of help to one of my patients.

When I told Harriet I had arranged for James Kanner to represent her and that he would so inform Mr. Abbott, she shouted, "Are you crazy? How can I afford James Kanner? It costs about $50,000 just to say hello to him!" I said that for reasons I could not divulge it would cost her very little.

The next day I went to the court and sat near the front. To my left were three men. I instantly recognized Jack from some photos Harriet had shown me. The other two were obviously his lawyers, and I guessed correctly that the one with a handlebar mustache was Benjie Joseph. If I were the casting director for a movie, I'd pick Mr. Joseph to play the villain. But where was Jimmy? Harriet sat alone to the far right of Jack and his lawyers who snickered and smirked at her. I grew very concerned when the judge entered the courtroom and Jimmy was nowhere to be seen. Could the famous James B. Kanner have stood Harriet up? I do not recall the exact sequence of events, but I do remember Benjie Joseph and his associate stating their names and saying that they were Jack's lawyers. I also recall the judge asking Harriet, "And where is your counsel, Mrs. Peters?" at which moment Jimmy, always interested in drama, entered the courtroom and said,

> I will be representing Mrs. Peters, your Honor, James Kanner. I apologize to the court and to my learned colleagues for failing to give prior notification, but I was only retained late last night. I would ask your Honor for a continuance so I can familiarize myself with the facts of the case.

In most states, surprises are not only frowned on by the court, but they also subject the surprising attorney to discipline. To cover himself, Jimmy had sent a fax to Benjie Joseph that he had obviously not yet received. Jack and his attorneys stood gaping for several seconds until Benjie Joseph blurted out, "May we approach your Honor?" It seemed obvious that Mr. Joseph was not about to go up against Mr. Kanner. The judge said he'd see all the attorneys in his chambers. I don't know exactly what transpired, but the case was quickly settled out of court, and Harriet received considerably more than 10 times the amount of Jack's initial offer.

Harriet continued working with me at fortnightly intervals to consolidate and extend her gains. She was notably more self-confident, less apologetic, and less submissive; she had stopped taking Paxil and had cut back on most of the other medications. At this juncture, we were tackling her residual feelings of personal failure and endeavoring to enhance her self-image, mainly by the use of positive imagery and rational disputation. She continued her physical exercise regimen and was taking good care of herself. Her sons, who had always been much closer to her than to Jack, expressed their approval concerning the divorce.

Several months after the divorce, at a dinner party, Harriet happened on Paul, a man she had dated before Jack had come on the scene and whose wife had left him for another woman. She and Paul dated, and Harriet subsequently moved into his condominium. She commented, "Paul is such a sweetheart. If only I had married him instead of Jack, my life would have been so much better." Formal therapy ended around the middle of 2003. Harriet and I have kept in touch via intermittent e-mails, mainly consisting of salacious jokes.

WHAT DOES THIS CASE ILLUSTRATE?

Some readers may be unclear about what this case illustrates about MMT. It could be argued that much of the positive outcome hinged on the strings I was able to pull in securing a high-powered attorney for my client. Didn't this factor override the other significant therapeutic gains?

Remember that Harriet suffered from many problems across the BASIC ID dimensions. She was a timid, overapologetic, anxious, depressed, unassertive, and self-effacing woman who felt inferior and who suffered from health problems and chronic pain. By addressing and mitigating each of these issues, she was then capable of standing up to her malevolent husband and was ready to face the process and consequences of an acrimonious divorce rather than stay in the marriage. In other words, she had to be multimodally primed to take the final necessary steps to enhance the quality of her life.

Explicitly going beyond the usual cognitive–behavioral therapy parameters, the MMT approach tends to pay greater attention to various sensory and mental imagery techniques and includes explicit liaisons, when necessary, with experts inside and outside the mental health profession. Thus, my friendship with a celebrated lawyer played a pivotal role. In football parlance, the attorney scored the final and winning touchdown for us.

It is always most pleasant to treat cooperative and nonresistant clients. Harriet and I quickly formed a good working alliance: She trusted and respected me and our level of rapport flowed easily. I consider it important to match the selection of techniques and the relationship style to each client's individual needs and expectancies. For example, had Harriet received purely reflective or exploratory therapy, the outcome probably would not have been so favorable. She required and responded well to a directive, didactic, and at times pedagogical stance.

Above all, this case depicts the use of psychotherapy as an educational and problem-solving process. It also clearly underscores the advantages of drawing on the power and talents of whoever is likely to aid and abet the resolution of clients' problems. Reverting to football analogies, I see good therapists as quarterbacks who are likely to know to whom the ball must be thrown downfield and who feel no need to score final touchdowns themselves.

REFERENCES

Bandura, A. (1977). *Social learning theory*. Englewood Cliffs, NJ: Prentice Hall.

Bandura, A. (1986). *Social foundations of thought and action: A social cognitive theory*. Englewood Cliffs, NJ: Prentice Hall.

Fay, A. (1998). *Making it as a couple*. New York: FMC Books.

Lazarus, A. A. (1967). In support of technical eclecticism. *Psychological Reports, 21*, 415–416.

Lazarus, A. A. (1995). Different types of eclecticism and integration: Let's be aware of the dangers. *Journal of Psychotherapy Integration, 5*, 27–39.

Lazarus, A. A. (1996). The utility and futility of combining treatments in psychotherapy. *Clinical Psychology: Science and Practice, 3*, 59–68.

Lazarus, A. A. (1997). *Brief but comprehensive psychotherapy: The multimodal way*. New York: Springer Publishing Company.

Lazarus, A. A. (2001). *Marital myths revisited*. Atascadero, CA: Impact.

Lazarus, A. A. (2005). Multimodal therapy. In R. J. Corsini & D. Wedding (Eds.), *Current psychotherapies* (7th ed., pp. 337–371). Belmont, CA: Brooks/Cole.

Lazarus, A. A., & Beutler, L. E. (1993). On technical eclecticism. *Journal of Counseling & Development, 71*, 381–385.

Lazarus, A. A., & Lazarus, C. N. (1991). *Multimodal life history inventory*. Champaign, IL: Research Press.

Lazarus, A. A., & Lazarus, C. N. (1997). *The 60-second shrink*. Atascadero, CA: Impact.

Lazarus, A. A., & Zur, O. (2002). *Dual relationships and psychotherapy*. New York: Springer Publishing Company.

London, P. (1963). *The modes and morals of psychotherapy*. New York: Holt, Rinehart & Winston.

Rotter, J. B. (1954). *Social learning and clinical psychology*. Englewood Cliffs, NJ: Prentice Hall.

3

SYSTEMATIC TREATMENT SELECTION AND PRESCRIPTIVE THERAPY

LARRY E. BEUTLER, T. MARK HARWOOD,
MATTEO BERTONI, AND JIMENA THOMANN

Systematic treatment selection (STS; Beutler & Clarkin, 1990; Beutler, Clarkin, & Bongar, 2000) is an empirically developed procedure for identifying the mix of therapist, treatment strategies, and psychotherapeutic interventions that are most likely to produce a favorable response in any given patient. Two basic assumptions underlie this approach: (a) There is no treatment method or model that works well on all patients, and (b) most treatment methods work well on some patients (e.g., Beutler & Harwood, 2002; Howard, Krause, & Lyons, 1993). The effects of most (if not all) treatments range from very positive to mildly negative, depending on the patient observed. STS seeks to identify which patients will respond positively to various mixes of interventions from different treatment models. Treatments are not mutually exclusive, however. Regardless of whether they are identified (e.g., by similar labels or brands), treatments are distinguished more by the pattern of interventions used than by the exclusivity of the procedures used (e.g., Malik, Beutler, Gallagher-Thompson, Thompson, & Alimohamed, 2003). Moreover, the procedures used are more closely related to the therapist's training and beliefs than to the procedures' scientific validity (Beutler et al., 2000).

Contemporary efforts to construct research-informed guidelines do not as a rule address the commonalities among treatments; practitioners prefer instead to think of each treatment model as a discrete and identifiable entity that can be applied to all patients with the same diagnosis. However, the presence of a shared diagnosis occludes the presence of important differences among patients. Thus, the appropriateness of any given treatment model depends both on the pattern of interventions used and the fit of these interventions to both the diagnostic and nondiagnostic characteristics of the patient.

In contrast to the broad approach of fitting a treatment model to a patient's diagnosis, STS seeks to identify the specific pattern of patient traits and states (*dimensions*) that best fit with a corresponding pattern of demand characteristics that constitute the amalgamation of a treatment strategy and a therapist's particular relationship style. Rather than identifying the treatment received by a patient purely in terms of the theoretical model that guides it (e.g., cognitive therapy, psychoanalytic therapy, interpersonal therapy) or the techniques that it contains (e.g., interpretation, thought records, evidence analysis), all of which may reveal more about a particular therapist's beliefs than about in-therapy behavior, STS is constructed around principles of behavior change—guiding theorems of change and relationship that cut across treatment models and theories and that can be applied by individual therapists from different perspectives (Beutler et al., 2000).

In the strictest sense, STS is not an "integrative therapy"; it does not attempt to combine theoretical concepts or to derive a unified theoretical approach of any type. To the degree that it falls within the domain of current descriptors, it is a "technical eclectic" approach, but even that label is imprecise because STS does not specify any particular set of techniques but rather allows the therapist to use procedures from any particular approach that are consistent with the application of cross-cutting principles of change and influence (e.g., therapeutic change is most likely when the therapeutic procedures do not evoke patient resistance).

The principles and applications of STS have been defined and developed through a four-step process (Beutler et al., 2000). The first step was a series of literature reviews designed to identify predictors and moderators of therapeutic change. The second step was to collapse and combine these predictors and moderators into a smaller set of clusters, each of which identified a particular fit or match between patient qualities and treatment strategies that reliably relate to change and improvement. The third step was to develop means for measuring the patient qualities and treatment strategies that emerged from the prior steps. The fourth step tested a series of hypotheses that had been extracted from the reviews of literature, all of which bore on the question of what factors accounted for optimal therapeutic change. A detailed review of these steps is contained in Beutler et al. (2000).

The application of the original STS dimensions for the task of planning treatment is illustrated in the next section, as applied to the case of Frank, a patient experiencing comorbid depression and chemical abuse disorder and who was seen as part of a randomized trial study of the efficacy of STS predictions (Beutler et al., 2003).

CASE DESCRIPTION

Frank was a 39-year-old Caucasian male with 14 years of education who had been married for about 3 years and had no children. He had just started a home-based business with his wife, after having held several jobs in the past few years. He decided to see a psychologist because he was experiencing severe financial problems caused by his drug abuse (he was in debt to pay for his drugs), and his wife was threatening to leave him if he did not find a definitive solution to his addiction. He also reported symptoms of anxiety, sometimes feeling "overwhelmed by a lack of motivation," and talked about having "no desire to do anything," all of which are characteristics of severe depression. He was "tired of lying to himself and to others."

Frank was 15 minutes late for the first interview. His language was logical and coherent, but he was sometimes distracted. He claimed slight memory impairment because of the drug use, and therefore he was vague and found some dates and events difficult to remember. The following information was extracted from the initial evaluation interview and administration of standardized intake procedures, which included the Minnesota Multiphasic Personality Inventory—2 (MMPI–2; Butcher, Dahlstrom, Graham, Tellegen, & Kaemmer, 1989), the STS Clinician Rating Form (Fisher, Beutler, & Williams, 1999), and the Beck Depression Inventory (Beck & Steer, 1987).

The therapist learned that Frank was still taking approximately a quarter gram of heroin at least three times a week and approximately a half gram of cocaine almost every day. He reported using them together or alternately and stated that he was able to stay clean from one drug or the other just for few days. He was trying to self-titrate the doses but felt that he could not "go any lower." He had been treated twice for drug abuse, including a treatment consisting of detoxification only, but he was not able to remember the specific dates. Frank tried numerous 30-day outpatient programs but never methadone because, as he said, "It's just synthetic heroin, but with a third of the power. If I want that, I can just take less dope." He attended several Alcoholics Anonymous and Narcotics Anonymous meetings, claiming a preference for the first.

Frank reported difficulties with various cognitive functions such as concentration and decision making. He was experiencing frequent loss of appetite and insomnia; soon before starting therapy, for example, he had spent an entire week without sleeping. Everything went from bad to worse after visiting his stepbrother, who had reminded Frank of early traumatic experiences. Nonetheless, before the sessions described here, he "didn't feel like going to a shrink," and he tried to "get into a better mood" by consuming more drugs and alcohol.

Frank was raised by his biological parents until he was 14, when they divorced and he stayed with his mother. She remarried soon after the divorce. His father disappeared, and Frank never learned if he was dead or alive. Frank reported that his father had alcoholism and that his mother had a "paranoid phobic" personality. He always suspected that she had worked as a prostitute. She committed suicide 16 years prior to this intake. Frank stated that his mother had physically abused him and his brothers. He did not remember his father abusing him, but he was hurt because of all the times the father ignored what the mother was doing to his brothers and to him. A few months after his mother's suicide, Frank had a terrible car accident.

Frank started drinking when he was a teenager and continued to abuse alcohol after that time. Sixteen years before entering treatment on the occasion under discussion, and in reaction to both the physical problems that followed his car accident and the nearly concomitant suicide of his mother, he started using heroin to "get out from the physical and emotional pain." In a short period, he developed an addiction to heroin, and he started consuming regular amounts of cocaine as well. After 6 years of drug abuse, he was arrested for the first and only time and charged with drug possession. He entered or was committed by the court to several 30-day outpatient treatment programs. He successfully stopped using drugs and remained "clean" for 4 years, during which time he started seeing a psychiatrist. He was dissatisfied and left psychotherapy without further benefit.

Seven months before initiating the treatment effort described here, he went to visit James, an older stepbrother he had not seen for a long period. James helped Frank remember some physical and emotional abuse that they both had experienced in childhood at the hands of their parents, especially the patient's mother. When he returned home, Frank felt depressed and began having suicidal thoughts. He subsequently slashed his wrists. At the time of the current admission, however, he reported no suicidal ideation. He did report continuing depression and anxiety and indicated that this had been relatively constant for more than 6 months. He reported a recurrent fear that he might "go crazy."

Frank had many friends among drug abusers and only two "good pals" who were not drug users or dealers. These two friends and his wife were the only persons he trusted. One of these friends was a physician who had sometimes helped him by prescribing narcotic drugs to cope with withdrawal symptoms.

DIMENSIONS DESCRIPTION AND CASE FORMULATION

A series of intensive analyses of the variations among commonly used psychotherapies (Beutler & Clarkin, 1990; Beutler et al., 2000; Castonguay

& Beutler, 2006), followed by research on these psychotherapies (Malik et al., 2003), has revealed that most psychotherapies can be represented by mapping the therapist's actions against the following dimensions: (a) variations in intensity of treatment, (b) variations in the focus on insight versus behavior and skill change, (c) variations in the level of directiveness used, and (d) variations in the way that patient affect is managed. In STS, it is proposed that each of these variations in therapy implementation tends to be most suitable for a patient who has a particular and corresponding quality of personal or situational attribute. In other words, variations of patient styles and environments tend to serve as indicators (and contraindicators) of different classes of therapy procedures. An analysis of Frank's history, using the cross-cutting STS dimensions of patient variations, and the associated assessment procedure, suggested the following treatment plan.

Assessment of Level of Functioning

An assessment of the level of functional impairment serves as the basis for the assignment of an appropriate level of care. A thorough assessment of functional impairment, within the STS model, includes a consideration of the patient's problem complexity (i.e., comorbidity and personality disorder) and chronicity as well as an assessment of the patient's available social support system. The level of impairment determines the level or intensity of the treatment to be provided. Intensity of treatment, in turn, may be varied by increased length, the use of multiple formats and modalities, and by increased frequency. Our reviews failed to find outcome differences among these alternatives.

Frank displayed a moderate level of impairment as indicated by his chronic history of drug abuse combined with a diagnosis of depression and a previous suicide attempt. Additionally, his MMPI–2 Social Introversion (Si) and Paranoia (Pa) scales indicated some feeling of being alienated from others. Thus, current levels of social support were considered weak, and his problem was characterized as complex because it was negatively impacting numerous areas of functioning; at the time he sought treatment, he was in danger of losing both his job and his marriage. Frank had been able to establish satisfying attachments to his wife. MMPI–2 (Butcher et al., 1989) and various indicators of work and family disturbance suggested a moderate disturbance in functioning; accordingly, the intake clinician gave Frank a Global Assessment of Functioning (GAF; American Psychiatric Association, 2000) rating of 56.

Treatment was scheduled at the rate of twice a week for the first 4 to 6 weeks of the therapy. At the end of 6 weeks, if Frank's impairment had been adequately stabilized and problematic symptoms had been addressed (e.g., the drug abuse noticeably declined, he was less depressed and anxious), the frequency of the sessions were to decrease to once a week, supplemented by phone calls and emergency sessions if needed.

The primary goal of therapy and the initial focus of treatment was to reduce the risk posed by self-destructive behaviors (substance abuse and suicidal behavior). The need to provide a protective environment (e.g., by using inpatient treatment) was given serious consideration and remained an option throughout treatment. Eventually, however, it was decided that frequent outpatient visits would be adequate to the patient's needs.

The level of functioning also suggested that the therapist assign and monitor the patient's attendance at Narcotics Anonymous and Alcoholics Anonymous meetings on a regular, perhaps daily, basis. Antidepressant medication was considered as an eventual adjunct to psychotherapy (specifically, an antidepressant that may also help reduce the patient's symptoms of general anxiety). In the long run, Frank was encouraged to enter psychotherapy in order to learn psychological change procedures as a first-line treatment before prescribing biochemical agents in an effort to help maintain his focus on developing a chemical-free lifestyle.

In the service of this latter goal, Frank was encouraged to decrease his use of substances on the basis of a realistic schedule of reduction and titration. A medical specialist in substance abuse was consulted about the titration schedule, and a physical exam was conducted to clear him for gradual withdrawal from drugs. Additionally, Frank was provided with educational material describing the possible withdrawal effects and specific behaviors (e.g., exercise, diet, vitamin supplements, sleep hygiene, stress reduction techniques) that have proved helpful in reducing the symptoms of withdrawal.

Because of the chronicity and complexity of Frank's problems, the STS model indicated a need for long-term outpatient care. The frequency of treatment was adjusted as Frank succeeded in reducing drug use, but the therapist knew to expect periods in which Frank's symptoms would flare up, necessitating temporary increases in treatment frequency.

Coping Style

In the STS model, an assessment of the patient's coping style is designed to inform the focus of treatment, encouraging the therapist to select procedures that vary along a dimension that ranges from a focus on gaining insight to a focus on symptom, skill, and behavior change. Within the STS model, externalizing and impulsive behaviors indicate the value of problem and behaviorally focused interventions while internalizing and restraining behaviors indicate the potential value of insight and emotional awareness.

Frank presented with a mixed pattern of internalizing and externalizing symptoms. Specifically, he had a history of acting out (externalizing) through drug use and substance abuse. Additionally, his history of suicidal acts accompanied by a self-reported claim of "interpersonal conflict," suggested the presence of impulsiveness, which accompanied a correlated pattern of self-blame emotional restriction. The MMPI–2 confirmed the presence of mixed personality features, including both internalizing and externalizing behaviors. Specifically, Frank exhibited elevations on several internalizing scales like the Depression (D), the Si, and the Anxiety (Pt) subscales. Additionally, he scored high on the Impulse (Pd) scale, and he exhibited a moderate elevation on the Pa scale, which indicated a potential to externalize.

The symptoms that placed this patient at risk for continued drug use and for suicidal behavior were given priority in the STS model and served as the initial focus of intervention. Because he presented with both externalizing and internalizing coping patterns, early therapeutic work focused directly on developing impulse control; long-term goals included achieving insight into his motivations and awareness of his unmet emotional needs.

The following example illustrates the therapist's effort to help the patient gain control over "helpless" feelings by insight and emotional awareness.

Therapist: When you take a lower dose, and you believe that nothing is happening and that you need to have another "hit," how do you feel?

Frank: I don't know—*helpless* I guess is the word.

Therapist: Because that's actually what you are likely to feel when you are at the detox program. You are not going to get the feeling that you have to have your stuff to help you feel more powerful!

Frank: That's true.

Therapist: What do you think? What do you tell yourself, when you are in that spot? Something like, "The stuff is not working, I've gotta get more"?

Frank: I don't know. Maybe.

Therapist: Let's assume that this is the feeling and thought you have—of being helpless and needing something to pull you out of it. How does that sound?

Frank: It's uncomfortable—I feel lost. I hate it.

Therapist: It feels like you don't have any options at that point?

Frank: It does! Yeah! Actually, I feel that way about a lot of things right now! I feel like my options are very limited, I feel helpless, and I don't like what I see. What I've been left with . . .

Therapist: So, even though you feel helpless and don't like that, maybe there are some options, but you just don't like them!

Frank: Probably . . . yeah, you're right!

Therapist: This is important because the more you can get an understanding of how those feelings make you do things, before going to the detox program, the easier it will be for you.

Level of Resistance

An assessment of the patient's level of resistance informs the selection of the therapist's level of directiveness. Within the STS framework, high resistance is taken as an indicator for the use of procedures that deemphasize therapist control and vice versa. *Resistance* may be defined as the level of patient opposition to perceived efforts on the part of the therapist to control the patient's behavior. Managing resistance by the selection of procedures that are either nondirective or directive and skillfully adapting to changes in resistance levels minimizes the occurrence of negative interactions in therapy and enhances the development and maintenance of the therapeutic alliance.

At the beginning of treatment, Frank showed a strong will to quit his drug abuse and his motivation seemed high—good signs with respect to treatment compliance. On the basis of quantitative assessments, Frank scored just above the mean on the Dowd Trait Reactance Scale (Dowd, Milne, & Wise, 1991), but he scored below the mean on the MMPI–2 Readiness for Treatment Scale. Taken together, these scores suggested that Frank possessed a low-to-average level of resistance; therefore, the use of therapist-directed procedures was indicated. For example, early in treatment, the therapist offered a directive homework task:

Frank: Change apartments, go to work, talk to my doctor, detox . . . I should make a list! I keep making lists, but every time my priorities change . . .

Therapist: Maybe you should make a short list and a long list. The long list is what you have to do in the next couple of weeks or so; the short list is what you have to do today. Keep it simple. Just one thing at a time, commit to one thing each day. You have to say to yourself: Today I'm definitely gonna do this for me! Can you do that?

Frank: Yeah.

Therapist: So, what can it be today?

Frank: Well, calling the detox program!

Therapist: Okay. So next time you can tell me how it went and what's your next choice.

Frank's homework assignment was reviewed and monitored in each session. His cooperation and compliance confirmed that he had a relatively low level of resistance. Thus, he continued to benefit from the structure and guidance provided by symptom-focused strategies. Nonetheless, the therapist remained vigilant to any signs of increased resistance (e.g., being repeatedly late for therapy, becoming argumentative, not completing homework) throughout the course of therapy and adjusted directiveness levels accordingly.

Motivation and Subjective Distress

Motivation and subjective distress, as assessed in the STS system, involves an assessment of current levels of emotional arousal. The strategy of treatment is to maintain moderate arousal levels throughout treatment. In psychotherapy, patients usually seek treatment to reduce the intensity of painful emotional states; however, if emotional arousal levels are too low, patients may lose their incentive to continue the therapy, and they may not persist in making positive changes in their lives. Conversely, when anxiety is high, the patient may be too distressed to approach treatment in a planned and receptive manner.

An examination of Frank's State–Trait Anxiety Inventory State score (Spielberger, Gorsuch, Lushene, Vagg, & Jacobs, 1983) indicated that his distress levels were in the average range. An examination of his treatment history revealed that he usually entered treatment in an acute state of anxiety that dissipated rapidly, after which he had little motivation for change. On the basis of this assessment, it was decided to use a modest amount of confrontation in therapy to maintain Frank's anxiety and hence his motivation for change.

The high levels of initial distress suggested that establishing a stable routine and life structure would be needed to reduce the patient's anxiety to manageable levels. A decrease in anxiety through the development of a supportive structure and safe environment was used to enhance the development of the therapeutic alliance—a necessity for continued involvement and successful treatment. Also, because of the intensity of anxiety symptoms and the history of suicidal thoughts and behavior, the therapist was encouraged by the STS supervisor to give Frank his phone and pager numbers and encourage him to use them any time he felt the need to do so. Drawing on extant research and specific findings, the STS model emphasizes that initial goals should be directed toward symptoms and aimed at reducing risk and increasing social activity. Achieving these goals requires direct and immediate interventions that should be applied before proceeding to the longer term treatment of more chronic aspects of the patient's presentation.

The following exchange illustrates the therapist's efforts to manage and control Frank's discomfort.

> *Frank:* I'm doing better. My work, my behavior, my being with other people, the sensation of being sober and clean instead of drug motivated . . .

Therapist:	When you say that you are doing better, I don't think that you completely believe that, but . . .
Frank:	I believe that I'm going in the right direction and I have more desire to get clean and sober. But, like you said, it's not entirely true.
Therapist:	What is really better right now?
Frank:	I have that desire and, at the moment, I'm off the coke . . . and right now it just disgusts me! You know, I disgust me! When I think about using it . . . I just wanna be out of that!

From an STS perspective, the level of confrontation that produces arousal must be balanced against and integrated with the focus of treatment—in this case, the focus on insight and awareness of feelings.

Therapist:	These experiences have been really, really dramatic.
Frank:	You know, the drugs don't scare me one tenth as much as the idea of some of this stuff reoccurring.
Therapist:	The drugs have been an escape from those memories.
Frank:	I guess so. I don't remember the time when I was home . . .
Therapist:	Unconsciously, they have always been there.
Frank:	Sure. I would say that I didn't think about that until the day I talked to my stepbrother.
Therapist:	I think it's gonna take time to process all those memories.

In an effort to manage and maintain optimal levels of emotional arousal, the therapist remained vigilant to changes in distress level throughout therapy, providing reassurance as Frank became more distressed and providing confrontation when stress became too low. The therapist attended to in-session cues regarding moment-to-moment changes in arousal levels and adjusted his therapeutic stance accordingly. For example, if in-session distress is maintained at a high level for an extended period, specific procedures for relaxation and reducing cognitive or muscular tension may be helpful for reducing discomfort (Harwood & Williams, 2003).

SUMMARY AND OUTCOME

STS defines classes or groups of interventions, on the basis of common demand characteristics and objectives, that are fitted to patients according to their personal qualities and living environments. Variations in levels of severity (functional impairment) are used to set the level of treatment intensity for the patient. However, in the spirit of basing treatment on principles rather than recipes, the way in which therapy is intensified may vary from patient to patient. In our case example, the therapist chose to vary the frequency of sessions, but one could add treatments, extend treatment, or do some combination of these things. In all cases, how one follows the principles defined by STS is guided by available research, not by preferred theory or personal bias. Because research has not yet provided persuasive evidence that these individual ways of intensifying treatment produce different effects, therapists are left to select their own methods.

Similarly, patient coping style is used as an indicator for selecting methods of intervention that rely on insight or on direct behavioral and cognitive training. In the example used here, an insight-focused approach to the use of interpretations and working with dynamic themes was used, along with some behavior change procedures (scheduling, thought monitoring) to encourage change. This selection of procedures was based on the patient's mixed coping style, in which he vacillated between internalizing and externalizing coping behaviors.

Patient resistance level helps determine the level of directiveness to be used in implementing the interventions. Directiveness level defines the therapist's role as either teacher and authority or collaborator and student. On one hand, the therapist may assume the role of authority as in behavioral or psychodynamic therapies, and on the other, he or she may assume a reflective and questioning role, much like that used by cognitive and client-centered therapists. In the case study presented in this chapter, the therapist adopted a largely teaching and guiding role with Frank, recognizing his relatively low level of resistance.

Finally, the patient's level of distress is assessed and, in STS systems, determines how much structure is used to reduce anxiety as opposed to providing structure that confronts and arouses anxiety. It is assumed that moderate levels of distress are motivational. Thus, in the case presented here, the therapist focused initially on providing structure to help reduce Frank's anxiety to more manageable levels. This structuring comprised homework, assurance, and here-and-now discussions. This was a necessary first step that allowed Frank to engage meaningfully in treatment. Additionally, the relief or reduction in anxiety that structure provided, combined with his subsequent receptivity to various interventions, served to enhance the development of a good therapeutic alliance.

After a few sessions, Frank and the therapist were able to start establishing insight and targeting specific behaviors or skills such as drug abuse, impulse control, and the development of healthy social interaction skills. At this point, the therapy was tailored to track Frank's drug use; drug cravings; and his unique pattern of depressogenic events, thoughts, and behaviors. Considering his low resistance and his mixed coping style, the therapist elected to use primarily insight-focused and directive interventions like homework, providing information and psychoeducation, and scheduling healthy (non–drug-use) activities and goal deadlines.

After fewer than the scheduled 20 sessions of therapy, Frank was able to begin a methadone detox program and attend Narcotics Anonymous meetings on a regular basis. By the end of this time, Frank had abstained from all drugs, and he was able to establish new social networks and increase his social contact within non-drug-using contexts. He successfully moved from his previous residence, and he started a new job in a completely new environment. Frank reported improvements in his marital relationship, and he managed to solve his financial problems through careful counseling and skills gained in budget management. All these changes gave the therapist the opportunity to partially shift his attention to Frank's life-long threatening memories and his history of loss and abandonment, very likely the primary causes of his depression and suicidal attempt. At follow-up (6 months after treatment) Frank reported that he was "on the right track," he acknowledged the therapist as an important and trusted figure, and he was ready to slowly discuss and face what he had experienced in childhood.

REFERENCES

American Psychiatric Association. (2000). *Diagnostic and statistical manual of mental disorders* (4th ed., text rev.). Washington, DC: Author.

Beck, A. T., & Steer, R. A. (1987). *Beck Depression Inventory: Manual*. San Antonio, TX: The Psychological Corporation.

Beutler, L. E., & Clarkin, J. (1990). *Systematic treatment selection: Toward targeted therapeutic interventions*. New York: Brunner/Mazel.

Beutler, L. E., Clarkin, J. F., & Bongar, B. (2000). *Guidelines for the systematic treatment of the depressed patient*. New York: Oxford University Press.

Beutler, L. E., & Harwood, T. M. (2002). What is and can be attributed to the therapeutic relationship? *Journal of Contemporary Psychotherapy, 32*, 25–33.

Beutler, L. E., & Harwood, T. M. (2000). *Prescriptive psychotherapy: A practical guide to systematic treatment selection*. New York: Oxford University Press.

Beutler, L. E., Moleiro, C., Malik, M., Harwood, T. M., Romanelli, R., Gallagher-Thompson, D., & Thompson, L. (2003). A comparison of the Dodo, EST, and ATI factors among co-morbid stimulant-dependent, depressed patients. *Clinical Psychology & Psychotherapy, 10*, 69–85.

Butcher, J. N., Dahlstrom, W. G., Graham, J. R., Tellegen, A. M., & Kaemmer, B. (1989). *Minnesota Multiphasic Personality Inventory—2 (MMPI–2): Manual for administration and scoring*. Minneapolis: University of Minnesota Press.

Castonguay, L. G., & Beutler, L. E. (Eds.). (2006). *Principles of therapeutic change that work*. New York: Oxford University Press.

Dowd, E. T., Milne, C. R., & Wise, S. L. (1991). The Therapeutic Reactance Scale: A measure of psychological reactance. *Journal of Counseling and Development, 69*, 541–545.

Fisher, D., Beutler, L. E., & Williams, O. B. (1999). Making assessment relevant to treatment planning: The STS Clinician Rating Form. *Journal of Clinical Psychology, 55*, 825–842.

Harwood, T. M., & Williams, O. B. (2003). Identifying treatment-relevant assessment: Systematic treatment selection. In L. E. Beutler & G. Groth-Marnat (Eds.), *Integrative assessment of adult personality* (2nd ed., pp. 67–81). New York: Guilford Press.

Howard, K. I., Krause, M. S., & Lyons, J. (1993). When clinical trials fail: A guide for disaggregation. In L. S. Onken & J. D. Blaine (Eds.), *Behavioral treatments for drug abuse and dependence* (NIDA Research Monograph No. 137, pp. 291–302). Washington, DC: National Institute of Drug Abuse.

Malik, M. L., Beutler, L. E., Gallagher-Thompson, D., Thompson, L., & Alimohamed, S. (2003). Are all cognitive therapies alike? A comparison of cognitive and non-cognitive therapy process and implications for the application of empirically supported treatments (ESTs). *Journal of Consulting and Clinical Psychology, 71*, 150–158.

Spielberger, C. D., Gorsuch, R. L., Lushene, R., Vagg, P. R., & Jacobs, G. A. (1983). *Manual for the State–Trait Anxiety Inventory.* Palo Alto, CA: Consulting Psychologists Press.

4

INTEGRATING THE PSYCHOTHERAPIES THROUGH THEIR EMPHASES ON THE FUTURE

BERNARD D. BEITMAN, ANGELA M. SOTH, AND GLENN E. GOOD

Despite marked distinctions in the underlying premises, theoretical constructs, and clinical techniques of the various camps of psychotherapeutic thought, all schools intersect in an ultimate concentration on the client's future. The effective psychotherapist helps clients rework disruptive expectations, anticipations, and intentions in order to develop realistic, adaptable, and achievable visions of the future. This process is necessarily shared by all psychotherapies because each orientation advocates the capacity to change and acknowledges the concrete nature of the past. A future-oriented approach to psychotherapy recognizes that human beings are teleological creatures and that behavior is controlled by its consequences: "A person's processes are psychologically channelized by the way in which he anticipates events" (Kelly, 1955, p. 46). Individuals are influenced to think, feel, and act through their images of the future: a panoramic vision composed of reassembled memories. Overlaid on developmental landmarks and cultural worldview, the individual's idiosyncratic history and patterns of response become the foundation of what is expected; in this sense, the future is remembered. Psychotherapy integration is achieved when therapists and clients collaborate to reshape problematic expectations of the future images that are based on debris of the past.

Some schools of psychotherapy are highly specific in articulating tones of a future-oriented approach to psychotherapy integration. Psychodynamic psychotherapy examines underlying client motives and formulates symptoms as projections of the future, such as impulses, wishes, and fears. Maladaptive defense mechanisms are conceptualized in psychodynamic theory as learned mechanisms for protection against imagined rather than real threats (Freud, 1927). Person-centered therapy attempts to modify negative self-expectations through clinical congruence, genuine acceptance, and positive regard (Rogers, 1951). Interpersonal therapists use here-and-now processing to provide clients with corrective emotional experiences so they may relinquish maintenance of aberrant relational patterns (Teyber, 2000). Cognitive–behavioral therapy views dysfunctional core beliefs as the lens through which clients predict future interactions and events (Ellis, 2001). Beck interpreted the process of anticipation as central to human action and emotion: "The role of anticipation in influencing feelings and actions is far more dominant than is generally recognized. The meaning of a person's experiences is very much determined by his expectations of their immediate and ultimate consequences" (Beck, 1976, pp. 40–41). Psychotherapists of feminist and multicultural orientations concentrate attention on the content and structure of clients' past learning and on sociocultural influences in particular in developing belief patterns better adapted to present and future functioning (Good & Mintz, 2001; Worell & Remer, 2003).

Across these theoretical foundations of a future-oriented approach, it is evident that in imaging potential futures, individuals regularly make plans to achieve intended or desired results. When these outcomes result in the anticipated goals, positive and optimistic emotions are typically experienced. When plans do not meet one's expectations, however, one's predominant emotional response is commonly dysphoric. Mismatches between anticipated and actual outcomes may be seen in disappointments and surprises such as foreshortened futures (early deaths and debilitating illness), catastrophic events like accidents or natural disasters, interpersonal conflict such as divorce or surrendered friendships, or disrupted developmental expectations like impediments in social or career goals. The unpleasant emotion of grief is typically associated with loss of a future; regret often represents a feeling correlated with "what might have been will not be," and anger is linked with an emotional response that "what should be is not or will not be." Within a future-oriented approach, such mismatches between that which is expected and the actual experiences of life form the basis of clients' distress and psychological symptoms.

Individuals formulate expectations of the future from prior experiences within their history, developmental norms, and cultural worldview. The brain registers the sum of one's experience and uses this material to rehearse future ways of thinking–feeling–doing–living; this procedural memory becomes the foundation for mental movies of one's future, or *expectation videos* (Beitman, Soth, & Bumby, 2005). Although some individuals may only be dimly aware of these expectations, others are cognizant of experiencing precise images of their plans and intentions. These future-oriented videos, occurring consciously or subconsciously, may be limited from an immediate short term (what is expected within the next few minutes) or may span a time continuum that reaches to long-term potentials (Madsen, 1999; O'Hanlon & Beadle, 1994). Expectation videos are composed of speech, images, thoughts, emotions, plans, and goals, with a template of scripts, actors, setting, and action.

Although these "movies" project themselves automatically in the mind, their component parts may also be summoned to active consciousness through deliberate self-awareness for examination, review, and revision. The protagonist of the expectation video is also its writer and director, selecting, organizing, and enacting the internal and external elements of a yet-to-be realized drama. As rehearsals for future events, expectation videos may be considered instruments for psychotherapeutic change. Therapists of all theoretical orientations try to relieve the intrusive impediments created by problematic mismatches between clients' expectation videos and their actual experiences. They typically do this by imagining alternative futures with the client. This reformulation of clients' thoughts, feelings, and actions, supplemented by controlled rehearsals of therapeutic experiences, provides the basis of a future-oriented approach to psychotherapy integration.

FUTURE-ORIENTED PSYCHOTHERAPY INTEGRATION MODEL

The process for this approach to psychotherapy integration entails a four-step model interlaced with a conceptualization of an integrated psychotherapeutic interpersonal relationship that moves through the stages of engagement, pattern search, change, and termination (Beitman, 1987; Beitman et al., 2005). The future-oriented supplement to this template involves, sequentially, activation of the client's observing self, identification of problematic expectations, modification of problematic expectations, and coconstruction of new expectations. Termination of psychotherapy emerges as the client acts independently in forming expectation videos, requires diminishing intensity and frequency of therapeutic collaboration, and can both maintain what has been learned and apply it to a widening breadth of experience to reality (Beitman et. al., 2005). The various psychotherapeutic schools, along with specific future-oriented integrative strategies, use a multitude of techniques to address the therapeutic goals within each stage of this model.

Activating the Observing Self

When individuals recognize troublesome symptoms and present for therapy, psychotherapists help them activate their self-awareness to identify patterns in their thoughts and behaviors (Deikman, 1982). In doing so, the therapist becomes an alternate observer of the client's self. With a practitioner co-observing the landscape of clients' minds, clients become better able to view themselves from a different perspective; such supplementary attention to subjective experiences helps guide self-awareness, assessment, visualization of opportunities, and choice of what to change (Beitman et al., 2005; Beitman & Soth, in press). This cognizance of self is a critical prerequisite for therapeutic change and may be activated through several techniques. Psychotherapists may call attention to the immediate dynamics of the therapeutic dyad, encouraging the client to "step back" in order to examine inner representations of role expectations and projections. Self-awareness may also be activated through therapeutic techniques such as relational restructuring, empathetic reflections, the empty chair technique, behavior monitoring, thought records, guided imagery, and journaling.

Identifying Problematic Expectation Videos

Faulty images of the future can precipitate such undesirable results as dysphoric emotions, maladaptive behavioral patterns, or troubled interpersonal relationships. Examining these outcomes can elucidate the underlying expectation videos. Psychotherapists of all orientations seek targets for change by working backward from signals of distress and forward from situations to identify the psychological variables connecting stimulus (trigger) with response (symptom). Theorists of the various schools have divided these intervening variables into several overlapping categories of symptom causation, such as wishes, fears, and conflicts in psychodynamic theory, cognitive distortions and dysfunctional automatic thoughts in cognitive–behavioral theory, and maladaptive interpersonal schemas in interpersonal theory. The concept of expectation videos weaves together these theoretical distinctions: Etiologic models within each of the schools can be consolidated within a word-image–based focus on the future.

The key to identifying expectation videos is detection of the unusual, excessive, or dysfunctional emotions or behaviors that emerge as a result of mismatches between clients' past experiences, current reality, and expectations of the future. Once recognized, these atypical responses can be conceptualized through the manner in which they are "reasonable" reactions to how the client perceives and interprets prior life experiences and, accordingly, anticipates the future. The diagnostic nature of expectation videos arises from their content: Although congruent with the past, the video message is incompatible with ongoing situational demands and present circumstances.

The psychotherapist helps clients to identify why particular visions of the future were learned and how these responses may be unlearned or modified to preclude creating further distress and undesirable situations. Psychotherapeutic techniques, varied according to theoretical approach, may work as amplifiers, illuminating the structure, quality, and composition of such videos. When expectation videos are identified, clients may choose to restructure their realities in accordance with these anticipatory films or erase inadaptable mental images and reconstruct new visions of the future.

Modifying and Coconstructing Expectation Videos

Modification of problematic expectation videos and coconstruction of new ones is a simultaneous process: As clients are relieved of undesirable visions, new realistic and adaptive expectations may be concurrently developed. This process begins when a client acknowledges a need and willingness to change, which may be augmented through the psychotherapist's use of value clarification and motivation enhancement techniques (Miller & Rollnick, 1991). Most school-based psychotherapeutic strategies indirectly help to erase problematic expectation videos without providing sufficient guidance in generating the new ones to replace them. The theoretical approaches that most directly provide clients with means to create new expectations are training packages that promote such specific skills as assertiveness, anger management, and basic interpersonal skills. These modules teach clients new ways of acting, reprogramming the procedural memory encoded in the brain's basal ganglia; through a future-oriented psychotherapeutic lens, this process helps produce new expectation videos. Systematic desensitization techniques expose clients to feared circumstances in a safe, controlled, and progressive manner until they are able to independently replace their old anxiety-laden expectation videos with new, less ominous ones. Instead of turning away from the dreaded situation of the old expectation video, the client is encouraged to slowly approach the fear until its actual harmlessness can be demonstrated; the client's expectation is proven erroneous by his or her actual experience and new expectations are concomitantly formed. When the therapeutic approximation is applied to a real situation, the client's memory of this experience becomes the basis for an expectation video displaying personal mastery and success.

Other more explicitly future-oriented methods intend to erase (rather than supplement) rigidly held expectation videos by creating new, adaptable ones. Tactics include forgiveness (dissolution of videos of punishment, regret, and revenge); "next day imagining" of small success experiences; and collecting effective, satisfactory videos (recognizing knowledge gained from previous negative experiences). Pretending that one's desires are realized, visualizing a future with nothing changed, projecting ahead 6 months, and looking back at the present from 10 years ahead are all effective exercises in helping clients understand the possibility of change and appreciate the availability of alternative expectation videos (Beitman et al., 2005).

In coconstructing a possible future expectation video with clients, psychotherapists should empower them to generate their own sense about what is sought from therapy, how to achieve this end, and what the ultimate outcome should look like. Therapists collaborate during this process by asking guiding questions to help clients sharpen their sense of what is desired and providing a neutral, nonjudgmental standard for healthy psychological functioning in interpersonal relations, thought patterns, emotional responses, identity formation, and symptom control. Different schools of psychotherapy view successful change, human ideals, and emotional well-being through differing lenses that color their specific theoretical orientation; future-oriented psychotherapy encourages integration of any and all theoretical elements, techniques, methods, and ideas that suit the needs of an individual client in terms of how expectations for the future influence current and future functioning. Once modified or new expectation videos are formulated, clients may "road test" their validity and durability in a variety of real-life situations. This involves extrapolating such new visions to present situations in order to refine, generalize, and assimilate therapeutic work to the external environment.

Changing personal perspectives on the future can be hard work, consuming time and emotional energy. One's old expectations are well ingrained and automatic: "I am who I have been." A person who characteristically ignores successes and discounts compliments tends to perpetuate the ongoing "I am incompetent" film by casting actors to speak the expected derogatory lines and editing out positive words and actions. Expectation videos continue to move by inertia in the same direction until sufficient psychological force knocks them off of their tracks and onto new ones. This is typically a jarring and scary process for clients, but at the same time, it is validated by the sense of safety and sanction inherent in a strong therapeutic relationship. Through therapist–client collaboration on new visions of the future, movement is created to release clients' old, maladaptive videos and form functional expectations.

CASE STUDY

A case study provided the original foundation for the aforementioned four-stage model of future-oriented psychotherapy integration. Kathy G. was the future-oriented theoretical impetus for development of the new psychotherapeutic framework, conceptualization for understanding symptoms, and honing of therapeutic change techniques. By filtering Kathy's presenting concerns, life history, cultural worldview, and patterns of behavioral and emotional responses through the construct of expectation videos, a theoretical integrative basis was formulated. This framework illuminates how expectations of the future influence experiences in the present, the distress caused by mismatches between expectations and reality, and the methods by which one can change and create different visions of the future.

Kathy, a 22-year-old, European American, heterosexual, middle-class woman, presented with reports of panic attacks and depressed mood of 6 years' duration. She also reported a history of difficult interpersonal relationships. Kathy had grown up in a small midwestern town that she described as a sheltering, conservative, and community-oriented environment. She reported that she had one older brother and that she had a mother who dominated her father. When Kathy was 5 years old, her father had an affair, divorced her mother, and remarried, often leaving Kathy under the care of a new stepmother. This woman, "the bitch my father sleeps with," physically and emotionally abused Kathy throughout her developmental years. Kathy reported that her father consistently sided with his new wife's criticism of Kathy and that her birth mother was only superficially supportive. Kathy's closest childhood friend, through whom she escaped the pressures of home, died after falling off of a rooftop when he was 13. When Kathy was 17, preparing for a dance recital, her best male friend was rushed to the hospital where he died of a rare virus. At age 20, Kathy's brother died suddenly while wrestling with his roommates. She described her romantic relationships as nongratifying, imbalanced, and short-lived. Kathy was a senior theater major at a large midwestern university when she came into psychotherapy.

Kathy reported that she knew she had been affected by her experiences but lacked insight into how they specifically influenced her current functioning and distress. Although seemingly motivated and determined to make therapeutic changes, she reported that the therapists and psychiatrists she had seen in the past offered little guidance for stimulating any perceivable psychological improvement. She had been maintained on 40 milligrams of Prozac daily and sought a new psychiatrist for medication maintenance and another attempt at psychotherapy. Her diagnoses were recurrent major depression and panic disorder without agoraphobia.

Activating Kathy's Observing Self

In the process of building a working alliance during the early engagement period, the therapist concentrated on helping Kathy activate her observing self so that she could better understand her subjective experiences. The theme of loss was evident in Kathy's reported history: her parents' divorce and the deaths of a childhood companion, best friend, and brother. The therapist helped Kathy to explore this issue more deeply and asked her to prepare a chronological timeline for the unusual scenes of death she had experienced so young in life. This homework assignment stimulated Kathy's active processing of her loss experiences. She began to ruminate about not being present at the time each of these persons, all male, had passed away. Her therapist selected the empty chair technique to enhance Kathy's self-awareness of this distress; when Kathy "spoke" to those for whom she grieved, it became apparent that in her subjective reasoning, her absence was the cause of the deaths. Her guilt was pervasive, and she tearfully apologized to the lost souls occupying the empty chair.

Kathy's sense of interpersonal shame was also magnified in the context of a developing conflict with her roommate, Jenna, who had been contributing less and less to her half of the rent in recent months. Jenna had been further irritating Kathy by becoming increasingly noisy in the apartment when Kathy needed to study quietly. Although Kathy had attempted to remedy these irritations by leaving timid notes, she could not bring herself to confront Jenna about her inconsiderate behavior. The therapist used cognitive–behavioral techniques to assist Kathy in activating her self-awareness of her core beliefs associated with resisting the process of directly approaching her roommate. Incrementally, Kathy became aware that her passivity reflected fears that assertiveness would cause Jenna to move out and, more poignantly, that Jenna would be unable to survive without her. Kathy discovered that she dreaded feeling guilty for causing this seemingly inevitable outcome. Activation of Kathy's observing self helped her understand more deeply the cognition and affect related to her current roommate difficulties and to extrapolate these observations to a more comprehensive view of her characteristic interpersonal style. This process also encouraged Kathy to trust her psychotherapist, feel confident about therapy itself, and prepare her for identifying and changing her problematic expectation videos.

Identification of Kathy's Problematic Expectation Videos

Kathy's growing cognizance of her underlying fears suggested to her therapist that they concentrate on Kathy's anticipations, expectations, and intentions for the future. To identify Kathy's behavioral, emotional, and cognitive patterns and understand how they intertwined with her images of the future, the therapist explored additional relationships in Kathy's life. In discussing her romantic experiences, Kathy reported that they all seemed to end abruptly despite her desire to develop a deep and lasting loving relationship with a man. She became furious when relating the varieties of requests men had made of her and described her terror at surrendering her individuality to be dominated by a romantic partner. Kathy described how she had ended her last relationship with a man after she had seen him at a coffee shop with an unknown female and how she had terminated the one before that when the man did not call her one evening. In both circumstances, Kathy reported she suffered what she believed to be panic attacks, in the former case after concluding that she had been abandoned for another woman and in the latter because she felt certain that her partner had been in a terrible accident. Consequently, she broke off both relationships to relieve her fears and anxiety. As a transference supplement to these feelings and reactions, Kathy eventually revealed that she felt fearful each time she left the therapy office, imagining that her psychotherapist might die. Kathy apparently saw her attention, presence, and nurturance as essential to the lives of those with whom she was close. She tied her presence to these persons, such as her therapist, roommate, and romantic partners, subconsciously expecting that her physical leaving of these individuals, parallel to her prior experiences of loss, would result in their deaths.

This clinical information contributed to a synthesis of Kathy's experiences, wherein her therapist was able to more comprehensively conceptualize her problematic expectations and differentiate the forest (Kathy's patterned responses) from the trees (events and details in her life). This formulation recognized how Kathy's exaggerated thoughts, emotions, and behaviors, such as reacting passively toward her roommate and impulsively to the presumed slights of lovers, corresponded with her early experiences of grieving unexpected deaths, being emotionally estranged from her parents, and observing her mother control others. Kathy's problematic expectation videos thus adopted four predominant themes: the inevitable and sudden death of any individual, particularly a male, to whom she felt close; romantic betrayal and abandonment; fear of lost identity as the price of affection; and finally, that she would grow old and die alone.

Modifying and Coconstructing Kathy's Expectation Videos

These painful and terrifying expectations dominated Kathy's world and were the source of her feelings of panic and chronically dysphoric mood. The therapist recognized that these thematic visions emerged from Kathy's life experiences and set about to help her eliminate and replace these expectation videos with ones more positively adaptive to the conditions of her life. Using cognitive–behavioral techniques, her therapist encouraged Kathy to consider alternative evidence to counter her inadaptable thoughts and emotions, which triggered behaviors causing undesirable outcomes. Kathy and her therapist reviewed her extreme responses to her recent romantic partners and entertained other possible scenarios accounting for the events she interpreted so catastrophically. The woman in the coffee shop could have been a relative or a friend, the missed phone call the result of a family emergency or a late business meeting. The therapist asked Kathy to imagine reacting differently to interpersonal interactions, perceiving situations through the filter of alternative dynamics, and acting in unfamiliar roles.

Because of the reflexive and obstinate nature of Kathy's accustomed pattern of expectations, she was initially highly resistant to a changed way of thinking, feeling, and behaving. By regularly reminding Kathy that her response patterns were the product of her prior experiences and not necessarily representative of current reality, the therapist was slowly able to encourage Kathy to understand the possibility of other interpretations, outcomes, and expectations. Combining these reformulations with breathing exercises to relieve her anxiety, Kathy slowly learned to envision the future differently.

Kathy's empowerment to define and construct her own realistic ideals was a significant part of this intervention. The therapist collaborated with Kathy on the development of alternative future visions, but Kathy was the ultimate writer and producer of her own expectation videos. She reported that she wanted to perceive the intentions and actions of others, such as men and her roommate, realistically. In doing so, Kathy imagined herself speaking assertively to her roommate without ensuing tragedy and being involved in a committed, egalitarian romantic relationship that did not regularly threaten her independence or provoke her anxiety. She was thereby able to imagine herself remaining calm if a date did not show up to meet her on time, understanding that extenuating circumstances were a more realistic interpretation than death or betrayal. Her expectation videos of future relationships were relieved from preponderant visions of domination, abandonment, sudden death, and lonely old age, to be newly characterized by images of calm reaction to minor relational infractions, comfort in discussing anxiety-arousing issues with partners, and trust in others. As she became less frightened at the prospects catalyzed by her old visions, Kathy was also better able to relinquish her subconscious idea that others' lives depended on their closeness to her. Relief from this burden lifted her sense of doom and assuaged her panic.

Kathy's new expectation videos cleared dysfunctional pathways in her mind so she could perceive, think, feel, interpret, and act differently. She thereby released herself from problematic self-fulfilling prophecies and was better prepared to cope with external stressors. After coconstructing new expectation videos with her therapist, Kathy began dating a man in whom she developed a romantic interest. When he began displaying highly dependent behavior, suggesting a fear that Kathy would leave him, Kathy used her newly activated self-awareness and psychological insight into how expectations can elicit distress to handle this situation in an improved manner. She perceived her own old movies running in her partner's mind and was able to recognize a reenactment of her old maladaptive relational patterns in his interpersonal mannerisms. Having disentangled herself from her own undesirable expectations, Kathy encouraged her romantic interest to explore his own darkened forecast of the future; when he was unwilling to do so, she reluctantly but thoughtfully extracted herself from the relationship. After maintaining distant contact over time, Kathy eventually recognized a gradual improvement in his readiness to change, and she renewed what became a satisfying relationship for both of them. Using the tools imparted by future-oriented psychotherapy, Kathy was able to mobilize her abilities to define and enact realistic boundaries without depriving herself of opportunities to prosper and feel empowered to make healthy decisions.

The therapeutic relationship was terminated when Kathy no longer experienced panic attacks, reported abated depression, gained the capacity to scan possible futures, and completed her college education. Kathy left the therapeutic dyad reportedly understanding that negative events, although inevitable, may be responded to in a variety of ways. Through running different expectation videos about her future, Kathy gained the ability to replace distressful anticipations with adaptive ones, thus allowing her to act differently in the present. She was no longer emotionally constrained by a sense of certainty that the future could only repeat a disappointing past.

CONCLUSION

Kathy's case study, illuminating the form and shape of this future-oriented approach to psychotherapy, was the foundation for a systematic theory of integrated design. In activating her observing self and reconstructing problematic expectation videos, Kathy was armed with the tools she needed to change detrimental patterns and alleviate distress, not only during psychotherapy, but also throughout her life. Kathy's story, although perhaps colored with details more unusual than the average client's, is not exclusively applicable to the use of a future-oriented approach to psychotherapy integration. Her case is shared, carefully chosen by us and shaped through the context of the readers, to open gateways into the psychotherapeutic integrative landscape, expose the future-based undertone of all theoretical schools, and reveal the usefulness of expectation videos enfolded in therapeutic details and unfolded through theoretical meta-analyses.

REFERENCES

Beck, A. T. (1976). *Cognitive therapy and the emotional disorders*. New York: International Universities Press.

Beitman, B. D. (1987). *The structure of individual psychotherapy*. New York: Guilford Press.

Beitman, B. D., & Soth, A. M. (in press). Activation of self-observation: A core process among the psychotherapies. *Journal of Psychotherapy Integration*.

Beitman, B. D., Soth, A. M., & Bumby, N. A. (2005). The future as an integrating force through the schools of psychotherapy. In J. Norcross & M. Goldfried (Eds.), *Handbook of psychotherapy integration* (2nd ed., pp. 65–83). New York: Oxford University Press.

Deikman, A. J. (1982). *The observing self*. Boston: Beacon.

Ellis, A. (2001). *Overcoming destructive beliefs, feelings, and behaviors: New directions for rational emotive behavior therapy*. Amherst, NY: Prometheus Books.

Freud, S. (1927). *Inhibition, symptom, and anxiety*. Oxford, England: Psychoanalytic Institute.

Good, G. E., & Mintz, L. B. (2001). Integrative therapy for men. In G. Brooks & G. E. Good (Eds.), *The new handbook of psychotherapy and counseling with men: A comprehensive guide to settings, problems, and treatment approaches* (Vol. 2, pp. 582–602). San Francisco: Jossey-Bass.

Kelly, G. A. (1955). *A theory of personality*. New York: Norton.

Madsen, W. C. (1999). *Collaborative therapy with multi-stressed families*. New York: Guilford Press.

Miller, W. R., & Rollnick, S. (1991). *Motivational interviewing: Preparing people for change*. New York: Guilford Press.

O'Hanlon B., & Beadle, S. (1994). *A field guide to possibility land: Possibility therapy methods*. Omaha, NE: Center Press.

Rogers, C. (1951). *Client-centered psychotherapy*. Boston: Houghton-Mifflin.

Teyber, E. (2000). *Interpersonal process in psychotherapy* (4th ed.). Stamford, CT: Wadsworth.

Worell, J., & Remer, P. (2003). *Feminist perspectives in therapy: Empowering diverse women*. Hoboken, NJ: Wiley.

5

ASSIMILATIVE PSYCHODYNAMIC PSYCHOTHERAPY INTEGRATION

GEORGE STRICKER

Assimilative psychodynamic psychotherapy integration has been described in great detail previously (Gold & Stricker, 2001; Stricker & Gold, 1996, 2002). It is a particular application of assimilative integration (Messer, 1992), an approach in which a central theory is maintained but techniques from other theoretical approaches are incorporated as they appear to be useful. Assimilative integration is one of the four key approaches to psychotherapy integration (Stricker & Gold, 2003) and perhaps the one used most frequently by practitioners, although not always acknowledged as such.

Assimilative psychodynamic psychotherapy integration begins with a relationally oriented approach to psychodynamic formulation in order to understand the patient. The technique of choice is a standard reflective psychodynamic set of interventions, but techniques borrowed from cognitive, behavioral, and humanistic approaches are incorporated. The assimilation of these techniques expands the boundaries of traditional psychodynamic approaches, perhaps facilitating a more immediate and rapid change in the patient. The key is to do this assimilation in as seamless a way as possible so that the introduction of new techniques is experienced as part and parcel of a consistent approach rather than an arbitrary intrusion on the ongoing work.

The meaning of the intervention changes along with the change in theoretical context, and the therapist must be aware of this. For example, the meaning of role-playing, which is a typical part of cognitive–behavioral treatment, is altered when a therapist who is usually reflective assumes such an active role.

Although many practitioners are able to assimilate techniques into their "home" theory, it is unusual to also engage in accommodation and alter the theory to take into account the value of a technique that would not have been suggested by that theory. Stricker and Gold (1988), rethinking the notion of a one-dimensional theory of change, have instead taken an approach to accommodation that involves a circular model, in which changes in behavior can lead to changes in understanding, just as changes in understanding can lead to changes in behavior.

This circular model has been developed using a three-tier approach to understanding and treating the patient (Gold & Stricker, 1993; Stricker & Gold, 1988, 1996). The three tiers are the behavioral, which is the most observable and conscious; the cognitive and affective; and the psychodynamic, which is the least observable and most unconscious. Each tier influences the other two, interventions can occur at any point in the tiers, and an intervention at one tier is likely to reverberate in the other two.

One of the key concepts of the relational framework is that of the corrective emotional experience (Alexander & French, 1946), in which a patient is in a familiar situation but receives an unfamiliar response. In this way, the patient's expectations, which are consistent with destructive images of the self and others, are met by unfamiliar and more comforting responses, and the self-images and patterns of behavior can be altered. The corrective emotional experience was initially conceptualized within the framework of transference, and it was thought that change was accomplished through the therapist's responses, discrepant with the patient's expectations. Such corrective emotional experiences also may occur outside the therapeutic relationship, and the discontinuity between expectation and reaction in therapy may encourage the patient to test these expectations outside of the consulting room. In this way, meaningful change can be accomplished as relationships become less difficult and more rewarding.

The concept of corrective emotional experience initially was developed within a traditional one-person psychodynamic model, and it was met with great resistance because of the activity it required of the therapist. The importance of the therapeutic relationship as an exchange between two active participants makes the two-person relational model a more comfortable paradigm for the therapist. Closely related is the notion of an enactment or a re-creation of earlier relationships that the patient attempts to develop with the therapist (and with others in the patient's external world). The ability of the therapist to disengage from the enactment, help the patient to understand it, and provide a different and corrective emotional experience is critical to the patient's ability to understand what is happening, relate to it more comfortably, extend it into the external world, and ultimately arrive at important change.

There are many times in a routine treatment where such exploration is not sufficient to achieve the desired gains. In these instances, the introduction of techniques that are designed to accelerate behavior change can be helpful, and these are assimilated into the therapeutic interaction. These techniques not only are useful in producing behavioral change, but consistent with the three-tier formulation, they also can be an impetus to achieving further understanding. Thus, the relationship between understanding and change is cyclical, and the emphasis can be on either one, depending on the stage of treatment and the needs of the patient.

My general approach is to begin with psychodynamic exploration and then introduce more behavioral interventions as may seem helpful. It should be noted that there is solid evidence for this sequence (Shapiro & Firth, 1987; Shapiro & Firth-Cozens, 1990), although, another sound method (Fensterheim, 1993) reverses the sequence. It is likely that the preferred sequence depends on the patient's presenting problem. The behavioral–psychodynamic sequence is more likely to be helpful with patients with focused symptoms, whereas the psychodynamic–behavioral sequence was developed for use with patients with more characterological problems.

CASE HISTORY

Saul was a 50-year-old man, married for 20 years to Sharon, with two sons, 16 and 11. He was a practicing attorney, initially in a family firm operated by his father Eli and his older sister. In the preceding year, the firm had gone out of business and he found himself given less favorable treatment in the division of assets. He was in a heated battle with Eli (as he referred to his father) over one remaining account and subsequent payments from Saul to his father (per their agreement when the business closed), which Saul did not want to provide because of the unfair division of accounts. Saul described himself as depressed, short-tempered, and unmotivated; he was tearful, had trouble sleeping, and was gaining weight. He did not want to consider medication. He also described himself as an honest, straightforward man with little pretense, soft and easily taken advantage of, and now being victimized by his father and sister. He initially talked about how he could prevail and how much confidence he had, but he had trouble speaking concretely about his situation and clearly felt that Eli had never appreciated him and had mistreated and exploited him in business; Saul did not feel that he was able to extricate himself. He now wanted to establish himself but did not have the energy to do it effectively. He came to treatment at Sharon's urging.

The tone for the treatment was set at the first session, as is often the case. Saul did not come of his own volition and, because of his conflicted relationship with his father, was distrustful and wary. I responded to this by listening carefully, speaking gently, only asking necessary questions, and never making any judgments about what he was telling me. Gradually, he seemed to relax slightly, agreed to weekly sessions aimed at helping him with the depression, and said he did not want to talk about the past (he had been in treatment as an adolescent because his parents thought that there was something wrong with him). I explained the structure of treatment to him, including his responsibility for a $15 co-pay according to the terms of his insurance contract, and he agreed and left two bills on my desk. (He never gave the money directly, always leaving it for me in the same manner, apparently so as not to contaminate our relationship with the crass appearance of payment.) As he was leaving, I looked at the money and called after him. He asked what I wanted, and I told him that one of the bills was not a 10. He angrily wondered what it was, and I told him it was a hundred-dollar bill. He sheepishly exchanged it, but his bristly front disappeared, and he was very cooperative and involved in treatment after that time. I did not inquire about the motivation behind the overpayment, because there was no need to challenge him or to invite defensiveness, and at that time he had not yet developed curiosity about his actions.

In the next session, Saul said that he felt very upset and angry after the first session, then felt a fog rolling over him and was too depressed to work the next day; finally the fog lifted and he felt better until it was time to come to his next session, when he felt the fog coming in. We spoke about the problem not being depression as much as his difficulty with anger, his defense being the fog, and the depression being subsequent to it. This made sense to him, and we spoke about various ways he had dealt with anger. Foremost among these were taking walks and secluding himself, which he had not been doing. Saul seemed much lighter, left feeling somewhat better, and vowed to do more to take control of his life.

Almost immediately, Saul spontaneously began to talk about some of his early experiences, despite his initial expression of a wish not to do so. The most interesting experience was an emblematic incident in which he ran away from home as a teenager, functioned well in California, but then returned to go to college when Eli asked him to do so. I wondered whether there were any colleges in California, and he recognized how he had abandoned his independence to return to the safety and security of his father's shelter. This incident captured the conflict between his desire for independence, his apparent ability to function well on his own, yet his insecurity about that ability and his reliance on his father for assurance about that ability. Unfortunately, his father always favored Saul's sister and expressed his disappointment with Saul. Saul's internalization of this view of himself was behind the anger he felt over the unfair division of the firm, but he was unable to deal comfortably with the prospect of being on his own.

Saul related a prophetic dream early in treatment, in which his father threatened to sell the firm out from under him unless he complied with his financial wishes. Saul felt that he had been threatened and that he might have to give in but that if he did so he would feel that he had lost. Over the years, he had made several decisions, starting with returning from California, in which he acceded to his father's wishes, but this did not get him the acceptance he craved. He also was sensitive to what others, even virtual strangers, thought of him, and this resulted in a loss of control of his life direction that he found intolerable.

The early portion of treatment followed the structure of traditional exploratory treatment. Saul talked about many of his early experiences, usually with his father, and his subsequent sense of inadequacy and disrespect. These were related to his current experiences with his father, with others in his life, and with me. The key to the therapy was his experiencing of these events and connections in the context of his relationship with me. In me, he found an older man whom he experienced as understanding, accepting, and affirming of his worth. This allowed him the freedom to explore his feelings and to experiment with new behaviors. It represents a good illustration of the corrective emotional experience, and Saul enjoyed and profited from it.

From the beginning, Saul was extremely reactive to events around him. If he lost an account, he would assume that Eli would have retained it, and his father did not help by reiterating that criticism of his son. We discussed how this experience was rooted in his early experiences with his father and that he was inclined to recreate the early experiences but that he did not have to do so if he was aware of the origin of this inclination.

At this point, with some clarity about dynamic issues, I began to introduce some behavioral interventions designed to make his dynamic insight more conscious and able to be translated into action. The first of the two major verbal touchstones that he was given was not to take things personally. Saul felt that he gained immensely by keeping this in mind and often would pause before responding to realize that some slight he had received was not about him, and he could go forward without recalling the deep sense of inadequacy that he carried with him.

The second of the verbal touchstones was not to expect people to be what they were not. In his dealings with Eli (and with Sharon), he constantly found himself expecting them to be more responsive to his feelings and needs but always feeling disappointed that they were not and then hurt and rejected when they behaved as they always had. Much of treatment held his feelings and reactions up to this awareness of the need not to take things personally and not to expect people to change.

The depression that brought Saul to treatment lifted rapidly as soon as he began to take more responsibility for himself and to realize that he could do so. He also began to deal more constructively with his father, standing up for himself and not caving in to the pressure to make a deal that would not be in his best interests. Even when an initial deal fell through because Eli backed out, Saul did not become depressed but instead recognized that his father had been at fault rather than he, and he was able to move forward in a productive manner.

Although Saul was functioning in better ways, he initially questioned whether we were getting anywhere but continued to work hard and to try to make connections between his early experiences and his current predicament. He saw these connections as being expressed in his social relations as well as the familial ones, and he began to be a little more assertive, and with that, more comfortable in situations he previously had avoided. Later in treatment, he came to accept the need for patience while working toward change and was determined to be true to himself, act with integrity, and be pleased whatever the outcome.

Saul referred to his mother as an example of someone who was always a victim, something he did not want to be. We then reviewed situations in which he saw himself as a victim. These seemed to be ones in which he had done nothing wrong but that Eli would have handled better. His authority for this was Eli himself, who always told him how inadequate he was and how much better he, Eli, would have handled it. Saul then began to work on learning to quiet the Eli voice in his head that reinforced his sense of inadequacy and did not allow him to experience the success he deserved.

Saul began one session by saying that no catastrophes happened during the week and that he was trying to preplan what he should do so that he would not get caught in uncomfortable situations. He then gave an example, I began to comment positively, and he explained what he had meant. I remarked on how he had become defensive before I finished, and he noted that I had just gotten a glimpse of the real Saul. We then spoke about his discomfort with the praise he craved but never received, and that his discomfort was because it always had been the other way. He saw the self-fulfilling prophesy aspect of his view of praise and the world and how he expected to be a lonely old man, just like his grandfather, and now was acting in a way to assure that it would happen.

In general, the sessions were conducted in a predominantly exploratory way, and Saul proved to be an involved and cooperative patient. At various times I introduced cognitive tasks, such as the verbal touchstones mentioned earlier. I also helped him by role-playing situations that were in the offing, a more behaviorally oriented intervention to which he responded well. He often remarked that he was happy about the disappearance of his symptoms and his better way of handling things but still felt the same nagging doubts that always beset him. This contrast between behavior, which changed nicely in response to specific interventions, and underlying change, which occurred slowly, is typical of the course of assimilative integrative treatment.

When I asked Saul for permission to write this case up, his immediate response was that it would be all right with him, but he did not want to read it because he did not need to be reminded of all his problems. I asked him whether he realized that I also would be including something about how much I liked and respected him and about his decency and competence. He said he realized that but always focused on the negative. However, in the next session he said that he would like to read the report and to show it to Sharon so that she would be aware of some of his good qualities.

When Saul returned after reading the report, he mentioned several areas where I had not done justice to him, often because space did not allow a full exposition or because disguising particular details led to what he saw as a distortion of who he was. He was pleased that Sharon had read it and agreed that it was accurate in many places, and he did not ask for any changes. In many ways, this unusual exercise of allowing the patient to read a report about his progress and dynamics was reminiscent of Ryle's (Ryle & Low, 1993) Good-Bye Letter to the patient, an intervention taken from cognitive analytic therapy. It was successful in that it indicated respect for the patient, a nice summary of the course of treatment, and a means of helping the patient organize the experience of the past year.

CONCLUSION

Saul's treatment followed a traditional pattern of assimilative psychodynamic psychotherapy integration, inasmuch as any treatment can be traditional within this framework. Saul's condition was understood from a psychodynamic theory viewpoint, and the general approach was reflective and expressive. When I deemed it necessary, I introduced various interventions from other orientations. This is where treatment varies from patient to patient. For Saul, there were some cognitive interventions (the exhortations not to take criticism or negative situations personally and not to expect more from others than they could do), some role plays, and the Good-Bye Letter. The entire treatment was conducted within the framework of a therapeutic relationship that was sound and facilitative from the beginning and that allowed Saul to experience corrective emotional experiences at many different points in treatment. These experiences then were generalized outside the consulting room, as Saul experimented with behaving differently with Sharon and Eli. To the extent that his new behavior drew different responses, he learned and grew. Where his responses could not elicit anything different, as was often true with Eli, Saul fell back on the mantra not to expect more of others than they could deliver.

The relationship of the treatment to the three-tier model seems clear. The initial approach to treatment focused on the third tier, psychodynamic, and illuminated many of Saul's problems and concerns. The introduction of cognitive interventions (second tier) clarified the psychodynamic issue and helped Saul to translate his insight into behavioral change. The role play was a more direct behavioral intervention (first tier) and also helped directly with behavior change, but the subsequent change led to further exploration of Saul's feelings and thoughts.

My formulation was that Saul had developed a self-concept of being inadequate and a potential victim, both from the way he was treated by Eli and the way he saw his mother respond to his father. The goal of treatment, then, was to help Saul, a competent man with many fine personal qualities, to recognize his ability and give it the opportunity to flourish. The beginning of this was in our relationship, and as he could experience the extent to which I valued him, he began to look at himself differently. At this point, it was necessary to expand that recognition to the world around him, and the role-playing and cognitive interventions encouraged this. Although I was not particularly active throughout the treatment, my assumption of a more active role was not jarring for Saul because he experienced it as part of my attempt to be helpful to him and was consistent with his wish for clear guidance. However, even when he got the response from others that he hoped for, he did not always feel better, and so an extended period of working this through was necessary. When the response from others was inconsistent with his hopes, he used the cognitive interventions (a) to avoid taking it personally and thus having his low self-concept confirmed and (b) to recognize the shortcomings of the people he was dealing with. As he was able to make some changes in his world, his sense of being a victim diminished, and this allowed him to become more assertive. The cyclical way in which one gain can feed on others was noteworthy and also typical of psychotherapeutic progress.

If I had to select a single change agent in the course of treatment, I would point to the corrective emotional experiences, both within and outside the treatment room. However, it would be simplistic to credit this single influence; it is clear that these experiences simply facilitated the ways in which Saul took a more active role in shaping his life and began to think better of himself. In the critical way in which these things happen, both the active role and the improved self-concept reinforced and fed into each other. Saul was grateful for the gains he made, but more important, he recognized the role he played, and could continue to play, in making his life more rewarding.

REFERENCES

Alexander, F., & French, T. (1946). *Psychoanalytic therapy*. New York: Ronald Press.

Fensterheim, H. (1993). Behavioral psychotherapy. In G. Stricker & J. R. Gold (Eds.), *Comprehensive handbook of psychotherapy integration* (pp. 73–85). New York: Plenum Press.

Gold, J. R., & Stricker, G. (1993). Psychotherapy integration with personality disorders. In G. Stricker & J. R. Gold (Eds.), *Comprehensive handbook of psychotherapy integration* (pp. 323–336). New York: Plenum Press.

Gold, J., & Stricker, G. (2001). Relational psychoanalysis as a foundation of assimilative integration. *Journal of Psychotherapy Integration, 11*, 43–58.

Messer, S. B. (1992). A critical examination of belief structures in interpretive and eclectic psychotherapy. In J. C. Norcross & M. R. Goldfried (Eds.), *Handbook of psychotherapy integration* (pp. 130–165). New York: Basic Books.

Ryle, A., & Low, J. (1993). Cognitive analytic therapy. In G. Stricker & J. R. Gold (Eds.), *Comprehensive handbook of psychotherapy integration* (pp. 87–100). New York: Plenum Press.

Shapiro, D., & Firth, J. (1987). Prescriptive vs. exploratory psychotherapy: Outcomes of the Sheffield Psychotherapy Project. *British Journal of Psychiatry, 151*, 790–799.

Shapiro, D., & Firth-Cozens, J. (1990). Two year follow-up of the Sheffield Psychotherapy Project. *British Journal of Psychiatry, 157*, 389–391.

Stricker, G., & Gold, J. (1988). A psychodynamic approach to the personality disorders. *Journal of Personality Disorders, 2*, 350–359.

Stricker, G., & Gold, J. R. (1996). Psychotherapy integration: An assimilative, psychodynamic approach. *Clinical Psychology: Science and Practice, 3*, 47–58.

Stricker, G., & Gold, J. R. (2002). An assimilative approach to integrative psychodynamic psychotherapy. In J. Lebow (Ed.), *Comprehensive handbook of psychotherapy: Integrative/eclectic* (Vol. 4, pp. 295–315). New York: Wiley.

Stricker, G., & Gold, J. R. (2003). Integrative approaches to psychotherapy. In A. S. Gurman & S. B. Messer (Eds.), *Essential psychotherapies: Theory and practice* (2nd ed., pp. 317–349). New York: Guilford Press.

6

AN INTEGRATIVE PERSPECTIVE ON THE ANXIETY DISORDERS

BARRY E. WOLFE

Over the past 2 decades, I have developed an integrative perspective on the anxiety disorders. The term *perspective* in this context refers to two interrelated theories, an integrative etiological theory of anxiety disorders and an integrative psychotherapy for anxiety disorders. This division is based on the assumption that an etiological theory directs the therapist to the targets of change, whereas a theory of psychotherapy specifies how to bring about change in these target areas (H. Arkowitz, personal communication, March 10, 1986). Both theories represent a synthesis of the major extant perspectives of anxiety disorders and their treatment, including psychodynamic, behavioral, cognitive–behavioral, experiential, and biomedical perspectives (Wolfe, 2005b). This particular perspective therefore represents an example of a theoretically driven integration of existing etiological and therapy models.

ETIOLOGICAL MODEL OF ANXIETY DISORDERS

The guiding premise of the etiological model is that anxiety disorders are based in patients' chronic struggles with their subjective experiences.

The experience of severe anxiety in selected situations gives rise to conscious anticipations of impending catastrophe, which at an implicit level reflect a fear of exposing unbearably painful views of the self. The exposure of these self-wounds is accompanied by overwhelming affects such as humiliation, rage, and despair. Thus, anxiety disorders appear to possess a conscious layer and an implicit layer in terms of what the anxiety symptoms mean to the individual.

The external and internal cues that provoke anxiety are developed through one's perception of relationships between certain life experiences and intense fear. That is, certain experiences are perceived as self-endangering. The cues themselves often function as a kind of shorthand for the painful memory that exists beyond the individual's conscious awareness. Thus, for example, an agoraphobic woman's fear of losing control is signaled by a feeling of lightheadedness, which is the same feeling she had when she panicked at the sight of physically disabled people years before.

All painful views of the self suggest a perception and experience of the self as being unable to cope with—and therefore needing protection from—the rigors and realities of everyday living. Because these realities are unavoidable, anxious individuals must create indirect coping strategies that both protect them from intolerable affective states and keep them from facing these realities head on. Such strategies range from behavioral avoidance to cognitive ritual and emotional constriction, and they usually produce unintended interpersonal consequences that have the paradoxical effect of reinforcing the patient's painful core beliefs about the self. Self-wounds result from the interaction of damaging life experiences and the cognitive and emotional strategies designed to protect individuals from their feared catastrophes. These strategies, however, keep the person from facing his or her fears and self-wounds head-on. In response to the initial anxiety, patients typically engage in cogitating about being anxious (i.e., self-preoccupation), avoiding the fear-inducing objects and situations, and engaging in negative interpersonal cycles. These strategies result in the temporary reduction of anxiety and the reinforcement of the patient's underlying maladaptive self-beliefs. Psychological defenses in this model serve as self-defeating efforts to protect one's image of the self (see Wolfe, 2005a).

With respect to social phobia, the specific self-wounds tend to involve core self-perceptions as socially inadequate, unlovable, or unworthy (Wolfe, 2005b). These wounds often derive from frequent shaming messages received from the person's original family or his or her expanded social environment. The individual internalizes these toxic opinions, which result in a generalized view of self as defective or inferior. Social situations and public-speaking opportunities, for example, produce the experience of self-endangerment. The self-endangerment experience is the intense anxiety or panic that "protects" the individual from having to experience the excruciatingly painful feeling of inadequacy. The extreme humiliation that a person feels when faced with his or her sense of inadequacy is unbearable and is thus avoided by experiencing instead the often more painful panic attack.

Self-endangerment leads to a shift of attention and from there to a preoccupation with one's social—or in the case presented later, public-speaking—limitations and with imagined rejecting reactions of a hostile or disdaining audience. This self-preoccupation, or what I call *obsessive cogitation*, about the potential catastrophic meaning of one's immediate anxiety is a major maintaining factor in public-speaking phobia. Self-preoccupation results in the awareness of a discrepancy between the experience of "the way one is versus the way one ought to be." The experienced gap between the actual self and the idealized standard produces anxiety or pain (Higgins, 1987).

A second major maintenance process is avoidance. Individuals with social phobia avoid speaking opportunities and social engagements. Avoidance leads to a short-term reduction of anxiety, but it reinforces the underlying self-wounds and therefore the social phobia.

A third maintaining factor is the interpersonal strategy of impression management, which is basically to present oneself in such a way as to elicit a positive impression from others. When a positive impression is communicated to the anxious individual, he or she experiences a temporary reduction of anxiety because it is not necessary to face the feared negative self-image. This reassurance is only temporary, however, because the anxious individual "knows" at some level that he or she is "fooling" the other person. Because the individual believes the other person has been fooled, the latter's credibility as an accurate judge of the anxious individual has been undermined. Anxious people, therefore, have great difficulty believing positive feedback from others. Finally, because of these above-mentioned strategies, the self-wounds remain unhealed, resulting in the continuation of the social phobia.

AN INTEGRATIVE PSYCHOTHERAPY FOR ANXIETY DISORDERS

The psychotherapy model envisions four phases: (a) establishing the therapeutic alliance, (b) treating the symptoms, (c) eliciting the tacit self-wounds, and (d) healing the self-wounds. Typically, this psychotherapy initially focuses on symptomatic change to give the patient a sense of control over the anxiety symptoms. Relaxation strategies, exposure to the feared object or situation, and cognitive restructuring are the first line of treatment for anxiety symptoms as soon as the therapeutic relationship is solid enough to support this often harrowing work. When patients gain some control over their symptoms, they may opt to explore and modify the underlying causes of their anxiety disorder.

A deeper level of change is achieved by having patients confront, experience, and ultimately revise the extremely painful self-views they morbidly fear. This work may be done by (a) analyzing and gently confronting patients' defenses against direct experience and (b) conducting experiential work that allows patients to emotionally process their feared self-views. Wolfe's focusing technique (Wolfe, 2005b), Socratic questioning (Beck, 1995), and the downward arrow technique (Beck, 1995) are often useful in helping patients contact their self-wounds. Wolfe's focusing technique, which involves a strict attentional focus on the internal or external anxiety stimulus, is usually effective in eliciting the tacit self-wounds and their associated painful emotions (Wolfe, 2005a). After patients contact the painful feelings, experiential interventions are frequently used to emotionally process the painful self-views. The tasks include (a) differentiating the painful self-views that are based in fact from those that are based in inaccurate or toxic opinions, (b) learning to experience and tolerate the painful realities of their lives and begin to develop a remediation plan to transform their liabilities into strengths, (c) transforming the toxic and inaccurate self-views, and (d) resolving the catastrophic conflicts that have helped maintain their self-wounds. The techniques used for this depth-oriented work include the empty chair dialogue, the two-chair dialogue, guided imagery, focusing, and the use of transforming metaphors. Behavioral experiments are then designed to help patients enact the emerging new sense of self.

This integrative psychotherapy can serve both as a short-term or long-term treatment. It is typically conducted once a week. If the treatment focuses only on the surface-level symptoms, patients should experience improvement in 6 to 20 sessions. If, however, treatment is extended in order to identify and heal the underlying self-wounds, the treatment may take anywhere from a year to 18 months. These figures are in keeping with the findings of research by Ken Howard and colleagues, which showed that behavior change can be achieved fairly rapidly but that change in core self-beliefs may take much longer (Howard, Kopta, Krause, & Orlinsky, 1986).

The advantage of this therapy over mainstream therapies for anxiety disorders is that it often leads to more comprehensive and durable change. Its long-term focus is the amelioration of the underlying determinants of an anxiety disorder, which makes relapse less likely.

CASE STUDY

Glen was a 45-year-old university economics professor who presented with a moderately severe case of social phobia, which primarily involved public speaking. He was afraid of revealing any signs of anxiety such as his voice cracking or tremors in his extremities. He construed such symptoms of anxiety as incontrovertible proof of his incompetence. However, he was most fearful of having a panic attack, expressing the idea that panicking in such a situation was extremely humiliating and felt to him like an annihilation of self. Glen experienced high levels of anticipatory anxiety, which could begin as long as a month or more before he was to give the talk. If he could begin his talk, within a few minutes, the anxiety subsided and he was able to perform.

Glen was born to parents who originally were from El Salvador. He was the eldest of three brothers, one of whom was mentally handicapped. His father was a businessman who was not particularly successful. His mother was a housewife. The explicit and implicit rules of this family were based on traditional gender roles. According to Glen, it was his father's wish that he become a very masculine man. Any behavioral deviation from a traditional concept of masculinity was viewed as shameful. Glen had always felt like a disappointment to his father because he was not a good enough athlete and not tough enough. Glen's relationship with his mother was also difficult. He did not remember her ever saying that she loved him. She apparently was not particularly affectionate with him, and she held at bay any of his affectionate overtures. Glen possessed an ambivalent relationship with his mentally handicapped brother. On the one hand, he loved him very much; on the other, he was resentful of the attention his brother received and fearful that his brother's mental retardation meant that his own intelligence was limited.

Case Formulation

Glen's primary self-wound was the view of self as weak and unmasculine. A related part of the network of images and beliefs was the self-view as an intellectual imposter and of "not being good enough" in any field of endeavor. It was hypothesized that his public speaking phobia was based in a fear of being exposed as a weak, insufficiently masculine intellectual imposter. Having a panic attack while speaking was incontrovertible proof to Glen that this painful self-view was true.

Characteristics of Self-Experiencing

Glen usually experienced significant anticipatory anxiety well before he was scheduled to speak. This anxiety could build to a significant level and, on occasion, could prevent him from speaking altogether. The anticipatory anxiety was almost exclusively focused on his fear of having a panic attack while he was speaking. Glen construed his experience of anticipatory anxiety to be a cue that a panic attack was very likely. He feared that if a panic attack were to occur, many—if not most—members of the audience might change their opinion about his intellectual capabilities.

As is typical with individuals suffering from a public-speaking phobia, Glen's attention would automatically shift out of the immediate experience of his task (i.e., what he was trying to communicate) to worrying about the significance of his anxiety. As his talk approached, his attention automatically switched to cogitating about the potentially catastrophic meaning of having a panic attack, which interfered with his being able to carry out his talk smoothly.

Underlying Feared Catastrophes

Our imagery work uncovered two closely interconnected fears that appeared to drive Glen's public-speaking phobia: that people would view him as both intellectually incompetent and insufficiently masculine. Thus, he considered having a panic attack while giving a talk the ultimate emasculating experience. The basis for this interconnection, as mentioned above, lay in Glen's family background. During his development, he had learned from many different family members that shame is a major catastrophe and that the most shameful behavior was to be unmanly or unmasculine. Hypermasculinity was prized above all. Therefore, for Glen to reveal any sign of weakness was despicable. Glen was the first member of his family to receive a college degree (much less a doctorate). Thus, he expressed his "masculinity" through intellectual achievement and created for himself a novel pathway, within the context of his family, to masculine achievement. It became clear during our work that any challenge to his intellectual competence was also a challenge to his sense of masculinity. It also became clear that despite his secure reputation in his field as a respected and productive scholar, Glen harbored significant doubts about his intellectual capabilities. Before certain groups of scholars, he often had the feeling that he was an imposter. To be discovered as a fraud was yet one more feared catastrophe.

Glen had one major hobby: He raced cars. He was often invited to speak before groups of auto-racing enthusiasts. He was as fearful of panicking in this context as when he needed to give a major academic address. In both contexts, the feeling of panic had the same meaning: that he was a weak and pathetic man who had no right to lecture, much less belong to, this masculine group.

Impression Management as an Interpersonal Strategy

When I asked Glen to imagine the scene in which he was about to give a talk and he had a panic attack, he became aware that his carefully nurtured illusion of intellectual superiority would come tumbling down. The imagery work also revealed that Glen had substantial doubts about his intellectual capacities, even though he had published often and his colleagues valued his work. He often felt like an imposter whenever he was invited to give a talk.

In addition, he became aware of his terror that his colleagues would come to view him as an "intellectual lightweight." He also became aware of the various stratagems he used for presenting himself as intellectually superior. Thus, his continual need to perform perfectly conflicted with his self-belief that he was far from perfect, and this conflict produced a wide gap between the view he actually held of himself and the way in which he presented himself to others, that is, between his self-belief and his self-presentation. At the same time, however, he often felt like an imposter and was acutely aware that he believed he was "not enough of" a man, a scholar, or a lover. In fact, he believed he was not enough in any field of endeavor that was important to him. During his development, his father and uncles harshly criticized him if he did not display appropriate masculine behavior and achievements. Glen had internalized this harshly critical attitude and consequently was now extremely critical of himself and his loved ones.

Interpersonal Consequences

Glen's harshly critical behavior had produced a severe strain in his 15-year marriage. His wife, who was a practicing social worker, had often felt intimidated by Glen's criticisms and now found it difficult to relate to him in a loving manner. Glen attributed malevolent motives to her growing indifference and became enraged at her "manipulativeness." In fact, she had emotionally withdrawn to protect herself from Glen's critical outbursts. If, however, she tried to express her concerns to him, he typically disagreed. He feared that to agree with her criticisms and to alter his behavior in response to her concerns would represent a shameful lack of masculine assertiveness. Glen construed such self-imposed behavior modification as "capitulation" and therefore as a pitiable sign of weakness. He therefore felt he must present to her an image of himself as a man who could take charge, one who was in control of the situation. On the other hand, the attrition of his wife's displays of love and passion toward Glen had raised doubts in his mind concerning whether he was "enough" of a man, lover, or husband for her.

Glen's Psychotherapy

Glen's therapy can be divided into four separate but interrelated stages. They include (a) establishing a therapeutic alliance, (b) managing the symptoms, (c) eliciting the self-wounds, and (d) healing the self-wounds.

Establishing a Therapeutic Alliance

I did not have an easy time establishing a therapeutic alliance with Glen. Because shame was a central issue in his social phobia, Glen allowed access to his most vulnerable experience at a slow pace. He was concerned about my opinion of him, particularly about whether he was an interesting enough patient. Perhaps the first rupture in our alliance came when he noticed my becoming heavy-lidded while he was talking. I had had insufficient sleep the night before, and I was struggling to be alert for Glen. His response was telling. Without a hint of sarcasm, he said, "I am sorry that I am not a more interesting patient today." This response bore the imprint of a family history filled with shaming responses from his father and uncle. His response was also a major clue to the implicit meaning of his panic attacks and anticipatory anxiety. Although he assumed a deferential stance with me during the therapy hour, he would go home angry. It was a significant indication of therapeutic progress when he finally could allow himself to express his anger toward me for my almost falling asleep while he talked. As the therapy progressed, the alliance strengthened and we were able to maintain a solid working partnership throughout the therapy.

Managing the Symptoms

After several sessions during which Glen described the nature of his problems and the implications of his public speaking fears for both his career and personal well-being, he was ready to participate in the symptom management phase of treatment. We began with my explaining the rationale of my integrative psychotherapy and segued into my teaching him diaphragmatic breathing (DB). The breathing technique became his most important tool for coping with anxiety, and he continued to use it frequently and successfully.

In anticipation of giving a talk, Glen would cogitate about the audience's likely reaction to his having a panic attack. This attentional shift made it difficult for him to focus on giving the talk. Thus, the second technique that I taught Glen was to retrain his attention away from cogitation toward a focus on what he wanted to communicate to the audience. In conjunction with DB, attention retraining gradually enabled Glen to reduce his anxiety. A third technique involved his preparing short talks during which he could use both DB and attention retraining as coping skills. Eventually he rehearsed with me the actual talk he was planning to give.

Attention retraining in conjunction with DB provided significant relief to Glen, and it convinced him that he could control the level of his anxiety both before and during his talk. One mark of this progress was that before therapy he would begin to cogitate and obsess a month before he had to give a talk. After about 12 sessions, he did not start cogitating until a day or two before the talk. He also clearly experienced the reciprocal relationship with respect to anxiety between focusing his attention on the talk and cogitating.

Eliciting the Self-Wounds

With these improvements in the management of his anxiety symptoms, Glen wanted to explore the roots of his anxiety. We began with imaginal probes using Wolfe's (2005a) focusing technique. I asked him to imagine having a panic attack while giving a speech and to notice the feelings and thoughts that arose. He began to experience intense feelings of humiliation and to harshly criticize himself for being weak and pathetic. He also imagined the audience coming to his aid and being sympathetic. This also humiliated him because it made him feel weak and needy. As we continued the probe, he began to encounter feelings of being an intellectual imposter and thoughts that he really was not as intelligent as he would like others to think.

When we explored the network of images associated with his self-perceived level of intelligence, we found that he had a split in his self-view. One view was that he was very bright; the other view was that he was an intellectual imposter. I asked him to engage in a two-chair dialogue between the two self-views in an effort to help him integrate these two perspectives. This work helped him to entertain the possibility that he was smart enough to be successful in his field. As he began to assimilate this self-view, his public speaking anxiety decreased.

The most difficult challenge in working with Glen at this level was the attempt to modify the shameful connotations of panic. If he were to have a panic attack while giving a talk, Glen would harshly condemn himself as pathetic, weak, and an intellectual fraud. He would then imagine his colleagues revising their good opinion of his abilities and his being paralyzed by the resulting shame. The imagery probes revealed that the harsh, condemning voices originally belonged to his mean-spirited uncle and his disappointed father. His father in particular, Glen believed, was disappointed that Glen was not a better athlete and that he was not a star achiever in traditional masculine endeavors. These kinds of experiences and memories produced in Glen a core self wound that he was not a good enough athlete, man, husband, and academic. For Glen, to panic was to confront this unbearably painful self-view as "not enough."

Healing the Self-Wounds

In our effort to heal this self wound, we encountered a number of startling obstacles. One of these involved Glen's relationship with his father. Glen was angry and hurt that his father rarely listened to him. A core memory involved Glen trying to have a conversation with his father and the latter having his face in a newspaper. At the same time, however, Glen was unable to tell his father about his achievements. I asked Glen to do some empty chair work with his father. I asked Glen to tell his father about his achievements and to also tell him that in some ways he had surpassed what his father had been able to achieve in his life. This request terrified Glen. He could not do it. He was afraid that such declarations would deeply hurt his father. In fact, Glen was afraid that he might permanently damage his father psychologically. This fear was still prominent in Glen's mind even though his father had been dead for many years. Thus, Glen had constructed a conflict of the "damned if you do, damned if you don't" kind. He was in pain because he continued to believe that his father was disappointed in his achievements, but he could not own those achievements in his father's presence for fear that his father would be shattered.

Because Glen could not confront his father in actuality, we engaged in work to restructure his memories of their relationship. Glen worked hard during the empty chair procedure to tell his father that he had made a success of his career and of his life. Eventually, he was able to do this comfortably and to subsequently imagine his father responding with the following statement: "I always knew you would be successful, but it was difficult for me to tell you how much I respected you and how proud of you I really am." These, by the way, were the actual words his father uttered on his deathbed. The empty chair work resulted in Glen feeling less conflicted about owning and accepting his real competence.

As mentioned above, Glen attempted to present himself as a superstar academic who should be considered one of the leading authorities in his field. However, he was painfully aware of the gap between the image that he was trying to project and how he actually felt about himself. To modify this defensive tendency, Glen engaged in imagery exercises in which he had a panic attack and told his audience that he had a problem with public speaking. This letting go of his secret began to undermine his impression management strategy. We continued to work on his accepting whatever his abilities were and doing the best he could. I encouraged him to tell someone he trusted that he was in therapy because he had a public-speaking problem. As Glen became more and more willing to risk these disclosures, he discovered just how much his secrets were helping to keep him anxious.

Glen began to realize that the impression management strategy was yoked to his tendency to constantly compare himself with other academics. Attention retraining was reintroduced to help him replace social comparisons with intrinsic motivations. Consequently, we worked on keeping his focus on the task of delivering his ideas and on why he considered these ideas useful or important rather than on the constant self-diminishing comparisons with other academics. This combination of self-acceptance and attention retraining went some way toward reducing his anxiety about speaking in general. Over time, he was virtually anxiety free when he had to prepare and give a talk.

Another aspect of the self-acceptance strategy involved his experiencing the feelings connected with acceptance of his limitations. When he tried to face the fact that he might not be as intelligent as he would like others to think, he experienced a great deal of sadness and pain. Through the emotional acceptance of his limitations, Glen was able to come to the realization that despite his limitations, he was still intelligent enough to make contributions to his field that would be respected and valued by his colleagues.

A final piece of the therapeutic work concerned reframing the meaning of panic per se. Even after our work on self-acceptance, attention retraining, and allowing and accepting the feelings associated with the acceptance of one's limitations, Glen still found the idea of having a panic attack unbearably humiliating. To address this problem, we took two different tacks. The first was to have Glen experience and survive being humiliated. This approach was based on the safe assumption that humiliation is an ontological given. We all experience it. We all can survive it. The second tack was to redefine panic as a problem that represented one small aspect of his being, a problem that he was living with and trying to solve but one that did not represent a total characterization of him as a person. By the end of therapy, Glen had made some headway in redefining panic's meaning, but he was still uncomfortable with the idea. The healing of his self-wounds continued, and he was able to approach the task of giving a talk with much greater self-confidence and much less apprehension that he would be viewed as a pathetic imposter if he should happen to have a panic attack.

By the time Glen terminated therapy, he was able to give his talks virtually free of anxiety. His anticipatory anxiety had been reduced close to zero. Moreover, he engaged less and less in impression management and was able to catch himself when he occasionally felt the urge. He had made great progress on detoxifying the shameful meanings of a panic attack. The thought of panicking before his peers still carried a significant emotional charge, albeit one that no longer debilitated him. It was conceivable that he would return to therapy someday to finally complete this task.

SELECTION AND SEQUENCING OF INTERVENTIONS

Although I have suggested a prototypical sequence of interventions in the four-phase model of psychotherapy, it is obvious that different patients may require a different sequence, because different patients possess different access points for the process of change. For a variety of reasons, patients differ in their comfort level in the initial focus of therapeutic work. Some patients prefer to respond to life's challenges through action, others by thinking and planning, and still others through gaining a "feel" or emotional sense of a problem. Behavior change is the initial access point for most patients, but for some patients, it is cognitive change, and for a few patients, therapeutic work may begin with a focus on bringing about corrective emotional experiences (Alexander & French, 1946). Selecting the wrong initial access point can seriously impede the progress of therapy. For example, I once attempted to use imagery work with a depressed patient who, after several failures, finally told me, "I am not comfortable with the language of feelings." I immediately switched to cognitive–behavioral interventions. For Glen, we followed the typical sequence of interventions, beginning with behavioral interventions, adding cognitive techniques, and eventually moving to experiential procedures supplemented by psychodynamic inquiry and cognitive–behavioral techniques.

CHANGE MECHANISMS

My clinical experience suggests that different change processes may be associated with different foci of change. Behavior change, for example, can occur with or without changes in the cognitive or emotional realms. Individuals with phobias can learn to approach their feared object but may continue to experience significant anxiety. People can also rationally reevaluate their beliefs and change those at a cognitive level. This may or may not be accompanied by behavior change. Change at the level of self-belief and self-experiencing, however, appears to require corrective emotional experiences. These experiences necessarily embed cognitive changes, and they increase the possibility that any future behavior change will be experienced as congruent with a revised perspective on the self. Change at this level results in an individual feeling and thinking differently about self and others. In other words, some kind of emotional processing seems to be a necessary ingredient of an enduring change process.

Glen, for example, was able to reduce his public-speaking anxiety by applying a relaxation strategy (i.e., DB) and changing his behavior (i.e., attention retraining). Later, he began to entertain the idea that he was smart enough to make valued contributions to his academic field of endeavor. A variety of emotional processing tasks helped him have a corrective emotional experience with respect to the toxic meaning of having a panic attack. These included tasks that helped Glen (a) accept and express painful and threatening feelings; (b) experience himself as an equal to his father without destroying himself or his father; (c) eliminate his impression management strategy, thereby reducing the gap between his experience and his presentation of self; and (d) emotionally accept the painful reality that he was not as intelligent as he would like to believe.

SUMMARY

Glen's public-speaking phobia represents a prototypical illustration of the self-wound model of the etiology of an anxiety disorder. His treatment is an example of an integrative psychotherapy that initially focuses on the symptoms and only later attempts to elicit and modify the underlying determinants of the disorder. His self-wound clearly was based in significant doubts about his intellectual ability that he attempted to hide from both himself and others. In every encounter, the public-speaking setting represented for Glen the context that automatically generated anxiety about the possibility of his "secret truth" becoming exposed. To publicly display signs that he was having a panic attack was the ultimate humiliation, one that he believed would lay bare for all to see his utter worthlessness and insufficiency as an adult human male.

The integrative psychotherapy illustrates that empirically supported techniques were available to help Glen become more comfortable in a reasonably short period of time with public speaking by helping him stay focused on the task of communicating his ideas and by undercutting the catastrophic thinking that generated his anticipatory anxiety. The more depth-oriented phase of the therapy provided other integrative techniques and clinical strategies that elicited and repaired the underlying self-wounds that appeared to be the ultimate source of Glen's public-speaking anxiety. This case study illustrates a fact that therapists have known for some time: It is possible to treat the symptoms of an anxiety disorder in a short period of time, but it takes a long-term treatment to bring about change in its underlying determinants.

REFERENCES

Alexander, F., & French, T. M. (1946). *Psycho-analytic therapy: Principles and applications*. New York: Ronald.

Beck, J. S. (1995). *Cognitive therapy: Basics and beyond*. New York: Guilford Press.

Higgins, E. T. (1987). Self-discrepancy: A theory relating self and affect. *Psychological Review, 94*, 319–340.

Howard, K., Kopta, M., Krause, M., & Orlinsky, D. (1986). The dose–effect relationship in psychotherapy. *American Psychologist, 41*, 149–164.

Wolfe, B. E. (2005a). Integrative psychotherapy of the anxiety disorders. In J. C. Norcross & M. R. Goldfried (Eds.), *Handbook of psychotherapy integration* (2nd ed., pp. 263–280). New York: Oxford University Press.

Wolfe, B. E. (2005b). *Understanding and treating anxiety disorders: An integrative approach to healing the wounded self*. Washington, DC: American Psychological Association.

7

CYCLICAL PSYCHODYNAMICS

JERRY GOLD AND PAUL L. WACHTEL

Cyclical psychodynamics (Wachtel, 1977, 1997) is the name of an integrated theory of personality and of psychopathology as well as an integrative psychotherapeutic approach. Cyclical psychodynamic theory offers a model of personality in which behavior, interpersonal relationships, and unconscious motivation and conflict mutually determine each other. From this vantage point, unconscious motives, fantasies, and representations of the self and of others can best be understood in the context of the person's actual life circumstances and ongoing transactions with others rather than from a narrower internal or strictly intrapsychic perspective. This expanded, contextually oriented theory assists therapists in understanding how meaningful changes in psychodynamics could lead to or follow from changes in behavior and in interactions with others rather than deriving exclusively from insight obtained through interpretation.

Cyclical psychodynamic theory (Wachtel, 1977, 1997) is an integration of interpersonal and relational psychoanalytic concepts with ideas from social learning theories, experiential theories, and family systems theories. It adds to the standard psychodynamic understanding of the historical origin and nature of unconscious processes by conceptualizing the patient's seemingly regressive unconscious wishes, fantasies, and images as schemas that evolve in a context of continuing interaction with other people (Wachtel,

79

1981). These psychodynamic variables may thus be seen to be as much the result of repetitive and skewed ways of looking at the world, of processing emotion, and of interacting with others as they might be the causes of such behavior. Further, these unconscious issues are understood to be maintained and reinforced by the responses of the persons with whom the patient is interacting.

Inferred unconscious processes are assigned an extensive role in cyclical psychodynamic psychotherapy: They are a key source of information about unnoticed or unacknowledged aspects of significant interpersonal relationships, as well as a possible remnant of unresolved issues from the past. The latest iteration of cyclical psychodynamics has expanded the theory to include concepts drawn from family systems theory, relational psychoanalysis, experiential theories, and cognitive theory (Wachtel, 1997).

Cyclical psychodynamic psychotherapy includes the usual psychodynamic concerns with the clarification and understanding of the patient's past and present psychological life through inquiry, clarification and interpretation, and an examination of the therapeutic interaction and the processes of transference and countertransference. However, in cyclical psychodynamic psychotherapy this psychodynamic orientation is expanded to include the use of techniques drawn from the full range of behavioral, cognitive, family systems, and gestalt therapies, among others, as well as through traditional exploration, interpretation, and insight. It is assumed that insight often is the outcome of psychological change rather than simply and exclusively being the precursor to change and that important insight into the patient's history and psychodynamics frequently follows spontaneously from the successful use of active interventions such as desensitization, assertiveness training, the empty chair technique, or reframing, to name just a few. Any effective therapeutic intervention, regardless of its origin, may reach and change unconscious conflicts, fantasies, and depictions of the self and of other people, and thus a wide range of interventions is potentially useful within an integrative, psychodynamically informed psychotherapy.

Anxiety is a critical variable in the development and maintenance of psychopathology, and therefore exposure to the causes and sources of anxiety is a significant change factor in treatment. Any intervention that identifies the intrapsychic or interpersonal sources of the patient's anxiety and assists the patient in gradually facing that anxiety may be used (Wachtel, 1977).

A central concern in this therapy is the possible impact on the patient of pathogenic relationships with a parent, spouse, employer, or other significant person that may potentially be more powerful than the impact of the new experience with the therapist. At times, these persons may be highly invested, consciously or unconsciously, in keeping things as they have been despite the patient's wish for change (Wachtel, 1977, 1991). The patient's symptoms, for example, may stabilize the relationship or keep the patient in a dependent, powerless position. Often, however, neither patient nor accomplice wish the relationship to proceed as it has, yet each ironically ends up drawing from the other the very behavior that perpetuates it. Cyclical psychodynamic therapy is thus strongly based on an ironic perspective that suggests that people unwittingly recreate pathogenic childhood experiences despite their earnest intentions to find new sorts of relationships, because these early experiences skew and limit their ability to make new and better choices (Gold & Wachtel, 1993). This is in contrast to the tragic perspective that is typical of traditional psychodynamic therapies, which assumes that the patient is unconsciously trying to recreate the past in order to obtain those gratifications that remain ever elusive and tantalizing. (See Messer's [1992] discussion of the ironic and tragic perspectives in psychotherapy as well as chap. 21, this volume.)

A key aim of the cyclical psychodynamic therapist's use of active interventions is thus to empower the patient and assist the patient in learning new interpersonal skills that may allow her or him to minimize the impact of these ironic perpetuations of old patterns. As the patient uses this new learning to change the interpersonal context in which he or she lives, the motivations, wishes, and fantasies that both shape and are created by these problematic encounters often become more accessible to consciousness and less of a troubling presence in the patient's mind. New experiences of interpersonal competence may also make the patient more aware of, and less affected by, some of the historical experiences that may have limited her or his ability to make other and better types of choices in relationships.

CASE STUDY

Silvana was a married White woman in her 50s who lived in a middle-class suburb.[1] She came to therapy complaining of recent feelings of hopelessness, dejection, and sadness that she could not link to any specific incidents or circumstances in her current life situation. She also noted that she felt as if she had "lost herself," by which she seemed to mean that her ability to identify what she wanted in life and to go after it with enthusiasm had waned significantly.

Silvana was a successful, self-employed professional who worked as a consultant to agencies in her area. She noted that her business required her to do a fair amount of networking to maintain the contacts that generated referrals. In the past she had enjoyed these activities, but her recent distress had made it difficult for her to find the confidence to call established contacts or to make the "cold calls" through which she usually obtained new business. Silvana had been married for about 3 years when she entered therapy. Her first marriage of about 15 years' duration had ended a decade earlier

---

[1]Silvana was a patient of Jerry Gold's.

because of her first husband's substance abuse. She described her current spouse as a warm, dependable, athletic, and competent but somewhat insecure man who was prone to "pout when he feels neglected." This was his second marriage as well. The couple had no children from any of their marriages and had the financial resources, time, and shared eagerness to engage in many sports and cultural activities together.

Silvana agreed to a course of psychodynamically oriented psychotherapy on a once-per-week basis. We discussed the role of patient and of therapist in this type of therapy and also the possibility of incorporating other techniques, experiments, and homework assignments as they might seem advantageous at various points in the future. Silvana was enthusiastic about this possibility. She often brought a notebook to sessions, identified issues about which she wanted to think further between sessions, and frequently asked about ways to use in the time between sessions ideas and insights that had been generated in sessions.

In the beginning phase of therapy, the work was exclusively exploratory. Silvana spoke freely about all aspects of her life: her work, her marriage, her dreams, her friendships and leisure activities, and her history. Occasionally, the focus of the sessions moved to the therapeutic relationship when a transference issue emerged, but these issues were mild and relatively transient, usually focused around a nagging feeling that Silvana had somehow displeased the therapist by slacking off as a patient, or by not making "enough progress quickly enough." These issues were explored and helped Silvana learn how she perceived the therapeutic relationship, and perhaps other current relationships, from the somewhat demanding perspective out of which she evaluated herself. In psychodynamic terms, we found that she projected an internal critic onto the people with whom she interacted.

As these issues were explored, their sources in Silvana's relationships with her parents became more visible. She recalled many scenes from her childhood in which she had observed her mother "criticizing and nagging" her father for not working hard enough, and she remembered her fear that her mother would turn on Silvana as well. Her father was a more benign presence in her life but not an active giver of support. Silvana recalled that he seemed beaten down by her mother and by life in general and that she had felt sorry for him and would try to entertain him in the evenings by telling him amusing stories about her day at school. As a result, Silvana concluded, "That's how I became a perfectionist and a people pleaser, to placate and appease my mother, and to try to bring my father back to life and to help him cope with his depressions." These discussions became the central focus of an extended phase of therapy, during which Silvana investigated the extent to which her energy, time, thoughts, and emotions were invested in anticipating the needs of others in her life and the cost of investing in the pleasure of others at the expense of her own authenticity and goals.

These discussions also made Silvana more aware of the resentment, anger, and jealousy that were evoked by her people-pleasing activities. She gained considerable insight into the role that these suppressed and disavowed emotions played in her presenting symptoms of depressions and hopelessness and in the recent lack of confidence that she had felt at work. The most profound discovery, according to Silvana, was making the connection between

> being a people pleaser, being secretly angry about putting everyone first, and feeling that I'm losing myself and becoming invisible and transparent. I guess to feel solid and real, we have to be able to put what we want first sometimes, and not worry so much about other people and how they feel.

Silvana was pleased with these insights and experienced some mild and transient relief from her dejection and anxiety. However, the improvement was not as great as she or the therapist had hoped. It was apparent that insight alone could not change this longstanding pattern of relating to herself and to others. It also became clear that there were interpersonal pressures, in- and outside of the therapeutic relationship, that were interfering with Silvana's tentative steps toward change.

She and the therapist began to look at these relationships and their influence on Silvana's intrapsychic life and her efforts to put herself first. It became obvious to us both that her people-pleasing demeanor had manifested itself in the therapeutic relationship, in the form of pleasing the therapist and of making him feel good about himself. In her typically astute, sensitive, and competent way, Silvana had sized him up and had recognized that an enthusiastic response to psychodynamic exploration, and expressions of appreciation for the insights gained, was an excellent way to stroke a psychodynamic therapist. They began, in a tentative and uncomfortable way, to look at the cues that Silvana read from the therapist that signaled her to be appreciative and enthusiastic and to talk about her fears of being more real in the sessions. At the same time, they looked at her current relationships, particularly with her husband and close friends, and the ways in which her sensitivity to their moods impeded her attempts to change. When they compared the interactions in therapy to her everyday interactions, there seemed to be a great deal of similarity. In her daily life, Silvana's uncertain and timid attempts to speak her mind or to act independently were met with puzzlement, vague and subtle disapproval, or, more frequently, ignored and treated as if they had not occurred. In particular, it became clear that her husband's "pouting" and feelings of being neglected when she attempted to take care of herself not only were reminiscent of her father's depressions but were powerful reinforcers in the present. Eventually, she would give up and go back to her familiar, pleasing ways and would observe a restored positive tone to the interaction. Silvana would experience a short-term sense of relief and lessening of anxiety, which would be followed by the return of her sadness, anxiety, and sense of being "not all there, or not really a whole person." Often these experiences would be followed by reveries or dreams in which she found herself in some unpleasant interaction with her mother or other person from her past.

At this point, she and the therapist were able to formulate Silvana's psychological difficulties and some potential solutions with the expanded framework of cyclical psychodynamics. They postulated that Silvana had unwittingly recreated the environment and emotional climate of her childhood home by involving herself with people, including her husband and close friends, who seemed warm and giving but who quickly became dependent on her cheeriness and energy to ward off their own feelings of insecurity, depression, and anxiety. Though these individuals clearly cared for and about Silvana, they could not tolerate her tentative efforts to change, and together they had created an interpersonal system of rewards and punishments in which Silvana was positively reinforced for returning to old, caretaking patterns of behavior and was negatively and aversively responded to when she tried to behave more assertively. This pattern had emerged in the transference–countertransference interaction as well.

These interaction cycles not only kept her feeling stuck interpersonally but also stymied any attempts to resolve the psychodynamic issues that had been explored in therapy. She could not integrate or lessen her feelings of anger and resentment because these emotions were consequences of the actual unsatisfying relationships in which she was involved. Because she believed that the expression of such feelings would be entirely threatening to those to whom she was attached, she was left with no choice but to suppress and disavow her angry and hurt feelings, and as a consequence continued to be depressed and to feel "unreal." She and the therapist began to understand that her retreat to the past in dreams and fantasies and the continuing attachment to anger and resentment toward her parents were as much a symbolic expression of the emotions that she could not use in the present as they were leftovers from her childhood.

This formulation led to a dramatic technical shift in the therapy. They began to work on ways that Silvana could assert herself more effectively and could lessen the impact of the negative messages that she received when she stopped putting everyone else first. They worked on this primarily through the use of variants of behavioral rehearsal and assertiveness training, the largest components of which were in-session role-playing and graduated homework assignments.

At first, they focused on the therapeutic relationship, with the goal of enabling Silvana to speak more freely about her perceptions, opinions, wishes, and feelings. They did this because she felt that the therapist was less invested in "keeping her in her place" than were her husband and friends, and because she felt she had less to lose if he were hurt or offended than if someone else in her life were to feel this way. Because Silvana was an avid note-taker and diarist, they evolved the plan that she would write a description of each session soon after it occurred and include in that description any thoughts, feelings or reactions that would have made her feel more authentic had she talked about them with the therapist. They would then begin each session with a review of these diary entries and a discussion of the anxieties connected with admitting more of her true experiences into the sessions. As Silvana became more comfortable with this process, they began to role-play interactions in which she re-created segments of the previous session, including the disavowed thoughts and feelings that she had reported in her diary. These periods of behavioral and cognitive work flowed easily and naturally in and out of sequences of psychodynamic exploration of the impact and meaning of the interventions as well as of other significant events in her current life.

Eventually, Silvana was able to talk without overwhelming anxiety about the more negative and uncomfortable aspects of the therapeutic interaction in the here and now. These experiences generally were concerned with momentary feelings of irritation at the therapist, of seeing aspects of his personality that she felt were silly or selfish (she usually had a point), or of getting wrapped up in some idea or interest to the point that she forgot about him and whether he was interested. They then turned to her relationships with her husband and friends and used a similar sequence of techniques. Silvana observed herself in interaction with these individuals and brought to the sessions detailed notes about her behavior and the aspects of the interactions that she wanted to change. They then practiced these changes through role-playing and explored the impact and meaning of attempting to make such changes. Silvana experienced a great deal of anxiety about the possibility of upsetting her husband and friends and noted the similarity of her current fears to those she had experienced as a girl when faced with her irate and critical mother. She concluded, "It's time to put Mom to rest and for me to grow up. If they [husband and friends] don't like it, it can't be as bad as things feel now." She and the therapist added to the assertiveness training explicit work on anxiety management through diaphragmatic breathing and soothing self-talk and practiced a kind of cognitive–perceptual reorientation, in which Silvana guided herself to focus on her own inner experience, thoughts, and feelings, rather than on the verbal and nonverbal feedback that she might get from her husband and friends. This last intervention arose from her request to find a way to become less sensitive to, and therefore influenced by, their distress and potential criticism.

There then followed a period of several weeks during which the therapy was devoted to examining Silvana's progress in dealing with her "neurotic accomplices" as she gradually and gently introduced more of her needs, ideas, and interests into her significant close relationships. Her path was gratifyingly successful, expectedly uneven, and fraught with deep and painful potholes. A couple of friends made it clear that they had no use for this new version of Silvana, and she thought long and hard about whether the cost of losing those relationships was worth the gain of feeling more like herself. She decided that friendship needed to be more mutual than it had been with these people, and moved on. Other friends made the adjustment, and the relationships with these individuals became more nuanced and symmetrical. Her husband was baffled, hurt, irritated, and yet sometimes supportive of her efforts. He felt neglected and pushed aside and yet at times recognized that she was happier and that as her people-pleasing diminished, she had become a more complex and interesting person as well. Their relationship became somewhat stormier during this period but also more gratifying, and eventually her husband decided to begin psychotherapy to deal with his feelings of insecurity and neglect.

The ups and downs of these interactions were reflected in the ebb and flow of the psychodynamic material that Silvana brought to her sessions. When feeling confident about her new ways of coping with other people, Silvana was able to perceive and to experience herself in newly autonomous ways. When her accomplices pushed back hard and angrily, as for example when her erstwhile friends expressed their disapproval, her fears of loss and abandonment and her attachment to the critical image of her mother, became dominant themes. Her husband's loving but often bewildered and hurt response to her assertions of self evoked many issues connected to her father's passive resignation and impotent love, until she made it clear to both men (her husband in real life, and her father in the subjective realm of memory and emotion) that she no longer was invested in treating them like children in need of protection. As Silvana solidified this stance in her marriage, she was able to grieve for her father and to move beyond the sadness of that relationship.

At the end of this period of therapy, Silvana reported that she felt "more real than I've ever felt in my life. I'm sometimes tempted to be that old people pleaser, and do fall into it, but the unreal feelings are such a warning that it doesn't last long." She had established a new friendship that she thought was promising, because this person seemed comfortable with Silvana's expression of her own interests and desires. She was aware of and wanted to be prepared for the periodic emergence of undermining behavior by old friends and family, and it was this issue that was the most important focus of the last part of the therapy. The therapist used a form of relapse prevention as they role-played possible interactions in which she was pressured to conform to the need of the other person.

Silvana was moderately anxious about termination. Her main concerns mirrored the important themes of the therapy: She was afraid that the therapist would be offended by her wish to stop, and she worried that she would be too vulnerable without regular contact. Interpretation of the former issue led to immediate recognition, then to a great deal of laughter on her part, and to a seeming resolution of the issue. Her fear of vulnerability was handled by the response prevention exercises mentioned above and by a gradual increase in the time between sessions (from weekly to bimonthly to monthly) over the course of about 3 months. The therapy was ended by mutual consent after about 2 years.

CONCLUSION

This case illustrates the interplay of insight, exposure, new learning, and alteration of the interpersonal context of the patient's world in producing important and profound changes at several levels of psychological life. These improvements were gained in a painful and painstaking way, with the usual stops, starts, and missteps that typify all psychotherapies. Cyclical psychodynamic psychotherapy allows patient and therapist access to all spheres of psychological and interpersonal experience without privileging or devaluing any sphere or any set of psychotherapeutic ideas or techniques. Integrative psychotherapy of this type is conducted in an experimentally oriented, symmetrical, and collaborative atmosphere in which patient and therapist explore the past, look for its effects on the present, examine the ways in which the current situation keeps the past alive, and try out new ways of influencing change in all these spheres.

REFERENCES

Gold, J. R., & Wachtel, P. L. (1993). Cyclical psychodynamics. In G. Stricker & J. R. Gold (Eds.), *Comprehensive handbook of psychotherapy integration* (pp. 59–72). New York: Plenum Press.

Messer, S. (1992). A critical examination of belief structures in integrative and eclectic psychotherapy. In J. C. Norcross & M. R. Goldfried (Eds.), *Handbook of psychotherapy integration* (pp. 130–168). New York: Basic Books.

Wachtel. P. L. (1977). *Psychoanalysis and behavior therapy: Toward an integration.* New York: Basic Books.

Wachtel, P. L. (1981). Transference, schema, and assimilation: The relevance of Piaget to the psychoanalytic theory of transference. *The annual of psychoanalysis* (Vol. 8, pp. 59–76). New York: International Universities Press.

Wachtel, P. L. (1991). The role of accomplices in preventing and facilitating change. In R. Curtis & G. Stricker (Eds.), *How people change: Inside and outside therapy* (pp. 21–28). New York: Plenum Press.

Wachtel, P. L. (1997). *Psychoanalysis, behavior therapy, and the representational world.* Washington, DC: American Psychological Association.

8

RESOLVING TRAUMA IN PROCESS-EXPERIENTIAL THERAPY

JEANNE C. WATSON

Emotion-focused therapy (EFT) is an empirically supported, humanistic treatment that is designed to foster clients' emotional intelligence and their emotional processing skills to help them better regulate their affect (Elliott, Watson, Goldman, & Greenberg, 2004; Greenberg, Rice, & Elliott, 1993). Emotion-focused therapists view affect as primarily adaptive; however, problems arise if people have not been able to develop the necessary processing skills because of past trauma or early attachment experiences and have developed ways of coping that result in poor treatment of self and others. Emotions tell people what is significant for their well-being and alert them to what they need and want, which provides a guide to appropriate action. In process-experiential therapy (PET), clients learn to become aware of their emotions, label them, express them, and reflect on them to come up with ways of behaving that are consistent with their needs, values, and goals. Emotion coordinates experience, provides it with direction, and gives it a sense of unifying wholeness. In PET, therapists use clients' emotions like a compass to guide them to what is relevant and important for them to focus on in clients' narratives. Central to EFT theory is the organizing function of emotion schemes and how emotion processes function in the person. *Emo-*

tion schemes refer to ways of behaving that people develop as a result of experiencing different types of emotions. Although these emotion schemes are not necessarily conscious, they can be activated by recalling specific experiences that can then be explored, expressed, and reflected on (Greenberg & Safran, 1987). The sequence of recollection, emotional arousal, exploration, expression, and reflection is central to process-experiential theory (Elliott et al., 2004; Greenberg, 2002). Emotion schemes consist of a number of different elements, including perceptual–situational, bodily–expressive, symbolic–conceptual, motivational, and behavioral, which are organized around a particular emotion. Emotion schemes are understood as dynamically constructive; they are not viewed as static entities but are constantly being reorganized as people synthesize them to create different self-organizations for different situations.

TREATMENT PRINCIPLES

EFT is an integrative treatment that draws on a number of sources, including the work of Carl Rogers (1951), Fritz Perls (1969), attachment theory (Bowlby, 1969), interpersonal theory (Benjamin, 1993; Lietaer, 1984), and emotion theory (Greenberg & Safran, 1987; Kennedy-Moore & Watson, 1999). Two sets of treatment principles guide process-experiential therapists' approach to psychotherapy: relationship principles and task principles. The relationship principles embody the relationship attitudes identified by Rogers (1951). These include empathic attunement, the therapeutic bond, and task collaboration. Empathic attunement requires the therapist to enter and track the clients' immediate subjective experience. This requires that the therapist try to capture the essence of what clients are saying and to mirror the intensity and quality of their affective experience. In addition to demonstrating that the therapist understands the client's subjective world as it evolves moment to moment in the therapeutic encounter, empathic responding also helps clients deconstruct this subjective world so they can reflect on it and develop alternative ways of acting (Watson, 2001).

As in other humanistic approaches, process-experiential therapists see the therapeutic relationship as an active ingredient that facilitates healing insofar as it communicates empathy, prizing, acceptance, and genuineness. Process-experiential therapists learn early to be fully present with their clients so that they can accurately mirror their clients' experiences and promote feelings of being cared for and respected. Feeling accepted is viewed as an important component of healing; it communicates a strong belief by the therapist in the client's ability to change. An effective therapeutic relationship also requires that the client and therapist be able to establish agreement on the tasks and goals of therapy.

Emotion-focused treatment has three significant task principles: a process-guiding relational stance, an exploratory response style, and a marker-guided strategy. A process-guiding relational stance requires the therapist to integrate the process of leading and following. Although the therapist's task is to follow the client's track and remain empathically attuned to the client's inner experience and respect the client's agency and autonomy, it is also important for therapists to guide the process. This does not mean specifying what the client should do but rather that each therapeutic response should have specific objectives, the three main ones being to (a) communicate an immediate intention (e.g., to communicate understanding or facilitate exploration), (b) facilitate a within-session task (e.g., resolve a conflict, integrate vulnerable feelings), and (c) facilitate the overall treatment goal (e.g., to alleviate the client's depression; Mahrer, 1983).

One way that process-experiential therapists facilitate clients' exploration of their experience is by using an exploratory response style. The tentative probing and exploration characteristic of this type of responding is distinctive to EFT and is best exemplified by a number of different types of responses, including empathic exploration, evocative empathy, and empathic conjectures (Bohart, Elliott, Greenberg, & Watson, 2002; Greenberg & Elliott, 1997; Watson, 2001). These are typically exploratory reflections that are attempts by the therapist to convey understanding and to facilitate clients' exploration of their inner subjective experience.

In addition to providing a healing therapeutic relationship, emotion-focused therapists use marker-guided interventions to help their clients resolve specific cognitive–affective problems. *Markers* consist of clients' verbal statements and their nonverbal expressions. These markers guide therapists to intervene in particular ways, for example, suggesting systematic evocative unfolding at a problematic reaction marker or a two-chair exercise when the client presents a self-critical split (Greenberg et al., 1993; Perls, 1969; Rice & Greenberg, 1984). Four types of markers have been identified as important in formulating ways of working with clients in EFT (Elliott et al., 2004; Watson & Bohart, 2001): micro markers, mode of engagement markers, markers of characteristic style, and task markers. *Micro markers* are the moment-to-moment behavioral indices like vocal quality, language use, and style of speech that alert EFT therapists to clients' immediate experiencing. Micro markers are the cues that guide therapists' responses by facilitating therapist empathy to help clients process their inner experience in more productive ways.

In addition to attending to clients' micro markers, experiential therapists listen for clients' characteristic style of treating themselves and others. To do this, it is essential to have some sense of clients' early attachment histories in order to understand how they learned to process their affective experience and express it to others (Bowlby, 1969; Kennedy-Moore & Watson, 1999). Clients usually reveal how they treat themselves and others in their descriptions of their current problems (Benjamin, 1993). Therapists can recognize when clients invalidate their feelings or when they allow others to take advantage of them. These markers of characteristic style guide therapists in choosing relevant task markers. For example, process-experiential therapists would be alert for clients' statements indicating that they were invalidating their feelings, and this type of therapist might suggest a two-chair exercise as a way of helping his or her clients to change their ways of responding to themselves. Emotion-focused therapists tie in these markers of characteristic styles with clients' presenting problems so the therapists can facilitate the development of the therapeutic alliance by obtaining agreement on the tasks and goals of therapy.

The third types of markers that experiential therapists listen for are those that indicate clients' modes of engagement in therapy. This has to do with how clients are processing their emotional experiences in the session (Kennedy-Moore & Watson, 1999; Leijssen, 1990). For example, some clients may be analytical and disengaged from their emotional experience; alternatively, they may be overwhelmed by their experience and have difficulty reflecting on and containing it. An important objective in experiential therapy is to turn clients' attention inward (to their inner subjective experience) so that they can label it and express it in words in the presence of a supportive other and reflect on it to change problematic aspects of their experience.

The fourth types of markers that experiential therapists attend to are specific task markers. These are the client statements that indicate clients' readiness to deal with particular cognitive–affective problems, such as negative feelings toward a significant other or self-critical statements that are undermining their sense of well-being (Greenberg et al., 1993; Perls, 1969). These markers help clinicians develop relevant problem foci. In successful cases, clients are able to resolve these specific cognitive–affective problems; formulate alternative views of themselves, others, or problematic situations; and develop alternative ways of processing and expressing their affective experience.

CASE STUDY

Jenny was a young graduate student in her mid-20s when she first came to see me. She was concerned about the quality of her intimate relationships and particularly the feelings of anger and hurt that she was experiencing with her current boyfriend. She reported feeling sad and desperate when he left her to return to his apartment or go to work, and she worried that they would split up. She seldom expressed her feelings, preferring instead to put on a mask of loving kindness, and used alcohol to ease the pain. When she first came to see me she felt that she was unraveling; she found herself crying unexpectedly and was extremely dissatisfied with her life.

Jenny had poor memories of childhood but did recall that her father was emotionally and psychologically abusive. She described her father as controlling and explosive. He would beat her and make derogatory and insulting comments about her appearance and behavior. She provided one example where her father would make her kneel in front of him and beg for forgiveness if he was displeased with her behavior. As a teenager, she had engaged in self-harming behavior by cutting herself to ease the intense feelings of anger and hurt. She continued cutting herself until age 16, at which time she saw a psychologist and discontinued the behavior. Jenny was highly motivated to change her behavior. She realized that if she was to build a happy life for herself and realize her dream of marriage and children, she needed to deal with the feelings of pain that were emerging for her in her current life situation. She also expressed a strong desire to stop drinking and to develop alternative ways of coping with her pain. Jenny was an articulate and creative young woman. In addition to her graduate studies, at which she was excelling, she was an accomplished artist and had exhibited a number of works in local art shows. At the end of the first session, we agreed to use therapy to help her become more connected to her feelings, process her feelings of hurt and anger toward her boyfriend, and address her contradictory feelings in the relationship.

Case Formulation

Jenny was highly intellectual and analytical in terms of her presentation of the events in her life. She lacked awareness of her feelings except for the intense ones that seemed to flood over her at times. In the early sessions, she found it difficult to focus on her feelings; instead she described the behavior of others. When I asked her how she felt about specific events, she was uncertain and confused. Jenny had a strong need to remain calm and in control. Early in therapy, she expressed a fear of becoming vulnerable and of breaking down in the session. Although she was adamant about remaining impassive, it was clear that her emotions were overwhelming her and she did not understand what sparked them or how to express her feelings to significant others. Jenny wanted to become more aware of her feelings and to process them and regulate them better so as not to be ambushed by them when she least expected it. To achieve this, I considered it highly likely that Jenny would need to explore and process her relationship with her father both to label and express the feelings that were suppressed as a child and to understand the impact on her of his behavior so that she could see how it might be affecting her currently, especially in her intimate relationships. An important goal was to have Jenny access her vulnerability in a safe environment so that she could develop alternative ways of being with others and of treating herself. Like many victims of abuse, Jenny assumed a lot of responsibility for the well-being of others while neglecting her own needs. Moreover, she was punitive with herself and blamed herself for her father's treatment of her.

The Therapeutic Process

At the beginning of therapy, Jenny focused on her feelings of confusion and anxiety about her boyfriend, Daniel. He was a graphic artist who had initially been ambivalent about becoming involved in a relationship for fear that it would interfere with his work. His ambivalence manifested itself in that he would be loving and involved for a few days and then withdraw. Jenny experienced him as disconnected at these times and became anxious and worried that the relationship was about to disintegrate. She was finding these feelings intolerable and wanted to change them. We agreed to explore them; however, Jenny acknowledged that she had a hard time exploring her feelings.

Forging the Alliance

Initially, we focused on Jenny's fears about engaging in therapy and allowing herself to be vulnerable. She had worked so hard to protect herself that it was difficult for her to change. During the next four sessions, Jenny tried to resolve her ambivalence about exploring and expressing her feelings. Often she would agree to proceed, but by the following week she would be overcome once again by fear. During this period, my primary objective was to help her feel safe and to establish a connection with her that would enable her to explore the vulnerable, painful aspects of her experience.

To try to help her resolve her ambivalence, I suggested two-chair work. During the exercise, two sides of Jenny that governed her behavior became clearer. One side was contemptuous of any weakness. This side was domineering and angry that Jenny wanted to express and explore her feelings of vulnerability. As we explored this strong, contemptuous side of her, it became clear that this side was scared that Jenny could not cope with the pain and was trying to protect her; it reminded her that the way she had survived her childhood and defeated her father was to hide her feelings and pretend she did not care. For the strong side to agree to be in therapy, it needed reassurance that Jenny would not fall apart and that she would be able to handle her painful feelings and not engage in any self-harming behaviors. Jenny was able to reassure the strong side and promised to go slowly and not rush things. I supported her in this decision and reassured her that we would work at her pace.

We continued to work with Jenny's conflict between the strong side and the side that wanted to express feelings. After acknowledging the strong side's fears, Jenny was able to negotiate a way to enable the strong side to feel protected as she explored her feelings. Jenny told the strong side how helpless and overwhelmed she was by her feelings. She expressed how difficult and unhappy she was in her relationship and asked the strong side to acknowledge that it was not useful to continue to run away from painful, negative feelings. The strong side agreed that Jenny needed to explore and express the pain if she was to feel better about herself and stop feeling depressed. She resolved that she could not continue to run away from the pain or cover it up. This session marked a turning point. Jenny seemed more willing to confront the difficult feelings she was experiencing in her relationship with Daniel. However, the struggle to confront and process the painful aspects of her experience would resurface periodically throughout our work together, and each time we would examine it so that she could work out a satisfactory way of proceeding.

Attending to Feelings

As we continued to explore how Jenny treated herself, she became aware of how self-critical she was. She also noted that she felt responsible when Daniel pulled away. She realized how harsh she was with herself, blaming herself when Daniel withdrew, seeing herself as weak and contemptible when she felt sad or scared, dismissing her painful feelings, and telling herself to stop whining and smarten up. She also attempted to control the expression of vulnerable feelings by telling herself that she was disgusting and that nobody would love her if she whined. As we explored her feelings, she became aware that she often had a drink to ease the pain, especially after a negative incident with Daniel. I suggested that she needed to learn to be more compassionate with herself. She said that she did not know how. Knowing that she was training to work with children and had shown herself to be compassionate and caring in her interactions with them, I asked her to imagine what one of them might need if he or she was in pain. This helped her think of some behaviors that were particularly comforting to her, like painting, getting into a pair of warm snuggly pajamas and watching a movie, making herself some soup, and going for a walk with her camera. At the end of the sixth session she resolved that she would try to go for a walk instead of having a drink the next time she felt angry or sad.

Early in therapy, Jenny expressed impatience that she was unable to access her sadness and pain about her childhood. However, after engaging in the two-chair exercise, she realized that she needed to go slowly. I urged her to respect her need for a slower pace because this would be treating herself with compassion. She was able to admit that she was ashamed of her father's behavior and that it was difficult to share some of her memories with me. I reassured her that she was not responsible for her father's behavior and that I would be patient until she felt ready to open up.

Over the next few sessions, we continued to explore her interactions with Daniel. Jenny was pleased to report that she had gone for a walk after a difficult interaction with him. She was relieved that she had chosen this alternative over alcohol and began to feel more optimistic about being able to change. She continued to feel hurt and anxious by Daniel's withdrawals. We explored her anger and hurt, and she became aware of how much she held herself responsible for his moods. She realized that she was not only highly sensitive to them, in that any sign of disconnection made her feel very anxious, but that she also felt that she must do something to remedy the situation. A two-chair exercise enabled her to see how much she blamed and punished herself for Daniel's moods. She resolved to stop blaming herself and to become more aware of her negative self-statements when he expressed a need for more space and less involvement with the relationship.

For the next 10 sessions, we focused on her relationship with Daniel. She acknowledged how painful it was that Daniel seemed unable to commit to the relationship. She was worried that she was being more self-destructive and drinking more than she would have liked. The intensity of Jenny's feelings was a clue that she might benefit from exploring the issue further. In EFT, intense feelings are often seen as an indication of unresolved emotional material. Consequently, I asked her if the feelings of anxiety reminded her of anything. She recalled feeling that way as a child when her father was due to return from work. When she hid in her bedroom to stay out of his way, he became angry that she was being rude and ignoring him. On the other hand, if she did appear to say hello and greet him, he would often turn on her angrily, demanding she get him the newspaper and stay out of his way because he was tired from having to work all day to provide for her and her sisters. This prompted me to suggest an empty chair exercise with her father.

During this exercise, she expressed some of the anger and rage she felt at how she was treated as a child. She imagined ways that she might hurt her father so that he would know how hurt and humiliated his behavior had made her feel. In the empty chair exercise, Jenny's imagined father was contrite and acknowledged that he had been tough on her. He apologized and noted how proud he was of her achievements. Jenny found it difficult to hear his positive feedback. She was mistrustful of him and felt that he did not deserve to feel proud of what she had accomplished because he had made her life so difficult. Before ending the session, we explored ways that she could care for her angry, hurt part instead of being self-destructive. Soon after this session, Jenny decided to take a break from Daniel. She recognized that his moodiness and ambivalence were not good for her. This was an important recognition for Jenny as she slowly began to assert her own needs and began to take responsibility to protect herself with significant others.

As Jenny became more aware of her feelings, she began having nightmares. One night she awoke trembling with fear and, although she could not remember the content of the dream, she broke down and wept freely. As we explored her feelings, she realized that part of her was waking up as she began to become aware of and express her feelings in therapy. She realized how conflicted she was about crying and feeling vulnerable. I suggested a two-chair exercise. During the exercise, Jenny identified a part that wanted to feel and be able to cry for all the painful things she had suffered and another part that wanted her to remain stoical and hide her pain. The stoical part realized that she needed to release her pain but was fearful of being overwhelmed by it and drowning in grief. She realized that part of her was afraid to emerge from the shadow of the strong, stoical side of her personality. Jenny was able to reassure her stoical side that she would take care of herself as she was already doing by coming to therapy, resuming yoga, and building her support network. Toward the end of the session, she felt a sense of excitement at allowing herself to be more expressive and in touch with her feelings.

At a subsequent session, she reported being startled awake and feeling frightened. We explored her feelings, and she was able to access some of her pain around her childhood. She felt sorry for the little girl who had been so browbeaten. She recalled living in terror of her father's next attack of rage and his beatings. She was glad that she was able to break through her numbness and feel some of the pain. Before concluding the sessions, we explored ways that she could take care of herself until our next appointment.

Jenny resumed seeing Daniel after this session, but she was cautious and guarded with him. She felt unsettled. After a focusing exercise, she realized that she was afraid that the relationship would not survive. At one session, Jenny reported that she had had a difficult weekend with Daniel. He had been moody and had decided to opt out of a dinner engagement they had made with friends. Jenny recalled feeling stifled and confused. She did not understand her reaction. We explored it using systematic evocative unfolding. She realized that she had felt needy and vulnerable when he stood her up on the dinner date but could not express her feelings to him. Instead she had shut down her feelings and made a joke about it. As we explored her problematic reaction, she acknowledged that she found it difficult to ask and receive but easy to give. She became aware of a tendency to deny her own needs and not to make demands or have expectations of other people. We agreed to explore this issue further in subsequent sessions.

At the following session, Jenny informed me that Daniel had decided to leave the country to take an art course. Although she felt hurt and rejected, she recognized that this was important for Daniel and did not want to stand in his way. However, she resolved to be more self-assertive and protective. She decided that she would regard his absence as an opportunity to take a break from the relationship and explore other options and that she would reassess the relationship when he returned in the fall. In the meantime, she made plans to visit friends on the east coast and to relax and have some fun. When she returned from her vacation, Jenny looked more relaxed and seemed more confident and self-assured. She had enjoyed reconnecting with friends and was excited at the prospect of seeing Daniel, who was coming up for the weekend. However, the meeting did not go well; Daniel once again expressed ambivalence at spending time together. Jenny decided to end the relationship. However, she wanted to continue in therapy to work on the abuse she had suffered as a child. She realized that she needed to come to terms with the abuse she had suffered as a child so that she could form intimate relationships that were healthy and nourishing for her and not become involved with people who activated her insecurities and anxiety.

Processing the Abuse

The breakup with Daniel started a new phase of therapy. For the next 30 sessions, Jenny and I processed her feelings about her childhood; she took the time to grieve and to explore new relationships. She spent more time observing her reactions to how she felt and what made her feel good and what contributed to her feeling hurt, angry, and uncomfortable in her interactions with others. At first Jenny was uncertain about how to process her feelings about her father. To facilitate this, I suggested that she begin by describing some of the events that she recalled from her childhood. This brought up intense feelings of hurt. I suggested we do an empty chair exercise so that she could express these feelings to her imagined father. Jenny agreed. She was able to express how hurt and devastated she had been by his moods and his anger when she was a child. For the first time, she was able to tell him that his behavior to her had been unacceptable. She also said that she needed to distance herself from him and was not going to tolerate any put-downs or belittling comments he might make in the future. Jenny felt much stronger after this session. She felt more able to protect herself. Shortly after this session, Jenny reported that she had had a dream about me in which she felt cared for. I saw this as important in terms of the alliance we had built over the previous few months and as an indication that she was ready to confront her painful feelings in therapy. Unfortunately, I was unable to meet with her the following week. I empathically explored her feelings of distress at my unavailability and reassured her that she had done nothing wrong; a prior commitment had simply (and unavoidably) intervened.

This rupture may have contributed to the material that emerged in the subsequent session, when Jenny reported that she felt angry that her mother had not protected her more as a child. We did an empty chair exercise with her mother, during which she expressed her confusion and anger about the events of her childhood. Her mother responded that she was sorry. She acknowledged that Jenny's dad had been difficult and that they had all lived in fear of his rage and moods. She said that she had tried to pacify him and had worked to keep the peace but realized in retrospect that she should have set firmer limits and not allowed him to take his anger out on the children. She asked Jenny for forgiveness, which Jenny gave. She recalled how hard her mother's life had been and how her father had yelled at and mistreated her, too. She acknowledged that her mother's life with her father had not been easy and said that in spite of it all, she knew her mother loved her.

Jenny continued to work on changing her relationship with her parents. She wished that she had a normal family; instead, she felt isolated and cut off from her parents. She wondered why they did not call her more frequently or try to stay in touch. We continued to empathically explore and process her sadness and her grief about what she had lost in terms of her childhood. She mourned the loss of feeling safe and loved at home and the sense of carefree abandon that she imagined other children experience when they live with a less volatile parent. Jenny recalled a particularly painful memory during a family vacation when her father had humiliated her in front of her friends after he became angry about how much noise they were making when playing Ping-Pong while the adults were eating. We agreed that it was important to process these memories in order to become aware of and label the pain in the presence of a caring other so that she could learn how to process her emotions and learn ways of protecting herself so that she could form more satisfying intimate relationships.

In the following session, we did an empty chair exercise so that Jenny could express her pain to her father and begin to establish a different type of relationship with him. Jenny was able to express her anger and to tell her father that she did not deserve to be treated so cruelly. She told him that his behavior was out of line. As she recalled the painful memories from her childhood, Jenny began to cry for the little girl she had been. I suggested that she imagine herself as a little girl in the empty chair and tell herself how she felt. She did so, and Jenny told herself as a little girl how sorry she was that she had not been able to protect her from her father's rages. She expressed her sorrow that the child had had to endure such treatment and told her that she would not let that sort of thing happen again. We then explored ways that Jenny could nurture and comfort the little girl over the next week until our next appointment. She recalled how much she had enjoyed listening to folk music as a teenager while she strummed along on her guitar. She resolved to go home, play some music, and get herself a tub of her favorite ice cream as a treat.

Transforming the Client

As we continued to work, Jenny began to note a number of changes. She observed that she was feeling good and that her paintings were changing. Previously, her subjects had been dark and menacing, but recently this had changed and she was using brighter colors and depicting more light in her paintings. She was thinking seriously of taking a watercolor class so that she could capture lighter moods and subjects. She realized that she was demanding of herself regarding her school work and that she kept to very strict timelines. After a session in which we explored how controlling she was with herself and how she invalidated her feelings, she resolved to give herself more time to complete her degree and take some time to travel and try to be more attuned to her inner self. She wished she could forgive her father so that she could establish closer ties with her family, but after a two-chair exercise she realized that she was not yet ready for this and that she needed to respect her feelings. Jenny's appearance also changed during this time. She cut her hair and looked brighter and more relaxed. She no longer felt the need to hide behind her hair and enjoyed the freedom of the shorter style. She said that friends had noticed a difference. She was better able to express her anger and to assert boundaries with friends, and she did not feel as if she was letting them take advantage of her good nature. We continued to explore her wish that her parents would phone her more often. She expressed her sadness that her family was so disconnected. She wished that she had a greater sense of belonging and that they cared for her more. As I empathically explored her feelings with her, she recalled a negative memory of being punished by her father for her reluctance to visit friends of the family. She felt angry as she recalled his treatment of her, but she was able to reassure herself that it was not her fault and that she had not deserved to be treated in that way.

For the next three sessions, we continued to work on Jenny's feelings of sadness and loss. She noted that she was dreaming more and that she felt better able to tolerate her feelings. She realized that she needed to cry for the little girl she had been and acknowledge her pain but that she was not yet ready to do so. She recognized how much she had tried to cover up her feelings as a child so that her father would not have the satisfaction of seeing her defeated. Also, there had never been anyone to comfort her after he beat her and she was sent to her room. She recalled having angry fantasies of hurting him in an effort to dull the pain.

During this time, she learned of a colleague's death. She felt sad and wanted to process those feelings as well as the feelings of sadness about her father. She realized how difficult it was for her to experience sadness and that she often tried to avoid such feelings by making a joke or laughing instead. Jenny recognized that she often expressed the opposite of what she was feeling in an attempt to cover up and conceal her emotions from others. She observed that she would change her anger into sadness and vice versa. She expressed a wish to clearly express what she was feeling. At that point in the therapy, Christmas was approaching and Jenny decided to go home to see her sisters and parents. She was looking forward to it.

When she returned, Jenny reported that she had been more assertive at home and that she even gently challenged her father and set limits when he became impatient and controlling. Her mother supported her in this behavior, for which Jenny felt touched and grateful. Over the holidays, she started dating David and was excited and optimistic about the new relationship. At this juncture, we entered a new phase of therapy as we started processing not only her feelings about her abuse but also began to examine its impact on her relationships with the people she dated.

The affair with David did not last long, but while it did, Jenny gained a number of important insights into her behavior in romantic relationships. She noticed that she often felt hurt and worried in the relationship. She was vigilant and continually tried to monitor how the other was feeling. We explored different situations to see if she could better understand what triggered her reactions. It was difficult for her when David retreated to his own space or became more involved with his surroundings. At these times, Jenny became anxious, fearing that she had done something wrong. However, because of the effects of therapy, she now behaved differently. Whereas before she would have tried to coax the person back into the interaction, now she tried to observe how she was feeling and to calm herself in other ways. She became aware of how easy it was to sacrifice her own comfort for the sake of the other. She told me how difficult it had been for her one night to shift her position on the sofa where she and David were cuddling even though her foot was going numb. She had never realized the extent to which she silenced herself before and resolved to try to balance better her own needs with those of the other. Jenny became aware that David would ridicule her and make demeaning comments. She attended to her sense that she did not feel loved and appreciated. She began to question the relationship, and shortly thereafter broke it off.

We explored why it was difficult for her to find a relationship in which she felt valued. She noted that she looked for excitement and sexual attraction and became quickly involved with the person emotionally in the hope of being loved in return. As we explored her behavior, she realized that she needed to allow herself more time to assess and get to know the person before becoming emotionally involved. However, it was difficult to stop investing herself from the beginning. She observed that she frequently made herself anxious when she first became involved with someone. We did a two-chair exercise to see how she made herself worry. She realized that she put herself down and kept her attention focused on the other's needs. I suggested she try to keep her attention focused on her own feelings. To help her, I suggested she keep a diary of her feelings and to record salient events and her reactions so that she could attend to her experience and label it to come to know it better. Because she lacked an adequate yardstick of what it felt like to be in a good relationship, I suggested she pay attention to her body when she felt warm, safe, and comfortable either in therapy or after her yoga class. I suggested she might use these feelings as indicators that she was feeling comfortable and safe with a partner. Jenny agreed and resolved to observe herself more closely the following week.

Jenny canceled the next session because her grandfather passed away. We explored her feelings about his death at the next session. Her grandfather's death brought up a lot of memories from her childhood. She realized that her father had had a difficult relationship with his father, who had also been abusive and critical. At first Jenny was reluctant to share the memories that had come back to her following the funeral because she was afraid that she would be overwhelmed by them. To help her feel safe, I suggested that she might consider talking about and exploring the memories with me and then before leaving put them away in a locked box that she would leave behind in my office. That seemed to reassure her and she agreed. She talked about the tension at home and her father's unpredictable temper and how he would lash out at her, her sisters, and her mother at the dinner table. She recalled that to this day she often had difficulty at meal times, especially if there was any form of tension. Her breathing would become shallow and she would feel nauseated. I suggested that she monitor her breathing in the future to help her identify when she was feeling tense and encouraged her to deliberately deepen her breathing at those times in order to calm herself. At the end of the session she stored away the memories and resolved to go to her yoga class that evening as a way of soothing herself.

For the next three sessions, we continued to explore Jenny's childhood memories and her feelings toward her father. She was more in touch with her deep sadness and the pain she had suffered as a child. She was more attentive to her shallow breathing and concerned about her eating difficulties. I suggested that we explore ways that she could nurture herself by managing her digestive problems and changing her breathing patterns. She began to make sure that she set time aside to eat and to make sure that the environment was soothing and relaxing. She also began to pay attention to her breathing at these times and made sure that she was relaxed before she sat down to eat.

A month after breaking up with David, Jenny became involved with Steven, whom she had met at school. She felt that he was sensitive and responsive to her, and she felt appreciated and highly regarded. These feelings restored her belief that she was not asking for too much to find someone who could make her feel special and treat her well. However, she was aware that Steven was not as compelling as her previous partners. She felt that there was not enough chemistry and that he was not as good-looking as David and Daniel. We explored what the pull of the other two had been. She wondered if it was just because they made her feel anxious because she was not certain of their commitment or regard for her. The uncertainty made her focus all her energies on them in an attempt to maintain the relationship. By comparison, a relationship in which she was secure of the other's attention and regard seemed somewhat flat and lacking in excitement. I suggested that perhaps in the past she had mistaken anxiety for chemistry. She agreed and decided she needed to wait and see whether her feelings for Steven would grow.

Over the next month, Jenny came to appreciate and value Steven's gentleness and to revel in his appreciation of her. Her feelings did grow, and she found that she was more attracted to him as time passed. She was aware that the relationship did not have the extreme highs and lows of her previous relationships but that she felt safer and more comfortable in the narrower emotional band that she and Steven were exploring together. Jenny began to talk of terminating therapy. She was feeling very content in her relationship; however, she wanted to talk to her parents and finally have them acknowledge what had transpired when she was a child.

No one in her immediate family spoke about her father's rages, and everyone seemed to pretend that they were an ordinary happy family. Jenny did not want to pretend any longer. She wanted her father's behavior acknowledged so that she could forge different and more loving relationships with her parents in adulthood. She was uncertain about how to talk to them. I suggested that she use "I" language and speak about how what had happened affected her so that they would hear her and be less defensive than they would if she used blaming statements. She agreed and asked if we could role-play what she wanted to say. We did so, after which she felt more confident. She went home the following weekend and spoke with her mother. On previous occasions, her mother would ask her to try to forget the past and live in the present; however, this time she listened carefully to what Jenny had to say and expressed her sorrow that Jenny had taken so much abuse as a child. She said she wished she had done more to stop it and supported Jenny's wish to speak to her father. At the next session, Jenny felt very relieved and pleased with how she had handled the subject, but she had not found time to speak to her father. She realized she was still feeling constrained and fearful around him. We did a two-chair exercise to try to ease her conflict. She realized that part of her was still afraid that her father would turn on her. Jenny was able to reassure herself that she was a grown woman with more physical strength than her father, whose physical health was failing. She realized that he would not be able to attack her in the ways that he had when she was a child. She felt freer and more confident at the end of the session.

Subsequently, Jenny said she had spoken with her father. He was genuinely remorseful and asked her to forgive him for his behavior. He said he did not realize what a terrible impact it had had on her and her sisters and that he would take it all back if he could. He also told Jenny how much he loved her and how proud he was that she was his daughter. For the first time, Jenny allowed herself to hear his pride and taste a little of his genuine regard. She doubted whether she could ever be really close to him but felt that their relationship had taken a turn for the better and that it would be easier to be around her parents in future. She said that she did not feel so isolated or disconnected from her family and that things continued to go well with Steven.

At the next session, she announced that she was ready to leave therapy. At first she said she wanted to stay for another month or two. After we explored her feelings, she decided that she was ready to leave as long as she knew that I was there and that she could return if things became difficult for her. I agreed and expressed my pleasure at seeing how much she had grown in her time with me and wished her all the very best in the future, reassuring her that she could return at any time if she chose.

CONCLUSION

I regard this as a successful case. It was not easy for Jenny to engage in therapy and access her vulnerability and painful experiences. At various times throughout the treatment, we returned to her fear of processing and experiencing her feelings as she acknowledged the pain of her childhood and confronted its full impact. It seemed to me in our time together that Jenny successfully processed her feelings about her childhood: She became aware of the impact of events, labeled the impact in conscious awareness, and learned to identify her needs and express these and her feelings to significant people in her life. As we explored her feelings, she came to see how she treated herself and how she let others treat her. She saw that she kept herself from naming or expressing her feelings and often invalidated her needs with significant others. In therapy, she learned to listen to her feelings in her interactions with others so that she could use them as a guide to her own needs and behavior. Together we developed alternative strategies for her to care for herself and manage her negative emotions so that she was able to give up her dependence on alcohol. She became more spontaneous and playful, aspects of herself that had been stifled and constrained when she was a child.

The active ingredients that I would identify as having facilitated these changes were the therapeutic relationship and the specific therapeutic tasks, including my use of experiential empathy and chair work and examination of her interpersonal functioning in romantic relationships. It was clear from the beginning that Jenny needed to feel safe in order to explore her feelings; she also needed to know that I would respect her pace and not push her to experience feelings or examine events until she was ready. Jenny herself noted the importance of having someone witness her pain and tell her that it was not her fault and that she did not deserve to be treated as she had been. It provided her with relief, released her from the responsibility and shame she had carried since childhood, and helped her become more compassionate toward herself. No one had been available when she was a child to whom she could go for comfort or to help her process the feelings of anger, sadness, humiliation, and betrayal that she experienced as a result of her father's behavior. Thus, these feelings had remained confusing, overwhelming, and raw.

The therapist's use of experiential empathy facilitated Jenny's emotional processing and helped her come to terms with her childhood experiences of abuse. The two-chair exercises allowed Jenny to resolve her ambivalence about engaging in the tasks of therapy and gave her insight into how she regulated her feelings and how she treated herself. They also provided her with the opportunity to listen to her feelings and develop alternative ways of behaving. The empty chair exercises provided her with a safe place in which to express her negative feelings toward the significant people in her life who had injured her. As she expressed her feelings, Jenny came to see clearly the impact of her father's behavior and what she needed instead. By expressing her feelings, she was able to draw back from him and hold him accountable for his treatment of her. She became more self-protective and compassionate toward her current and childhood selves.

As she saw the impact of her father's behavior, Jenny was able to see how his abuse and her coping responses played out in her current relationships. She developed the ability to be more attentive to her feelings, became more self-protective, and was able to modify her interactions with friends and romantic partners. Finally and perhaps most important, Jenny's readiness and motivation to engage in treatment facilitated the dramatic changes she was able to effect. Her intelligence, motivation, courage, and indomitable spirit allowed her to fundamentally change her way of being with herself and others. My hope is that she no longer merely survives but continues to bloom and flourish.

REFERENCES

Benjamin, L. S. (1993). *Interpersonal diagnosis and treatment of personality disorders.* New York: Guilford Press.

Bohart, A. C., Elliott, R., Greenberg, L. S., & Watson, J. C. (2002). Empathy. In J. Norcross (Ed.), *Psychotherapy relationships that work* (pp. 89–108). New York: Oxford University Press.

Bowlby, J. (1969). *Attachment and loss: Vol. 1. Attachment.* New York: Basic Books.

Elliott, R., Watson, J. C., Goldman, R. N., & Greenberg, L. S. (2004). *Learning emotion-focused therapy: The process-experiential approach to change.* Washington, DC: American Psychological Association.

Greenberg, L. S. (2002). *Emotion-focused therapy: Coaching clients to work through their feelings.* Washington, DC: American Psychological Association.

Greenberg, L. S., & Elliott, R. (1997). Varieties of empathic responding. In A. Bohart & L. Greenberg (Eds.), *Empathy reconsidered: New directions in psychotherapy* (pp. 167–186). Washington, DC: American Psychological Association.

Greenberg, L. S., Rice, L. N., & Elliott, R. (1993). *Facilitating emotional change: The moment-by-moment process.* New York: Guilford Press.

Greenberg, L. S., & Safran, J. D. (1987). *Emotion in psychotherapy: Affect, cognition, and the process of change.* New York: Guilford Press.

Kennedy-Moore, E., & Watson, J. C. (1999). *Expressing emotion: Myths, realities and therapeutic strategies.* New York: Guilford Press.

Leijssen, M. (1990). On focusing and the necessary conditions of therapeutic personality change. In G. Lietaer, J. Rombauts, & R. Van Balen (Eds.), *Client-centered and experiential psychotherapy towards the nineties* (pp. 225–250). Leuven, Belgium: Leuven University Press.

Lietaer, G. (1984). Unconditional positive regard: A controversial basic attitude in client-centered therapy. In R. Levant & J. M. Shlien (Eds.), *Client-centered therapy and the person-centered approach: New directions in theory, research and practice* (pp. 41–58). Westport, CT: Praeger.

Mahrer, A. R. (1983). *Experiential psychotherapy: Basic practices*. New York: Brunner/ Mazel.

Perls, F. S. (1969). *Gestalt therapy verbatim*. Moab, UT: Real People Press.

Rice, L. N., & Greenberg, L. S. (Eds.). (1984). *Patterns of change*. New York: Guilford Press.

Rogers, C. R. (1951). *Client-centered therapy*. Boston: Houghton Mifflin.

Watson, J. C. (2001). Revisioning empathy: Theory, research, and practice. In D. Cain & J. Seeman (Eds.), *Handbook of research and practice in humanistic psychotherapies* (pp. 445–473). Washington, DC: American Psychological Association.

Watson, J. C., & Bohart, A. (2001). Integrative humanistic therapy in an era of managed care. In K. Schneider, J. F. T. Bugenthal, & F. Pierson (Eds.), *The handbook of humanistic psychology* (pp. 503–520). Newbury Park, CA: Sage.

9

UNIFIED THERAPY WITH A PATIENT WITH MULTIPLE CLUSTER B PERSONALITY TRAITS

DAVID M. ALLEN

Unified therapy (UT; Allen, 1988/1994, 1993, 2003) is an individual psychotherapy treatment for self-destructive and self-defeating behavior patterns. It is based on the idea that ambivalence over role functioning in parents within a patient's family of origin results in a situation in which other family members are faced with contradictory demands. These contradictory demands intermittently and unpredictably reinforce (in a manner analogous to the learning theory concept of a variable intermittent reinforcement schedule; Reese, 1966) the patient's intrapsychic conflicts and the resultant dysfunctional behavior. The patient's conflictual behavior then simultaneously reinforces ambivalent, dysfunctional behavior in the rest of the family. Thus, the basis for integration of family systems, cognitive–behavioral, and psychodynamics schools is a dialectic process involving patterns of behavior in the patient's family of origin that operantly reinforce psychodynamic conflicts. Concepts from existential psychotherapy and techniques from experiential therapy are also integrated into the treatment, and medications are used for symptom relief. The therapy is designed particularly for adults in their early 20s through late 40s who exhibit Cluster B personality disorders (with behaviors that appear primarily dramatic, emotional, or erratic) or Cluster C personality disorders (with behaviors that appear primarily anxious and fearful) or traits (American Psychiatric Association, 2000) and who have at least one living parental figure.

UT accepts the concept of *kin selection* (Wilson, 1998), which posits that individuals within coherent social groups are altruistic in many contexts. People inherit a tendency, created by the process of natural selection, to be willing to sacrifice their own needs whenever such needs appear to be in conflict with the needs of the kin group. Seemingly oppositional behavior results from an individual's perception that the family requires it. In some circumstances, parents may also sacrifice their own children if the group seems to deem it necessary. If individuals attempt to ignore this tendency, they are subject to a terrifying sense of existential anxiety.

Parents or other family system leaders are thought, for genetic reasons, to be the most potent of all environmental influences in shaping and reinforcing role-relationship behavior in all humans. UT posits that any patient insights or behavioral changes that develop within the context of the patient's relationship with the therapist do not generalize to outside relationships unless the usual way that the family-of-origin members respond to the patient also changes significantly. The therapist is no match for the family in directly altering, positively or negatively, the patient's patterns of interpersonal behavior in social or occupational settings.

According to the theory behind UT (Allen, 1988/1994), ambivalence about role behavior within the family is created by homeostatic family rules that lag behind changes in cultural expectations. As first described by Fromm (1941), in general, the ambient culture has been evolving away from collectivism and more toward individualism. Individuals may be torn between introjected family values and demands from the larger culture for increasingly less role-driven, more flexible behavior. The idiosyncratic experiences of individual families within their ethnic and cultural group over several generations create a milieu in which once-useful family roles and rules are maintained. Therapy is designed to interrupt this process so that family members validate new, adaptive behaviors for one another instead of working to reinforce old, maladaptive patterns.

A prevalent example of how cultural changes lead to ambivalence in parental role function that then leads to contradictory demands on progeny derives from the changing role of women in Western culture over the 20th century. (This process is illustrated concretely in the case example that follows.) The traditional female role of having many children was once adaptive in an agrarian society in that family wealth and security were dependent on it. During these times, when infant mortality was high and labor-saving technologies nearly nonexistent, women had little time to think about how they might be more fulfilled by roles other than wife and mother. With the advent of a technological, urban society, this situation gradually reversed so that family wealth and security became dependent on women working outside the home and having fewer children. Women who had never been validated for being ambitious but who got a taste of what it was like to have a career during World War II became ambivalent about traditional female roles. In some women, this ambivalence would be manifested by an overt dependency on the males in the family coupled with covert attack on any male who would dare try to actually take care of them. For instance, a widow might demand that her son cater to her every need yet do so in such an annoying away that it would have the effect of punishing her son's efforts to be helpful.

The process of cultural evolution has sped up so much that individuals may learn one set of rules growing up but face a new set by the time they have children themselves. In some families, the resultant role confusion becomes amplified through a process (described elsewhere; see Allen, 1988/1994), leading to marked parental instability caused by ambivalence about what the parents want for themselves. In such cases, children are induced to attempt to stabilize the parents. They may sacrifice their own idiosyncratic desires and act out one side or the other of their parents' ambivalence. Through the child, the parents vicariously experience impulses and desires forbidden to them by the rules of their own family of origin.

However, if the adult child is too successful at living out the parents' forbidden impulses, the parents react negatively. Seeing their child succeed at what they themselves would have liked to do, they become acutely aware of their own lost opportunities. They are often reluctant to admit to anything like this (Allen, 1988/1994), but they begin to invalidate the very behavior they had helped to induce in their child in the first place. In addition, they may begin to act out in a self-destructive manner or become more depressed, which then frightens the child caught up in the bind as well as the rest of the family. Other family members may then also invalidate the offending individual. A similar process occurs if the offspring attempts to overtly challenge or ignore any family rules regarding acceptable behavior; other family members powerfully relay the message "you are wrong, change back."

The behavior necessary for family members to stabilize the role functioning of the parents is partially determined by the precise nature of the parents' conflicted roles. Particular combinations of dysfunctional traits cluster together in many individuals with similar family issues. This results in the specific combinations of traits that characterize the personality disorders. The case example in this chapter was chosen because the patient exhibited symptoms of several disorders, illustrating several common conflict areas in families and some of the reasons for their existence.

Although invalidating behavior often appears malicious, a hidden altruistic motive is usually present. Dysfunctional behavior by all family members is usually mutually reinforced by every other member of the family, often on the mistaken assumption that everyone else wants or needs the patterns to continue in their current form.

To alter this process, UT aims to achieve the following strategic goals:

1. Frame the patient's chief complaint and current difficulties as a response to family-of-origin issues.
2. Gather information identifying interpersonal relationship patterns that cue or reinforce self-destructive behavior.
3. Gather information about the patient's genogram for the purpose of understanding family misbehavior so that the patient can develop empathy for targeted family members.
4. Make a hypothesis about both the patient's current role in the family and the reasons the family seems to require this role.
5. Plan a metacommunicative strategy designed to help the patient confront the problem with his or her family so that the reinforcing behavior is diminished or extinguished.
6. Implement the strategy and obtain feedback about its effectiveness.

Ideally, patients learn to get past the defenses of each primary family member to effectively discuss the context of problematic family interactions and mixed messages and their effects. They request concrete, behavioral changes in the relationship. The primary vehicle for developing and teaching specific strategies is the experiential therapy technique of role-playing.

CASE EXAMPLE

In the following case example, the men in the patient's family had failed in their traditional breadwinner roles because of ethnic discrimination and feelings of inadequacy. In an environment of changing cultural expectations for both men and women, this led to dysfunctional interactional patterns between a mother and her son, the patient, which in turn reinforced the son's narcissistic conflicts and dysfunctional behavior.

Vance, a married White male in his 30s, came to therapy complaining of recent worsening of a depression that dated back many years. He was diagnosed with dysthymia. He also complained of episodic rage; a history of suicide attempts but no current suicidal ideation; and transient, seemingly stress-related paranoid ideation. Currently in professional school, he described a history of troubles at school and on jobs because of a pattern of provocatively overreacting to any injustices he perceived. He wanted therapy to help him with his mood, his suspicious nature, and his conflicts over success.

He met the full criteria for both narcissistic personality disorder, albeit with overtly low self-esteem, and a mild borderline personality disorder. The narcissistic traits were paramount. Over the course of therapy, he also exhibited histrionic and paranoid personality traits as well as significant conflicts over intimacy with his wife. He was seen for 45 psychotherapy sessions over approximately 18 months and for 3 follow-up sessions spaced every 4 to 6 months over 14 months.

Vance reported a complex family history that showed dysfunction over four generations. He was unusually well-informed about behavior patterns in his extended family. Vance readily talked about family issues, obviating the need to use the typical UT procedure of gradually tying family issues to the patient's symptoms. Data about both family interactions and their genogram were collected from this patient at a rate that exceeded the usual rate for patients exhibiting this degree of personality difficulty. Although at times summarized in this report, the family history was elicited over the entire course of therapy. Of note is that the mother's family may have been part of a persecuted minority at one time but hid their ethnic background.

During much of his childhood, Vance's mother oscillated between being physically abusive and subtly seductive with him without overt sexual abuse. Throughout his life, she tried to kiss him on the lips and called him "honey." She once remarked when Vance was an adolescent that she would punish him if he ever started to date. His father had died several years prior to Vance's entering therapy; the mother did not date anyone after her husband's death. The father had been away a lot when Vance was young and seemed indifferent to the mother's abuse. During most of his last years he was depressed and had seemingly given up on life.

When Vance was an adult, his mother flatly denied that any physical abuse had occurred. If he brought up problems from his childhood, she would whine about how horrible a mother she must have been. Despite being quite capable, she often acted helpless. Vance thought she was being manipulative to get him to take care of her, but he would nonetheless usually do the favors she asked for. When he refused, she would try to make him feel guilty. Both his mother and his wife made sudden demands on him at highly inopportune times, knowing full well how this angered him. His younger brother, who may have been schizotypal, was unable to work. He lived with and was dependent on the mother for many basic needs. Conversely, the mother was dependent financially on the brother's disability check.

The father had been close to Vance until the birth of the brother, but then seemed to favor the latter. The father himself always seemed to live in the shadow of his own older brother, who had been labeled by the family as the "successful one" despite a history of alcohol abuse. The father frequently gambled away the family money. At one point, he tried to start his own business; unsuccessful, he blamed the "old boy network" in his city. The father seemed jealous of Vance's accomplishments.

Vance felt that he did not fit in with any social group. In school, he would draw the ire of teachers because of his outspokenness over such things as racial injustice. When a high school dance was canceled because of resistance to integration, he organized his own integrated dances. Later, when he attempted to run with a Black crowd, he often felt himself to be a victim of reverse discrimination. His family would frequently make bigoted remarks but seemed to like a girlfriend of his who was Black.

Vance was aware that he often acted as if he were wearing the proverbial "don't kick me" sign. He was overly suspicious in annoying ways and subverted himself at various vocationally oriented academic endeavors through what he termed "stupid mistakes." He was nonetheless the first member of the family to graduate from college.

He had been married for a number of years to a woman he chose impulsively. Seductive before marriage, his wife quickly let her appearance lapse. Their sex life was minimal. She was the couple's primary breadwinner because of Vance's ongoing employment difficulties. The two of them rarely had sustained conversations about anything. If he protested about her lack of interest in him, she would complain, much like the patient's mother, about what a bad wife she was. Vance often felt like leaving her but never made any concrete moves to do so.

Genogram data revealed that Vance's paternal grandfather was married twice and had 14 children, the youngest of whom was Vance's father. He married the paternal grandmother, a babysitter for the children from his first marriage, when she was only 13. His first wife had left him. The grandmother kicked the grandfather out of the home after the father's birth because he had become physically abusive; they never divorced. The grandfather dropped by from time to time intoxicated and beat the grandmother. He had been physically abused by his own father. Later in his life, the grandfather went broke. Vance's father would send money to him, but the grandfather was unappreciative.

The grandmother supported the family with odd jobs, often sending the father to live with one of her siblings. She refused financial support from her husband. Instead, she was supported by her older sons—the father's brothers—who often seemed to resent the cost of the father's care. The mother's siblings also complained about what a financial burden the father was to them.

Vance's maternal grandmother was still living. She often told Vance that he would end up a failure just like his father. Her husband, the maternal grandfather, had actually been her second choice of mates. She believed she had lost out on her first love, a wealthy man from the minority group to which they may have belonged, because of an act of deceit by her own mother. Vance's mother idolized and idealized her own father, who was deceased by the time Vance entered therapy. The maternal grandfather often leaned on the mother for emotional support. The grandfather's father was killed in a fight and his mother committed suicide; he spent considerable time as a child in an orphanage. After being wiped out financially in the Depression, the grandparents had had to move in with the grandmother's parents; the grandfather then developed a drinking problem. When young, the mother and her siblings would frequently sleep in the same bed as their father. As an adult, the mother would call him daily, trying to make him feel better about himself by feigning dependence on him.

The case formulation from the UT perspective will become clear in the descriptions below of hypotheses offered to the patient during the course of therapy. The first few sessions focused on gathering family history. After the sixth therapy session, Vance decided, with no input from the therapist, to again try to talk to his mother about the abuse. In response, she once again did not "remember" specific incidents he mentioned and whined that she "could do nothing right." He told her she was right on that last point, but softened the barb by adding that she had mellowed during the previous decade. In the next session, the therapist cautioned the patient to avoid such confrontations until they had figured out the best approach for getting past his mother's denial. During this session, Vance also reported feeling alienated at school; he was already developing enemies in class for some of his provocative views.

In Session 8, the therapist offered the hypothesis that Vance's conflicts over success resulted from his having become a "savior with a double bind on achievement" (Slipp, 1984), which also contributed to his dysthymia. Most of the men in his family had failed as breadwinners for various reasons. The strong family women had had to lead the family covertly while appearing to be overly dependent so as not to further diminish the self-esteem of their partners. This led to their feeling conflicted about their own strength. Vance's mother would vicariously live through his attempts at success, but if he truly succeeded, both parents would become envious and the father's ongoing depression would worsen. In later sessions, the therapist offered another hypothesis about the related issue of the patient's narcissistic conflicts: that Vance was in the additional role of the "Little Man" (Allen, 2003). His mother acted helpless and dependent on him but would subtly undercut his attempts to take care of her and react negatively to his successes, because she covertly wanted to be independent and successful herself. The mother's apparent helplessness and whining self-blaming behavior are examples of the behavior through which she would overtly protect the self-esteem of the men while covertly and simultaneously express her anger about the need to do so.

In the following session, an incident occurred that served as an impetus for the therapist to begin role-playing possible approaches to confronting the mother about her various mixed messages to Vance. The therapist started with role reversal in which he played the patient while the patient played the mother, and the therapist tried different strategies. Once a strategy with a high likelihood of success was devised, the therapist and patient changed roles. The patient practiced the strategy while the therapist acted out worst-case scenarios to help the patient learn to stick with the strategy in the face of invalidation. The mother had asked Vance to come over and fix something. When Vance had pointed out that it required a professional repairman, his mother then cried about how broke she was, complaining that his father had left her with nothing. The therapist tried a strategy of directly pointing out to the mother how this statement affected the patient's self-image, but this led to problematic responses. The therapist then tried an alternate strategy of responding to the mother's statement about the father with the statement, "It's hard to depend on people who aren't very dependable." Vance did not know how his mother would react to this, because he had never tried to be empathic with her before.

In Session 11, Vance admitted that he was reluctant to confront his mother in any way that might actually lead to change. He stated he would not know who he was if he stopped acting out these roles. The therapist reassured him that this manifestation of existential groundlessness was natural and time limited. The therapist and Vance tried to construct a plan for getting the mother in a place where she could not just walk out on a conversation, a defensive maneuver she frequently used.

In the next session, Vance reported that his wife seemed to be escalating her negative behavior. The therapist wondered aloud if she might be doing so to interfere with the therapy plans secondary to fears about how the patient might react to a confrontation with his mother. Vance then admitted that in fact it was he who provoked the escalation. The therapist recommended continuing to focus on the mother. The therapist tried the strategy of having Vance focus on the mother's strength rather than her negative behavior. She had in fact carried the family when the father was ill. Vance replied that she would respond to this by becoming more seductive and trying to kiss him. The therapist said he would have to give more thought to how he might respond to that. The therapist also suggested ways to directly inform the mother that the way in which she requested favors from Vance was making him think she really did not want him to do the chores in the first place.

By the next session, Vance described a conversation he had had with his mother based on strategies he had adapted from those discussed in the previous session. It went much as predicted. He asked her, "Why, when you are such a capable woman, do you ask me to do things for you that you can do yourself?" The mother wanted to know why he asked; he replied that this behavior made him so angry that he did not want to help. The mother promised to stop. After he did a chore he had previously agreed to do, she immediately broke her promise and asked for another one. He replied nicely that he did not have time. The mother accepted this and then went over and tried to kiss him on the lips. He turned so she kissed him on the cheek; she then stormed off. In the next session, Vance reported that the mother had stopped, at least temporarily, asking for favors, except one. When he went to help her with a task, he found that she had in fact already accomplished it! He also told her clearly he would not kiss her on the lips. In the meantime, his wife had started to exhibit a small increase in affectionate behavior.

Before Session 15, Vance's mother started to complain about his new behavior, saying he was acting "like an asshole." He replied, "No, mom, I'm not. I let you kiss me on the cheek. What's wrong with that? And I did one chore for you but not another, because the second was not part of the plan." The mother became quiet in response. Vance also told his wife that if two people are miserable in a relationship, they should break up. His wife suddenly became more affectionate and for the first time expressed an interest in one of his hobbies. The therapist hypothesized that the wife's apparent coldness was in part a response to Vance's own discomfort with intimacy, which stemmed from his mother's inappropriate behavior as well as her jealousy of their relationship.

Before the next session, the maternal grandmother passed away. Vance worried that the mother would passively allow her sister, who had lived with the grandmother, to get all the money from the estate. He also began to complain about how the old boy network at school and work was always blocking his ambitions; the therapist expressed concern he might be feeling pressure to follow in his father's footsteps. Vance then revealed that the maternal grandmother had bailed the mother and father out of financial problems numerous times. The grandmother would then criticize everyone for using her. She also had criticized Vance and his brother for not earning enough money to "help your mother so I wouldn't have to."

Later, the mother did inherit some of the estate. She also admitted for the first time, without prompting, to two of the incidents of physical abuse of Vance, but justified them rather lamely. Despite the inheritance, she remained on the brink of financial disaster. Vance was coached to express concern about his mother but then to say, "It seems like you're almost afraid to be strong and successful; I wonder if the only time your mother would let you get close to her was when you needed money from her." Vance, playing the role of his mother, responded to this intervention with bewilderment. In this and the next session, the therapist also explored the additional hypothesis that the mother had learned to hide her competence for because, as mentioned earlier, when she acted dependent on her father it would help his shattered self esteem.

The therapist then hypothesized that Vance's strange mix of macho posturing and feelings of inadequacy stemmed from his being so central to everyone's life but not being able to stop their self-destructive behavior. One form of his posturing—fighting injustice and discrimination—was linked to repressed family anger over having to hide their ethnic heritage.

Five months into the therapy, Vance reported (in Session 20) an extensive conversation with his mother. He had maintained empathy throughout most of it but had become somewhat angry as abuse issues arose. He had started by bringing up the mother's relationship with her father. She revealed that both her parents wished she had been born a boy. When Vance was born, he was supposed to take the place of the son the grandfather never had.

This led to a discussion of how the men in the family were often seen as saviors but turned out to be weak or disappointing to their wives and how this led to the mother's pattern of subverting her own competence. The mother admitted that the patient and her brother seemed like millstones around her neck and that this had led to her abusive behavior. In UT, parents' ambivalence over the parenting role has been postulated as leading to traits characteristic of borderline personality disorder in their children; Allen, 2003). Although she admitted to some incidents of abuse, she denied others and sugar-coated the rest. She then offered an apology but made it sound like she thought he was making a big deal out of nothing. She ended the conversation with a prediction that Vance would "screw up" his own kids.

Vance was coached to tell his mother, "I'm not trying to make you feel bad by bringing up the abuse, but we need to clear the air so we can have a better relationship." Vance and the therapist also discussed ways to detriangulate the brother, who was beginning to interfere with Vance's attempts at metacommunication. Vance had by then told his wife what he was trying to do; she was supportive. He also for the first time talked to his wife about her appearance.

By Session 21, Vance felt that his mother was easier to be around. The next few sessions focused on his deceased father and how his experiences with the father affected his problems at school, where another student was getting angry with him. His school problems were tied to the negative predictions he had heard over the years from his mother and maternal grandmother about ending up a disappointment like his father. Vance continued to blame others for his problems, however, cataloging a list of how everyone had mistreated him. The therapist did not dispute this—there was, of course, some truth to his stories—but was instead empathic with how Vance must have felt.

Vance then spoke with his mother about how the father's gambling had kept them poor and dependent on the maternal grandmother. He also began to talk to his wife about their lack of intimacy; she began to discuss some of her own family dynamics and how they had affected the relationship. They began to have sex more frequently. The therapist connected the patient's discomfort with his mother's seductiveness to his discomfort in his marriage.

By Session 29, Vance reported increased depression, probably a manifestation of existential groundlessness caused by his relinquishment of old roles. He agreed to take an antidepressant. The therapist then began to clarify the issue of the relationship between the family dynamics, social class, and Vance's tendency to subvert his own success. Both parents had been obsessed with the issue of being poor. The paternal grandmother was a country girl who came to the city to escape poverty. The maternal grandfather, raised in an orphanage, was an unsuccessful lawyer. He married into a wealthy family that looked down on him. The father, much like the patient, had sabotaged his own success on a number of occasions, blaming it on the unfairness of the world.

Session 34 was devoted to a conjoint session with Vance and his wife, which confirmed the therapist's hypothesis about how they were misreading one another's motives. In the following session, Vance talked about a complaint about him at school made by the student he had angered; he maintained that he was innocent and that she was retaliating for remarks he had made that she did not like. He was preoccupied with this for several sessions. In a drawn-out process, he was initially found guilty of harassment but later exonerated. This unfortunate occurrence provided the therapist with an opportunity to focus on Vance's tendency to purposefully annoy peers and superiors. He began to see how he panicked at the prospect of financial success because of the double bind on achievement.

By Session 39, he was again depressed. He expressed reluctance to talk to his mother about the success issue, even though his mother was no longer asking for his help all the time and had admitted that perhaps she had over-idealized her own father. The patient gradually became more willing over the next few sessions to talk with his mother about what the grandfather was really like and how their relationship had affected the patient's relationship with her. His resistance, it became clear, had arisen because his mother had told him that she was thinking about suicide. The therapist expressed the opinion that the mother was strong enough to face the issue, particularly if he remained empathic. He was coached to be careful about being overly critical of his grandfather.

Following that session, treatment was unavoidably interrupted for a few weeks. During the interim, Vance had had an argument with the mother's sister, who warned him to stop criticizing his mother. Instead of reacting with anger, Vance tactfully stood his ground. She then yelled that he should not expect the mother to act responsibly, because she was incapable of it, and left in a huff. In Session 44, he was coached to share with his mother his aunt's concern that the mother could not act responsibly.

The following session was the last regular session. By then Vance's problems at school had been resolved in his favor; he had passed his professional exam and was about to take a job. He expressed determination to avoid provoking others into anger at him. The frequency of the mother's negative behavior remained low. She still gave out the occasional double message, but he did not react to them. His aunt was refusing to even speak to him, but she was asking other family members about him. When told of her sister's remarks about her lack of strength, the mother replied, "Look who's talking!"

In follow-up visits over the next 14 months, Vance was getting along better with his wife. Their sex life was still infrequent but much better than it had been. He was still making a few provocative comments on his jobs and was fired from one after he pointedly refused to send a dishonest bill. However, he had been steadily employed for some time by the last follow-up visit. He was not reacting as strongly as he once did when people criticized his sense of fairness. His mother was rarely coming to him for help and was in better shape financially. She seldom got on his nerves as she had before.

This case illustrates how a patient was coached to have metacommunicative discussions of family dynamics with a member of his family of origin. This led to change in dysfunctional family interactions that had previously triggered and reinforced his dysfunctional behavior and allowed him to experiment with more adaptive behavior without being invalidated.

MECHANISMS FOR CHANGE AND SELECTION OF INTERVENTIONS

UT attributes the improvement in this patient's self-destructive behavior to a basic alteration in reinforcement patterns within his family of origin. The patient was not expected to "fix" the negative behavior of the mother in contexts outside of their own relationship (nor does anyone really have the have the power to do so). However, changes in his own responses to the mother forced the mother to alter her responses toward him. An individual cannot change another person, but he or she can change a relationship. The patient successfully negotiated a metacommunicative strategy that was designed in psychotherapy using knowledge of the patient's interactional patterns and his family's sensitivities and history. Assertiveness techniques were modified to address those sensitivities. He was able to induce his mother, as well as his wife, to stop behavior that reinforced his conflicts over success, his low self-esteem, and his difficulties with emotional and sexual intimacy with his wife. This freed him up to experiment with more functional behavior patterns. Although antidepressant medication helped reduce his dysthymic symptoms, the more gratifying nature of his new behavior might over the long run decrease his need for medication. In this case, as a side effect of discussing the family dynamics, he helped his mother become a little more comfortable with her own independence. In UT, such events are happily quite common, even though they are not the primary goal of therapy.

THERAPEUTIC RELATIONSHIP

UT attempts to minimize transference reactions and motivate patients to focus on patterns of interaction with members of their family. Transference in UT is conceptualized as acting out the patient's family role function behavior with the therapist. This is a systems-oriented view of the analytic concept of a "false self." Transference is not ignored, because it may also serve as a resistance to problem solving within the therapy, and also because it illustrates for the therapist patterns the patient has learned from the family. It therefore gives clues to the family dynamics.

In this case, Vance may have initially expected the therapist to either invalidate his somewhat paranoid-sounding justifications for his behavior or to join him in vilifying his mother and blaming her abusive behavior for all of his problems. Instead, the therapist validated the kernel of truth in Vance's observations while slowly introducing alternate ways of thinking about the behavior of everyone in question. Vance formed a trusting relationship with the therapist rather quickly and readily accepted the therapist's focus on family dynamics, possibly because he had been covertly validated by his family for becoming a sort of family therapist for them. In other cases, patients have more trouble with this aspect of the treatment, requiring patience by the therapist.

Vance vacillated between resisting homework assignments and impulsively attempting to do them before strategies had been worked out and rehearsed in therapy. Fortunately, with the therapist's help, he was able to design and proceed with his own strategies, which were often successful. There was usually no need for the therapist to intervene to stop that; instead, he offered refinements that the patient could use the next time a particular subject came up. If Vance had attacked the mother more, or if the mother had responded with more acting out, he would have been told more forcefully to hold off homework attempts until he and the therapist had agreed on strategies. His eagerness to proceed would have nonetheless been validated and even admired by the therapist. When he was resistant to homework assignments, the therapist elicited his concerns about them, validated them, and addressed them.

Another important aspect of the therapeutic relationship occurred when the therapist recognized Vance's increased depression as a sign that the patient was making important changes in his life rather than as a sign that he was worsening. Using a psychoeducational approach, the concept of existential groundlessness over a loss of role function was discussed with the patient.

This case illustrates how intermittent yet ongoing family relationship patterns may continue to trigger acting out behavior and chronic affective symptoms in an adult patient with considerable personality dysfunction. I believe that teaching patients how to metacommunicate with family members in a tactful manner tailored to the individual family's sensitivities has a powerful potential to interrupt dysfunctional interactions. When such interactions cease or become attenuated, positive behavioral changes become much less difficult for the patient.

REFERENCES

Allen, D. M. (1993). Unified therapy. In G. Stricker & J. R. Gold (Eds.), *Comprehensive handbook of psychotherapy integration* (pp. 125–137). New York: Plenum Press.

Allen, D. M. (1994). *A family systems approach to individual psychotherapy*. Northvale, NJ: Jason Aronson. (Originally published as *Unifying individual and family therapies*, 1988)

Allen, D. M. (2003). *Psychotherapy of borderline personality disorder: An integrated approach*. Mahwah, NJ: Erlbaum.

American Psychiatric Association. (2000). *Diagnostic and statistical manual of mental disorders* (4th ed., text rev.). Washington, DC: Author.

Fromm, E. (1941). *Escape from freedom*. New York: Avon.

Reese, E. P. (1966). *The analysis of human operant behavior*. Dubuque, IA: William C. Brown Communications.

Slipp, S. (1984). *Object relations: A dynamic bridge between individual and family treatment*. New York: Jason Aronson.

Wilson, E. O. (1998). *Consilience: The unity of knowledge*. New York: Knopf.

10

COGNITIVE ANALYTIC THERAPY

ANTHONY RYLE AND LOUISE McCUTCHEON

Cognitive analytic therapy (CAT), as its name suggests, originated in linking ideas and methods from cognitive and psychoanalytic sources (Ryle & Kerr, 2002). To be more exact, it emerged from two simultaneous activities: (a) the practice of dynamic psychotherapy based on object relations ideas and (b) research into the impact of that therapy on individual patients using the repertory grid techniques derived from Kelly's personal construct theory (Kelly, 1955). In completing repertory grids, patients systematically rate a range of elements against a range of constructs. Elements are commonly known people, but in the dyad grid they are relationships between people, commonly self to others and others to self. Thus, information, entirely derived from the patient, is transformed into measures of association and plotted as maps; discussing the relationships of these to their experiences and behaviors with patients has been found to have a profound therapeutic impact. This work was summarized in Ryle (1975).

The use of pre- and posttherapy grids to describe the effects of therapy led to research in which predictions were made about how specified measures in the pretherapy grids should change if therapy were effective. The specification of individual goals was then extended to small group studies in which predicted grid changes were accompanied by other measures. This work was

We are grateful to "Kerry" for permission to describe her therapy.

part of an attempt to develop measures of change in psychodynamic psychotherapy. Attention was focused on the following question: Why do patients continue to behave in ways that are punishing or ineffective? This led to the delineation of three explanatory concepts:

1. *Traps*. These describe how negative assumptions lead to ways of thinking and acting that confirm the assumptions. This is a familiar pattern in behavioral and cognitive psychotherapies, but in addition to descriptions of faulty cognitions or ineffective actions, the responses evoked from others were highlighted.

2. *Dilemmas*. These represent the implicit assumption that opportunities for actions or relationship roles are confined to polar opposites; individuals may alternate between these, but more often they adhere closely to one pole as if the only alternative were the other. When therapists are faced with rigid and dysfunctional activity, it is important to consider what the apparent alternative might be. The concept can be related to psychoanalytic descriptions of splitting and reaction formation.

3. *Snags*. This pattern is manifest in the abandonment of appropriate goals or the dismantling of success. In some cases, this represents the avoidance of the anticipated responses of others, for example the pain or envy of handicapped siblings or the disruption of stressed family systems; in other cases the problem arises from the past, as when irrational guilt has resulted from the perception of having done harm—for example, when hostility toward a parent or partner was followed by their death. Both systems theory and psychoanalytic understandings of unconscious guilt offer parallel ideas.

Traps, dilemmas, and snags offer a way of describing how patients cause or fail to modify dysfunctional ways of living, and their resolution is an appropriate (and measurable) goal of therapy. These descriptions have been incorporated into a more general model of goal-directed activity, in which the descriptive unit is called the *procedural sequence* that unites the following elements: (a) the context or stimulus; (b) its appraisal in terms of overall needs and aims, involving affects and cognitions; (c) the choice of action from the available repertoire of action plans; (d) the more or less effective enactment; (e) evaluation of the consequences; and (f) the confirmation or revision of the procedure. This sequence organizes the perception of experience and activity and operates largely without conscious awareness. Key features of this model are that the basic descriptive unit combines environmental, behavioral, and mental phenomena and considers cognitive, affective, and behavioral factors as functionally inseparable.

Clinical practice and small-scale research have confirmed the utility of reformulating patients' presenting problems in these ways. Although initially intended to define the aims of psychodynamic therapy, the impact of the joint creation by therapist and patient of descriptions in these terms was so striking that practice changed and early descriptive reformulation became— and remains—a defining feature of CAT. Two further developments in practice were significant: (a) the initial summary of goals in terms of traps, dilemmas, and snags was supplemented by the writing of a reformulation letter, offering an account of how past experience had been dealt with in ways reflected in current dysfunctional procedures and (b) the drawing of sequential diagrams tracing how particular procedures led to outcomes either confirming the procedure or involving ineffective avoidance or symptoms.

The joint work of elaborating these reformulation tools usually generated an active working relationship, and the tools themselves provided understanding of problems arising in the further course of therapy. Over the ensuing years, object relations ideas were systematically restated. The procedures of concern to psychotherapists are those involved in relationships with others; in these, the aim is to elicit the expected or wished-for reciprocation. The key descriptive unit is therefore the *reciprocal role procedure*, a stable pattern of interaction originating in early childhood and manifest in relations with others and in patterns of self-management. This concept, incidentally, had been named many years earlier when considering diagrams based on the dyad repertory grid. Moreover, it was clear that the self–other reciprocal role relationships were paralleled by self-management patterns. The explanation for this lay in early development, where caretaker–child interactions shape interpersonal patterns but are also internalized and provide the basis for later self-care and control. These patterns are largely automatic and not reflected on; they are also stable because others can usually be found who provide or can be induced to offer confirmatory reciprocations.

Further theoretical developments followed (see Ryle, 1990, 1995), involving a systematic restatement of object relations ideas, in particular by an emphasis on the actual experience (as opposed to fantasy) of the developing child and by the application of the model of internalization proposed by Vygotsky (see Leiman, 1992; Ryle, 1991), who argued that what is internalized is neither a "representation" of another nor an "object." Formative experiences are accompanied by intense preverbal and verbal communication between child and caretaker (a view supported by the developmental studies of recent decades), and these communications involve the use of both individually created and culturally transmitted signs. Thus, the internalization of early experience involves the acquisition of the meanings and values conveyed by the signs accompanying early joint activity. CAT therefore proposes a "semiotic object relations theory" in which reciprocal roles and sign-mediated outer and inner dialogues are central concepts.

Just as early development involves sign-mediated communication in the context of a relationship, so the practice of CAT is based on a therapeutic relationship in which focused signs evolved in the reformulation process play a central role. This model makes no use of the complex and often arbitrary constructions of unconscious mental processes of the various schools of psychoanalysis, but it does place a central emphasis on the therapy relationship. When therapists enter the patient's field of consciousness, they are seen and related to in ways reflecting the patient's repertoire of reciprocal roles. Therapists' personalities, habitual practices, and elicited reactions all serve to confirm or challenge dysfunctional procedures. At the same time, the therapist's conscious provision of serious and concerned attention can serve as the source of a new, constructive voice in the patient's inner dialogue. At the most obvious level, working with patients to derive the best possible descriptions of their problematic procedures is both a useful example of teaching and an experience—often the first—of being treated with respect. Beyond that, however, the therapist's awareness at all times of the inner and outer directed reciprocal role procedures of the patient and of the ways in which these provoke or invite reciprocations allows therapists to avoid or repair unhelpful interactions. They can then offer a relationship to the patient that is reparative rather than collusive in the specific areas where the patient's problems arise.

Therapy is based on joint work and accurate descriptions and interpretations of supposed dynamically unconscious processes are largely avoided by CAT therapists or are tentative and up for discussion. The work with grids and with the procedural sequence model have demonstrated the power of accurate description, and the developed semiotic object relations model allows such an approach to be applied to the highest levels of self-processes. This has involved developments in the techniques of sequential diagrammatic reformulation, where core reciprocal role patterns, abstracted from observed and reported role procedures, are shown as the core from which dysfunctional behaviors and misinterpretations of experience are derived. Detailed analysis of segments of experience or conversation may involve tracing the shifting reciprocal patterns (dialogic sequence analysis). It is of interest that some psychoanalytic writers have recently noted the need to work with descriptions of procedural patterns as well as with interpretations.

Descriptive reformulation with an emphasis on reciprocal role patterns is of prime importance in working with borderline patients, whose propensity to destroy relationships, including those with their therapists, is well known. The reformulation of borderline personality disorder in CAT is based on the multiple self states model, which identifies three aspects of this diagnosis:

1. Adverse early experiences are reflected in a basic reciprocal role pattern of abuse and neglect in relation to victimization

or revenge. The latter roles are often accompanied by somatic symptoms.

2. Severe abuse generates, in predisposed individuals, the formation of a range of partially dissociated self states. In these patients, the perceived threat of abuse or abandonment may still lead to the original reciprocation, including in some cases states of primitive rage, which can lead to violence toward self or others. However, borderline patients who have survived in the world have a repertoire of alternative responses and usually respond to threat with a switch to patterns such as depressed coping, zombielike states without feeling, or the search for or fantasy of ideal care.

3. Early deprivation may have led to an impaired capacity for self-reflection, and this capacity, insofar as it is present, is disrupted by the switches between states. The clinical management and therapy of these patients is made difficult by the intensity of the negative roles and the reactions they induce, by the confusion generated by state switches, and by the patients' lack of ability to self-reflect. Diagrammatic reformulation describing the reciprocal role patterns of the different states and tracing the switches between them provides a basis for integration and control. This is illustrated in the case example described in this chapter.

In summary, CAT describes self processes as developed and maintained by reciprocal role patterns manifest in relationships and self-management. Accurate description and principled noncollusion are the underlying therapeutic principles. Reformulation aims to generate adequate, accessible descriptions of dysfunctional procedures. For relatively simple problems, descriptions at the "tactical" level of traps, dilemmas, and snags may be adequate, but many more disturbed patients and especially individuals with borderline personality disorder need reformulation in terms of the reciprocal role repertoire and of dissociated states. Such descriptions provide patients with a basis for continuing self-awareness that can lead to greater control, and they provide therapists with a guide to all the ways in which they may be drawn into unhelpful reciprocations. The development of CAT has drawn on a wide range of sources; although it avoids the reductive view of humans offered by cognitive–behavioral approaches and the mystifications provided by psychoanalysis, it takes the value of their contributions into account. CAT enhances the ability of patients to reflect on their own processes. It incorporates the factors common to most psychotherapies, above all emphasizing the importance of the therapy relationship. Its main contribution may be to spell out, in theory and practice, how to understand, describe, maintain, and make best use of this relationship.

CASE EXAMPLE

Kerry, a depressed, personality-disordered adolescent, was treated by Louise McCutcheon. An account of her therapy follows.

Referral, Assessment, and Case Formulation in Cognitive Analytic Therapy Terms

Kerry, a 16-year-old girl, was referred by an adolescent counselor from the local community health service who was concerned about how depressed she seemed. Kerry reported that although things had deteriorated a lot over the past 3 to 4 years, most of her current problems had followed the family's discovery that she was having a sexual relationship with the boyfriend of one of her sisters. They had all been angry with her, and Kerry was left feeling isolated, upset, and guilty.

Kerry lived in a small house with her mother. For the previous 6 months, her two sisters (ages 24 and 30), with their children and current boyfriends, had also lived in the house. Her parents had separated when she was 2 years old because of conflict and domestic violence. Kerry reported that the fighting continued to occur even after her father left. Kerry attempted to avoid the family fights whenever possible and was the one who usually tried to smooth things over. As a child, she had always looked up to her eldest sister, following her around and doing everything to try and please her. Kerry was described by her mother as a child who befriended others and cared for stray animals. Since the age of 12, however, she had been prone to angry outbursts, in some of which she had threatened others with knives.

During the assessment interview, Kerry sat slumped in her chair and was close to tears several times. She described herself as miserable and her home situation as intolerable. She felt guilty and hopeless and spent hours crying on the couch, wishing she were dead. Her appetite was impaired; she felt tired all the time and was avoiding socializing. When she did go out, she experienced increased anxiety and occasional panic attacks. She was in her 4th year at high school and was failing because of poor attendance. In recent years, she had occasionally harmed herself (by banging her head or cutting herself superficially), but she said she would never go through with actually killing herself. She was currently smoking cigarettes and marijuana daily and indulged in binge drinking at least once a week. Despite her hopelessness about the future, she appeared to be motivated to try therapy.

The home seemed to have been characterized by high levels of threat and violence for much of Kerry's life. In response to this, Kerry tried hard to please others but as a result did not convey to others what she needed, and she saw others to be depriving or abusing, leaving her disappointed. This seemed to have resulted on the one hand in her becoming unduly dependent on her mother and, on the other, especially recently, in her being rebellious, attacking others and harming and neglecting herself. The discovery of her affair with her sister's boyfriend left her feeling guilty and rejected by other family members.

In summary, the problems that had brought Kerry to therapy were the powerful emotions of guilt and depression reflecting the current situation and the longer term uncertainties about herself. Unhelpful strategies included her need to please others and her use of avoidance and substance misuse to deal with her negative emotions.

The focus in CAT is on the relationship and self-managing procedures underlying such problems, so these were further explored. A provisional list of reciprocal role procedures was made early in Kerry's therapy. Figure 10.1, which was constructed collaboratively with Kerry, shows these role procedures. The dominant pattern evident from the story was the perception of others as offering some mixture of threatening, abusing, hurting, and controlling (A). However, she herself also played this role, both in her betrayal of her sister and in the anger she directed toward herself. The reciprocal to A might be either being abused and hurt (B1), or being rebellious (B2). B1 was the role she was currently largely occupying, in which she felt deserted and abused. Her school failure and her episodes of violence in the family were examples of her playing B2. A linked negative pattern, also derived from her family experience, was rejecting and abandoning (C) in relation to being rejected, misunderstood, and unloved (D). D frequently led to a trap in which she desperately tried to please others in the hope of eliciting perfect care. A third, more positive pattern could be summarized as caring (E) in relation to dependent (F). Her care for others and for stray animals were examples of her enacting E, whereas toward her older sister and mother she played F but in ways that were inappropriately childish.

The therapist's recognition of these patterns from the history and as they were expressed in her developing relationship with Kerry contributed to the reformulation and served to guard against her being drawn in unhelpfully. Kerry's emotional neediness (F) and her self-destructive or rebellious behaviors (B2) generated a strong desire in the therapist to rush in and try to rescue her (E). This urge needed to be translated into the therapeutic aim of helping her see how her expectations of care were unrealistic while providing good enough but explicitly limited care and while helping Kerry learn how to care for herself. In addition to modifying her understanding of the E–F reciprocal role, the therapist was aware that she needed to anticipate that her anxious desire to protect Kerry against her self-destructive tendencies and the basic clinic procedures might be experienced as controlling or threatening (A), leading to Kerry's rejection of therapy (B2).

In these ways, the developing CAT reformulation provided an essential guide, alerting the therapist to sequential patterns such as the trying to please and avoidance traps and to the problematic reciprocal role procedures identified above. Its role in developing Kerry's capacity for self-reflection

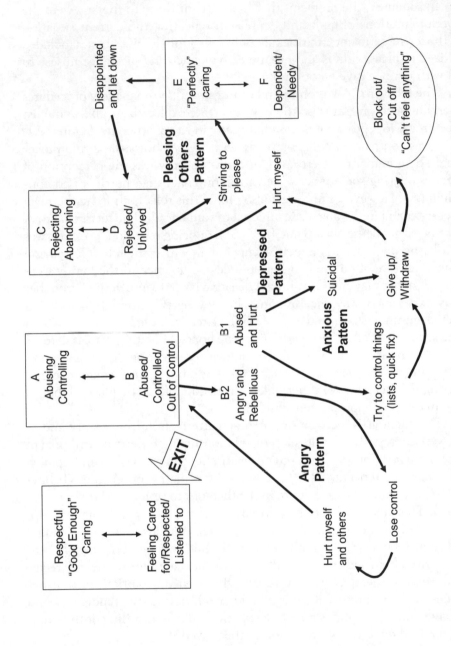

Figure 10.1. Kerry's reciprocal role procedures. A = threatening, abusing, hurting, controlling; B = being out of control; B1 = being abused and hurt; B2 = being rebellious; C = rejecting, abandoning; D = rejected, misunderstood, lonely; E = caring; F = dependent.

came later, however, because initially her depressive and anxiety symptoms were overwhelming and both symptomatic treatment and intervention in her social context were needed before she could engage at that level. Because she displayed a number of physical symptoms, she was referred to her doctor to exclude possible physical disorders. Three different antidepressants were tried, but Kerry disliked the side effects and did not take any regularly. Early on, the therapist taught her some simple psychoeducational and cognitive techniques. Her mood remained unstable, and the possibility of inpatient admission was raised several times, but Kerry did not want that; despite recurrent crises she managed without. Her distress had a major impact on the home, and both sisters and their families moved out, leaving Kerry and her mother alone. The therapist received a number of phone calls from Kerry's distraught mother. The pattern of each phone call could be described as mother's anxious E in relation to Kerry's demanding and threatening F and mother's F in relation to the therapist's E. During most of Kerry's treatment, basic support was offered to her mother, who was referred to a carer's support group. The situation at school deteriorated because of Kerry's poor attendance. Despite the therapist attending a meeting at the school to discuss more effective support, Kerry dropped out within a few weeks.

These various extratherapy interventions would not normally be a part of CAT with adult patients, but in Kerry's case were essential in the early weeks if a working alliance was to be established. At this time, the following general goals of the therapy were set: (a) to develop a better understanding of the patterns that were causing her problems and why things did not seem to get much better, (b) to learn to use the pattern descriptions to help her identify where she was, and (c) to begin to develop ways of doing things differently. Kerry's ambivalence about attending therapy and the possibility that she might drop out when disheartened was acknowledged early on. At the same time, given the history of Kerry wanting others to fix things for her, it seemed important to emphasize that it was Kerry rather than the therapist who must take responsibility for the process of change. At the 4th therapy session (of the agreed 24), the reformulation letter was given to Kerry, and it was read out to her. Kerry sat quietly listening to her story retold in terms of patterns and reciprocal roles. When asked what she thought of the letter, she said she felt it described her life well and that she felt understood.

Sessions 6 to 11

During this period, there were frequent cancellations and missed sessions. Kerry formed a relationship with a young man of 19, and he soon moved in with Kerry and her mother. After several weeks, it began to emerge that despite Kerry's idealized descriptions (boyfriend as E), he was proving to be challenging to live with. Kerry began to suspect him of using heroin and sedatives, which he denied, despite Kerry finding evidence of empty tablet packets and syringes in his possession. Kerry tried to ignore this, often using alcohol or marijuana to help block out her problems. She continued to try to see him idealistically, but as the weeks progressed she was not always able to maintain this and would become suspicious and angrily confront him. This usually resulted in a big argument during which he would threaten to leave (C). Kerry would immediately feel guilty and then set about trying to please him. She and the therapist summarized her difficulties in the form of the dilemma "either I stick up for myself and feel rejected or I give in but feel exploited and angry" and discussed how she might learn to assert her own needs more clearly, without either giving in (B1), rushing to please others, or becoming abusive (B2). In this way, an alternative to the family's shared patterns of A to B and C to D was proposed, based on proper assertion of her needs and respect for her own and others' rights.

During this time, the therapist felt both a strong urge to protect Kerry from exploitation by her boyfriend as well as concern and frustration with Kerry's increasing risk-taking (especially her own substance use). There were several ways this could be related to the diagram. The therapist discussed with Kerry the former's feeling that things were out of control (B) and how this seemed to provoke others (including the therapist) to want to take some control (A). It could also have been identified as her abandoning and rejecting the therapy, herself, and the therapist (C).

Sessions 12 to 16

Kerry ended her relationship with the boyfriend and transferred her dependence to a new close female friend who was experiencing similar life difficulties. They both left home impulsively for several weeks, hoping to "make a new start" but without any thought of finding a job or a place to stay. She did manage to contact the therapist several times during this phase, as did her mother. The few therapy sessions held at that time were focused on this general shared sense of the situation being out of control. She and the therapist used this analogy to understand how others, especially her mother, were also feeling forced to intervene in her life to try to prevent the possible disasters they felt were likely to happen. The therapist also offered some practical help during this phase, registering her for an independent youth allowance (a modest Australian government benefit that is paid to adolescents ages 16 and 17 years if they are able to demonstrate they are fully independent of their families and have no other income) and helping her work out how she might find some part-time work and emergency accommodation, because she seemed so set on not returning to her mother's house.

Gradually the situation began to settle, and Kerry was able to attend therapy more reliably. Her learning over the past few months was reviewed. Kerry still had difficulty using her diagram to quickly identify the patterns being enacted. However, she was starting to see that her needy and dependent role (F) often led to disaster, and she was beginning to imagine how she might be able to care for herself more. Kerry was also practicing how to communicate her needs more assertively, particularly to her mother. She and the therapist refined the diagram during this phase so that it was simpler for her to use, and she began to take on more responsibility for the direction of her therapy.

Sessions 17 to 20

During the last third of the therapy, Kerry began a new intimate relationship, having fallen out with her female friend. As before, Kerry used idealized terms to describe her new boyfriend and would go to extraordinary lengths to try and please him in the hope that he would realize she wanted the same attention and devotion in return. Through discussion, Kerry began to see her behavior as a pattern of feeling rejected (D), seeking perfect care (E) by pleasing others, being disappointed when that did not work, feeling exploited, and feeling abandoned and rejected (D). Work on the diagram began to incorporate more discussion of possible exits from such patterns. In addition, she and the therapist began to prepare for the coming termination. They noted as Kerry began to feel more depressed again that endings were likely to provoke her dependent and needy role (F). This helped Kerry to manage the episodes of hopeless crying with a little more objectivity, and she found they were less intense and did not last so long.

Plans were made for her support when CAT therapy ended, with meetings scheduled four times during the 6-month follow-up period at 1, 2, 4, and 6 months posttermination. Kerry and her mother both wondered whether she might need ongoing therapy. This anxiety about coping following the end of the therapy was normalized. The agreed-on plan involved referral to a drug clinic for treatment of her marijuana dependence as well as referral to a vocational support service.

Sessions 21 to 24

During the last four sessions, Kerry suddenly seemed to realize that the events of the week could all be expressed in terms of the diagram. She felt increasingly confident about using the diagram to help her avoid falling into previous patterns. Kerry felt more independent and more able to be assertive with her boyfriend and others around her. Her risk-taking had diminished considerably, and she was beginning to plan how to give up marijuana regardless of whether her boyfriend changed his daily use or not. These decisions were framed in terms of Kerry learning to care for herself. At the penultimate session, the therapist read out her good-bye letter (see Appendix 10.1). She also noted what had changed and what needed further work; this included her account of the relationship, and they were able to speak about how important this had been to Kerry. In the final session, Kerry also brought in a good-bye letter to the therapist (see Appendix 10.1), describing how she felt more responsible for her moods and behavior.

Follow-Up Sessions

Four follow-up sessions set at 1, 2, 4, and 6 months were offered after completion of the 24-session CAT intervention (Ryle, 1997). Kerry and her mother were both nervous about how they would cope during this phase. Having a clear agreement about the number and timing of the follow-up sessions was reassuring to them both. The aim of follow-up is to provide support and assistance in helping the patient retain the progress made during therapy.

One Month

Kerry was depressed and anxious and wondering about having more therapy. The therapist encouraged her to use the skills and knowledge she had developed and to use as necessary the supports that were in place. There was one particular crisis during which Kerry felt unable to cope on her own, and a psychiatric admission was discussed. In the end, she decided to return home and felt she had coped.

Two Months

By the 2nd month after termination of therapy, Kerry reported feeling that things were more in perspective. She reported being able to cope better, especially with her depressive moods. Kerry had reduced her marijuana use, even abstaining for several days at a time, but then relapsing into daily use.

Four Months

Kerry was feeling on top of her moods and more in control of herself in her relationship, and she reported two 10-day periods without cannabis. At this time, Kerry spoke with some sadness about her boyfriend; the relationship was not working out as she wanted. In particular, she felt that her boyfriend wanted to keep her dependent on him. She and the therapist spent some time speaking about how Kerry might help him understand her need for self-sufficiency.

Six Months

Kerry had decided that her boyfriend was not able to support her move toward the goals she deemed important, and they had separated. She had managed several more marijuana-free periods and now felt she was likely to continue to move toward giving it up completely. Her job had fallen through, and she had finally taken up the referral to the vocation support program; it seemed this might offer some assistance. This was the last meeting. Kerry was able to express some sadness about the ending of the therapeutic relationship, but she also expressed her optimism about her future and her plans.

REFLECTIONS ABOUT THE USE OF THE
INTEGRATIVE THERAPY MODEL

The goal of therapy in CAT is procedural revision. In Kerry's case, the aim was to resolve her symptoms and depressed mood by developing her capacity for self-reflection so she could gain greater control over her life. The reformulation letter and diagram were worked out in the early sessions, but she could make use of the diagram independently only toward the end of therapy. The diagram, however, allowed the therapist to offer a clear account of what she, the therapist, could and could not do, especially in maintaining awareness of Kerry as a whole person and to keep the goal of integration in mind. Without the clear model of Kerry's key procedures, the symptomatic treatments, involvement of her mother, and the use of other agencies, the treatment might easily have represented inadvertent reinforcement of one or another of her established reciprocal role procedures and might have led to her dropping out of therapy. Although they began working on the development of Kerry's self-reflective skills from the beginning of the therapy, Kerry's ability to understand, control, and care for herself only became apparent during the follow-up period. This is commonly the case in time-limited therapy and is aided by the availability of the reformulation tools and the use of good-bye letters to address the feelings around termination. The CAT model of Kerry's role procedures allowed the therapist to help Kerry see how her ability to care for animals and others needed to be extended to caring for herself, and they were able to make her dependence on others (including the therapist) more realistic and appropriate. Kerry was able to see how she played a part in drawing others into caring and controlling relationships with her and how this led to her disappointment or rebellion and to her unhelpful blanking off from her feelings through marijuana use. Through these understandings she began to take responsibility for her life.

CONCEPTUALIZATION OF THE THERAPEUTIC RELATIONSHIP

The model of learning in CAT places a central emphasis on the therapy relationship experience as offering both new understandings and a reparative emotional experience aimed specifically at modifying the patient's most dysfunctional procedures and at encouraging integration. The therapist's understanding guides every interaction, and the emphasis is less on the origins of problems than on describing, recognizing, and challenging their manifestations in daily life and in the therapy relationship. From the first interview, Kerry placed her trust in and depended on the therapist, who felt drawn to rescue her from her distress. While recognizing the need to resist offering care that could be idealized, the therapist was able to use cognitive and behavioral strategies for symptom relief. Resisting pressures to collude with Kerry's procedures was aided by the therapist's use of the diagram and by her supervision, but there were many points at which decisions were difficult. In particular, there were times when she felt compelled to become more controlling, and the analogy of being in Kerry's recklessly driven car allowed the therapist to share the dilemma she felt about that and to explore different understandings and actions. The brief crisis that occurred during the follow-up period was another challenging time for her as therapist. The CAT contract with more disturbed patients usually suggests four follow-up sessions at 1, 2, 4, and 6 months, but crisis appointments can be offered if necessary, as they were with Kerry. At various points during this posttermination phase, the therapist wondered whether other, more supportive arrangements might suit her better. In any event, Kerry was able to cope better than expected, and the experience of managing was valuable.

Overall, the alliance between Kerry and the therapist was strong. However, this was most threatened during the second quarter of therapy, when Kerry was most chaotic and there were many cancellations and missed sessions. Standard clinic practice with young patients is to discharge them if the gaps between face-to-face meetings exceed 6 weeks, but during unscheduled breaks, therapists actively contact clients and encourage them to complete their therapy contract. The therapist assumes more of the responsibility early on in the therapy and gradually hands this over as time goes by. This policy defined the relationship of the clinic to Kerry and minimized the risk that she would feel controlled (leading to B1 or B2) or abandoned (leading to D) while not encouraging undue dependence (F).

CONCLUSION

In this chapter, the basic theory and practice of CAT has been presented and illustrated. Derived from psychoanalytic, cognitive, constructivist, behavioral, and Vygotskian sources by a process of assimilation and transformation and based on a developmental model that describes the social and interpersonal origins of self processes, CAT now represents an integrated model of the psychological processes on which psychotherapy is based. Practice is clearly derived from this theoretical basis and although sharing many features with other approaches is unique in the joint creation and use of written and diagrammatic conceptual tools. These are then used to strengthen the capacity of patients for self-reflection and to guide therapists in the provision of reparative, noncollusive relationships.

APPENDIX 10.1: THERAPIST'S AND PATIENT'S GOOD-BYE LETTERS

THE THERAPIST'S LETTER

Dear Kerry,

This is the letter that I spoke to you about, that would be a chance to summarize and reflect on our work over the past 14 months.

I recall when you came in you were feeling very depressed, and often spent hours or even days curled up in a ball, crying, and feeling very overwhelmed. At that time, we spent some time trying to get at what was happening and why things might have got to this point. We drew the diagram and I wrote you a letter in which we tried to understand things from your history as well as from recent events.

There were a few times when you were able to come in regularly, and at other times your life was so chaotic that getting in here was the last thing you could think of. Despite this, we managed to catch up often enough to keep things going, and now it feels like you have learned all sorts of things.

The most important thing, it seems to me, is that you've learned how to think about your thoughts and feelings. The skill of reflecting on how you interact with others (and how you think) is essential if you want to change things. You said that you feel like you know what to do to manage feeling depressed or anxious, but the job ahead is to practice these skills until they become familiar habits (to replace the old, unhelpful patterns). You are already well on the way with this, and monitoring these patterns in your notebook has been one step that has helped with this. Learning to be more assertive about what you need from others (like your Mum and your boyfriend) has also been hard work, but you are taking steps and have been able to feel pleased with your progress.

I'm sure that there have been (and will continue to be many more) ups and downs, and at times progress won't feel very fast. We have discussed how "hoping for perfect care" can be a disappointing trap to fall into. Particularly when it ends up that you do everything else to please others the way you hope they will care for you—but they never do. So this will continue to be something to look out for in the future.

Kerry, I have really enjoyed working with you, and have felt privileged that you have been able to trust me with your story and your feelings—both the good and the bad moments. I know that coming in here and sharing these struggles with me has been difficult and confronting at times. It has also been an important time for you to learn all sorts of things about yourself. I know we have also shared a special trust that has been important to you and that you probably feel a bit sad about this finishing as well as an excitement about taking the next step "out on your own."

In the time I have known you, I have seen you take many steps like this, and you have not only survived but done well. This is another step that I'm sure will be one you learn from too.

I look forward to hearing about your progress (and even the setbacks) at your follow-up appointments.

THE PATIENT'S LETTER

Dear Louise,

Over the past year or so of having therapy with you I feel I have achieved a lot. The time we have together I used to step out of my body and look at the emotions, moods and situations I go through. When I first started coming here I felt that I could not be helped and I was going to stay sad forever. But I have now realized I can be happy and calm and all those things I wished I could be. It just takes time and plenty of understanding of myself. I can now blame my mood and say sorry to people for blaming them coz it was all my negative thinking (eg. Mum/boyfriend). I know I still have a very long way to go and I'd be lying if I said I wasn't scared. There are still big steps that need to be taken. But I know I'll get there one day. Thank you for listening, not judging me and helping me through a lot of tough stages. I feel if I didn't come at all I would either be completely insane or lying in a gutter somewhere. Because I couldn't cope at all. Thank you for all your help. You have probably saved my life. Kerry.

REFERENCES

Kelly, G. A. (1955). *The psychology of personal constructs*. New York: Norton.

Leiman, M. (1992). The concept of sign in the work of Vygotsky, Winnicott and Bakhtin: Further integration of object relations theory and activity theory. *British Journal of Medical Psychology, 65*, 209–221.

Ryle, A. (1975). *Frames and cages*. London: Sussex University Press.

Ryle, A. (1990). *Cognitive–analytic therapy: Active participation in change*. Chichester, England: Wiley.

Ryle, A. (1991). Object relations theory and activity theory: A proposed link by way of the procedural sequence model. *British Journal of Medical Psychology, 64*, 307–316.

Ryle, A. (Ed.). (1995). *Cognitive analytic therapy: Developments in theory and practice*. Chichester, England: Wiley.

Ryle, A. (1997). *Cognitive analytic therapy for borderline personality disorder*. New York: Wiley.

Ryle, A., & Kerr, I. B. (2002). *Introducing cognitive analytic therapy: Principles and practice*. Chichester, England: Wiley.

11

CHRONIC DEPRESSION AND THE COGNITIVE BEHAVIORAL ANALYSIS SYSTEM OF PSYCHOTHERAPY

JAMES P. McCULLOUGH JR.

The cognitive behavioral analysis system of psychotherapy (CBASP; Keller et al., 2000; McCullough, 1984a, 1991, 2000, 2001, 2003a, 2003b, 2003c) integrates several theoretical traditions into its formulations of patient psychopathology and treatment methodology. The social learning theory of Albert Bandura (1977) provides the essential view of human behavior whereby cognitive activity, motor behavior, and environmental influence are inextricably connected in an unbroken chain of reciprocal reactivity.

The psychopathology of the early-onset chronically depressed patient is based on Jean Piaget's (1923/1926, 1964/1967, 1954/1981) view of cognitive–emotive development, described in *Intelligence and Affectivity* (1954/1981). According to Piaget, heightened emotive stimuli may derail or retard cognitive–emotive maturational development in the young child. His description of maturational disruption aptly characterizes the developmental history of many early-onset chronically depressed adults who present with both (a) a primary child's structural view of reality in the social–interpersonal arena and (b) a longstanding and heightened out-of-control mood state. The developmental history of many chronically depressed patients is filled with trauma and abuse (e.g., Horwitz, 2001; McCullough, 2000; Nemeroff et al., 2003).

Late-onset patients typically present with an out-of-control mood state that begins in their mid-20s (McCullough & Kaye, 1993) following an unresolved episodic major depression that takes on a chronic course (Keller & Hanks, 1994; Keller, Lavori, Rice, Coryell, & Hirschfeld, 1986). The unabating and pernicious mood state undercuts normal cognitive–emotive patterns (Cicchetti, Ackerman, & Izard, 1995). Late-onset patients, like their early-onset counterparts, return to a childish level of cognitive–emotive functioning. In summary, preoperational structural functioning (Piaget, 1923/1926, 1964/1967, 1954/1981) in the social–interpersonal sphere characterizes both early- and late-onset chronically depressed adults.

Preoperational patients are perceptually disengaged from the environment in essential ways. An egocentric perceptual focus blocks the informing influences of the environment resulting in a refractory orbit of misery. CBASP posits that the patient's perceptual disconnection from his or her environment is the essential maintaining variable for chronic depression (McCullough, 2000). A primary CBASP treatment goal is to connect the individual perceptually with his or her environment, which modifies behavior in two ways: (a) Perceptual connection makes behavioral consequences explicit, resulting in an awareness that one's misery is self-produced, and (b) perceptual connection also mitigates the overwhelming feelings of helplessness and hopelessness associated with the disorder by showing patients that the way they behave clearly affects how they feel.

CBASP also incorporates Kiesler and colleague's (Anchin & Kiesler, 1982; Kiesler, 1983, 1996; Kiesler & Schmidt, 1993) interpersonal psychotherapy procedures to measure the patient's interpersonal effects on the therapist. These ratings make the patient's stimulus value explicit so therapists can pinpoint the interpersonal strategies to enact as well as to avoid.

The rationale for teaching CBASP therapists how to arrange in-session contingencies so that the content of psychotherapy is learned derives from operant psychology (McCullough, in press; Skinner, 1953, 1968). Negative reinforcement conditions are highlighted during sessions and used to modify behavior. Adaptive behavior is strengthened when change is accompanied by felt reductions in discomfort and distress (McCullough, 2000, in press).

Systematic measurement of patient change is an integral part of therapy administration (McCullough, 1984a, 1984b, 1984c; 1991; McCullough & Carr, 1987). CBASP is an acquisition learning model (McCullough, 2000, 2002, in press) in which patients are taught a problem-solving algorithm (situational analysis [SA]); then, they are assisted in applying what they have learned in daily encounters. I measure the degree to which in-session learning occurs using a reliable instrument, the Patient Performance Rating Form (McCullough, 2000). Evidence suggests that CBASP treatment outcomes reflect the degree to which patients learn SA (Manber et al., 2003; Manber & McCullough, 2000).

In summary, CBASP approaches the helplessness and hopelessness symptoms of chronically depressed patients as a natural consequence of their lack of perceived environmental connection. Perceptually establishing (in the early-onset case) and reestablishing (in the late-onset case) the Patient × Environment connection means that the social–interpersonal environment can now inform and shape behavior. Attainment of this perceptual goal (called *perceived functionality*; McCullough, 2000) is usually accompanied by heightened motivation to change as well as by a feeling of personal empowerment.

CASE STUDY

Sally was an attractive 42-year-old woman, in good health, mildly overweight, who had been married for 10 years to an alcoholic man, whom she had divorced 8 years prior to presentation for therapy. She had custody of their two teenaged boys (ages 14 and 15). For the past 15 years, Sally had worked at a law firm as a certified public accountant where she consistently obtained above average performance ratings.

Sally was diagnosed at screening as having been in a major depressive episode of 6 months' duration, which included two vegetative symptoms of overeating and sleeping more than usual. Sally reported that she went to bed tired and woke up tired. She also disclosed that she had been depressed since high school. I used a timeline procedure (McCullough, 2001) to determine the course of her depression. Sally met criteria of the *Diagnostic and Statistical Manual of Mental Disorders* (4th ed. [DSM–IV]; American Psychiatric Association, 1994) for early-onset dysthymia, which began during her 1st year in high school. She also described three episodes of major depression during the past 10 years, which included the current episode. Her clinical course denoted that she was suffering from a *DSM–IV* "double depression" (Keller & Shapiro, 1982, 1984). The periods between the major depressive episodes resulted in Sally returning to the mild dysthymic disorder baseline. Each major depression followed the breakup of a love affair. The first episode began during her divorce proceedings; the next had occurred 5 years before the beginning of therapy when she ended a relationship; and the present episode had started 6 months before, following another breakup. No other psychopathology, including personality disorder, was identified. Sally had not sought treatment before, and when asked why, she replied that the previous episodes never lasted more than 3 months, had not caused her to miss work, and had not interfered with child care.

In the most recent episode, Sally had been depressed for 6 months, she had had to call in sick several times because of her mood, and she was worried that she was neglecting her sons. Sally reported having two female friends whom she met several times a month, but she indicated that they were not very close. She and her sons attended Episcopal church services weekly, but she did not feel close to anyone at church. She also said she used to exercise at a local gym several times a week; however, she quit when the last depression episode began. Sally stated that nothing she did or tried seemed to affect the course or intensity of her depression (helplessness); she also disclosed a long-standing fear that she would always feel this way (hopelessness). Her conclusion was an oft-heard complaint of chronically depressed adults: "It really doesn't matter what I do, I'll always be depressed."

Theoretical Formulation of the Case

Sally's chronic helplessness and hopelessness signaled a dysfunctional relationship with the environment (McCullough, 2000). Over the years, environmental feedback had not exerted an informing influence on her life, nor did Sally report doing anything of value with her life. She had existed for many years in an orbit of solitary chronic misery uninfluenced by the world and unaware that she affected others in any way. This perceptual outlook illustrates the environmental disconnection (McCullough, 2000). CBASP can correct the patient's perceived disconnection using SA. SA repeatedly demonstrates behavioral consequences in an explicit manner.

I completed the Kiesler Impact Message Inventory (IMI; Kiesler & Schmidt, 1993) on Sally following Session 2 and found that she had a specific and negative interpersonal impact on me. Sally's highest scores were on the Hostile–Submissive Octant (H-S; denoting that she remained detached and anxious during Sessions 1 and 2), the Submissive Octant (S; signifying she wanted the therapist to take the lead and tell her what to do to make things right), and the Hostile Octant (H; an impact suggesting she wanted the therapist to keep his distance). Sally's stimulus value for the clinician was not pleasant, and it was easy to see why she reported few positive experiences with others. Her interpersonal impacts as measured on the H-S, S, and H octants, respectively, can be described as follows:

1. I'm nervous about getting close to you (H-S).
2. If I do get close, then I want you to tell me what to do (S).
3. I want you to stay away from me or at least keep your distance (H).

Sally's interpersonal style frequently pulled complementary hostile and dominant (D) reactions from others (Kiesler, 1988, 1996); this means people often reacted to her in a counterhostile manner (H) as well as told her what to do (D). Being perceptually disconnected from her environment, she was not aware that she pulled these reactions from others. When they occurred, Sally was driven into greater isolation and despair.

My IMI ratings warned me that I must not react to Sally in a complementary manner (that is, react with H-D out of frustration over her hostile avoidance or with D because of her submissiveness). By remaining friendly and helpful throughout, I would be responding interpersonally in ways that were new for her and that would not lead to isolation and despair. The best therapeutic stance would be a task-focused position on the friendly side of the interpersonal circle (Kiesler, 1983, 1988, 1996) denoting behavior that was neither too dominant nor too submissive (see McCullough, 2000, chap. 8).

Significant Other History During Session 2

Sally described a history of the significant other in which both parents had alcoholism, and she was the oldest of four children (the siblings had never been close; for a complete history, see McCullough, 2000, chap. 5). Whenever her father was drunk, he physically and verbally abused her with severe spankings and anger tirades. These outbursts occurred when she did not accomplish assigned household duties. The duties included age-inappropriate child-care expectations with her two younger brothers and sister. She said that her father expected her to act "grown up" when she was still in elementary school, and she had to meet his criteria for acting grown up to avoid the spankings. She cooked most of the meals, did the washing and mending, and watched and took care of her brothers and sister. She and her mother, who was intoxicated most of the time, were never close. Sally described her mother as "inadequate, very passive, and emotionally distant." She never remembered having a meaningful conversation with either parent. Her first intimate encounter occurred with a boyfriend during her senior year in high school. They spent long hours talking. She slept with him one time and became pregnant. The boyfriend's parents paid for an abortion, threatening to tell her parents if she did not comply. Her parents never knew about the pregnancy. The boy's parents forbade him to see her following the abortion.

She went to college and did well. Graduating on time with a degree in accounting, Sally passed the certified public accountant examination 2 years later. She did not date much in college and married when she was 24 "just to get away from my parents." The marriage was dysfunctional, and her husband, like her father, physically abused her when he was drunk and when she disobeyed him.

The material obtained from the significant other history is used to construct one transference hypothesis (McCullough, 2000). The hypothesis, stated as patient expectancies about a negative consequence that will occur, can be placed in one of four interpersonal domains: (a) interpersonal intimacy with the therapist, (b) disclosure of personal needs or problems, (c) making a mistake around the therapist, and (d) experiencing negative feelings toward the therapist. From Sally's history material, I constructed a transference hypothesis in the "making a mistake" domain: *"If I make a mistake around Dr. M, then he will verbally castigate and reject me."*

There were also thematic overtones in Sally's history suggesting that she would feel pressured to take care of me as well as meet my needs in some way to the neglect of her own. It should be noted that these specific interpersonal themes more than likely remained tacit knowledge for Sally (i.e., she had never thought about behaving this way around other people). It was obvious to me that she had always functioned as the "family caretaker" and that this early learning would more than likely play out in some way in our relationship. However, I made a clinical decision to target the "mistake" area, thinking that both interpersonal issues would be covered with the mistake hypothesis.

Using Sally's case, two CBASP techniques will be illustrated below: SA and the interpersonal discrimination exercise (IDE). SA, as noted above, is the major technique of CBASP and is a six-step problem-solving algorithm used to demonstrate behavioral consequences. It teaches patients to recognize the interpersonal effects they have on others. The exercise contains two parts: the elicitation phase and the remediation phase (McCullough, 2000, chaps. 6 and 7). SA is administered during every therapy session. The goal of IDE administration, the second CBASP technique, is to heal early emotional trauma by helping patients to discriminate the person of the therapist from maltreating significant others (McCullough, 2000, in press). The focus of the IDE exercise is determined by the transference hypothesis constructed from the significant other history material. As noted above, Sally's transference hypothesis suggested that "making mistakes" around the therapist would elicit strong negative emotional reactions in Sally as well as expectations of being castigated and rejected. This point will become clearer in a moment.

TWO TECHNIQUES

Session 4 Situational Analysis Exercise

SA was administered in two phases (elicitation and remediation), as described above. Descriptions follow below.

Elicitation Phase (First Part of Situational Analysis Exercise)

During the elicitation phase of SA, the therapist asks the patient to (a) describe an interpersonal situation or event, (b) interpret what the situation means to him or her, (c) describe how he or she behaved during the event, (d) describe the (e) actual outcome (AO) and (f) the desired outcome (DO), and (g) answer the question "Did you get what you wanted in the situation?" (i.e., did the AO = the DO?). My work with Sally during the exercise follows.

Step 1: Situational description (what happened?). Sally described the situation as follows:

> I spoke with the executive partner on Tuesday—I told you he's my boss. We reviewed some of my figures on a large corporation merger. I had overlooked adding some stock holdings into the total assets for one of the companies. Our firm drew up the final contract based on the wrong company value. My mistake had been caught by a lawyer who was representing that company. My boss said that he was embarrassed by my error, and he had to stop the merger proceedings until the error could be corrected and new figures put in the contract. My error meant that now a second meeting would have to be called to obtain the signatures and an "all-nighter" would have to be pulled by some of our firm's lawyers to fix the wording of the contract and print up new copies. I couldn't speak for a few seconds. When I finally said something, I asked him if he wanted me to resign. He looked at me like I was crazy. He said: "No, just don't make a mistake like this again!" I got up and left his office feeling like a fool and like I always screw up like this.

Step 2: Interpretation (what did the situation mean to you?). Sally made the following list:

1. I can't do anything right.
2. I'm totally stupid.
3. I'm no good, just a failure.

Comment. Notice how none of Sally's interpretations are grounded in the situational event; that is, they do not describe what occurred in the encounter between Sally and her boss. These interpretations prevented Sally from attending to the situation at hand and kept her focus on a global, general level of thinking. Effective problem-solving is precluded when one thinks this way. Remediating her interpretations in the second phase of SA will "ground" Sally in the situation and focus her attention on how she can respond directly to her boss.

Step 3: Response (how did you behave in the situation?). Sally described her response: "I was speechless for a few seconds. I couldn't think of anything to say. Then, I just offered to resign. After the look Mr. Smith gave me, I just got up and left the office."

Comment. Sally's behavior, like her interpretations, never dealt with what she had done and the consequences her error had had on the firm. A lack of focus on the problem at hand destined her to miss the mark, which meant she was unable to address the immediate problem and behave appropriately.

Step 4: Actual outcome (how did the situation come out for you?). Sally continued, "I never said another word after my resignation comment; I just got up and left."

Comment. The consequences (AO) in this interpersonal event were negative, like so many situational outcomes she reported. Because of the global, off-task way Sally cognitively constructed the situation and then subsequently behaved, problem resolution was precluded. Sally failed again, but this time her failure would not be the end of the story. SA would help her take another look at how she might have handled this slice of time and assist her in "fixing" a badly managed encounter. The next time something like this happened, she might approach the situation differently and obtain a different outcome. Over time, Sally learned that how she behaved with others directly affected the way situations came out. By repeatedly demonstrating the effects of her behavior in SA, she acquired a perceived functionality mind-set.

Step 5: Desired outcome (how would you have liked the situation to come out for you?). Sally said, "I wanted to tell Mr. Smith how sorry I was and ask if there was anything I could do to help the firm out."

Comment. Sally was surprised the first time she was asked to propose a DO for a situation. She had never thought of this possibility before.

Step 6: Actual outcome versus desired outcome comparison (did you get what you wanted in this situation?). Sally commented, "No! I acted like an idiot." I asked her why she didn't get what she wanted. She said, "Because I'm a loser, always have been, always will be."

Remediation Phase

In the remediation phase, the therapist works with patients to "fix" badly managed situations and to assist patients in obtaining their DO. My verbatim work with Sally during the remediation phase follows.

> Dr. M: Let's go back through this situation and see what must be fixed in order for you to get your desired outcome. Let's begin with your interpretations. Your first interpretation was "I can't do anything right." Is this interpretation anchored to anything which happened in this situation?
>
> Sally: Not really, it's just a general statement.
>
> Dr. M: Then what is an interpretative sentence that would indicate something that is actually happening?
>
> Sally: "I've made a serious error on this project."
>
> Dr. M: Good. I want you to understand what you missed and why we are revising your interpretations. It's important that you learn what I am doing here. Now, how does this interpretation contribute to your getting what you want?
>
> Sally: Well, it doesn't, but it's true.
>
> Dr. M: Yes, it is true. It helps you because it's anchored, grounded in the slice of time. You've got a much better shot at getting your

desired outcome as long as you stay grounded. Let's look at the next one. "I'm totally stupid." Is this interpretation anchored to anything that happened?

Sally: No, it's like my first one—just a general statement.

Dr. M: Doesn't do you much good, does it? What would be a better interpretation that would ground you in what was going on?

Sally: "I'm feeling terrible about my mistake."

Dr. M: That's a good interpretation. It certainly describes how you felt. How does it contribute to your getting your desired outcome?

Sally: It doesn't, but it was how I felt. Looking back on it makes me think I need to do something about this mess I made.

Dr. M: What would you like to do? Come up with something in place of your third interpretation, which was "I'm no good, just a failure." That one was just like your first two. Looking back now, what could you have thought right then?

Sally: "I've got to tell Mr. Smith what a mess I made, and ask him if there was anything I could do to help out."

Dr. M: Good. We call this an *action interpretation*, and it means that we think of something which we must do in order to obtain our desired outcome. Action interpretations usually precede assertive behavior. Now, had you interpreted the situation the way you just did when we revised your interpretations to make them relevant and accurate—"I've made a serious error; I feel terrible about it; and I've got to tell Mr. Smith what a mess I made and ask if I can help out"—how would you have behaved differently?

Sally: I would have told Mr. Smith I messed up and asked him what I could do to help.

Dr. M: Had you done this, would you have gotten what you wanted?

Sally: Yes, then I wouldn't have felt like such a fool, and I surely wouldn't have asked him if he wanted me to resign.

Dr. M: What have you learned here?

Sally: To focus more on what is going on instead of just running away. But I really messed up this SA. You had to help me all the way. I should have already learned how to do this. But I still don't know. I still make mistakes with it and need help.

Dr. M: Has anyone ever taken the time to teach you the things they wanted you to do?

Sally: No.

Dr. M: Well, I'm not surprised.

After repeated SA exercises in subsequent sessions, Sally began to focus more on the situation at hand instead of thinking globally and behaving inappropriately. Increasingly, her cognitive interpretations and behavior began to take on a problem-focused quality and less of an aimless, reactive pattern. Gradually, she realized that she could control many situational outcomes by thinking carefully about what was actually happening and what she wanted before doing or saying anything. Increasing situational mastery was accompanied with lowered symptom intensity and a greater feeling of personal empowerment.

I used the Patient Performance Rating Form to evaluate Sally's SA performance during each session. The ultimate criterion performance goal for SA is for the patient to be able to complete the entire exercise without any remedial help during two successive sessions. Sally reached the criterion performance level during her 19th and 20th sessions.

However, Sally's reaction to the mistakes she made in this fourth-session SA made me realize I was in a "hot spot" transference area. I was able to formulate a transference hypothesis for Sally: "If I make a mistake around Dr. M, then he will verbally castigate and reject me." I then administered the IDE. What follows is the verbatim dialogue taken from this exercise.

Session 4 administration of the interpersonal discrimination exercise.

> *Sally:*   I made a mess of that SA. You had to help me every step of the way, and I ended up having to revise all my interpretations and behavior. I can't get anything right. I try so hard and fail. One of my duties here is to get SA right—I've just messed it up again. You must think that I am an idiot and a failure. This is the story of my life—failure and screwing up.
>
> *Dr. M:*   Let's stop right here and focus on what you just said to me. What would have happened had you gone through the SA you just completed if your dad had been sitting where I am? Describe what his reaction to you would have been.
>
> *Sally:*   When I was a little girl he would have spanked me. After I got older, he just told me what an idiot and screwup I was, that I could never do anything right. That look of his was what cut me in two. He hated me, and that look said it. He thought I was a lowlife. I used to feel so guilty after his tirades that I couldn't sleep—it was like I was suffocating. I'm sorta feeling that right now. [*Sally began to cry softly.*]
>
> *Dr. M:*   What would have been your husband's reaction to you if he had been sitting in my seat?
>
> *Sally:*   He would have smacked me and cursed me and called me all sorts of names. He really hurt me and made me feel just like I

did with my father. I would go get in the car after one of his tirades and feel so physically weak that I could hardly push the accelerator pedal. I would just drive around aimlessly for hours and then go home. You must have a ton of discipline—I bet you want to lay into me and tell me what a real fool I am. I'm just worthless. [*Her crying became harder.*]

Now the IDE discrimination task begins:

Dr. M: I want to ask you something. You have made a lot of statements about how I must feel about you over the past 5 minutes. What was my behavior like while we were going through your SA?

Sally: I don't know.

Dr. M: Try to remember back a few minutes ago before you described your dad and ex-husband. What did I do while we worked together?

Sally: Well, you didn't hit me or yell at me.

Dr. M: What did I do?

Sally: You didn't seem to be that upset about my mistakes. You seemed interested in my understanding what we were working on. In fact, you said that to me—you wanted me to learn what I had missed on this SA and why. How can you react to me this way? You've got to be upset with me deep down.

Dr. M: Keep focusing on what I did and not what you're thinking might be going on in my mind. Did I do anything else that you can recall?

Sally: You wondered out loud if anyone had ever showed me how to do something before, and I said no. Then, you said that you were not surprised.

Dr. M: How did the tone of my voice sound? The look on my face? Do you remember?

Sally: You looked intense, like you were totally focused on me. I remember thinking at the time that this can't be real. Your voice remained calm, but supportive throughout the exercise.

Dr. M: What are the implications for you personally if I'm really different from your father and ex-husband?

Sally: I wouldn't have to walk around on eggshells waiting for the other shoe to fall. I could be myself more, warts and all. Maybe I could even learn to accept myself more. You seem to want to help me learn. Also, you don't seem to have a specific timetable or want to punish me if I screw up. That's it. You want me to learn from my mistakes. Now that's really different. No one has ever taught me anything. I was just always expected to know everything from the outset.

Comment. Learning to discriminate the person of the therapist from negative significant others is not easy, and I administered many IDE trials to Sally before significant loosening of these entrenched emotional patterns was achieved. Unless chronically depressed adults are taught to discriminate the clinician from negative significant others, the positive associations and feelings patients accrue toward the therapist during treatment are often not of sufficient strength to modify the older emotional ties with significant others. The IDE is specifically developed to break up these older bonds. Sally learned to respond realistically to me (free of her older emotional fears that I would ridicule or reject her for her mistakes). This resulted in her saying spontaneously that she felt greater freedom to be herself without fear of censure.

CONCEPTUALIZATION OF THE THERAPEUTIC ALLIANCE

At the end of Session 2, I defined my role with Sally in two ways. First, I completed an IMI (Kiesler & Schmidt, 1993). Identifying the negative complementary pulls for action is the first step in prevention. After my response tendencies were made explicit, I knew what I had to avoid. Second, my role was also informed by the construction of the transference hypothesis. In summary, I knew interpersonally both what not to do with the patient's complementary pulls for action and also what to do in interpersonal "hot spots" where Sally reported having made some mistake.

Unlike Bordin (1979) and the "revised" Bordin as described by Safran and Muran (2000), the CBASP therapist does not explicitly and verbally negotiate the tasks or goals of treatment with the chronically depressed patient using a sort of mutually agreed upon contract. The tasks and the goals in the model are both preset: Specific tasks have been designed to connect patients perceptually with their environments. During the first session, the therapist describes what needs to be done and how chronic depression is related to the way persons live their lives. The practitioner also points out how the patient is beginning a treatment that has been shown to be effective with his or her disorder (Keller et al., 2000). Instilling hope is an important goal for Session 1.

OUTCOME SUMMARY OF SALLY'S CASE

Sally was diagnosed in remission at Session 20 and at the 1-year follow-up interview. Her Beck Depression Inventory—II (Beck, 1996) symptom intensity scores steadily decreased over the course of treatment mirroring her

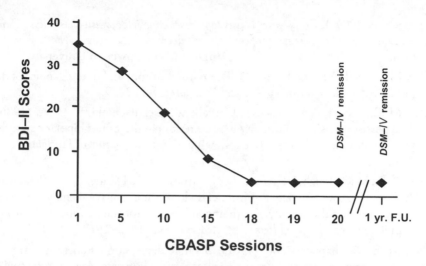

Figure 11.1. Sally's Beck Depression Inventory—II (BDI–II) scores over the course of therapy and at the 1-year follow-up session. CBASP = cognitive behavioral analysis system of psychotherapy; *DSM–IV = Diagnostic and Statistical Manual of Mental Disorders* (4th ed.); 1 yr. F.U. = 1-year follow-up.

diagnostic status (see Figure 11.1). I noted changed interpersonal impacts when I rated Sally on the IMI following Session 20. She moved from a predominately hostile and submissive interpersonal style toward a more friendly and dominant style. Sally had become more outgoing, sociable, and self-disclosing in the sessions, and she increasingly took a greater lead in setting the session agenda. Remission was achieved from Sally's lifetime chronic disorder, and the diagnostic and symptom intensity gains were sustained during a 12-month follow-up period.

REFERENCES

American Psychiatric Association. (1994). *Diagnostic and statistical manual of mental disorders* (4th ed.). Washington, DC: Author.

Anchin, J. C., & Kiesler, D. J. (1982). *Handbook of interpersonal psychotherapy.* Elmsford, NY: Pergamon Press.

Bandura, A. (1977). *Social learning theory.* Englewood Cliffs, NJ: Prentice Hall.

Beck, A. T. (1996). *Beck Depression Inventory—II.* San Antonio, TX: The Psychological Corporation.

Bordin, E. (1979). The generalizability of the psychoanalytic concept of the working alliance. *Psychotherapy: Theory, Research, and Practice, 16,* 252–260.

Cicchetti, D., Ackerman, B. P., & Izard, C. E. (1995). Emotions and emotion regulation in developmental psychopathology. *Development and Psychopathology, 7,* 1–10.

Horwitz, J. A. (2001). *Early-onset versus late-onset chronic depressive disorders: Comparison of retrospective reports of coping with adversity in the childhood home environment.* Unpublished master's thesis, Virginia Commonwealth University.

Keller, M. B., & Hanks, D. L. (1994). The natural history and heterogeneity of depressive disorders. *Journal of Clinical Psychiatry, 56,* 22–29.

Keller, M. B., Lavori, P. W., Rice, J., Coryell, W., & Hirschfeld, R. M. A. (1986). The persistent risk of chronicity in recurrent episodes of nonbipolar major depressive disorder: A prospective follow-up. *American Journal of Psychiatry, 143,* 24–28.

Keller, M. B., McCullough, J. P., Klein, D. N., Arnow, B. A., Dunner, D. L., Gelenberg, A. J., et al. (2000). A comparison of nefazodone, the cognitive–behavioral analysis system of psychotherapy, and their combination for the treatment of chronic depression. *New England Journal of Medicine, 342,* 1462–1470.

Keller, M. B., & Shapiro, R. W. (1982). "Double depression": Superimposition of acute depressive episodes on chronic depressive disorders. *American Journal of Psychiatry, 139,* 438–442.

Keller, M. B., & Shapiro, R. W. (1984). Double depression, major depression, and dysthymia: Distinct entities or different phases of a single disorder? *Psychopharmacology Bulletin, 20,* 399–402.

Kiesler, D. J. (1983). The 1982 interpersonal circle: A taxonomy for complementarity in human transactions. *Psychological Review, 90,* 185–214.

Kiesler, D. J. (1988). *Therapeutic metacommunication: Therapist impact disclosure as feedback in psychotherapy.* Palo Alto, CA: Consulting Psychologists Press.

Kiesler, D. J. (1996). *Contemporary interpersonal theory and research: Personality, psychopathology, and psychotherapy.* New York: Wiley.

Kiesler, D. J., & Schmidt, J. A. (1993). *The Impact Message Inventory: Form IIA Octant Scale Version.* Redwood City, CA: Mind Garden.

Manber, R. M., Arnow, B. A., Blasey, C., Vivian, D., McCullough, J. P., Blalock, J. A., et al. (2003). Patient's therapeutic skill acquisition and response to psychotherapy, alone or in combination with medication. *Journal of Psychological Medicine, 33,* 693–702.

Manber, R., & McCullough, J. P. (2000, November). *Patient Performance Rating Scale: The PPRS.* Paper presented at the 34th Annual Association for the Advancement of Behavior Therapy Convention, New Orleans, LA.

McCullough, J. P. (1984a). Cognitive–behavioral analysis system of psychotherapy: An interactional treatment approach for dysthymic disorder. *Psychiatry, 47,* 234–250.

McCullough, J. P. (1984b). The need for new single-case design structure in applied cognitive psychology. *Psychotherapy: Theory, Research, and Practice, 21,* 389–400.

McCullough, J. P. (1984c). Single-case investigative research and its relevance for the nonoperant clinician. *Psychotherapy: Theory, Research, and Practice, 21,* 382–388.

McCullough, J. P. (1991). Psychotherapy for dysthymia: Naturalistic study of ten cases. *Journal of Nervous and Mental Disease, 179,* 734–740.

McCullough, J. P., Jr. (2000). *Treatment for chronic depression: Cognitive behavioral analysis system of psychotherapy (CBASP).* New York: Guilford Press.

McCullough, J. P., Jr. (2001). *Skills training manual for diagnosing and treating chronic depression: Cognitive Behavioral Analysis System of Psychotherapy (CBASP).* New York: Guilford Press

McCullough, J. P., Jr. (2002). What questions are we trying to answer with our psychotherapy research? *Clinical Psychology: Science and Practice, 9,* 447–452.

McCullough, J. P., Jr. (2003a). *Patient's manual for CBASP.* New York: Guilford Press.

McCullough, J. P., Jr. (2003b). Treatment for chronic depression: Cognitive behavioral analysis system of psychotherapy (CBASP). *Journal of Psychotherapy Integration, 34,* 241–263.

McCullough, J. P., Jr. (2003c). Treatment for chronic depression using cognitive behavioral analysis system of psychotherapy (CBASP). *Journal of Clinical Psychology: In Session, 59,* 833–846.

McCullough, J. P., Jr. (in press). *Treating chronic depression using disciplined personal involvement: Cognitive behavioral analysis system of psychotherapy.* New York: Springer Publishing Company.

McCullough, J. P., & Carr, K. F. (1987). Stage process design: A predictive confirmation structure for the single case. *Psychotherapy: Theory, Research, and Practice, 24,* 759–768.

McCullough, J. P., & Kaye, A. L. (1993, May). *Differential diagnosis of chronic depressive disorders.* Paper presented at the 14th Annual Convention of the American Psychiatric Association, San Francisco.

Nemeroff, C. B., Heim, C. M., Thase, M. E., Klein, D. N., Rush, A. J., Schatzberg, A. F., et al. (2003). Differential responses to psychotherapy versus pharmacotherapy in patients with chronic forms of major depression and childhood trauma. *Proceedings of the National Academy of Sciences, 100,* 14293–14296.

Piaget, J. (1926). *The language and thought of the child.* New York: Harcourt, Brace. (Original work published 1923)

Piaget, J. (1967). *Six psychological studies* (D. Elkind, Ed.). New York: Random House. (Original work published 1964)

Piaget, J. (1981). *Intelligence and affectivity: Their relationship during child development.* Palo Alto, CA: Annual Reviews. (Original work published 1954)

Safran, J. D., & Muran, J. C. (2000). *Negotiating the therapeutic alliance: A relational treatment guide.* New York: Guilford Press.

Skinner, B. F. (1953). *Science and human behavior.* New York: Macmillan.

Skinner, B. F. (1968). *The technology of teaching.* New York: Appleton-Century-Crofts.

12

COGNITIVE–AFFECTIVE– RELATIONAL–BEHAVIOR THERAPY

MARVIN R. GOLDFRIED

Although my primary orientation is that of a behavior therapist, I find that I can readily incorporate contributions from other orientations by using common principles of change as an organizing format. After translating the theoretical jargon associated with different therapeutic schools of thought into ordinary English, one may discern principles at a level of abstraction somewhere between the observable methods of clinical intervention and the higher order, theoretical speculation about why these methods might be effective elsewhere (Goldfried & Padawer, 1982). Such common principles of change include (a) the presence of clients' expectations that change is possible, (b) the existence of an optimal therapeutic relationship, (c) providing feedback to help clients become more aware of aspects of themselves and others, (d) the encouragement of corrective experiences, and (e) facilitation of ongoing reality testing.

An initial *positive expectation* that therapy can help, along with a certain amount of motivation to engage in the therapy process, is essential to change. It is a promissory note and represents a necessary but probably not sufficient step in the change process. Another common change principle involves the existence of an optimal *therapy relationship*, providing a safe context within which change may be explored. The therapy alliance is particularly important in that it implicitly or explicitly functions to encourage clients to seek out new ways of functioning, both within and outside of the therapy session. Although they may do so in different ways, most approaches to therapy attempt to *increase clients' awareness*. Clients typically encounter problems in living because of antiquated and inaccurate views of themselves and others. Using different intervention procedures (e.g., reflection, interpretation, self-monitoring), therapy helps to provide clients with a clearer view of their perceptions, emotions, actions, and needs. This increased awareness can set the stage for what is perhaps the core principle of change, namely the *corrective experience*. When clients have become more aware of their own functioning and their relationships with others, they are in a better position to take such risks and learn to function more effectively. These corrective experiences may occur within the session (e.g., through the therapy relationship) or between sessions (e.g., homework). What is ultimately required for therapeutic change is for clients to continually become aware, have corrective experiences to support this new awareness, and use these experiences to give added meaning to their awareness, thereby providing a cycle of ongoing *reality testing*.

The specific methods by which these several principles of change may be implemented in the clinical setting vary from orientation to orientation and from case to case. In a sense, how these principles are implemented clinically may be thought of as reflecting the parameters of the more general principles. The following case illustrates how these general principles of change can guide a course of therapy that makes use of contributions from different orientations.

CLINICAL CASE

In thinking about providing a case to illustrate how I work integratively, I decided that a useful and true-to-life format would be to present the clinical material as it was presented to me. Thus, instead of beginning with a description of the client, relevant demographic information, a case formulation, and a general description of the therapeutic intervention, I begin with the client's initial phone contact and then describe, session by session, the way in which the assessment, formulation, and intervention unfolded.

Initial Contact

My first contact with Elaine consisted of a message she left on my answering machine, indicating that she had been referred by a psychiatrist friend that I knew professionally. I returned the call that evening and spoke with Elaine. She indicated that she had been in therapy off and on for the past few years, dealing with the deaths of both her parents. Unfortunately, this course of therapy had not helped her to deal with her grief, and other issues continued to persist. She indicated that I came highly recommended, which not only made me feel good personally but also provided some information about her positive expectations.

Session 1

Elaine appeared shortly before our scheduled session the following week. Sitting in the waiting room, she was busily reviewing material on her electronic organizer. She was an attractive, professionally dressed Caucasian woman who appeared to be in her mid-40s. I introduced myself, and we walked down the corridor to my office.

We began the session by my asking her to elaborate further on the reasons for contacting me. She openly described the issues that had been of concern to her and did so with somewhat pressured speech. She was articulate, and from the way she spoke, my overall impression was that she clearly was above average in intelligence.

She began by stating that she was dissatisfied with her relationship with her husband Mike, to whom she had been married for 22 years. Among the issues creating problems in their relationship was his criticalness, the decrease in frequency of their sexual contacts, and a general increase in emotional distance between the two. They had spoken about the possibility of couples therapy, but both agreed that additional individual therapy for her had a higher priority.

Additional reasons for seeking therapy at this time included "stress," concerns about aging and loss, and lingering negative feelings about the fact that she had been adopted. Elaine indicated that she had experienced an increase in stress a little under a year ago, at which time her father-in-law was placed in a nursing home. She also reported a number of other stressors, which seemed to center around the theme of death and loss (e.g., her mother had died 4 years earlier, her father had died 2 years ago, her husband's aunt had passed away about a year ago).

In describing more about her current life situation, Elaine indicated that she was 48 years old, had a 16-year-old daughter at home and a 20-year-old son in college, and was a real estate attorney in a law firm. Her husband, Mike, was 55, had an MBA degree, and worked in finance.

When asked if there were any other issues in her life that might be relevant, Elaine stated that for the past year, she had been suffering from lower back pain. Her orthopedist indicated that she might require surgery at some point, and the discomfort was currently being dealt with by means of cortisone injections. Her back problems occasionally affected her functioning, and she knew that she would need to face major surgery some time in the future.

As we got closer to the end of the session, I asked if she would like to continue our sessions. When she responded in the affirmative, I stated that I wanted to make use of the next two and perhaps three sessions to gather more information about her before discussing how we would proceed therapeutically. I indicated that I would be asking a lot of questions, at this point offering little in the way of information or suggestions. However, after I had a clearer understanding of the problems she wished to deal with (I hoped by Session 3 or 4), we would discuss how we might best proceed. When she nodded in agreement, I added that there were three factors that typically predicted successful therapy (i.e., the therapeutic alliance; Bordin, 1976). One was the existence of a good bond between client and therapist, which was reflected in her feeling that I was concerned about her welfare, that I understood her, and that we communicated well with each other. The second predictive factor was that we both agreed on the goals of therapy, and the third was that we both agreed on how to best reach these goals. I suggested that we could return to this once we were ready to plan the course of treatment.

My usual practice is to have the client complete a comprehensive personal data questionnaire before the second session, which asks for demographic information, a description of current life problems, past and current relationship with parents and siblings, past therapy experiences, and other assessment information that can be helpful in case formulation and treatment planning. I prefer not to have clients complete this information prior to the initial session, because I have found that asking to have this personal information described in such an impersonal format is best done after we have met in person. I gave Elaine the questionnaire and asked her to mail it back to me before our next meeting, explaining that it would help me to get more information about her without having to use as much session time. I also included a copy of the Beck Depression Inventory (Beck, Ward, & Mendelson, 1961) for her to complete.

Personal Data Questionnaire, Beck Depression Inventory, and Session 2

The personal data questionnaire reiterated some of what Elaine had told me in the initial session (e.g., age, education, occupation) but also provided additional information. Her concerns about getting older and dealing with issues of death had begun approximately 5 years before and had bothered her off and on since that time. To the question "What prompted you to seek help *now?*" she indicated that it was the result of discussions with her husband following her recent inability to attend a funeral. ("I was afraid I'd become too upset. It reminded me of my father's death.")

In describing problems in her relationships with her husband and children, Elaine indicated that she had withdrawn into herself during conversations. She had also found herself spending more time in the evening at the computer, which she recognized was a form of escape. Her Beck Depression Inventory score was 16, reflecting a mild level of depression. Her tendency to withdraw had resulted in arguments with Mike, which often took the form of his getting angry and her taking on the blame. On more than one occasion, her husband commented that their relationship mirrored the relationship she had with her father.

In the questionnaire, Elaine indicated that her father, who was a businessman, had died of a stroke 2 years before. She described him as "strong-willed, caring, but things had to be his way." Her mother, who had died of cancer 4 years before, was quiet and passive, typically deferring to her husband. Elaine indicated that she also wanted to work on her feelings about being adopted.

Additional demographic information provided on the questionnaire was the fact that she and her husband were Protestant and that she had a brother 2 years younger who lived on the west coast. Although she had been close to her brother when they were younger, most of their contact now consisted of periodic phone calls.

During the session itself, we reviewed the information provided on the questionnaire, and Elaine elaborated on a number of the issues. What became increasingly clear was a theme of loss in her life, consisting of the death of both her parents, the recent death of her husband's aunt, and the need to place her father-in-law in a nursing home the previous year. She also mentioned that through her professional work, she knew of people who had died in the attack on the World Trade Center, which had occurred a little over a year earlier. Also related to loss was the strain and reduced sexual contact with her husband over the past 5 years and the periodic disruption of her functioning because of her back problems. She spontaneously indicated that one of her fears was that her husband or children might suddenly die.

The session also revealed that Elaine was competent in her professional work and felt confident in her abilities to get things done. By contrast, she tended to be unassertive in social contacts, apparently mediated by a need to please others.

Session 3

We explored her relationship with her husband, the ways it seemed to parallel her relationship with her father, and how her concerns about approval often led to her putting other people's needs above her own. Although she recognized that her self-effacing stance often had a negative impact on Mike—he said he would like to have her take more of a stand on issues—she indicated that it was hard for her to openly express what she often felt or wanted.

Another problem Elaine raised was related to her future surgery, the date for which had not yet been set. She indicated that she had a blood phobia, experienced considerable anxiety when her blood was drawn, and would typically faint. In many respects, she dreaded this more than she did the actual surgery.

Toward the end of the session, we revisited the topic of the therapeutic alliance that I had introduced during our initial session. We both concurred that we seemed to have a good working relationship thus far and then focused on the goals of therapy. I suggested that her depression, fears regarding death, and the pattern of losses in her life might best be approached with grief work. When she agreed, I added that working on this might also involve possible unfinished business with her parents, especially around her reaction to having been adopted. We agreed that communication issues with Mike could be the focus of therapy, which would involve learning to better express and assert herself. They had discussed the possibility of couples therapy, but she wanted to see how much of their relationship problem might be resolved through her individual therapy. Because it was unclear how much her relationship issues and withdrawal were a function of a complicated grief reaction, we agreed to begin with grief work. We also agreed that her blood phobia was something to which we could return.

Sessions 4 and 5

In discussing the issues of death and loss, a number of factors emerged that may have been contributing to Elaine's difficulty in accepting the death of her parents. This included the ambivalent feelings she had toward them and her fear of becoming too emotional ("I'm afraid that if I start crying, I won't stop"). However, during the week prior to the fourth session, she had attended her cousin's funeral and allowed herself to cry. At the end of that session, I introduced the idea that an empty chair exercise might be effective in helping her sort out the different thoughts and feelings she had toward her parents, because these might be complicating the process of mourning. She was reluctant at first, but after I acknowledged that I recognized the unusual nature of the intervention and emphasized that it has been shown to be effective (cf. Elliott, Watson, Goldman, & Greenberg, 2004), she agreed to try it.

During the following session, Elaine spoke to her father in the empty chair, telling him that although she tried to be a "good daughter," she felt "frustrated" by his controlling and critical manner. In addition to hinting at some negative feelings toward him, she cried in the realization she was talking to an empty chair and that her father was no longer there. The exercise seemed to help to bring some of her thoughts and feelings into awareness.

Sessions 6 and 7

Elaine acknowledged that the previous session had been helpful and that she felt a little "freer" as a result of it. In continuing the empty chair exercise, she expressed confusion and annoyance to her father because of his emotional distance. In trying to help her better understand why her father had related to her as he did, I asked Elaine to sit in her father's chair and to explain why he was so distant (a useful method for helping clients reevaluate the motivation behind a significant other's actions). Although she initially had difficulty in verbalizing why he had treated her as he had, she (in the role of her father) eventually explained, "I was always afraid that you'd want to find your real parents and leave us."

We discussed how her relationship with her father was linked to the difficulty she had in expressing and asserting herself. She recognized that her tendency to emotionally distance herself from others was patterned after her father's interpersonal style. She was also able to appreciate her father's fear of rejection, because she saw this as a factor underlying her unassertiveness and her tendency to withdraw during disagreements with her husband. Although her father did not provide her with emotional closeness, Elaine acknowledged that he had cared about her welfare, worked hard to see that her physical needs were met, and supported her during college and law school. She also acknowledged that her passivity and unassertiveness in personal contacts were much like how her mother had related to her father.

Sessions 8 to 10

Elaine reported that she had been looking through some old pictures of her father, which brought back a number of bittersweet memories. While watching a TV program involving a daughter–father relationship, she had thought of him and cried. Because I had been to a particularly touching memorial service during the previous week, I disclosed to Elaine what was said and how I felt. (For the potential uses of therapist self-disclosure, see Goldfried, Burckell, & Eubanks-Carter, 2003.) Elaine related her own experiences during her father's funeral, started to cry, but then stopped herself. I commented on how she was interrupting her sadness and encouraged her to go with the sadness—which she did.

She became better able to forgive her father for not having given her what she needed emotionally. However, during an empty chair exercise, Elaine verbally expressed resentment toward him for never telling her directly that she had been adopted. She reported that she had learned of the adoption indirectly in her mid-20s, when she found her birth certificate. During the empty chair interaction, I encouraged her to ask her father why he had never told her about the adoption. I then asked her to switch chairs and, speaking as her father, to provide an answer (again, looking to see if she might be able to reduce her anger by reattributing his motive for remaining silent about the adoption). In speaking as her father, Elaine explained that he and her mother did not want to tell her about the adoption when she was younger, because they felt that she could not understand and would become too upset. However, they then felt awkward and fearful about telling her as she got older, because they were afraid she would be angry about never having been told. I asked Elaine what she would have done if her own two children had been adopted and when might have been a good time to tell them. After much thought, she confessed that she could not think of a good time, and perhaps there was no good time to tell them—or at least, no easy time.

Sessions 11 to 13

Elaine brought in pictures of her father and mother, which we used to have her recall some of the pleasant times they spent together. She was readily able to express her sadness over the loss of both her parents. Although she reported feeling sad during the process, her sadness was not mixed with resentment and was not overwhelming. My impression was that she was making progress on the working-through process associated with grieving. A potential complicating factor was that her father-in-law, who was in a nursing home, seemed to be deteriorating. Still, we agreed that a portion of our sessions might begin to focus on another agreed-on goal, namely her relationships with her husband.

As we explored the thoughts and feelings associated with her difficulties in asserting herself, Elaine indicated that she grew up with the image of being a "good girl." This meant that it was important for her to please people with whom she was close, not impose her own will or beliefs, and avoid conflict at all cost. The paradox, however, was that her attempt to please others (particularly her husband and children) by her lack of openness often *had* a negative impact on them. In addition to a negative interpersonal consequence, this lack of expressiveness typically resulted in her feeling annoyed with herself. I suggested she read Alberti and Emmons's *Your Perfect Right* (2001), a self-help book that can help to clarify frequent misconceptions about asserting oneself. I also suggested that she bring in a list of situations that involved the need for her to express her feelings, thoughts, and needs toward her husband.

During this period, Elaine's father-in-law passed away. She openly cried at the funeral, both for him and for her own father. She was able to support Mike in his grief and felt good about being able to do so. Her fear of crying and experiencing the pain of loss appeared to have lessened. As a result of several corrective experiences, she had learned that if she let go, she would not cry forever.

Sessions 14 to 17

Elaine continued to experience occasional waves of sadness when reminded of her parents. Of particular importance is that the symptoms associated with her failure to grieve (e.g., depression, fear of her husband and children dying) had deceased substantially. We therefore agreed to spend most of the session time dealing with her relationship with her husband.

We reviewed the situations in which she wanted to become more expressive with Mike. In doing so, we identified and reevaluated the anticipatory fears that could block her from speaking up, and we began to use roleplaying (with audiotaped feedback) to rehearse what she might say and how she might say it (Goldfried & Davison, 1994). To facilitate ongoing reality testing, each session involved a processing of the assertive and unassertive interactions she had had during the previous week and a preparation for what she would do during the following week.

From time to time, Elaine would manifest her unassertiveness in her interactions with me. When this occurred, I made a point of shifting the focus to her in-session behavior, thoughts, feelings, and wants and made the link to her inexpressiveness in her relationships with Mike and her children. I also encouraged her to be more openly self-assertive with me.

During this time, Elaine's back problems flared up. Although no date had yet been set for surgery, it was possible that it could occur within the next few months. We agreed that as the time drew nearer, we would spend more time on her blood phobia.

Sessions 18 to 21

Elaine continued to make progress in voicing her opinions to Mike. As before, the format of these sessions involved reviewing between-session corrective actions and their associated thoughts, feelings, and needs, noting both the interpersonal and intrapersonal consequences and preparing for new experiences.

Although the primary focus of our work on assertiveness centered on Elaine's relationship with her husband and children, she also became more aware that there were times when she held back voicing her opinion at work. It was also becoming increasingly clear to Elaine that her long-standing need to please others and the fear of not doing so continued to inhibit her expressiveness. We agreed that we would place additional focus on this issue.

Sessions 22 to 24

In dealing with Elaine's fear that something terrible would happen if she did not please other people(especially significant others), we made use of a gestalt two-chair exercise (Elliott et al., 2004; Samoilov & Goldfried, 2000). The rationale I provided for using this method was that she was experiencing an ambivalent internal dialogue, which could be externalized and made more explicit by having each side speak to the other in the opposite chair. Using recently acquired corrective experiences, the 48-year-old Elaine spoke to the anachronistic, schema-based "good little girl," helping to allay her fears that disagreement with someone does not necessarily result in an end to the relationship.

The two-chair exercise served to further increase Elaine's awareness that being more open was not as dangerous as it seemed (i.e., change in cognitive–affective meaning structures). This awareness helped her to risk having additional corrective experiences in her relationship with Mike, especially those situations in which she disagreed with him (e.g., how to spend the weekend). These corrective experiences and their associated impact on awareness (i.e., ongoing reality testing) further helped her to revise her belief that not deferring to her husband and risking displeasing him would mean an end to the relationship.

Sessions 25 to 28

Elaine reported that her ability to express herself to Mike (and others) was continuing to progress. Instead of having to deliberately reevaluate her unrealistic fears of displeasing someone before speaking up, it was becoming easier for her to spontaneously say what she believed. Her openness typically worked out well, and she was feeling better about herself and more equal in her relationship with Mike.

A date had been set for her surgery approximately 2 months from then, and we agreed that the therapeutic focus would shift to dealing with her blood phobia. Issues related to grieving and loss no longer seemed to be much of an issue, and we agreed to briefly check on that during our sessions. Because Elaine had become better able to deal with assertiveness on her own, we also agreed to simply monitor that from time to time.

In gathering further information about her blood phobia, Elaine indicated that it was typically triggered by receiving injections, getting blood drawn, and having an IV. In addition to experiencing anticipatory anxiety, she described what was a vasovagal reaction, in which she would faint. I proposed an intervention to which she agreed. We would use relaxation and in vivo desensitization to deal with the sympathetic reaction associated with the anticipatory anxiety, and we would use distraction to cope with the parasympathetic reaction resulting in dizziness and fainting (Penfold & Page, 1999).

The relaxation training followed the procedures outlined in Goldfried and Davison (1994), in which the goal is to learn to use the relaxation response as a method of coping with anxiety. As the training progressed, we identified situations that were likely to create blood phobic anxiety and trigger a vasovagal reaction (e.g., seeing a syringe, having blood drawn). I also encouraged her to expose herself to hospital situations (e.g., watching *ER* on television, visiting a hospital), because she was apprehensive about these situations as well.

The in vivo desensitization and distraction was implemented in the sessions by having her use her relaxation to cope with a simulated situation in which I drew a blood sample. I had an actual syringe and alcohol, and we repeatedly rehearsed the procedure (using a pencil to simulate the insertion of the needle). During this time, Elaine not only relaxed, but also closed her eyes and distracted herself by imagining that she was at a ballet performance, watching her favorite ballet. We continued this procedure repeatedly over several sessions until she no longer experienced the anxiety or dizziness associated with injections, having blood drawn, or having an IV inserted.

Session 29

Three months later, following some brief phone contacts in which Elaine reported that the surgery had gone well and that she was recovering with the assistance of physical therapy, we had a session to discuss her experiences in greater detail. Much to her surprise and delight, she had handled it well, adding that she had even enjoyed her imagined visits to the ballet!

This was not our last session. Indeed, at the time of this writing, I am continuing to work with Elaine on her relational issues. Although assertiveness and expressiveness training has clearly helped her in her interactions with Mike, certain problems continue to exist. Whether or not couples therapy will be needed remains to be seen.

CONCLUDING COMMENT

As can be seen from this case illustration, contributions from different theoretical orientations can readily be incorporated into a course of therapy. Although cognitive–behavior therapy served as my starting point, experiential interventions (e.g., empty chair, two chair, a focus on in-session process) and relational interventions (e.g., linking the client's relationship with the therapist to her unassertiveness with others) were used from time to time. The overriding rationale that holds these diverse procedures together is that they reflect certain common principles of change associated with different approaches to therapy: the expectation that therapy can be of help, the existence of an optimal therapy relationship, a facilitation of awareness, the encouragement of corrective experiences, and the presence of ongoing reality testing. The case of Elaine illustrates how these principles can be implemented. How I might implement them in another instance would be determined by the requirements of the case at hand.

REFERENCES

Alberti, R., & Emmons, M. (2001). *Your perfect right: Assertiveness and equality in your life and relationships* (8th ed.). Atascadero, CA: Impact Publishers.

Beck, A. T., Ward, C., & Mendelson, N. J. (1961). An inventory for measuring depression. *Archives of General Psychiatry*, 4, 53–63.

Bordin, E. S. (1976). The generalizability of the psychoanalytic concept of the working alliance. *Psychotherapy: Theory, Research and Practice*, 16, 252–260.

Elliott, R., Watson, J. C., Goldman, R. N., & Greenberg, L. S. (2004). *Learning emotion-focused therapy: The process-experiential approach to change.* Washington, DC: American Psychological Association.

Goldfried, M. R., Burckell, L. A., & Eubanks-Carter, C. (2003). Therapist self-disclosure in cognitive–behavior therapy. *In Session: Journal of Clinical Psychology*, 59, 555–568.

Goldfried, M. R., & Davison, G. C. (1994). *Clinical behavior therapy* (Expanded ed.). New York: Wiley-Interscience.

Goldfried, M. R., & Padawer, W. (1982). Current status and future directions in psychotherapy. In M. R. Goldfried (Ed.), *Converging themes in psychotherapy: Trends in psychodynamic, humanistic, and behavioral practice* (pp. 3–49). New York: Springer Publishing Company.

Penfold, K., & Page, A. C. (1999). The effect of distraction on within-session anxiety reduction during brief in vivo exposure for mild blood-injection fears. *Behavior Therapy*, 30, 607–621.

Samoilov, A., & Goldfried, M. R. (2000). Role of emotion in cognitive–behavior therapy. *Psychology: Science and Practice*, 7, 373–385.

13

ACCELERATED EXPERIENTIAL–DYNAMIC PSYCHOTHERAPY: THE SEAMLESS INTEGRATION OF EMOTIONAL TRANSFORMATION AND DYADIC RELATEDNESS AT WORK

DIANA FOSHA AND DANNY YEUNG

A bottom-up model that emphasizes dyadic regulation of relatedness and emotional arousal, accelerated experiental–dynamic psychotherapy's (AEDP's) conceptual framework integrates constructs, insights, and findings from attachment theory (e.g., Bowlby, 1982), clinical developmentalists' research into moment-to-moment mother–infant interaction (e.g., Beebe & Lachmann, 2002; Stern, 1985; Tronick, 1989), emotion theory and affective neuroscience (e.g., Damasio, 1999; Darwin, 1872/1965; Panksepp, 1998; Tomkins, 1962, 1963), experiential short-term dynamic psychotherapies (e.g., McCullough, 2003; McCullough Vaillant, 1997; Osimo, 2003), other experiential emotion-focused therapies (e.g., Greenberg & Paivio, 1997), and body- and trauma-focused therapies (e.g., Gendlin, 1996; Levine, 1997). AEDP's conceptualization of the phenomenology and dynamics of healing transformation has been informed and inspired by studies that document its nongradual, discontinuous quantum nature (James, 1902/1985; Miller & C'de Baca, 2001; Person, 1988; Stern et al., 1998).

With its focus on facilitating healing emotional transformations within an emotionally engaged therapeutic relationship, AEDP seamlessly integrates previously disparate theoretical constructs and clinical strategies of intervention. AEDP's fundamental assumption that change can and does take place reliably in therapy is informed by an understanding of the nongradual nature of affective change processes (Fosha, 2000b, 2002, 2004). The AEDP therapist seeks to catalyze a state transformation of the patient's emotional experience and harness the healing power of emotions. Key to achieving this goal is forming an affect-regulating attachment bond between patient and therapist from the get-go.

Dyadic Regulation of Relatedness

Attachment theory informs AEDP's focus on the patient–therapist relationship as a secure base from which to explore aversive experiences. Secure attachment enhances emotional resilience and optimizes the capacity to endure intense affective experiences without resorting to defensive exclusion (Bowlby, 1988). The establishment of a relationship where one dyadic partner operates as a secure base for the other is accomplished through optimal dyadic affect regulation, that is, the moment-to-moment coordination and dyadic regulation of affective states through psychobiological state attunement (Fosha, 2001; Schore, 2003a, 2003b). The process of moment-to-moment dyadic affect regulation is made up of endless iterations of the sequence of *attunement* (the mutual coordination of affective states), *disruption* (the lapse of mutual coordination), and *repair* (reestablishment of mutual coordination under new conditions). In securely attached dyads, disruption motivates repair, and negative emotions are metabolized rapidly while maintaining relational connection. By contrast, in pathogenic dyads, disruptions do not motivate dyadic repair efforts but instead lead to disconnection, withdrawal, and aloneness, with a reliance on self- rather than dyadic regulatory strategies to cope with the stress of dysregulated emotion (Tronick & Weinberg, 1997). These dyadic interactions, whether optimal or compromised, become internalized as the individual's *affective competence*—that is, the capacity to "feel and deal while relating" (Fosha, 2000b, 2001).

Dyadic Regulation of Emotional Arousal

The paradigm-shifting revolution in emotion theory and affective neuroscience emphasizes the fundamentally adaptive nature of affects and views them as complex, wired-in neurobiological programs with distinct arousal, appraisal, and physiological patterns and adaptive action tendencies. Core affect (Fosha, 2000b)—that is, affect not blocked by defenses or inhibited by anxiety, shame, or other aversive affects—is a powerful catalyst for healing transformation. Core affect, when (a) dyadically coordinated and regulated moment-to-moment with the therapist, (b) experienced viscerally, and (c) worked through to completion (Fosha, 2004), unleashes adaptive and self-righting capacities that are hard-wired in the patient's mind and body. The activation of these capacities and the resources and resilience they entrain translate into enhanced functioning and greater well-being for the patient; compromised access, on the other hand, sows the seeds of psychopathology.

Affective neuroscience demonstrates the centrality of the right cerebral hemisphere in emotional processing (Schore, 2003a, 2003b; Siegel, 2003; Trevarthen & Aitken, 1994). Dyadic affect regulation through psychobiological state attunement has been shown to be mediated through right-brain to right-brain communication between dyadic partners. Right-brain language codes use gaze, play, vocal tones and rhythms, touch, visual imagery, and somatosensory experiences; right-brain mediated processing of emotion and attachment occurs through this somatic, nonverbal lexicon. This somatic lexicon is what must be engaged in the therapeutic interaction.

Technical Integration

Four groups of strategies of intervention—relational, restructuring, experiential–affective, and integrative–reflective—specify how the dyadic regulation of relatedness and emotion is technically effected in AEDP (Fosha, 2000b; Fosha & Slowiaczek, 1997). They reflect the integration of elements from experiential, psychodynamic, relational, cognitive, reflective, and narrative-based approaches into a transformation-based treatment. Echoes of existential–humanistic psychology are encountered in AEDP's affirming stance and belief in patients as the experts of their experiences. The influence of somatic and body-focused treatments is reflected in the emphasis on the rootedness of emotional experience in bodily processes and thus the primacy of experiential interventions. Dyadic relational and affect-regulating strategies, somatic focusing strategies, and emotion processing strategies, all illustrated in the case vignette below, are AEDP techniques that are the focus of this chapter.

Psychopathology and Transformation: Representational Schemas

Difficulties in dyadic affect regulation and thus the individual's resulting aloneness in the face of overwhelming emotional experience are front and center in AEDP's understanding of how psychopathology develops. In dyads where the caregiver's affective competence is compromised, the child's intense emotions also disrupt the caregiver. The attachment bond becomes dysregulated, as does the smooth operation of its affect regulatory function. Failed dyadic experiences themselves evoke a second wave of intense emotions, the pathogenic affects of fear, shame, and distress. As a result, (a) the disrupted initial emotional experience; (b) the experience of aloneness as a result of the disrupted attachment bond; and (c) the pathogenic affects of fear, shame, and distress combine to give rise to yet a third wave of affects: the unbearable emotional state of aloneness. Feeling helpless, worthless, empty, broken, or lost are some of the wrenching feelings that characterize this "black hole of trauma" (van der Kolk, 2002), and individuals go to great lengths to avoid ever having these feelings. Procedural learning thus deems emotions dangerous. Eventually, just the hint of emotional activation evokes "red signal" affects, communicating to the individual that the direct experience of basic emotions needs to be defensively excluded.

Subsequently, multiple defense mechanisms are used to (a) avoid the havoc wreaked by dysregulated emotion and (b) maintain the attachment bond at all costs. Although necessary to emotional survival in the short term, long-term reliance on defensive mechanisms leads to constriction and distortion of the personality, compromised functioning, and the eventual emergence of psychopathology. This understanding is schematically represented in the revised triangle of conflict (see Figure 13.1, top panel), a schema initially derived from the experiential short-term dynamic psychotherapy tradition. It informs and guides moment-to-moment clinical work, whose aim is to (a) bypass defenses, (b) process fully previously evaded core affective experiences, and (c) reap their healing benefits.

However, AEDP's healing- and transformation-centered clinical understanding posits that side by side with the psychopathology-engendering processes just described, there also operate powerful tendencies toward healing and self-righting (Emde, 1988; Gendlin, 1996). These psychic forces exist in each individual not only as potential dispositions awaiting awakening under the right facilitating conditions but actually evident in those moments when individuals are at their best. Another schema is required to represent their operation (see Figure 13.1, bottom panel). Briefly, in conditions of safety, the caregiver meets the child's emotions with acceptance and empathy and shows a willingness to share and bear them along with the child, thus actively helping in their regulation. Dyadically regulated, emotions overwhelm neither child nor caregiver and instead enhance the adaptive repertoire of each partner. Such dyadic experiences lead to the security-engendering expectation that one's emotions can be processed and become procedurally internalized in positive unconscious attitudes toward one's own emotional experience. In such circumstances, hints of emotional activation evoke the "green signal" affects of hope, trust, curiosity, interest, and anticipation: These communicate that it is OK to approach emotional experience with mindful openness rather than with defensive exclusion and the tendency to shut down. Alone or with a trusted other, an individual can then process emotions to completion; the individual's functioning is enhanced.

Thus, AEDP features two schemas of the triangle of conflict: one schema, the *self-at-worst*, represents pathological functioning (see Figure 13.1, top panel), and another schema, the *self-at-best*, represents adaptive, resilient

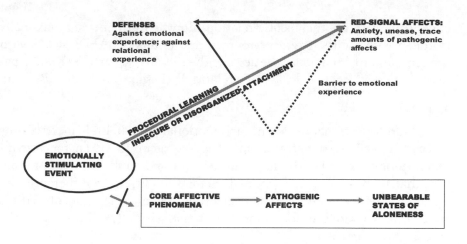

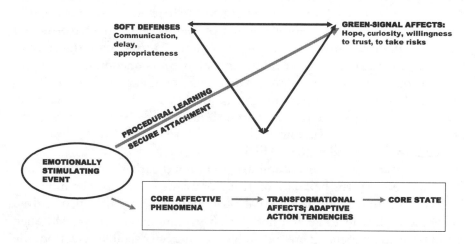

Figure 13.1. The two versions of the revised triangle of conflict. Top panel: Self-at-worst functioning—psychopathology. Bottom panel: Self-at-best functioning—optimal development.

functioning (see Figure 13.1, bottom panel). The nature of the emotional environment fundamentally contributes to which kind of functioning is accessed: emotionally thwarting conditions are more likely to activate self-at-worst functioning, whereas emotionally facilitating conditions make more likely the activation of self-at-best functioning. From the opening moments of the first session and from there on throughout the therapy, the AEDP approach seeks to dyadically entrain patients' self-at-best configuration. In this way, therapeutic work can be done with difficult pathological experiences from within a therapeutic relationship where patients are maximally in touch with their strengths, resources, and resilience. AEDP works with the self-at-worst from under the aegis of the self-at-best, striving to help patients not only "feel and deal (while relating)" (Fosha, 2000b) but also heal.

Transformational Work

Transformational work with an emotional episode is characterized by three states and two state transformations (see Figure 13.2). Therapeutic interventions are keyed to the state the patient is in and the state transformation that is the goal. Under optimal therapy conditions, the therapist can facilitate and expect the rapid emergence, and hence acceleration, of all three states and two state transformations in a single session (as illustrated by the case in this chapter).

Pervasiveness and predominance of defenses mark the first state in AEDP. Here, the patient unconsciously uses a variety of cognitive, affective, and behavioral strategies to exclude emotional experience. Mindful and respectful of the once-but-no-longer adaptive defensive strategies, the therapist acts collaboratively with the patient in the here and now to bypass the defensive wall. The unwavering presence of a protective nurturing other is a startling anomaly, provoking an intrapsychic crisis (first state transformation): The patient's internal working model, with its unconscious dire predictions of aloneness in bearing negative emotional experiences, begins to implode. The *heralding affects*, understood by AEDP to be the last hurrah of the resistance, signal the first state transformation and draw the therapist's attention to a crucial window of therapeutic opportunity to facilitate entrance into the second state of AEDP.

Unfettered access to visceral experience and expression of core affective experiences is the hallmark of the second state in AEDP. The moment-by-moment attunement and mutual coordination of the therapeutic dyad helps the patient feel safe and not alone with intense emotions. Although disruptions in attunement are inevitable in any deep dyadic interaction, the timely repair of disruption further deepens the therapeutic process (Fosha, 2003). As core affective experiences are processed, the therapeutic process unfolds; the patient's previously hidden emotional narrative emerges. Experiential affective strategies are most effective in this state to deepen and work through the experience of core affects.

With the completion of each wave of emotion, adaptive action tendencies are released: Authentic relief (vs. defensive avoidance) from intense negative experience is accompanied by a deep sense of joy, zest, and exuberance. There is a definite shift in the somatic sensory experience, frequently felt as sensations in the area of the heart or as a sense of warmth or energy emerging from the gut level.

As the patient feels better and increasingly resourced, *receptive affective experiences* (i.e., feeling seen, understood, and cared for) come to the fore,

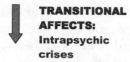

STATE 1: DEFENSE

TRANSITIONAL
AFFECTS:
Intrapsychic
crises

STATE 2: CORE AFFECT
Categorical emotions, coordinated
relational experiences, authentic
self states, receptive affective
experiences

TRANSFORMATIONAL AFFECTS:
Adaptive action tendencies
Mastery affects (pride, joy)
Emotional pain of mourning-the-self
Healing affects (gratitude, feeling moved)

STATE 3: CORE STATE
Flow, vitality, ease, well-being,
openness; relational experiences
of closeness and intimacy; bodily
states of relaxation; empathy and
self-empathy; wisdom, generosity;
clarity about the subjective truth
of one's own emotional
experience; the sense of things
being "right"; the truth sense

Figure 13.2. The three states and two state transformations of accelerated experiential–dynamic psychotherapy.

giving rise to the *healing affects* (Fosha, 2000a, 2000b)—the welling-up tears of "being moved" and "being touched," tears often accompanied by a deep experience of gratitude, love, and tenderness toward the therapist. The release of both adaptive action tendencies and healing affects mark the second state transformation and the transition from *core affect* (State 2) to *core state* (State 3). The wave of core affective experience gradually recedes only to be followed by the next wave: core state experience. Core state represents the culmination of the full experiential processing of emotion.

Core state follows the full and complete experience of any core affect. Characterized by a heightened sense of authenticity ("I feel at home with myself," "I feel like myself"), its affective marker is the *truth sense*, the sense the patient has of being in direct touch with the subjective truth of personal experience. Anxiety free, core state is experienced somatically as openness, vitality, relaxation, ease, and flow. Rather than being rocked by any emotion, there is a prevailing sense of calm. Authentic core relational experiences of love, closeness, intimacy, and compassion predominate. Patients often have deeply spiritual experiences of being in touch with ultimate reality and eternal truths: Here, AEDP crosses another boundary and integrates psychology with that which is at the roots of spirituality and aesthetic experience. The therapist, who often is also in core state by now, can act simply as a validating witness, being present with the patient, or as active participant. Reflective integrative strategies are useful in core state, as patients become capable of constructing coherent and meaningful autobiographical narratives, shown to be highly correlated with secure attachment and emotional resilience (Main, 2001; Siegel, 2003).

BRIEF DETOUR: FREQUENTLY ASKED QUESTIONS

Before going to the clinical case example, we wish to refer to a couple of questions often asked in workshops on AEDP. Given its emphasis on both the tender, affect-facilitating ministrations of the therapist and on the necessary emotional arousal of the patient, does the model privilege gender—in other words, is AEDP more suited to the allegedly more tender and more emotional nature of women? Another often-raised question is whether AEDP has any cultural bias toward the allegedly more emotionally expressive American culture.

In keeping with bottom-up orientation of the model, we address these questions through example: Our AEDP case illustration features a male therapist (Danny Yeung) with a male patient, both of them belonging to the Chinese culture, which is characterized by display rules for emotional expression that differ greatly from those that operate in American culture.

CASE HISTORY AND PSYCHODYNAMIC FORMULATION

Having felt depressed every day for the past few years, Gary, a 30-year-old insurance broker, sought psychotherapeutic help for symptoms that included lack of concentration, motivation, and confidence; short-term memory problems; hypersomnia; malaise; sluggishness; and paralyzing indecisiveness. Gary was also plagued by serious work impairment and moderate relational difficulties with his family of origin as well as in his marital life. In addition to meeting the full criteria in the *Diagnostic and Statistical Manual of Mental Disorders* (4th ed.; American Psychiatric Association, 1994) Axis I diagnosis of dysthymia, obsessive–compulsive, negative personality, and dependent personality traits were also in evidence. On the positive side—and resource assessment is a fundamental aspect of assessment in AEDP—Gary presented as intelligent, highly motivated for change, and possessing a high reflective self-function.

Gary's history of negative dysregulated emotional interactions with caregivers with compromised affective competence produced intense shame about emotions and needs. His defensive exclusion of these self-needs— through mechanisms such as reaction formation; aggression turned against the self; dissociation; and, most prominently, isolation of affect—became necessary to avoid the excruciating emotional pain, self-loathing, despair, and unbearable loneliness that would follow in the wake of massive shame-driven dysregulation of affect and attachment experiences. Gary's chronic reliance on these defense mechanisms blocked his access to the adaptive categorical emotions of anger, sadness, and joy as well as to the adaptive action tendencies that are released with the complete experience of each emotion and that eventually led to the development of the depressive symptoms for which Gary sought treatment.

The following clinical vignettes are edited excerpts from Session 12 of an AEDP treatment carried out by Danny Yeung. They are organized in three sections. The therapeutic work presented here illustrates AEDP's striven-for transformational journey involving three states and two state transformations taking place in a single session.

CASE ILLUSTRATION:
HEALING THE VULNERABLE SELF'S WOUNDED HEART

State 1 (Toward State 2): Enlarging the Glimmers of Affective Experience

Gary described a typical scene in his family of origin: His father, enraged, is yelling at him. The presence of such intense affect-laden material from the start is an opportunity on which AEDP tries to capitalize. The therapist immediately attempted to deepen the therapeutic change process by facilitating a felt-in-the-body affective experience. As often happens, there was moment-to-moment oscillation between defensive evasiveness and deepening affective expressiveness, which the therapist closely tracked, encouraging the latter.[1]

Therapist: (*Tender and compassionate tone*) Are you having any feelings at this moment?

Gary: (*Gazes at therapist. Soft and vulnerable tone*) Some woundedness at heart . . . [spontaneous somatic, affective language to express emergent emotional pain]

Therapist: (*Soft and tender tone*) What are the feelings in your eyes? [facilitate experience of emotional pain]

Gary: (*Maintains mutual gaze with therapist. Tender and vulnerable tone*) Somewhat moist . . . (I feel) my tears wanting to flow . . . (*Blinks eyes frequently. Breathes quicker*)

Therapist: (*Very soft and tender*) Blocked? Are your tears blocked? [explicit labeling of the defense of isolation of affect]

Gary: (*Maintains mutual gaze. Blinks eyes frequently. Nods head gently*) Yes.

Therapist: (*Very soft and tender tone*) Can I sit beside you . . . nearer to you? [asks permission]

Gary: (*Maintains mutual gaze. Very tender*) Okay. [permission granted]

Therapist: (*Moves and sits next to patient. Holds patient's right forearm gently and firmly. Very tender and soothing tone*) Try . . . [implicit support through the body language of holding and being near; explicit exhortation][2]

Seeking the patient's explicit consent, which he obtained, the therapist strategically intervened to reduce interpersonal distance; as a contralateral right-brain communication of emotional closeness, he moved from sitting opposite to sitting next to the patient. Through maintaining mutual gaze and a steady protective nurturing presence, the therapist sought to counteract the patient's aloneness with the painful experiences under exploration to help him regulate (dyadic affect regulation of unbearable states) rather than defensively exclude them.

---

[1]In what follows, we will use the following typographical conventions: The italicized text in parentheses describes the nonverbal and paraverbal aspects of communication (i.e., tone of voice; body posture; emotional expression, such as smiling or crying, etc.). The text in bold in brackets is our explication of the affective nature of the patient material that calls for particular interventions, and of the types of interventions used by the therapist.

[2]Although discussions of the role of therapeutic touch are becoming increasingly frequent in psychodynamic circles (M. Bridges, personal communication, October 2003; McCullough, 2003), this is not an issue that we will address here. In this case, the therapist was a family physician by training and had in fact been the patient's family physician prior to the undertaking of the therapy; thus, there was a naturalness of physical touch in their relationship. This is the context within which therapeutic touch was used in this session.

Therapist: (*Very soft and tender tone*) Describe this scene to me. [**encourages elaboration and clarification of the specifics of the emotional scene**]

Gary: (*Looks up at the ceiling. Softly*) Once I asked my old man for money . . . (*Nervous giggle*) I don't know why I asked him for money . . . (*Looks down. Appears dejected*) my old man was speaking with my mother . . . I called out to him several times . . . "Pa, Pa" . . . I was not sure whether he heard me or not . . . I was accused of interrupting their conversation . . . he yelled at me several times . . . then he said (*imitating father's demeaning and dismissive tone*) "Take it, take it."

Simple self-expression led to a humiliating, intensely negative experience with an emotionally dismissive parent. After repeatedly being the recipient of such "errors of commission" (Fosha, 2000b) from a rejecting caregiver, humiliation colored the experience of self; eventually shame functioned as a red-signal affect, triggering the institution of defenses to prevent reexperiencing the unbearable emotional pain associated with expressions of emotion and need.

Therapist: (*Very soft and tender tone*) Are you having any feelings? Any feelings in the body? [**maintains moment-to-moment tracking of bodily experience of affect**]

Gary: (*Long pause. Softly*) Somewhat tense in my chest . . . it was unfair . . . I called for him several times . . . he did not respond . . . I also felt humiliated. [**awareness of somatic correlates of anxiety; emergence of personal emotional narrative**]

Therapist: (*Very compassionate tone*) Are you blocked? [**empathic resonance with emotional pain through tone, explicit defense work through words**]

Gary: (*Long pause; looks down. Softly*) Last couple of minutes . . . I tried to let the tears flow . . . but I also felt as if my body was not listening . . . that it was blocked . . . [**recognizes defense and collaboratively joins with therapist to relinquish it**]

State 2: Uncovering Emotional Experience

As the patient's defenses became *ego-dystonic* (i.e., aware that what was adaptive there and then is maladaptive here and now), his motivation to overcome them rose, and patient and therapist were increasingly joined in the therapeutic enterprise. The therapist helped the patient recall in vivid detail scenes of "family feuding" where "screaming" and "swearing" were the order of the day. The therapist continued to seek to heighten the patient's emotional arousal by using highly specific imagery, sensation, and experience (i.e., speaking the language of the right brain). After a very long pause, the patient described another scene, which turned out to be critical.

Gary: (*Maintains mutual gaze. Softly*) I remember when they came here as immigrants . . . they arrived at the airport . . . my old man was shouting how easy it was, passing customs . . . but I saw Mom as somewhat like a zombie . . . zombie . . . rather crazy and insane . . . her hair turned all white . . . (*hand gesturing toward head*) what a big contrast.

Therapist: (*Holds patient's right forearm*) [**nonverbal communication of support**]

Gary: (*Maintains mutual gaze. Blinks eyes frequently. Shakes head*) I wanted to cry just now when I described Mom . . . [**on the threshold of core affective experience of grief**]

Therapist: (*Very tenderly*) Where is the feeling located? [**facilitating somatic correlates of affective experience**] (*The therapist touches patient's sternum*)

Gary: (*Blinks eyes frequently. Nods head*) Yes . . .

Therapist: (*Very gently lays right hand on patient's sternum. Applies pressure gradually*). Try . . .

Gary: (*Closes eyes. Breathing heavier*) [**physiological activation, signaling the imminent emergence of previously blocked affects**]

The first state transformation was in progress: About to enter into the realm of core affect, the therapist strategically prompted the patient to focus on his mother's eyes.

Therapist: (*Applies gentle pressure on patient's solar plexus with each out breath. Compassionate tone*) Look at her eyes . . . look at your mom's eyes . . . what do they look like?

Gary: (*Eyes closed. Facial melancholy. Soft voice*) Helpless . . . her eyes are helpless . . . she's looking at the new surroundings, but . . . [**facial expression of deepening grief**]

Therapist: (*Deeply compassionate tone*) Don't block it . . .

Gary: (*Very long pause. Eyes closed. Soft voice*) My heart hurts very much. [**somatic experience and expression of core affect of emotional pain**]

Therapist: (*Very compassionate tone*) Mmm . . . [**empathic attunement; nonverbal compassion to facilitate deepening of emotional experience**]

Gary: (*Very long pause. Eyes closed. Soft voice*) I am very afraid . . . (*Starts crying, tears flowing freely and fully*) [**experience of pain-**

ful emotions associated with witnessing his mother's suffering: helplessly witnessing the trauma of a loved one is itself traumatic]

Therapist: (*Very compassionate tone*) Mmm . . .

Gary: (*Eyes closed. Tears flowing. Long pause*)

Therapist: (*Very tenderly*) Any feelings in your body? [moment-to-moment tracking of shifts in the somatosensory correlates of emotional experience]

Gary: (*Opens eyes*) I feel some relief. After the tears flowed, the tense feeling in the chest seems to disappear [completion of first wave of adaptive grief; unprompted, the patient elaborates and deepens the exploration] At first, I thought it was the way I sat . . . I saw Mom in the scene . . . the people in the background were fuzzy.

Therapist: (*Tenderly*) Seems like there is more. [intuitive anticipation, encouraging the further unfolding of the affective experience]

Gary: (*Tenderly*) She seemed so lost, walking towards me . . . it seemed on the surface like a family reunion . . . [but] there is such unhappiness. (*More tears*) [absorbed in the experience] (*Deep sobbing. Long pause*)

Therapist: (*Tenderly*) Any feelings in the body? (*Long pause*) Don't block.

Gary: (*Eyes closed. Tears flowing*) She did not use to have that much white hair.

Therapist: (*Tenderly*) Any feelings . . . that she did not use to have that much white hair?

Gary: (*Eyes closed. Tears flowing. Tender voice*) Very sad.

Therapist: (*Very compassionate tone*) Mmm . . .

Gary: (*Very pained tone*) Very lonely . . . she looked so lonely.

Therapist: (*Intensely compassionate tone*) Mmm . . .

Gary: (*Eyes closed. Tears flowing. Sniffs*)

Therapist: (*Lays left hand behind patient's neck with gentle stroke*)

Gary: (*Pause; eyes closed. Tears flowing. Cracking, trembling voice*) Why would no one care for her?

Therapist: (*Very tender and intensely compassionate tone*) Yes . . . guai. [deep affirmation of the patient from the here-and-now attachment figure]

Gary: (*Head bend down. Eyes closed. Tears flowing. Deep sobbing*) I could not . . . help her.

The breakthrough of terrible pain was a key moment: The most personal, subjectively important aspect of what made the situation so unbearable now fully came to light. The patient's shame and pain about his helplessness and failure to alleviate his mother's suffering emerged immediately following the therapist's affirmation of the patient's value as a human being, *guai* being a Chinese expression for the prizing of a younger person by an elder. Being affirmed in his fundamental goodness by an attachment figure, someone perceived as "older and wiser" (Bowlby, 1988), was a profound corrective emotional experience: the toxic shame of the self, until that moment a closely guarded secret, could now come out to be detoxified and healed.

> Therapist: (*Very tender*) Guai . . . [**further undoing of shame experience through empathic affirmation**] (*Very tender*) Any other feelings?

> Gary: (*Eyes closed. Dreamy voice*) My mother loved me so much . . . all these years . . . I miss her . . . [**spontaneous emergence of positive receptive affective experience (i.e., feeling loved by his mother); the first marker of the emergent state transformation**]

> Therapist: (*Tender*) Yeah . . . *guai*. [**continued affirmation**]

> Gary: (*Eyes closed. Tears flowing. Deep breathing*)

> Therapist: (*Very tender*) Any other feelings?

> Gary: (*Eyes closed. Deep crying. Tender voice*) I remember she used to tell me to eat . . . I felt her care for me . . . she was worried that I might be hungry . . . (*More sobbing*) [**more memories of being cared for, congruent with a self worthy of being loved**] (*Eyes closed. Dreamy voice*) I feel warmth . . . [**sudden shift of bodily felt sense from negative to positive experience: second marker of emergent state transformation**]

> Therapist: (*Intrigued. Tender*) Where . . . where do you feel the warmth in your body?

> Gary: (*Gestures towards his chest*) She is smiling at me . . . [**positive affective marker: the third marker of emergent state transformation**]

> Therapist: (*Tender. Lighter voice*) Really!

Once the core affective experience was articulated and met with loving support, the second state transformation—that from core affect to core state—was heralded by the emergence of positive affect: "My mother loved me." The shame undone, the individual was now open to receptive affective experiences of feeling loved. The therapist, knowing that "nothing that feels bad is ever the last step" (Fosha, 2004; Gendlin, 1981), recognized these positive affects as signaling the completion of the wave of grief and the emergence of the next state. The patient opened his eyes, maintained mutual gaze, and noticed the tears in his therapist's eyes. This gave rise to the emergence of healing affects, here, gratitude for the therapist.

Gary: (*Tender*) Thank you! **[expression of healing affects]**

Therapist: (*Tender*) Not necessary . . . you are welcome! **[momentary defense on therapist's part; immediately corrected]**

Gary: (*Wipes tears off his face. Long pause*)

State 3: The Core State Experience and Its Revelations

The completion of the experience of core affect ushered in the experience of core state. The patient had a feeling of deep relaxation and expressed his wish for a good sleep, which the therapist accepted with continued care and tenderness. The session continued.

Therapist: (*Tender*) Yes . . . any other feelings? Can you describe your state of mind?

Gary: (*Maintains eye contact with therapist. Declarative tone*) Two things popped into my mind . . . my burden is light and my yoke is easy. **[simple declarative tone as marker of core state; spirituality as an aspect of core state experience]**

Therapist: (*Intrigued. Smiles*) Share with me.

Gary: (*Declarative. Matter of fact tone*) Usually . . . it would be many Sundays [of going to church] before I could hear such inspirations. I don't know why it would just pop up now.[3]

Therapist: (*Awed. Tender*) Amazing . . . very amazing. And the other thing? **[affectively resonant affirmation; encourages continued experiential unfolding]**

Gary: (*Long pause. Reflective and declarative tone*) The last few days, I tried to remember a saying . . . but I could not recall it clearly until just now . . . (*Gesturing toward his solar plexus*) "the kingdom of heaven is in your heart."

Therapist: (*Startled tone*) Whoa! **[affectively resonant affirmation]**

Gary: (*Maintains eye contact. Nods head*)

Therapist: (*Intrigued. Mesmerized tone*) Why is it that before you could not remember . . . and now you can?

---

[3]This is an example of spontaneous, unbidden, experience, the "passive" emergence as marker of quantum transformational experience of the mystical type (James, 1902/1985; Miller & C'de Baca, 2001) and core state phenomena with a mind of their own (Fosha, 2002).

Gary:	(*Very long pause. Puzzled tone*) I don't know why.
Therapist:	(*Chuckles*) We seem to have difficulty with such dogma . . . that we are bombarded by it. [**authentic self-expression**]
Gary:	(*Smiles. Declarative matter-of-fact tone*) It seems like other people could experience it . . . but I couldn't.
Therapist:	(*Very tender*) And now?
Gary:	(*Long pause; calm, declarative, and assertive tone*) It confirmed this experience.
Therapist:	(*Softly*) What experience?
Gary:	(*Calm, declarative, and assertive*) I can let go of my suffering. [**from within core state, the patient reflects and offers a spontaneous acknowledgment of therapeutic impact**]
Therapist:	(*Calm and intrigued tone*) What did you feel when I was pressing on your chest?
Gary:	(*Calm, reflective, and declarative*) I was thinking of my mother's face . . . that was the most touching moment. [**unimpeded exercising of reflective self function**]
Therapist:	(*Tender*) You saw my tears earlier too. [**explicit exploration of the impact of the therapist's expressed emotional experience on the patient**]
Gary:	(*Maintains eye contact. Nods head*) Yes.

In core state, the therapeutic relationship is one of authentic reciprocity. The patient is no longer a "patient" and the therapist is no longer a "therapist." They are mere human beings, fellow travelers sharing an authentic moment in this life journey. The true self of the patient is actualized in this moment of meeting with a true other, who responds to the real needs of the patient. True self to true other is AEDP's version of Buber's I–Thou relating (Buber, 1996).

Therapist:	(*Tender*) I notice the redness in your eyes now . . . it seems that there are still some feelings . . . [**maintains moment-to-moment tracking of patient's affect**]
Gary:	(*Softly*) Tears of sorrow are very tiring . . . but the tears at this moment seem to recover quickly.

Indeed, the phenomenology of depression is different from the phenomenology of core grief which, in turn, is different from the phenomenology of healing and transformation. Though tears are common to all three, the patient, deeply in touch with his own emotional experience, knew the difference and knew it in his body.

Therapist: (*Gentle*) How would you describe these tears . . . at this moment?

Gary: (*Tender*) "Healing tears" does not seem to fit close enough . . . **[the patient does not yet have the words for this affect, but his experience is his able guide]**

Therapist: (*Tender*) What pops into your mind now?

Gary: (*Calm and declarative tone*) Hope . . . I cannot visualize it, but I feel it . . . hope!

These three segments document a therapeutic journey. In the first segment, working from a highly empathic stance that is maintained throughout, the therapist used relational, restructuring and affective–experiential techniques to help the patient explore previously evaded feelings. The therapist's success in becoming a secure base for the patient renders the patient's defense mechanisms both anachronistic and ego-dystonic. The second segment illustrates State 2 work with core affect: The therapist facilitated the patient's bodily experience and expression of deep emotional pain, helping him viscerally access his grief, all the while maintaining the moment-to-moment dyadic regulation of affect. In the last segment, the patient's completion of an intense but corrective affective experience led to the emergence of healing affects; then, heralded and marked by several positive transformational affects, core state experiencing came to the fore, as the experience of healing transformation became solidified.

CONCLUSION

The nature of the integration that AEDP exemplifies—seamless, synthetic, organic—is by no means the result of deliberate effort to combine different clinical approaches. Instead, the drive toward optimal effectiveness and maximal efficacy and the search for further ways to deepen, enhance, and empower therapeutic work led to AEDP's de facto technical integration of different technical elements, each singly belonging to a different therapeutic modality.

Similarly, with regard to the theoretical integration that informs clinical action in AEDP, phenomena associated with the transformative affective experiences of relatedness and deep emotion were obtained initially by a conceptually psychodynamic therapy, stretching to use experiential techniques and an emotionally engaged stance to maximize therapeutic efficacy in an accelerated time frame. These transformative affective phenomena—sudden, discontinuous, sometime explosive quantum changes—transcended the explanatory bounds of psychodynamic theory and pleaded for an explanatory account that did justice to the dynamics by which they originated and operated. Different theoretical constructs from different disciplines—attachment research, emotion theory, neuroscience, transformational studies, and developmental models—helped AEDP develop such an account. The phenomenon-driven emergent understanding of heretofore unilluminated aspects of the clinical process, in turn, further extended AEDP's conceptual framework. The dialectic of phenomena in search of an explanatory theory, and the new evolving theory in turn informing, explicating. and sensitizing awareness to new phenomena and aspects of the clinical process describes integration achieved through praxis.

One last point: Our bodies, our brains, our minds, our psyches, and our selves are all seamless integration in action. They are entities in which the integration of emotion, cognition, relatedness, behavior, and communication is reflected in our moment-to-moment experience and functioning. It is how these master integrators operate when the physiology and energy of mind are reflected in fluidity and resilience (Kristi Foster, personal communication, February 4, 2004) that AEDP has sought to emulate. We continue to heed their integrative lessons.

REFERENCES

American Psychiatric Association. (1994). *Diagnostic and statistical manual of mental disorders* (4th ed.). Washington, DC: Author.

Beebe, B., & Lachmann, F. M. (2002). *Infant research and adult treatment: Co-constructing interactions.* Hillsdale, NJ: Analytic Press.

Bowlby, J. (1982). *Attachment and loss: Vol. 1. Attachment* (2nd ed.). New York: Basic Books.

Bowlby, J. (1988). *A secure base: Parent–child attachment and healthy human development.* New York: Basic Books.

Buber, M. (1996). *I and thou.* New York: Simon & Schuster.

Damasio, A. R. (1999). *The feeling of what happens: Body and emotion in the making of consciousness.* New York: Harcourt Brace.

Darwin, C. (1965). *The expression of emotion in man and animals.* Chicago: University of Chicago Press. (Original work published 1872)

Emde, R. N. (1988). Development terminable and interminable. *International Journal of Psycho-Analysis, 69,* 23–42.

Fosha, D. (2000a). Meta-therapeutic processes and the affects of transformation: Affirmation and the healing affects. *Journal of Psychotherapy Integration, 10,* 71–97.

Fosha, D. (2000b). *The transforming power of affect: A model for accelerated change.* New York: Basic Books.

Fosha, D. (2001). The dyadic regulation of affect. *Psychotherapy in Practice, 57,* 227–242.

Fosha, D. (2002). The activation of affective change processes in AEDP (accelerated experiential–dynamic psychotherapy). In F. W. Kaslow (Ed. in Chief) & J. J. Magnavita (Vol. Ed.), *Comprehensive handbook of psychotherapy: Vol. 1. Psychodynamic/object relations* (pp. 309–344). New York: Wiley.

Fosha, D. (2003). Dyadic regulation and experiential work with emotion and relatedness in trauma and disorganized attachment. In M. F. Marion & D. J. Siegel (Eds.), *Healing trauma: Attachment, mind, body, and brain* (pp. 221–281). New York: Norton.

Fosha, D. (2004). "Nothing that feels bad is ever the last step:" The role of positive emotions in experiential work with difficult emotional experiences. *British Journal of Clinical Psychotherapy, 11*, 30–43.

Fosha, D., & Slowiaczek, M. L. (1997). Techniques for accelerating dynamic psychotherapy. *American Journal of Psychotherapy, 51*, 229–251.

Gendlin, E. T. (1981). *Focusing.* New York: Bantam.

Gendlin, E. T. (1996). *Focusing-oriented psychotherapy: A manual of the experiential method.* New York: Guilford Press.

Greenberg, L. S., & Paivio, S. C. (1997). *Working with emotions in psychotherapy.* New York: Guilford Press.

James, W. (1985). *The varieties of religious experience: A study of human nature.* New York: Penguin Books. (Original work published 1902)

Levine, P. (1997). *Waking the tiger: Healing trauma.* Berkeley, CA: North Atlantic Books.

Main, M. (2001, March). *Attachment disturbances and the development of psychopathology.* Paper presented at the conference Healing Trauma: Attachment, Trauma, the Brain, and the Mind, University of California at San Diego School of Medicine, San Diego.

McCullough, L. (2003, October). *The experience of touch and the deepening of affect.* Paper presented at the conference Reaching the Affect: The Healing Force in Psychodynamic Therapy, Washington School of Psychiatry and International Experiential Short Term Dynamic Psychotherapy Association, Bethesda, MD.

McCullough Vaillant, L. (1997). *Changing character: Short-term anxiety-regulating psychotherapy for restructuring defenses, affects, and attachment.* New York: Basic Books.

Miller, W. R., & C'de Baca, J. (2001). *Quantum change: When epiphanies and sudden insights transform ordinary lives.* New York: Guilford Press.

Osimo, F. (2003). *Experiential short-term dynamic psychotherapy: A manual.* Bloomington, IN: First Books Library.

Panksepp, J. (1998). *Affective neuroscience: The foundations of human and animal emotions.* New York: Oxford University Press.

Person, E. S. (1988). *Dreams of love and fateful encounters: The power of romantic passion.* New York: Penguin.

Schore, A. N. (2003a). *Affect dysregulation and disorders of the self.* New York: Norton.

Schore, A. N. (2003b). *Affect regulation and the repair of the self.* New York: Norton.

Siegel, D. J. (2003). An interpersonal neurobiology of psychotherapy: The developing mind and the resolution of trauma. In M. F. Solomon & D. J. Siegel (Eds.), *Healing trauma: Attachment, mind, body, and brain* (pp. 1–54). New York: Norton.

Stern, D. (1985). *The interpersonal world of the infant: A view from psychoanalysis and developmental psychology*. New York: Basic Books.

Stern, D. N., Sander, L. W., Nahum, J. P., Harrison, A. M., Lyons-Ruth, K., Morgan, A. C., et al. (1998). Non-interpretive mechanisms in psychoanalytic psychotherapy: The "something more" than interpretation. *International Journal of Psychoanalysis, 79,* 903–921.

Tomkins, S. S. (1962). *Affect, imagery, consciousness: Vol. 1. The positive affects.* New York: Springer Publishing Company.

Tomkins, S. S. (1963). *Affect, imagery, consciousness: Vol. 2. The negative affects.* New York: Springer Publishing Company

Trevarthen, C., & Aitken, K. J. (1994). Brain development, infant communication, and empathy disorders: Intrinsic factors in child mental health. *Development and Psychopathology, 6,* 597–633.

Tronick, E. Z. (1989). Emotions and emotional communication in infants. *American Psychologist, 44,* 112–119.

Tronick, E. Z., & Weinberg, K. (1997). Depressed mothers and infants: The failure to form dyadic states of consciousness. In L. Murray & P. Cooper (Eds.), *Postpartum depression and child development* (pp. 54–85). New York: Guilford Press.

van der Kolk, B. A. (2002). Beyond the talking cure: Somatic experience and subcortical imprints in the treatment of trauma. In F. Shapiro (Ed.), *EMDR as an integrative psychotherapy approach: Experts of diverse orientations explore the paradigm prism* (pp. 57–84). Washington, DC: American Psychological Association.

14

CONTEXTUAL INTEGRATIVE PSYCHOTHERAPY

ANDRÉS J. CONSOLI AND ROBERT C. CHOPE

The approach articulated in this chapter is one perspective in the broad spectrum of integrative psychotherapies. We do not intend through the title and case example to offer a prototypical integrative approach; rather, we wish to illustrate how practitioners may operationalize an integrative perspective in their daily practice.

The approach that we have termed *contextual integrative psychotherapy* seeks to honor and articulate the following salient contributions and perspectives.

1. An essential component for a successful therapeutic relationship is the development of a shared worldview between patient and therapist. A shared worldview should be considered not only in the strengthening of the alliance and in the adherence to treatment but in the facilitation of a successful outcome (Fischer, Jome, & Atkinson, 1998). In other words, therapists must understand their clients' worldviews and work with such views systematically.

Partial support for this chapter was provided by National Institute of Mental Health Grant 3 R24 MH61573-01A1S1 to Andrés J. Consoli.

2. Rosenzweig's (1936) early conclusion regarding the differential effects of distinct psychotherapy approaches captured by the Dodo verdict in Alice in Wonderland ("Everyone has won and all must have prizes") is, without a doubt, one of the strongest arguments in putting forward a well-articulated common-factors, integrative perspective grounded in the centrality of the therapeutic alliance (Bordin, 1979). This perspective has been advanced by some brilliant elaborations such as that of Frank and Frank (1991) and, more recently, Wampold (2001), among many others. We believe, however, that although this argument is a crucial one, it remains only one side of the proverbial coin.

3. The other side of the coin has been eloquently argued by Beutler, resonating with the well-known clinical practice maxim, "different folks benefit from different strokes" (Beutler, 1991, 2002), or different clinical demands should, indeed, lead to differential treatment. The dynamics between the two sides of the coin are perhaps captured in the dialectics between nomothetic (rule-bound) and idiographic (case-specific) approaches, etic (universal) and emic (particular) values, common and specific factors—the yin and yang of psychotherapy.

4. The discernment of patient variables inclusive of diagnosis and on which to personalize treatment is perhaps one of the most pressing endeavors for psychotherapy development. We have found it beneficial to focus on coping style, resistance, problem severity and distress, problem complexity, chronicity, level of functional impairment, resources (e.g., social support), degree of resilience, and racial and ethnic identity development.

5. The psychotherapeutic contract is made up of a set of complex decision-making dimensions that include patient variables such as the ones above, the treatment context (e.g., setting, modality, intensity, format), relationship variables, and strategies and procedures (Beutler, Consoli, & Williams, 1995, p. 279).

6. The progress of psychotherapy has been hampered by a misguided and misleading focus on traditional theoretical "brands" of psychotherapy rather than on the principles of human change processes and stability that are affirmed explicitly and implicitly by the different approaches. It would benefit the field to make explicit such principles, and we welcome recent developments along these lines (Daya, 2001; Rosen & Davison, 2003).

7. The overwhelming majority of surveys that seek information about practitioners' theoretical orientations indicate that mental health professionals endorse an eclectic or integrative orientation. Furthermore, reputable professionals resort to differential therapeutics that are based on the nature of the clinical problem and the context. As practitioners progress in their professional development, they become less dogmatic and embrace complexity, resulting in a welcoming of perspectives previously shunned while affirming a more integrative stance (Castonguay, Reid, & Halperin, 2003).

8. The crushing complexity of human resilience and psychopathology has resulted in numerous reductionistic conceptual attempts. Congruent with Fernández-Alvarez's (1992/2001) taxonomy, we recognize four main and significant conceptual contributions in the field of psychotherapy that can be ordered on two axes. The horizontal axis represents the processes considered when explaining the origins and maintenance of psychopathology as well as strengths and resiliency of the person. The vertical axis represents the relative emphasis given to the person or the context in the generation of disorders and normalcy. These approaches are inevitably dynamic in that (a) they dialectically interact with one another, facilitating their evolution and resulting in a continual rapprochement over time, and (b) they are traversed by sociopolitical, economic, and cultural vectors that shape them and give meaning to their existence. The space generated by the intersection of the two axes bundles an integrative, pluralistic cluster of approaches that attempts to honor the main contributions of the four so-called "forces" (Pedersen, 1990) while seeking to articulate an evolving synthesis (see Figure 14.1).

In summary, our present synthesis of an integrative approach to psychotherapy embraces motivation and learning as two crucial organizing principles of change and stability. These are systematically moderated by the person's individuality expressed in a developmental lifeline. Our synthesis also emphasizes the interpersonal and cultural contexts in which the person's range of comportments is embedded. We view the process of psychotherapeutic change as significantly framed by a meaningful professional relationship with a trained practitioner characterized by empathic resonance, positive regard, collaboration, instilling hope, acceptance, and the development of a shared worldview. Moreover, it includes, as Bordin (1979) suggested, an alliance between the patient and the therapist on the goals of

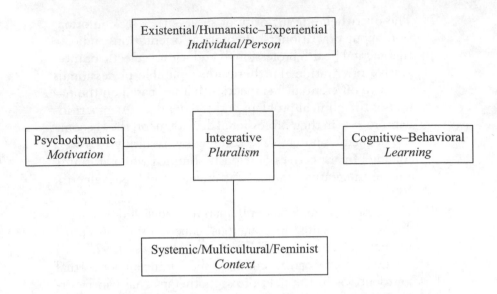

Figure 14.1. Ordering of main conceptual contributions by approaches. From *Fundamentos de un Modelo Integrativo en Psicoterapia* [Fundamentals of an Integrative Model of Psychotherapy], by H. Fernández-Alvarez, 1992, p. 46, Buenos Aires, Argentina: Paidós. Copyright 1992 by Paidós. Adapted with permission.

treatment, the tasks involved, and the bond that results when the two work together.

We view this relationship not as an end in itself but as a secure base for exploration, scaffolding for human change, and a springboard for risk-taking that will result in the expansion (rather than the "correction") of emotional experiencing, behavioral repertoire, and meaning making. Change and stability in psychotherapy come from strategies and procedures that generate support (e.g., empathy, collaboration), facilitate learning (e.g., insight, feedback), expand behavioral repertoires (e.g., assignments, coping strategies), and enhance emotional skills (e.g., activation, regulation). Different patients and different patient–therapist dyads will vary in their timing and readiness (i.e., stages of change; Prochaska & Norcross, 2002) and in their capacity, desire, and willingness to materialize changes and affirm stability.

CASE MATERIAL

The case of Federico illustrates some aspects of our approach. Specifically, we focus on the development of a shared worldview, the use of external support to structure change, and the distinction between problem severity and problem complexity to demonstrate an integrative method when treating a patient diagnosed with panic disorder with agoraphobia. In addition, the assumption underlying this case material is that the therapeutic process can be contextualized and made even more efficient and effective with the use of family members or other external supports in the treatment protocol. Therapeutic change needs to be conceptualized contextually, and clients' change processes are most likely to endure when they are accompanied by a supporting interpersonal world, installed, to some extent, by the therapist.

Demographic and Clinical Information

Federico was 26 when he entered treatment for a number of complaints, many of which could be summarized by a diagnosis of panic disorder with agoraphobia. He emigrated to the United States from Mexico City with his mother and sister when he was 18. He did not know his father. He had completed high school in Mexico City but struggled in the *favelas* (the Portuguese word he used referring to urban slums) and felt the stark contrast between his lifestyle and the lifestyles of those who grew up in more prosperous communities. He had anticipated that moving with his family to the United States and living near his mother's sister would improve his lot in life. However, he had to learn English and secure a job while trying to attend community college, and so he found life to be demanding. He resided with his mother and sister until he was 24, completing an associate of arts degree in liberal studies at a local community college. Meanwhile, he worked as a food server or cook in a variety of Mexican restaurants.

Two years before moving away from his mother and sister, "Freddy" (as he referred to himself) met Vera. He had had three other significant relationships before settling in with her, and he felt she was really special. Vera was a second generation Mexican American who identified more as "American" than as "Chicana." She had graduated from a state college and was an emergency room nurse at a local hospital; she aspired to be a head nurse.

Freddy felt a deep attraction and love for Vera in their 2 years of courtship. After their marriage, however, he experienced some degree of alienation from her. He became more sensitive to the fact that his worldview was more collectivistic than hers; she was more individualistic. He believed that relationships with his family of origin were central to his identity and existence, whereas Vera believed more in the importance of individual autonomy. He lived very much in the present; she focused more on the future. She wanted to have a home, children, and a lifestyle that reflected her "Americanized" perceptions of career and life planning success. He wanted to focus more on helping and serving others. She wanted to travel; he wanted to spend vacations with his family.

Although Vera had grown up in a lower middle class household in the San Francisco Bay area, she aspired to a standard of living that was a clear upgrade. Freddy was satisfied just to have steady work and use whatever resources he had to assist his mother, who worked as a domestic helper, and his sister, who was a hair stylist. He was committed to maintaining their health and well-being, and this represented a source of tension in the marriage. In addition, Freddy acknowledged a degree of difficulty in expressing his emotions, bordering on stoicism, which was another source of tension in the relationship.

While at work, Freddy met several diners from a local video and audio retailer who suggested that he consider advancing his career by working in their store. He decided to apply for the job, in part to better his income and in part to satisfy Vera's "powerhouse" aspirations. Freddy was hired by the retailer, was quickly promoted to a position in showroom sales, and was being groomed to be an assistant manager. He was a bit taken aback by this change in fortune, but Vera was thrilled. Two weeks after being told that he might become an assistant manager, Freddy had a mild panic attack at work as he was closing a large sale.

Three days after the first panic attack, Freddy had a more significant attack. He felt completely out of control, that he would die if he did not get some medical attention. He called Vera to come and take him to the local hospital emergency room. Vera complied. Freddy was in a corner office at the store waiting for her to come in to escort him, afraid to walk out of the store alone. Although Vera was relieved to see him, he reported she also appeared a bit annoyed. At the hospital, Freddy expected that the physicians would find something physically wrong with him. He had his share of life struggles, but he did not think he was a "nut case." Freddy was released from the hospital, told that he had experienced an anxiety attack and that he should go home and rest, even consider taking a day or two off from work on sick leave. Freddy returned to work in 2 days, had another panic attack, and was driven to his mother's house by a colleague from the store.

Freddy was able to continue to work but ruminated constantly about having another panic attack. He felt that with the next panic attack, he would faint in front of a customer or while driving to work. He also feared dying with no one available to help him. He felt safe with Vera because she was a nurse, but it was difficult for him to be away from her. Freddy had two milder panic attacks in the next 6 weeks and then had another disabling attack that frightened him significantly. He called 911 and Vera and was again taken to an emergency room, this time by ambulance. He did not return to work after that.

When Freddy arrived for counseling, he had been away from work for 3 weeks, would not go out of the house except with Vera, and needed to be taken to his mother's house by Vera when she left for work on her evening shift. His employer was reluctantly willing to see him through this, but he wanted Freddy to give him a definitive return date. Vera was also concerned that Freddy was not working, but she was more concerned that Freddy could not stand to be alone in their apartment. Freddy engaged in few activities at either his own apartment or his mother's, preferring to spend the day watching television or playing video games. He refused to drive his car, and because he had never had many friends, he was socially isolated.

Vera talked to several physicians at her workplace about Freddy's problem, and one of them suggested that he receive treatment for what appeared to be an anxiety disorder. He gave her a referral to a private psychologist who had a long-term relationship with the hospital and specialized in the treatment of anxiety. Freddy was resistant to psychological counseling, and he was unwilling to take any medications for psychological problems. He initially hoped to get another referral to a physician who would point out what was wrong with him physically and put him on medication that would resolve the problem. With Vera's encouraging persistence, however, he met with the psychologist.

Vera and Freddy attended the first session together because Freddy did not want to be alone talking with a stranger about personal matters. He gave a brief history of himself and his life in Mexico, characterized himself as comfortable alone prior to the anxiety attacks, and professed to enjoy caring for his mother. He had little contact with other members of his family and was not aware of any other psychological problems. He stated that although he had made the adjustment to living in the San Francisco Bay area, he still felt very much like an "alien" and wondered aloud whether he really belonged back in Mexico, where he said he felt "safer."

He professed to love Vera, whom he found to be "extraordinarily beautiful" but somewhat demanding regarding their lifestyle. He indicated that he was excited about selling at the video store but that he had some fear of being under a microscope, especially regarding store sales volume, should he become an assistant store manager.

Case Formulation

A variety of clinical issues emerge in the work with Freddy. He was an immigrant with a different worldview than his wife's and was not currently working ostensibly because of his panic disorder with agoraphobia. His relationship with his mother could be described as preoccupied and framed by an absent father figure for whom Freddy had tried to stand in, to some extent.

The case demonstrates the prioritization and integration of a number of factors:

- the development of a working alliance and the creation of a shared worldview between client and therapist;
- the development of a treatment plan that is agreeable to all parties, based on the client's motivation and preferences, available resources, urgent demands, and the therapist's professional opinion;

- the use of family members in the treatment process; and
- the distinction between problem severity and problem complexity.

Working Alliance and a Shared Worldview

Though the acquisition of advanced listening skills by a therapist precedes the therapeutic encounter, the actualizing of such skills in the context of a new therapeutic relationship is a process regenerated with every therapeutic dyad. The therapist must be especially attuned to this when the case involves multiethnic and cultural issues. For instance, Freddy's counselor was a specialist in anxiety disorders, but he did not speak Spanish, so Freddy initially felt that they might not be able to work together. Freddy's English was fluent, but he felt that a non-Spanish-speaking psychologist might not share the views and beliefs that he held dear. The therapist encouraged Freddy to express some of the key words of his discourse in the language of his preference. The therapist then invited Freddy to articulate the meanings of these key words. Freddy found this process emancipatory, because he discovered that even though he had used certain key words repeatedly, such as *favelas*, he had not paused to ponder the meaning of them. Furthermore, Freddy indicated the profoundly rewarding experience of having worked with a majority culture therapist whom he found inviting and accepting, an experience that filled him with hope and a new sense of self-appreciation and self-worth.

The creation of a shared worldview between Freddy and the therapist required the initial honoring of Freddy's view of his difficulties as exclusively physical, followed by a persistent and systematic invitation by the therapist to enlarge Freddy's somewhat inflexible ideas about the physical nature of his problems and Vera's conviction that it was within Freddy's control. The therapist presented a perspective of panic disorder with agoraphobia as a problem that could be addressed and solved and that had physical, cognitive, emotional, behavioral, and interpersonal dimensions. Freddy and Vera needed to be confident about this diagnosis. Moreover, a spirit of cooperation was essential. Freddy needed to believe that the therapist and Vera supported his interests. The therapist wanted to develop a balance between Vera and Freddy in how they viewed the world and the presenting complaints. Freddy believed to some extent that external forces drove the courses of people's lives. Vera believed that life throws challenges to people and that they are evaluated by how they respond. This posed an interesting dilemma. Because Freddy had an unexpected panic attack, he was convinced that superior forces were determining his stake in life. Vera thought that notion was unfounded. The therapist determined that having both Freddy and Vera become more familiar with panic attacks and agoraphobia could help them develop a shared worldview. Their first assignment was to watch *Finding Forrester* (Van Sant & Rich, 2000) to begin to enlarge their perspective of Freddy's difficulties and the importance of contextual forces in the maintenance as well as in the redressing of such difficulties.

Treatment Plan

Beyond the development of a working alliance and a shared worldview described above, the initial structure for the work would seek to redress the most pressing matters. The therapist and Freddy negotiated a contract for 10 initial sessions. They agreed to focus on the following objectives, which seemed congruent with a client ostensibly in an action stage experiencing significant distress:

- Educate Freddy and Vera about panic attacks, panic disorder, and agoraphobia and how specific ways of responding to these conditions could exacerbate or redress their present circumstances.
- Expand Freddy's and Vera's belief system to include psychosocial dimensions and balance optimism and acceptance in the process of change.
- Decide on a time for Freddy to return to work.
- Help Freddy and Vera learn and practice a variety of relaxation techniques.
- Select target behaviors for Freddy to change.
- Help Freddy learn new exercises to achieve target behaviors.
- Counsel Freddy about practicing the exercises with Vera as a coach.
- Expand Freddy's ability to read and give meaning to body signals.
- Encourage Freddy to develop coping skills for "dangerous episodes."
- Help Freddy and Vera take credit for the work that was being done.
- Explore Freddy and Vera's differences related to generational immigration status, life goals, and ethnic identity development.
- Help Freddy find meaning in the process, making the experience a rediscovery.

Vera was invited to attend part of each of the initial 10 sessions and was taught how to coach Freddy in the relaxation exercises and intervention techniques. Ten additional sessions were suggested for Freddy to attend alone. These would focus on some of the longer term issues Freddy faced that included his stand-in as a father figure and a preoccupied attachment with his mother, low self-esteem stemming from his upbringing in the *favela*, his ethnic identity development, and the expansion of his emotional expression and repertoire. The therapist could gently integrate some of these issues within the initial 10 sessions and beyond. Wallowing through the material could be difficult, and the therapist needed to ensure that it would not distract from getting Freddy back to some level of employment.

Use of Family Members in Treatment

The therapist had used a variety of techniques over the years to assist individuals who suffer from anxiety disorders. Predominant among these was the use of family members or caregivers in the counseling process to serve as coaches. This approach can improve the efficacy and efficiency of the therapeutic process (Chope, 2001). The therapist, however, must assess not only the patient but also the family members or caregivers to ensure that the tactics used in the therapeutic process would not be derailed by them. This can often be done by having the therapist ask some pointed questions of the caregiver; the following list provides examples:

- What did the caregiver first feel about his or her partner's problem?
- Did the caregiver minimize the problem?
- Did the caregiver fear that this could not be resolved?
- Did the caregiver believe the client?
- From whose perspective did the caregiver view the problem?
- How protective did the caregiver feel toward the client?

Using Chope's (2001) outline for working with a client and a family member, the therapist asked Freddy and Vera to (a) choose the target behaviors individually and then negotiate the targets together, (b) negotiate the timing for reaching the targets, (c) decide on a treatment strategy with professional consultation, (d) evaluate the progress after a predetermined time and set new targets, and (e) use appropriate rewards. Furthermore, Vera was encouraged to be predictable and patient, maintain optimism, limit or eliminate negative self-talk or marked criticism of Freddy, use concrete rewards for activities that were completed, continue her education about the difficulties faced by Freddy and herself, and become as good a listener as possible while projecting an appropriate attitude.

Distinguishing Problem Severity From Problem Complexity

Problem severity is often considered to be the acute, intense, situation-specific aspect of the problem that requires immediate resolution. It is typically expressed by intrapersonal and interpersonal distress. Freddy needed symptom relief, in the form of mobility, and the ability to return to work. Problem complexity is more thematic and enduring; it requires some longer term attention. Freddy needed to address his migratory process, his attachment issues with his family, his relationship with Vera, his restricted emotional world, and his persistent low self-esteem.

For the short term, the primary goal for the therapist was to relieve problem severity through the inculcation of hope, education, and the selection and meeting of targets. The targets were created with a timeline in mind. With the therapist, Freddy and Vera decided independently what short-, middle-, and long-term targets they would like to meet. After the listing of the targets, the therapist worked on having Vera and Freddy compromise on the targets in order to achieve agreement.

To address Freddy's perspective of his difficulties as physical, he learned physical relaxation strategies that he then practiced; Vera helped to coach and to monitor. Initially they learned diaphragmatic breathing, visualization, and Stroebel's (1978) quieting reflex. Later they learned Jacobson's (1970) progressive muscle relaxation. All of these were useful in and of themselves, but they became particularly useful in later techniques, which included systematic desensitization with reciprocal inhibition, role-playing, and real-life practice. Vera turned out to be a supportive coach and monitor.

In addition, Freddy was helped to expand his attribution style and expectations beyond negativity, a process facilitated by his early gains in therapy. Freddy's self-esteem issues often became internalized negative messages, which included worries that Vera might consider him weak and decide not to stay with him, that work colleagues might laugh at him, and that his employer might not have any confidence in him. Coping strategies included having Freddy keep and maintain positive visualizations of his success and recovery. Freddy and Vera were encouraged to remain upbeat and to refrain from criticizing each other. Both were encouraged to continue to learn as much as they could about panic disorder and agoraphobia.

As Freddy's symptoms began to lessen, the therapy focused on themes related to his emotional style and attachment issues with his mother and Vera. Some of the therapy work involved the use of a two-chair technique to encourage emotional enactments (Greenberg & Johnson, 1988; Johnson & Greenberg, 1987) and to expand Freddy's restricted emotional expression. Freddy's reactions in therapy were to some extent characteristic of parentified children, at times denying or minimizing his needs and expecting the therapist to do likewise, at others working extremely hard to be "the best client" while setting unrealistic expectations for the process. Similarly, therapy involved some linkage between Freddy's work and his personal issues.

Success at work was a source of meaning for Freddy, a signal that he was adapting successfully to the United States, but it also added stress and tension to his workplace placement. For this purpose, an integration of Bandura's (1977) self-efficacy theory with Betz's (1992) career self-efficacy theory was used. Freddy clearly had issues with his capacity to successfully perform demanding work tasks. The therapeutic work necessitated raising his expectations of the probability that he could be successful. Four sources of efficacy expectation were used to help Freddy. First, he was asked to keep a record of his accomplishments, beginning with his meeting the previously mentioned behavioral targets. In addition, he was asked to begin to document other accomplishments he had earlier in life (e.g., doing well in school, functioning as a cook, etc.). Second, he needed to understand the value of vicarious learning and modeling. He selected people at his work whom he felt he could learn from so that on returning to work he could shadow the activities of these individuals. Third, he was advised to select three people who could offer him regular encouragement regarding his value as an employee. Fourth, he was counseled to continue to maintain a steady state of appropriate arousal. He called this "getting back to the middle," sustaining equanimity by being neither too high nor too low.

Freddy successfully completed his therapeutic work in confronting his panic attacks. He was able to return to full employment at the prescribed time and continued to work on his personal issues, attending therapy once every 2 weeks. Although the interpersonal work that he had begun could have been continued for some time, Freddy terminated therapy after the 18th session. He did so unexpectedly; he believed that he had accomplished what was necessary to return to work and make peace with some of the issues he had brought to counseling.

CONCLUSION

The brief outline of contextual integrative psychotherapy and the case that followed illustrate a few aspects of the approach. Specifically, the case illustrates the importance of developing a working alliance and creating a shared worldview, the significance of prioritizing therapeutic goals, and the enlisting of family members as part of contextual forces that can facilitate or impede treatment. On the basis of this case formulation, however, it would be misleading to conclude that therapy progresses linearly from urgent matters to thematic issues because these two are dialectically related to one another and operate synergistically in facilitating change. The case material demonstrates the importance of prioritizing on the basis of urgency while maintaining a structural sense of the work to be done.

REFERENCES

Bandura, A. (1977). Self-efficacy: Toward a unifying theory of behavioral change. *Psychology Review, 84,* 191–215.

Betz, N. (1992). Counseling uses of career self-efficacy theory. *Career Development Quarterly, 41,* 22–26.

Beutler, L. E. (1991). Have all won and must all have prizes? Revisiting Luborsky et al.'s verdict. *Journal of Consulting and Clinical Psychology, 59,* 226–232.

Beutler, L. E. (2002). The dodo bird is extinct. *Clinical Psychology: Science and Practice, 9,* 30–34.

Beutler, L. E., Consoli, A. J., & Williams, R. E. (1995). Integrative and eclectic psychotherapies in practice. In B. Bongar & L. Beutler (Eds.), *Comprehensive textbook of psychotherapy: Theory and practice* (pp. 274–292). New York: Oxford University Press.

Bordin, E. S. (1979). The generalizability of the working alliance. *Psychotherapy: Theory, Research and Practice, 16*, 252–260.

Castonguay, L. G., Reid, J. J. J. R, & Halperin, G. S. (2003). Psychotherapy integration. In G. Stricker & T. Widiger (Eds.), *Handbook of psychology: Clinical psychology* (Vol. 8, pp. 327–366). New York: Wiley.

Chope, R. C. (2001). *Shared confinement: Healing options for you and the agoraphobic in your life.* Oakland, CA: New Harbinger.

Daya, R. (2001). Changing the face of multicultural counselling with principles of change. *Canadian Journal of Counselling, 35*, 49–62.

Fernández-Alvarez, H. (1992). *Fundamentos de un modelo integrativo en psicoterapia* [Fundamentals of an integrative model of psychotherapy]. Buenos Aires, Argentina: Paidós.

Fernández-Alvarez, H. (2001). *Fundamentals of an integrative model of psychotherapy* (A. L. LaBruzza, Trans.). New York: Jason Aronson. (Original work published 1992)

Fischer, A. R., Jome, L. M., & Atkinson, D. R. (1998). Reconceptualizing multicultural counseling: Universal healing conditions in a culturally specific context. *Counseling Psychologist, 26*, 525–588.

Frank, J. D., & Frank, J. (1991). *Persuasion and healing: A comparative study of psychotherapy.* Baltimore: Johns Hopkins.

Greenberg, L. S., & Johnson, S. M. (1988). *Emotionally focused therapy for couples.* New York: Guilford Press.

Jacobson, E. (1970). *You must relax.* New York: McGraw-Hill.

Johnson, S. M., & Greenberg, L. S. (1987). Integration in marital therapy: Issues and progress. *Journal of Integrative and Eclectic Psychotherapy, 6*, 205–219.

Pedersen, P. (1990). The multicultural perspective as a fourth force in counseling. *Journal of Mental Health Counseling, 12*, 93–95.

Prochaska, J. O., & Norcross, J. C. (2002). Stages of change. In J. C. Norcross (Ed.), *Psychotherapy relationships that work* (pp. 303–313). New York: Oxford University Press.

Rosen, G., & Davison, G. (2003). Psychology should list empirically supported principles of change (ESPs) and not credential trademarked therapies or other treatment packages. *Behavior Modification, 27*, 300–312.

Rosenzweig, S. (1936). Some implicit common factors in diverse methods of psychotherapy. *American Journal of Orthopsychiatry, 6*, 412–415.

Stroebel, C. (1978). *The quieting response training: Introduction.* New York: BMA.

Van Sant, G. (Director), & Rich, M. (Writer). *Finding Forrester* [Motion picture]. United States: Sony Pictures.

Wampold, B. E. (2001) *The great psychotherapy debate: Models, methods, and findings.* Mahwah, NJ: LEA.

15

A "STUCK CASE" AND A "FROZEN PERSON": SUMMARY OF AN INTEGRATIVE APPROACH

WILLIAM C. NICHOLS

The invitation to present and illustrate the features and use of my integrative approach with a case was the impetus for writing this chapter. The case chosen involved an emotionally "frozen" person suffering from unresolved and unrecognized conflicts. With her marriage and personal life and relations threatened, she was stuck in a therapeutic situation that was going nowhere at the time of referral. What was the course to take? Change was needed, and quickly.

A SUMMARY OF THIS INTEGRATIVE APPROACH

The integrative approach that characterizes my therapeutic work is drawn from the three major revolutions that have occurred in the broad field of mental and behavioral therapy—the psychodynamic, behavioral, and systemic. Wachtel and McKinney (1992) could have been speaking for me when they wrote that integrative family therapy selects from systems, behavioral, and psychodynamic perspectives the parts of each that can be put together in a new system. To this I would add that the "putting together" or integrative facet of this approach is a live and dynamic process in which the theory and application continue to be altered in the light of new findings. The development and functioning of human personalities in their most significant contexts have been my major concern for decades (Nichols, 1990). Personality theory, psychodynamic psychology, anthropology, social psychology, and family studies, merged with clinical observations and quantitative research, evaluation of the empirical research of others, and family systems theory guide the fluidity and ongoing integration that form the basis for my therapy practice (Nichols, 1996b, 2001).

Psychodynamic Theory

Adaptations of Sullivan's interpersonal theory (Sullivan, 1953a, 1953b, 1954, 1962, 1964) and Fairbairn's object relations theory (Fairbairn, 1952, 1954, 1963) furnish a two- (or more) person psychological model that emphasizes relationships and interaction between the person and his or her environment as well as internal functioning and development. Sullivan's focus on cultural content and the crucial role of communication gives an important "outside" emphasis. Fairbairn offered a more specific "inside" perspective. Together, they forcefully emphasized taking the troubled patient's relationships and environment into account when working with that patient.

The major psychodynamic emphases in this model, in addition to the "inside-out" dimensions (individual, intrapsychic), include unconscious processes (dream processes), interpersonal (Sullivanian emphasis), and object relations (dyadic and choice emphases), including the processes of projective identification, introjection, projection, collusion, splitting, and others (Nichols, 1996b, 2001; Nichols & Everett, 1986).

Behavioral Theory

How persons learn and the ways that learning can contribute to change in therapy have also long been important attributes of my integrative approach to therapy. Generally focusing on observable, individual behavior, behavioral approaches can be described as offering essentially an "outside-in" orientation (Nichols, 1996b). Specifically, learning processes include attention to cognitive emphases, a teaching–learning emphasis, and techniques for change, as well as a general emphasis on change. The behavioral part of this integrative approach offers practical help in assisting patients to develop social skills and adaptive behaviors. More recently, cognitive behavioral emphases have tended to move to the fore in my work involving behavioral approaches (Nichols, 1998, 2000).

Family Systems Theory

General system theory, as adapted to family systems theory and treatment and in contrast to traditional psychotherapy's focus on individual theory and treatment, brings in a new epistemological outlook that stresses the contextual dimension (interactive, systemic emphases). It also has a strong focus on change. The major parts of a systems perspective for my approach to family therapy include the constructs of organization, subsystems, wholeness, boundaries, hierarchy, open systems, *equifinality* (meaning briefly that the same results can be secured by different means and from different starting points), feedback, *nonsummativity* (the idea that one must attend to the pattern and not merely the parts of systems and behaviors), communication, stability and change, and structure and process (Nichols, 1996b, 2001). Family systems theory, in broad terms, accentuates connectedness and the systemic nature of human interaction. When merged with Fairbairn's idea that humans possess an active object-seeking ego from birth, family systems theory robustly supports the notion that the human person is a proactive creature (Allport, 1955), a significant element in my therapeutic approach.

An important part of family theory, family development (Nichols, Pace-Nichols, Becvar, & Napier, 2000), also is incorporated into my integrative family therapy model, especially with regard to the family life cycle and the marital life cycle. The major family development emphasis that is called on in this description of integrative therapy is the recognition that unresolved tasks from an earlier period from a family member's life may be carried within oneself and in one's relationships. The existence of various tasks and stages of the life cycle provide therapists with guidelines for determining some of the tasks that must be completed in order to achieve adequate functioning (Nichols, 1996b; Nichols & Everett, 1986).

Some Areas of Application

Integrative therapeutic work has been described and illustrated in a variety of therapeutic uses over the years, including family and marital cases (Nichols, 1985a, 1988a, 1988b, 1996b, 1998, 2000, 2001; Nichols & Everett, 1986); family-of-origin work (Nichols, 2003); children and families (Nichols, 1999); antisocial personality disorder and histrionic relationship disorder (Nichols, 1996a); and family stress, divorce, children, and postdivorce adjustment (Nichols, 1984, 1985a, 1985b, 1989).

CASE EXAMPLE

This case began for me when I received a telephone call from an attorney colleague of mine who occasionally referred adults and children for either psychological evaluation or therapy. "Could you see a divorce client of mine who can't decide what to do?" he asked. He explained that a female client and her husband had been involved in working together with a pair of co-therapists for several months. "She wants to marry somebody else and he wants to continue the marriage," he continued. "The people they are seeing have been trying to get them to agree to a separation/postmarital contract, and they are totally stuck. Can you see her? He's seeing another therapist, individually, and is not available. It's pretty confused."

"I can see her once on a consultative basis and see if we can sort out the situation, but, as you know, I won't see her more than once so long as she is in treatment with somebody else," I responded. "If that's workable, go ahead and give her my number and let her call me, and we'll see what seems appropriate."

Demographic and Clinical Information

Marilyn (a pseudonym is used for the patient and some details have been changed in order to protect her identity) was a young woman in her 30s who had been married for 12 years, since her graduation from college. Nicholas, 2 years older than his wife and also a college graduate, was a stockbroker. Their children, two young boys, were 8 and 10 years old. White and Protestant, the family lived comfortably in an upper middle class neighborhood. Marilyn was in good health, except for some "recent depression," and was not taking any medication. She was an only child whose parents lived less than an hour's drive away from her. Her presenting complaint was the inability to work out a divorce agreement with her husband so that she could have full custody of their children.

Case Formulation Within the Theoretical Model

The systemic perspective in the theoretical model used holds that what affects one part of a system affects all parts. Initially, Marilyn's symptoms were assessed as a case of depression, stemming from an unresolved grief reaction to bereavement. It was deemed necessary to deal with the individual depression and grief reaction before any responsible direct interventions could be considered regarding her marriage. Although I recognized that her problems reverberated through her marital and family systems, it was not viewed as possible to make a firm assessment of the marital situation, nor was it deemed wise to assess the implications of her relationship with the person she said that she intended to marry (after divorcing her husband) until attention had been given to the unresolved grief. In the interim, the additional systems and relationships needed to be put on hold and protected as well as possible against unnecessary and undue harm.

From a psychodynanic and practical vantage point, it was important to bring the feelings of loss, which were being blocked from recognition, into awareness and to elevate Marilyn's consciousness regarding what was happening. Accompanying the result relief, I expected to find in the patient an increased ability to begin conceptualizing how to cope more effectively and to make better choices than she had been making in the recent past.

Clinical Interaction

Soon after the attorney talked with me, Marilyn telephoned for an appointment. She arrived 10 or 15 minutes early, as was requested, and completed the standard background information that I used, which provided a considerable amount of information and saved time in the interview (Nichols, 1988b, 1996b).

Marilyn manifested a deep sadness from the moment she entered my office, sitting virtually frozen on the sofa, continuing to wear her coat, and with her head slightly bowed most of the time, her face partially obscured by her shoulder-length black hair. I told her briefly what little I knew from the attorney and from my telephone conversation with her when she made the appointment. Reiterating that I was seeing her on a consultative basis, I asked, "What brings you in? What are you looking for?" Marilyn slowly explained that she and her husband were seeing a pair of therapists and that they were at an impasse, that they could not agree on how they were going to handle arrangements with their two children after they divorced and she remarried, and that her husband did not want a divorce.

When I asked her to tell me more about the situation, she related a story essentially as follows. She and her family had been very close to her dearest friend and her family and had spent a good bit of vacation and holiday time with them over the years. The previous summer, her friend had died after a short illness. Marilyn and her friend's husband had always been "kind of attracted" to each other, and a couple of months after the death, they decided that they were in love with each other and wished to get married. Nicholas did not want a divorce and insisted that he would not give up the children, so the couple began consulting with a therapy team that saw them together. The therapists began to work with the couple on a divorce agreement, constructing a proposed custody and visitation contract and strongly insisting that the arrangement for custody of the children had to be fair to the husband. The process had been stuck at this point for nearly 6 months.

Marilyn pulled a four-page, single-spaced copy of the document out of her purse and handed it to me. I scanned it quickly, noting that it involved a complex schedule in which the children would fly back and forth several times a year between their present home in Florida where the father planned to continue living and Colorado, where Marilyn said that she would live with her intended husband and his two children on the ranch that he owned. She explained that the therapists insisted on splitting the time and contact with their children equally between herself and Nicholas, because they said that was necessary to be fair to her husband. (I wondered about fairness to the children.)

We explored briefly where things stood with regard to her husband: He had recently started working with an individual therapist, who was providing him with some emotional support, and he had no desire to go back to the therapists they had been seeing.

"Tell me about your friend," I requested, adding, "She obviously was very important to you. It's been very painful. You miss her a lot."

"She was my 'sister' . . . the closest thing I had to a sister," Marilyn declared. Going on, she spoke in an almost mechanical way of how they had been friends since childhood, how they had maintained a closeness between their families after marriage, and then, choking slightly, how it had hurt when the friend unexpectedly became ill, and what a vacuum had resulted.

"And I don't think that you are through dealing with your feelings of grief and loss. Whatever you do or whoever you work with, you need to work through the process and get rid of some of the pain you're carrying inside," I observed.

When she asked some questions, I briefly described the stages of reaction to loss that people typically go through, using a framework that I have used effectively many times with patients (Nichols, 1988b, pp. 244–247, 1996b, pp. 236–237). Answering Marilyn's query as to whether I would work with her, I indicated that it would first be necessary for her to work out a responsible termination with the persons that she had been seeing.

A couple of weeks later, Marilyn called to say that she had closed out her work with the therapists amicably and to request an appointment. When she came for the first session, we examined the bereavement reaction process she was experiencing and discussed the normality of the numbness, anger, confusion, and other feelings that she had experienced after the loss of her friend. Afterward, I sat silently supportive as she quietly wept without speaking for nearly 10 minutes. Before she left the session we explored her feelings gently and sympathetically We talked about how it was all right to let the feelings get out as she had and about some practical steps that she could take to deal with the reactions that emerged.

During the third meeting, she became pensive, sitting quietly for a little while and then looked up from the bowed head position that she had assumed to ask, "Do you think that it's possible that I transferred my feelings from my friend to her husband?" Gently, I said, "I not only think it's possible, I think that's what happened," affirming the conclusion I perceived that she had already reached. We soon left the matter there and moved on to other things.

Much of the time in the next few sessions was spent in talking about her friend. I noted how important the friend had been to her—consciously using the past tense—as she described how "inseparable" they had been growing up, how as teenagers they had talked on the telephone continually when they were not together and how they had continued to talk on the telephone frequently after they became adults, even when they lived hundreds of miles apart. As Marilyn was able to explore and express her thoughts and feelings more freely, a noticeable change in references from speaking of the friend in the present tense to the past tense occurred.

When she came in with a dream that she requested that we talk about, we worked with it using what I regard as a contemporary approach, viewing it as reflecting her current life problems and incomplete emotional issues from daily life rather than as expressions of unconscious wishes (Mishne, 1993). Our exploration of that dream disclosed that she was beginning to accept the fact that her friend was dead. The small amount of dream work that we did then and subsequently played a brief but important integrating, organizing, problem-solving role (Glucksman, 1987) in helping her to move along toward resolving the loss.

While this was occurring, there was no indication of any change in her plans regarding possible divorce and remarriage. During the next few weeks she continued to mention plans to divorce, remarry, and move to Colorado, but after making a trip there with her children, she canceled a scheduled second visit and terminated the relationship with her intended new husband. By this time she clearly recognized that they had used their contacts and that relationship as a means of trying to avoid accepting the pain of loss. Together with some examination of what had happened with her in that relationship, we began to work on effecting some new life patterns for her, including how she could take practical steps to find new replacement activities and new meanings in her life.

Marilyn decided, appropriately, that she needed to "go home again" to work on some new understandings and relationships with her parents. Without getting into detail, it is sufficient to say that we were able to form a short list of unresolved questions and issues, and I coached her in ways to present and discuss them with her parents. She was able to examine with me some of the family developmental tasks that had not been satisfactorily completed and to work on them with her parents with a fairly good degree of success (Nichols, 1996b). For several reasons, coaching her to go home and talk with her parents at their residence seemed to be more appropriate than taking the path of asking the parents to come in for couple or family-of-origin meetings, as is often done in integrative therapy (Nichols, 1996b, 2003).

Issues that Marilyn delved into with her parents included why she had been an only child ("they tried [to have more children] but it just never happened") and why they had been so protective of her ("I was an only child and they were perhaps overprotective, they said, because they were afraid something might happen to me"). The parents had never talked with her about these matters before, but disclosed that they had realized that they had been overprotective and that that had been a mistake; they apologized. Marilyn and her mother began to spend some time together occasionally, going shopping and having tea, taking steps toward establishing a more active adult relationship. The work done in Marilyn's return home was soon followed by more comfortable social interaction between Marilyn's family of procreation and her parents. At the same time, we did some cognitive–behavioral work, and she began getting involved in some meaningful volunteer activities.

No work was done directly on Marilyn and Nicholas's marriage; it was not necessary, given the changes that had transpired with her. The marital partners worked out any issues between them on their own.

At a brief encounter 4 years later when I spoke to a large meeting of a volunteer group (in which I subsequently learned Marilyn was involved), she sought me out following my presentation to let me know that everything was "all right" and that things were still "going very well."

Effect of the Integrative Approach on the Patient's Psychopathology

Thinking back over the case, it seems clear that the psychodynamic aspect of this integrative theory pointed to the probability that Marilyn's sadness and depression were reactive to the loss she had suffered of a significant person and relationship (object relations). This was borne out by the changes that occurred, including the lifting of the emotional "heaviness" and frozenness of Marilyn as we looked at the typical stages of acute grief reactions and examined what was happening with her as well as the working through of the delayed reactions to the loss of her long-time friend and the termination of the transference attachment to the friend's widowed husband.

Careful listening to the descriptions of the relationship and interaction with the person Marilyn was planning to marry following a proposed divorce raised doubts in my mind that given the nature and degree of commitment and other important marital relationship factors, the relationship would eventuate in a marriage. (For a description of the five "Cs" of marital relationships—commitment, caring, communication, conflict/compromise, and contract, see Nichols, 1996b, 1998.) Conversely, the quality of the relationship between Marilyn and her husband, including his steadfast stance that he loved her and wished to continue the marriage, gave the impression that their marriage had a good chance of surviving if she could be helped to deal with her loss and resume relatively normal functioning and personal growth.

Essential Change Mechanisms

Two major change mechanisms were evident in this case.

Relationship and Alliance With the Patient

As seems to be the case in virtually all successful therapy, the therapeutic alliance formed between the therapist and the patient is a major factor in achieving change (Nichols, 1996b). In the case under discussion, I observed that two facets of the therapist's stance and behavior were crucial in achieving a workable and effective alliance. First I made clear from the outset that I was not going to get involved in issues pertaining to any proposed postdivorce arrangements, and, at least at that time, in dealing with whether Marilyn continued or terminated the marriage. Second, I focused on the pain that the patient was experiencing and emphasized the need to alleviate that pain. Evidently this was the first time that anybody had seriously attended to Marilyn's unresolved grief, which was etched in her frozen countenance and body but was seeping out in her marked sadness and depression. Although she was not conscious of the source of her pain and confusion, she recognized it readily enough and responded appropriately when it was pointed out.

Respectful Treatment and Responsibility for Change

This therapeutic work followed the usual principle in my integrative therapy of encouraging the patient to exercise the greatest degree of self-determination she could with the professional assistance of the therapist (Nichols, 1996b). I provided support and guidance, but I am convinced that we do not change others and that patients change themselves in therapy (Nichols, 1996b). The initial change followed a path much like what has been referred to as "intentional change" by Prochaska and DiClemente (1992). Not only do I regard respectful treatment and patient responsibility for change as important in all therapy, but I felt that they were crucial for a patient who had been overprotected and who needed freedom, encouragement, and opportunity to continue growing in self-determination ability.

Resistance or Noncompliance and Patient's Perception of the Therapist (Transference)

Marilyn never expressed resistance to or noncompliance with therapy. This evidently was the case because of the status of the dynamics and processes at the juncture at which I entered into work with her as well as the nature and strength of the therapeutic alliance and the focus of the treatment. Enough time had elapsed since she had lost her friend and there had been sufficient pressure from the therapists to follow a given path during several months of nonproductive work on concluding a custody and visitation contract to make it clear to her that another course might be preferable. The stance mentioned above, namely, that of respect for the client's right to self-determination and personal responsibility for change, also contributed to the absence of resistance. Simultaneously, her pain was being recognized, and she was being afforded a supported and uncontested path for working out her problems with grief.

Marilyn seemed to view me as strong enough to help and as a fair and benign figure whom she could trust. This had been facilitated by learning that she could trust the attorney, who had recognized her obvious confusion rather than ignoring her emotions and had urged her to seek additional help, referring her to me with positive statements. After treatment began, Marilyn used me and therapy as a safe base from which she departed to tackle her living problems and to which she returned to emotionally "fill up" regularly, in much the same way that young children do with a supportive parent as they practice new skills and development.

My Reactions to the Unfolding Therapeutic Interaction

Marilyn's early responses to therapy consisted, as indicated above, of getting in touch with her grief; letting go of previously denied feelings; and, following her relief from the outpouring of tears and sharing her verbalizations of pain and meaning, beginning to seek ways to cope more appropriately with the situation. A major question for me was how much strength she possessed and what capacity she had for growth and coping with what faced her. The path I tried to follow was that of listening carefully, being as supportive as possible during some periodic outpouring of feelings, and offering observations and asking questions without attempting to be more than a consultative guide.

The growth perspective embodied in my integrative approach was part of the guidance in the family of origin and skill development work. Rather than discussing directly and in depth the fact that she had been as dependent as she had on her friend from childhood and had lost that security base, we focused on replacing that lost security through renewing and expanding family relationships and helping her to obtain sufficient freedom to move on as a more fully functioning adult. I attempted to provide consultation on how to view the issues and engage in ways to move from one state to another (Prochaska & DiClemente, 1992).

Selection of Interventions

A combination of psychodynamic and cognitive behavioral interventions was used in dealing with Marilyn's reactions to the death of a close friend. The keys to affecting the reactions were essentially intrapsychic in nature, the loss resulting in depression and frozenness as she attempted to emotionally hang on to her lost friend by denial and attachment to the friend's widowed husband. Cognitive–behavioral intervention was used through the explanation of and exploration of the typical stages in normal grief reactions of significant objects.

Family systems–based interventions were used in dealing with the patient's relations with her parents. The purpose there was to address as adequately as possible some unresolved issues pertaining to tasks in cross-generational child–parent stages of development and relationship. Cognitive–behavioral work was done to assist her in developing some new understandings, and general learning theory was drawn on to facilitate the learning of effective adult skills and attaining more self-confidence in social relationships.

REFERENCES

Allport, G. W. (1955). *Becoming: Basic considerations for a psychology of personality*. New Haven: Yale University Press.

Fairbairn, W. R. D. (1952). *Psychodynamic studies of the personality*. London: Routledge & Kegan Paul.

Fairbairn, W. R. D. (1954). *An object relations theory of personality*. New York: Basic Books.

Fairbairn, W. R. D. (1963). Synopsis of an object-relations theory of the personality. *International Journal of Psycho-Analysis, 44*, 224–225.

Glucksman, M. L. (1987). Introduction. In M. L. Glucksman & S. L. Warner (Eds.), *Dreams in new perspective: The royal road revisited* (pp. 11–21). New York: Human Sciences Press.

Mishne, J. M. (1993). *The evolution and application of clinical theory: Perspectives from four psychologies*. New York: Free Press.

Nichols, W. C. (1984). Therapeutic needs of children in family system reorganization. *Journal of Divorce, 7*(4), 23–44.

Nichols, W. C. (1985a). A differentiating couple: Some transgenerational issues in marital therapy. In A. S. Gurman (Ed.), *Casebook of marital therapy* (pp. 199–228). New York: Guilford Press.

Nichols, W. C. (1985b). Family therapy with children of divorce. *Journal of Psychotherapy and the Family, 1*(2), 55–68.

Nichols, W. C. (1988a). An integrative psychodynamic and systems approach. In H. A. Liddle, D. C. Breunlin, & R. C. Schwartz (Eds.), *Handbook of family therapy training and supervision* (pp. 110–127). New York: Brunner/Mazel.

Nichols, W. C. (1988b). *Marital therapy: An integrative approach*. New York: Guilford Press.

Nichols, W. C. (1989). A family systems approach. In C. R. Figley (Ed.), *Treating stress in families* (pp. 67–96). New York: Brunner/Mazel.

Nichols, W. C. (1990). Tear down the fences: Build up the family. In F. W. Kaslow (Ed.), *Voices in family psychology* (Vol. 1, pp. 177–191). Newbury Park, CA: Sage.

Nichols, W. C. (1996a). Persons with antisocial and histrionic personality disorders in relationships. In F. Kaslow (Ed.), *Handbook of relational diagnosis and dysfunctional relational patterns* (pp. 287–299). New York: Wiley.

Nichols, W. C. (1996b). *Treating people in families: An integrative framework*. New York: Guilford Press.

Nichols, W. C. (1998). Integrative marital therapy. In F. M. Dattilio (Ed.), *Case studies in couple and family therapy: Systemic and cognitive perspectives* (pp. 233–256). New York: Guilford Press.

Nichols, W. C. (1999). Family systems theory. In S. W. Russ & T. Ollendick (Eds.), *Handbook of psychotherapies with children and families* (pp. 137–152). New York: Kluwer Academic/Plenum.

Nichols, W. C. (2000). Integrative marital therapy. In F. M. Dattilio & L. J. Bevilacqua (Eds.), *Comparative treatments for relationship dysfunction* (pp. 210–228). New York: Springer Publishing Company.

Nichols, W. C. (2001). Integrative family therapy. *Journal of Psychotherapy Integration, 11*, 298–312.

Nichols, W. C. (2003). Family-of-origin treatment. In T. L. Sexton, G. R. Weeks, & M. S. Robbins (Eds.), *Handbook of family therapy: The science and practice of working with families and couples* (pp. 83–100). New York and Hove, England: Brunner-Routledge.

Nichols, W. C., & Everett, C. A. (1986). *Systemic family therapy: An integrative approach.* New York: Guilford Press.

Nichols, W. C., Pace-Nichols, M. A., Becvar, D. S., & Napier, A. Y. (Eds.). (2000). *Handbook of family development and intervention.* New York: Wiley.

Prochaska, J. O., & DiClemente, C. C. (1992). The transtheoretical approach. In J. C. Norcross & M. M. Goldfried (Eds.), *Handbook of psychotherapy integration* (pp. 300–334). New York: Basic Books.

Sullivan, H. S. (1953a). *The interpersonal theory of psychiatry.* New York: Norton.

Sullivan, H. S. (1953b). *Modern conceptions of psychiatry.* New York: Norton.

Sullivan, H. S. (1954). *The psychiatric interview.* New York: Norton.

Sullivan, H. S. (1962). *Schizophrenia as a human process.* New York: Norton.

Sullivan, H. S. (1964). *The fusion of psychiatry and social science.* New York: Norton.

Wachtel, P. L., & McKinney, M. K. (1992). Cyclical psychodynamics and integrative psychodynamic therapy. In J. C. Cross & M. R. Goldfried (Eds.), *Handbook of psychotherapy integration* (pp. 335–37). New York: Basic Books.

16

INTEGRATIVE COUPLE THERAPY

JAY L. LEBOW

My approach to psychotherapy is grounded in a multilevel biopsychosocial understanding of human functioning (Lebow, 1987b, 1997). Problems and strengths are seen as residing on multiple system levels, including the biological, cognitive, affective, and psychodynamic levels within individuals, and on various levels of the social system (couple, family, peer, society) in a relational context. Rather than viewing problems as uniquely nested in a single individual or relational subsystem, difficulties are regarded as typically having manifestations across a range of these system levels.

It follows, then, that there is no one "right" approach to working with clients (Lebow, 1984). Instead, many ways of working are likely to be viable and useful for the same individuals. Therefore, the prime task of therapy becomes the negotiation of a treatment plan that fits with clients' goals and with their sense of what is most acceptable to them within the range of interventions likely to be effective for dealing with their presenting difficulties. People enter therapy for many reasons, and I believe it is essential for the therapy to respond to the diversity of these motivations. For some clients, the primary goal is symptom change; for perhaps the majority of clients, however, other goals, such as better relational or individual functioning or better self-understanding, seem to be paramount. I see psychotherapy as highly consumer oriented, providing an experience that fits with client goals.

It is essential that psychotherapy be grounded in science (Lebow, 2000). A plethora of research findings speak to human experience and to what is effective in psychotherapy. The best psychotherapy incorporates and builds on these findings. The therapy I use draws from both the body of research that points to the broad factors at work in effective therapy (such as a positive therapeutic alliance and the generation of positive expectancy) and the more specific findings pointing to effective techniques for working with specific difficulties as well as the relevant research from social, family, personality, and developmental psychology that applies to a particular case. In my view, psychotherapy must create an effective context for change and then draw from the specific technologies that have been demonstrated to be effective in generating the particular kind of change that is sought, drawing from the breadth of knowledge about human psychology.

My integrative approach is not based on one or two theories of personality or the change process; instead, it has its foundation in a generic view of psychotherapy. Rather than mixing two methods of psychotherapy, my own method has its foundation in disaggregating many therapies that I have found useful in whole or in part into a core set of constructs, strategies, and interventions and reassembling my own version of what I believe to be most efficacious and which fits best with my own style as a therapist (Lebow, 1987a). The approaches that have been most influential in the generation of my thinking have been other integrative approaches (Norcross & Goldfried, 2005), especially those of Arnold Lazarus (1992), Clifford Sager (1976), William Pinsof (1995), Les Greenberg and Susan Johnson (1988), Froma Walsh (2002), Scott Miller and colleagues (Miller, Duncan, & Hubble, 1997), Paul Wachtel (1997), David Orlinsky and Ken Howard (1987), Marv Goldfried (Goldfried & Norcross, 1995), Howard Liddle (1995), Jim Alexander (Alexander & Sexton, 2002), Scott Henggeler (2001), Stan Messer (1991), and Alan Gurman (2002). Though these approaches are diverse in their conceptualization and strategies for achieving change, each has influenced my approach by highlighting a set of salient theoretical constructs, or strategies or interventions.

My approach draws on numerous specific school-based methods. I use a wide range of intervention strategies including ones with behavioral, cognitive, systemic, and psychodynamic roots. I find I most frequently use intervention strategies centered on altering cognitions (with roots in cognitive therapies) and the relational context of clients' lives (with roots in systemic therapies). However, the essence of my viewpoint is that most methods of psychotherapy offer something constructive that can inform my understanding and offer methods of intervention. There is no one "right" viewpoint but rather multiple lenses that can help guide understanding and intervention. People are their behaviors, their cognitions, their internal dynamics, and their interpersonal processes, and all must be attended to in psychotherapy.

I look to combine these viewpoints and strategies of intervention in a way that is solidly empirical, that fits with my strengths as a therapist, and that is internally consistent and can be easily followed by clients (Lebow, 1987a). My practice is strongly informed by the relevant science yet takes into account what I can do best (Lebow, 1987a, 2000). I also look to have what is a complex model of change and therapist decision making appear simple and straightforward to clients so they can understand the treatment plan and follow through with it during and after therapy.

Finally, I see therapy as open-ended (Lebow, 1995). The role of the therapist is to help clients accomplish their goals. The time frame for this work depends on the kinds of goals in focus, and thus therapy can involve only a few sessions or several years, depending on the kinds of goals set and the speed with which they are accomplished. Because people so readily encounter times of stress or trouble, an open-ended frame is created to work through the issues most relevant at a particular point in time and also to create a vehicle that can be used in the future when it seems that further therapy would be helpful.

COUPLE THERAPY

Following from these generic ideas about psychotherapy, I envision couple therapy as only in part a set of techniques for working with couples. Couple therapy also involves understanding the couple relationship in the context of both larger system levels (e.g., family and culture) and the individuals who make up the couple (e.g., each partner's internal processes). I also view effective couple therapy as being built on the foundation of the same core generic tasks in other psychotherapies (e.g., the development of the therapeutic alliance and the generation of the other "nonspecific" factors central to creating a context for change; Lebow, 1997). Yet, it is essential to grasp and respond to the special issues of this therapy format, such as the presence of more than one person and the likelihood of conflict between them. Couple therapy conducted as if it were two individual therapies rarely works. The frame of understanding and intervention must adapt to the specific treatment context.

My form of integrative couple therapy also builds on the foundation of the scientific knowledge available about what works and what does not work in couple relationships (Lebow, 2000). The science of couple relationships is able to tell us a great deal about such things as communication patterns, styles of arguing, the ways expectations are met, ratios in behavioral exchanges, and manifestations of attachment that distinguish those in satisfying relationships from those in distressed relationships. On the basis of these findings, many specific suggestions for how to improve the therapeutic process have been put forward and validated (Gottman, 1999; Lebow & Gurman, 1995).

I also consider successful couple relationships as depending on blending the idiosyncratic goals of two partners rather than on the existence of one set "successful" way of being part of a couple. There are some patterns that inevitably lead to difficulty but many possible roads to being in a satisfied relationship (Sager, 1976).

Couples seek help for a variety of reasons, most having to do with reducing relationship distress but many for other motives as well, ranging from wanting to dissolve a relationship, to hoping for constructive relationship development, to coping with life crises, to searching for help with specific individual problems. In the couple therapy I conduct, work can center on couple processes such as communication, on internal process within the partners, or on the couple's relationship with the outside world (such as with friends and family).

I view the couple therapist as making a series of complex clinical decisions about what to focus on and when, where, and how to intervene. Couple therapists become, in part, teachers of couple skills; in part, mediators between two human beings about their needs and desires; in part, helpers with individual difficulties; and in part, conduits for individual and relationship development.

THE CASE

The case described here is a couple therapy of 15 sessions that occurred over a 5-month period. Marcia and Scott were a Jewish American couple in their mid-30s who had been married for 10 years and who had two children under the age of 5. Neither identified any major individual issues in functioning except strong feelings of distress that accompanied the outbreak of high levels of conflict in their relationship.

When Marcia called to make the first appointment, she described herself as very upset about the state of her marriage. She said she had been married for 10 years and had been unhappy for 9 of those years.

The first phase of my integrative approach to working with couples focuses on two primary tasks: building a therapeutic alliance and assessment. First and foremost, I see the alliance as the crucial building block for successful couple therapy. Couple therapies are notoriously fragile (Lebow, 2000). Although the issues in focus are almost always highly salient for the participants (e.g., the state of their intimate life and, at times, whether they will stay in the relationship), clients typically enter couple therapy less because they want to than because they feel they must because one or both partners is sufficiently unhappy with the relationship. Usually, one partner is more invested in the therapy process than the other, leading at least one party (and perhaps both) wishing to end therapy early on, especially if alliances are not quickly solidified. Add to this the high likelihood that stressful moments will be almost inevitably experienced early in therapy as issues surface in treatment (e.g., the high likelihood of a fight occurring or someone's feelings being hurt), and the pattern of clients attending briefly and leaving feeling that the therapy has not helped (even though little real therapy has been done) is difficult to avoid.

The antidote to this possible scenario lies in active efforts to forge alliances with both partners and to create an alliance specifically focused on exploring the possibilities for their relationship. To create such a set of alliances, I try to provide enough structure and support to ensure that each partner will be able to speak his or her concerns and feel heard, enough control over those aspects of the sessions that can undermine the sense of building a positive alliance (such as arguments degenerating into cascades of bad feeling), and enough of a sense of hopefulness about the therapy being able to accomplish at least some goals.

During the first phase of therapy, it is also essential to assess the situation by engaging the couple in a discussion of their difficulties and how they are experienced. I look to gain a clear sense in the first few sessions of the issues that bring each partner to therapy, how they experience the problems that have been occurring, their respective goals and their expectations for the relationship, and some sense of each partner's individual functioning and the social and cultural context in which they live.

Often, these assessment and alliance building tasks conflict with one another. The sharing of information and disparate viewpoints at moments of relationship distress readily becomes the stimulus for conflict. Such in-session conflict can serve both to increase relationship distress (and thus move against what is the most frequent goal of treatment, to reduce this distress) and as stressors affecting the client–therapist alliance, placing the therapy itself at risk.

My primary goals for the first session with Scott and Marcia were to learn about their situation yet to do this in ways that built a working alliance rather than undermining it. I left the content of the first meeting primarily to them, merely asking them to explain the problems that brought them to treatment and the strengths of their relationship. A proximal goal here was to elicit the internal narrative of each partner about the relationship and about how they experienced themselves in the relationship.

Marcia and Scott were seeing me at Marcia's initiative. She felt that she could no longer live with the state of their relationship and that if this did not change soon, it would be necessary to end the relationship. Her major complaints were the frequent and difficult fights, which she blamed on Scott's volatile temper, Scott's frequent withdrawal into watching TV, Scott's low level of help with tasks at home, and Marcia's general sense of not being supported in the marriage. Scott agreed the fighting was a major problem, but he focused on Marcia's frequent barbs and complaints as the cause of the arguments. He also thought that Marcia wanted too much from him in the way of both help and time together.

When I asked about the history of their marriage, Marcia stated that she had felt very much in love with Scott for the first 5 years of their marriage and had over that time a very positive view of their connection. However, when she became pregnant with their first child, Michael, she felt that Scott withdrew into his work and spent more time with his friends and watching television. Continuing to work after Michael's birth, she felt highly stressed about her multiple commitments and that Scott showed little consideration in relation to the pressures that were building. She said that this feeling of being overly burdened led her to confront Scott on a number of occasions, leading to painful fights in which Scott became verbally abusive and then withdrew from contact with her. Scott's version of these same events shared Marcia's sense of distress about the fighting that occurred but accentuated what he saw as Marcia's highly demanding behavior, her frequent complaints, and her insistence that they keep talking about a subject well after communication had broken down. From his viewpoint, he rarely looked to do anything other than work or be at home with Marcia, but she was unwilling to allow him to have a life away from direct contact with her.

They described several other events as they argued about who had let the other down more, but the examples had a common thread: Marcia seeking more closeness and looking for Scott to participate more in family tasks; Scott feeling like he did his part and that Marcia's expectations were unreasonable and that she complained too much; and their process breaking down into frustrating arguments in which Marcia aggressively pursued and Scott withdrew, a cycle that never led to resolution of the conflict.

At several points in the first meeting, Scott and Marcia's description of their concerns began to degenerate into conflict. Marcia would make pointed criticisms of Scott with a good deal of sarcasm. Scott would respond by saying things like "See how she is," and Marcia would grow exasperated and attack further. When this happened, I interrupted this sequence, working to establish control over the session and a sense of safety. I let them know that I had no trouble seeing the problems that they both were describing but that their process was getting in the way of hearing one another and our being able to do something useful about their concerns. I highlighted to them that these communication patterns would have to change if we were to be successful and presented a simple version of a "speaker–listener technique" that they could begin to practice to build better ways of communicating. However, my goal in these early sessions was not to try to do too much too quickly but rather to build a working understanding with Marcia and Scott about the kinds of changes that would be needed to create a different sense of the relationship.

Early in therapy, I always ask couples about strengths. I find that focusing on strengths is particularly important in couple therapy because so much of the conversation in couple therapy naturally drifts toward discussing problems, often resulting in a sense of disheartenment. Scott thought that Marcia was a good person and a great parent and that he still had positive feeling for her. Marcia, in turn, identified much that she liked about Scott, stating that if only he could overcome his distance, she could regain her good feeling about him.

I concluded the first session by summarizing my thoughts, reminding them again that I had no trouble understanding why they were distressed but that I also had no trouble seeing their strong sense of attachment, and with that attachment there was hope. I pointed to the different paths their relationship could follow: either toward working through their problems and regaining their positive sense of one another or toward more dissatisfaction. I also offered them a bit of psychoeducation about couple therapy that I share with couples early in the process: People always feel challenged in early sessions, and success depends on staying in the conversation and finding constructive ways to talk about difficult issues. I asked whether they would like to proceed and, when they said they would, we set a once-a-week meeting.

When Scott and Marcia came for the second session, they were in the midst of an argument about Scott's failing to call and inform Marcia that he'd be home later than he told her to expect. Being concerned that therapy would degenerate into a series of frustrating arguments if we did not do something about this, I suggested that this was an opportunity to work on how they argued and discussed complaints. My formulation was that Marcia and Scott had some vitally important issues to explore: issues of how they brought their expectations together, issues of roles, and issues around their respective personalities and how they fit together. Moreover, if they could not find a vehicle to process their differences, we would never be able to get to those issues and would instead be stuck in the bad fight of the week. So I refocused their discussion on their communication process instead of the content, highlighting how far their arguments strayed from the ideal of the fair fight. Fortunately, because each manifested an equal level of difficult behavior in their arguments, it was easy to present this in a way that helped maintain my alliance with both. I presented to them a simple set of skills of fair fighting and good communication as alternatives, which I suggested they begin to try.

Much of our focus in the next few sessions continued to accentuate the process of their communication. The prescription for handling difficult moments, however, did not just center on what to do and not do to fight fairly and communicate better (i.e., on the behaviors), but also on how to manage to live with the powerful affects that emerged from such discussions. I identified that it seemed clear that neither wanted to engage in the difficult behaviors they manifested but that the old patterns seemed to flow from the powerful thoughts and feelings within each of them. In this way, I used the behavioral prescription of following the guidelines of fair fighting (no name calling, staying with one topic, etc.; Bach & Wyden, 1982) as a launching point for exploring the cognitions that lay behind the feeling states that generated these behaviors. As I helped Scott and Marcia identify the powerful cognitions that lay behind their affective states (e.g., "If he says that to me, he doesn't love me"; "I don't need to tell anyone what I'm doing"; "Someone who treats me like that deserves my disdain"), we were able to move into a rational analysis of these thoughts, and I suggested a few simple exercises for slowing down and examining their thoughts.

This exploration of their cognitions also created opportunities to begin to explore the impact on the problem of their experiences in their families of origin. When affects were particularly powerful, I would ask Marcia and Scott if they had thoughts about where the power of these ideas came from. Both were able to identify family-of-origin experiences that had direct bearing on these patterns. Scott, in particular, described witnessing how his own father's powerful explosions occasionally degenerated into physical intimidation. Although Scott had successfully been able to avoid his father's pattern of physical intimidation, he was not much better at managing his anger when provoked. The insights that evolved from Scott's exploration of this pattern led to a greater commitment on his part to manage his anger regardless of Marcia's behavior. This led us to spend a part of each of the next few sessions focused on his and their collective anger management, with my teaching them and their practicing cognitive and behavioral anger management techniques.

We thus set a frame for looking at behavior patterns and working to change those patterns, then looking for the cognitions that lay behind the patterns, then the early life experience that had led to the development of the cognitions, and then using each of the various levels of insight to help inform and enable the process of behavior change. We repeated such a multilevel consideration of what was going on in each of them many times, using the material that was in focus for them at the time of each session. For both Scott and Marcia, I developed a number of core themes they needed to keep in focus and work on. These themes moved across those emphasized in different schools of therapy, ranging from active efforts to directly create behavior change, to working on their self-talk, to continuing to keep in focus and increase their insights into the old powerful feelings that underlay their difficulties.

Another major focus in our early and middle sessions was on finding ways to experiment with the positive side of their life together. The science of couple relationships shows that couples with difficult histories of conflict often suffer from an erosion of the positive experiences they share. A feedback cycle is created in which the disappointment blocks engaging in positive experience, which, in turn, leads to difficulties being experienced that much more negatively. In John Gottman's (1999) terms, the "positive sentiment override" (p. 106) that allows for relationship happiness is diminished, and the cascade to relationship distress is accelerated. So I typically suggest efforts to reengage in aspects of life that at one time helped with connection.

In part, the goal of these tasks is to increase connection; the task also serves as an assessment tool, to see how readily connection can grow. Fortunately, Marcia and Scott did follow through with the fun tasks we considered in sessions and fairly quickly reported feeling better for the time they were so engaged. That they were able to achieve that sense so quickly, even for a short time, I took as a positive sign.

A core aspect of my approach to psychotherapy lies in the ongoing evaluation of the status of problems throughout therapy, a simple tracking of therapy progress (and ultimately a measure of treatment outcome). This monitoring keeps attention focused on the treatment goals and how well it is achieving them. Research shows that this kind of monitoring enhances treatment outcomes (Miller et al., 1997). On the simple indicators of treatment outcome we used, both Scott and Marcia indicated a considerable increase in their relationship satisfaction and a decrease in their assessment of their conflict by the fifth session, and the indications in our meetings were consistent with these reports. Marcia and Scott were adhering to the fair fight rules with only a few slips, taking greater responsibility for their own behavior, and rebuilding their emotional connection.

When Scott and Marcia occasionally regressed into more difficult patterns, we intensely examined what triggered this behavior. Much of this work was straightforward dyadic cognitive therapy having to do with the emergence of catastrophic thoughts about these events (most especially, the thought, "Here we go again!"). We deconstructed these moments, looking at the beliefs that emerged for each of them and working to substitute soothing thoughts and feelings that challenged or overrode such beliefs in focus as "my partner wouldn't challenge me this way if he [she] loved me." As we encountered such events, I digressed into a discussion of how trust is rebuilt ("inch by inch") and highlighted that overall they were showing that they were rebuilding such trust even though it could not be rebuilt in a day. This thought in turn became part of the self-talk that I suggested they try to engage in when moments of mistrust arose.

As Scott and Marcia's relationship satisfaction improved and the conflict abated, the focus of therapy moved beyond calming the conflict and reconnecting to examining and building a better mutual understanding of their core expectations as partners. One aspect of the work I do with almost all couples centers on building a shared sense of expectations. Typically, this work cannot be successfully completed until after couples create an environment in which they can communicate and respectfully process issues. Scott believed that his minimal participation in family life was acceptable because he earned most of the family income. Marcia believed that Scott should share equally in the care of the children and that Scott's priorities should be realigned to build more closeness. During this phase of the therapy, we discussed expectations through several lenses. One lens was that of mediation between their respective visions of the world, looking to find a point of agreement where both felt heard and empowered. In discussions of expectations, however, I also look to build an understanding of the core beliefs that lie behind behavioral expectations (about such matters as gender roles, or the expectations of who will be active and who will be passive about various matters, or about control, or about the nature of the world) and of the sources of these core beliefs about expectations (see Sager, 1976).

I therefore asked not only about their expectations but also about how they came to have such expectations. Scott was able once again to trace some of his expectations to the model he experienced in his family of origin, in which his father left all domestic responsibilities to his mother. He was able to process his early experience, namely, his father being angry and distant and his mother depressed, from a new perspective, and he did not want to repeat these patterns.

Marcia, having grown up in the midst of a highly acrimonious divorce and its aftermath, carried the equally powerful legacy of looking to have continual reassurance that she was in connection to reinforce her own sense of security. In our exploration, she was able to differentiate between her positive wish for connection and the anxieties that came with even momentary disconnection and to work through these feelings, allowing her to convey a less demanding yet still connected set of messages to Scott. Thus, each was able to label his or her own set of subconscious expectations, the intrapsychic issues and transferences they brought to one another, and the progress each had made in freeing themselves from these powerful legacies.

Marcia and Scott were also able to use the knowledge they were developing about themselves to create a shared sense of mutual expectations that was less encumbered by legacies from their families of origin. Scott agreed to participate more in household chores and cultivated a better sense of what might be gained from being in connection rather than isolation. Marcia, because of this movement on Scott's part, was more readily able to differentiate between her core expectations (that he participate in the family life) and her less important complaints (that he be neater) and was able to experience and express more empathy for Scott's need for time on his own.

At each of the later sessions in the therapy, both Scott and Marcia also reported high levels of relationship satisfaction, both in session and on the simple measures that were tracking therapy progress. In the 15th session, they reported that they felt satisfied with their relationship and "wanted to take a break" from the therapy. We reassessed their progress and their reasons for this decision, and there seemed to be no strong reason to continue the therapy. We explored the various tasks of termination I have described elsewhere (Lebow, 1995), especially emphasizing what they had learned and needed to do to keep their relationship alive. We ended with the couple in a positive frame of mind about their relationship and about the therapy. Because my approach to therapy is open-ended, I invited them to return when they felt it would be useful in the future.

CONCLUSION

In retrospect, it seems clear that the unresolved issues about subconscious expectations about closeness and distance created a substantial rift over what this marriage was supposed to be like. Moreover, given their lack of collective skill in processing their differences, a tug of war emerged. Both Scott and Marcia experienced considerable levels of frustration, which in turn led to opportunities for difficult sides of their personalities to flourish with one other, and the painful fights that ensued were ungoverned by rules. A downward cascade typical of those described by John Gottman (1999) was launched, in which negative behavior begat negative behavior, and the ratio of positive to negative behavior in the marriage was compromised. The inability to successfully argue or discuss core issues blocked all pathways to resolve the issues, and the arguments that emerged further contributed to the cascade.

This therapy began with my working to declare a truce about the arguing and help Marcia and Scott build skills for avoiding those acrimonious conflict patterns. The reduction in such conflict, coupled with the nonspecific factors emanating from being in what they regarded as a helpful therapy process, interrupted the downward cascade. These factors also allowed for this couple to begin to reengage in positive exchanges, which helped them feel more connected and reminded them (as I did directly in sessions) that they shared a great deal if they could allow themselves to engage in such connection. In this way, what John Gottman (1999) called the "fondness and admiration system" (p. 81) was reengaged, rebuilding trust. This, in turn, allowed a sharing of the fundamental individual issues that impacted their relational selves. Ultimately, Scott began to feel safe and even to benefit from the closeness, and Marcia felt better able to tolerate distance. With more of their needs met, they were better able to accept each other. From this basis, they were able to successfully renegotiate what Sager (1976) called their "marital contract," including not only simple behavioral exchanges but also deeper levels of exchange with one another. When I last heard from them, they were continuing to do well.

REFERENCES

Alexander, J. F., & Sexton, T. L. (2002). Functional family therapy: A model for treating high-risk, acting-out youth. In F. W. Kaslow (Ed. in Chief) & J. Lebow (Vol. Ed.), *Comprehensive handbook of psychotherapy: Vol. 4. Integrative/eclectic* (pp. 111–132). New York: Wiley.

Bach, G., & Wyden, P. (1982). *The intimate enemy*. New York: Avon.

Goldfried, M. R., & Norcross, J. C. (1995). Integrative and eclectic therapies in historical perspective. In B. M. Bongar & L. E. Beutler (Eds.), *Oxford textbooks in clinical psychology: Vol. 1. Comprehensive textbook of psychotherapy: Theory and practice* (pp. 254–273). London: Oxford University Press.

Gottman, J. (1999). *The marriage clinic.* New York: Norton.

Greenberg, L. S., & Johnson, S. M. (1988). *Emotionally focused therapy for couples.* New York: Guilford Press.

Gurman, A. S. (2002). Brief integrative marital therapy: A depth-behavioral approach. In A. S. Gurman & N. S. Jacobson (Eds.), *Clinical handbook of couple therapy* (3rd ed., pp. 180–220). New York: Guilford Press.

Henggeler, S. W. (2001). Multisystemic therapy. *Residential Treatment for Children and Youth, 18,* 75–85.

Lazarus, A. A. (1992). Multimodal therapy: Technical eclecticism with minimal integration. In J. C. Norcross & M. R. Goldfried (Eds.), *Handbook of psychotherapy integration* (pp. 231–263). New York: Basic Books.

Lebow, J. L. (1984). On the value of integrating approaches to family therapy. *Journal of Marital and Family Therapy, 10,* 127–138.

Lebow, J. L. (1987a). Developing a personal integration in family therapy: Principles for model construction and practice. *Journal of Marital and Family Therapy, 13,* 1–14.

Lebow, J. L. (1987b). Integrative family therapy: An overview of major issues. *Psychotherapy, 40,* 584–594.

Lebow, J. L. (1995). Open-ended therapy: Termination in marital and family therapy. In R. H. Mikesell, D. D. Lusterman, & S. H. McDaniel (Eds.), *Integrating family therapy: Handbook of family psychology and systems theory* (pp. 73–86). Washington, DC: American Psychological Association.

Lebow, J. (1997). The integrative revolution in couple and family therapy. *Family Process, 36,* 1–17.

Lebow, J. (2000). What does research tell us about couple and family therapies? *Journal of Clinical Psychology, 56,* 1083–1094.

Lebow, J., & Gurman, A. S. (1995). Research assessing couple and family therapy. *Annual Review of Psychology, 46,* 27–57.

Liddle, H. A. (1995). Conceptual and clinical dimensions of multidimensional, multisystems engagement strategy in family-based adolescent treatment. *Psychotherapy: Theory, Research, Practice, Training, 32,* 39–58.

Messer, S. B. (1991). The case formulation approach: Issues of reliability and validity. *American Psychologist, 46,* 1348–1350.

Messer, S. B., & Wampold, B. E. (2002). Let's face facts: Common factors are more potent than specific therapy ingredients. *Clinical Psychology: Science and Practice, 9,* 21–25.

Miller, S. D., Duncan, B. L., & Hubble, M. A. (1997). *Escape from Babel: Toward a unifying language for psychotherapy practice.* New York: Norton.

Norcross, J. C., & Goldfried, M. R. (Eds.). (2005). *Handbook of psychotherapy integration* (2nd ed.). London: Oxford University Press.

Orlinsky, D. E., & Howard, K. I. (1987). A generic model of psychotherapy. *Journal of Integrative and Eclectic Psychotherapy, 6,* 6–27.

Pinsof, W. M. (1995). *Integrative problem-centered therapy: A synthesis of family, individual, and biological therapies.* New York: Basic Books.

Sager, C. J. (1976). *Marriage contracts and couple therapy: Hidden forces in intimate relationships.* New York: Brunner-Mazel.

Wachtel, P. (1997). *Psychoanalysis, behavior therapy, and the relational world.* Washington, DC: American Psychological Association.

Walsh, F. (2002). A family resilience framework: Innovative practice applications. *Family Relation, 51,* 130–137.

17

CLIENT, NOT THEORY, DIRECTED: INTEGRATING APPROACHES ONE CLIENT AT A TIME

BARRY L. DUNCAN, JACQUELINE A. SPARKS, AND SCOTT D. MILLER

Riding home after her first therapy session, Anna felt like the weight of the world had been lifted from her. Since she had moved from another state, she had experienced one disappointment after another. Her parents insisted she could not make it on her own, the therapist she had been seeing before this one had abruptly ended the first session saying that she did not work with "borderlines," and her new doctor had told her to see a psychiatrist. She was beginning to think she needed a long hospital rest and some kind of medication. Instead, she was going home to her apartment with a renewed sense of hope—a belief that she was, in fact, a strong person who had overcome severe difficulties and had lived to tell about it. She felt that strange, forgotten sensation of actually liking herself. How could she make the most of this when she got back home? Maybe going through those piles of boxes and cleaning house would be a start.

Anna could be returning from her first session with a cognitive–behavioral therapist, a psychoanalyst, an eclectic combination of those or others, or a therapist who practiced a formal integrative approach. It apparently matters little. Despite extraordinary efforts, the preponderance of the data indicates that no one can declare any approach superior to any other. The fact that this finding, the so-called "dodo bird verdict," has emerged by accident—while researchers were trying to prove the superiority of their own models—makes it particularly worthy to consider (Duncan, Miller, & Sparks, 2004). But what does it mean? As Rosenzweig (1936) amazingly said some 70 years ago, because all approaches appear equal in effectiveness, there must be pantheoretical factors in operation that overshadow any presumed differences among approaches. Therapy works; however, how it works cannot be found in the insular explanations of the different theoretical orientations but rather in the factors common to all approaches

Research and writing on the common factors—dating back to Rosenzweig's (1936) and Frank's (1961) publications and forward to Lambert's (1992) scholarly and Wampold's (2001) meta-analytic reviews of the literature—provide the empirical backdrop for what we call *client-directed, outcome-informed* ways of working with clients. A client-directed, outcome-informed approach contains no fixed techniques, no invariant patterns in therapeutic process, and no causal theory regarding the concerns that bring people to therapy. Any therapy can be client directed and outcome informed. This comes about when (a) the factors across theories that account for successful outcome are intentionally enhanced, (b) the client's theory of change guides choices of technique and model, and (c) valid and reliable measures of the client's perceptions about the fit and progress of therapy direct options and provide the ultimate litmus test for success.

CLIENT-DIRECTED, OUTCOME-INFORMED CLINICAL WORK

The common factors can explain what opened the door for Anna to have a revived sense of herself and optimism about the future. Of the various factors identified, the data indicate that two, client–extratherapeutic factors and the therapeutic alliance, account for the majority of the variance in treatment outcome. Lambert (1992) suggested that 40% was attributable to the client–extratherapeutic factors and 30% to the therapeutic relationship. By comparison, model and technique factors and placebo were thought to contribute 15% each. Later meta-analytic research by Wampold (2001) confirmed and extended these findings, documenting larger roles for client–extratherapeutic, alliance, and placebo factors but a weaker contribution from models and techniques. For example, Wampold's analysis apportioned 54% of the variance of the impact of therapy to the alliance. Putting this into perspective, the amount of change attributable to the alliance is about 7 times that of specific model or technique. This view about change suggests a radical revamping of our ideas about clients and about what therapy should look like.

Such data, when combined with "the observed superior value, across numerous studies, of clients' assessment of the relationship in predicting the outcome" (Bachelor & Horvath, 1999, p. 140), make a strong empirical case for putting the client in the "driver's seat" of therapy. Successful treatment can be argued to be a matter of tapping into client resources and ensuring a positive experience of the alliance (Hubble, Duncan, & Miller, 1999). To these two elements, we add a third aspect, namely, the client's frame of reference regarding the presenting problem, its causes, and its potential remedies— what we term the *client's theory of change*.

Adopting the client's frame of reference as the defining "theory" for the therapy fits with several major findings from the extant, process-outcome literature. For example, researchers Orlinsky, Grawe, and Parks (1994) reported that "the quality of the client's participation in treatment stands out as the most important determinant of outcome" (p. 361). What better way to enlist clients' partnership than by accommodating their preexisting beliefs about the problem and the change process? Other data provide further support. Follow-up research from the landmark Treatment of Depression Collaborative Research Project showed that although outcome did not vary between treatments, congruence between a person's beliefs about the causes of his or her problems and the treatment approach offered resulted in stronger therapeutic alliances, increased duration, and improved rates of success (Elkin et al., 1999). In short, a client-directed approach calls for an elevation of the client's theory over the therapist's.

There is a good reason for this: Wampold's (2001) meta-analysis assigned only a 13% contribution to the impact of therapy, both general and specific factors combined. Of that 13%, a mere 8% is apportioned to the contribution of model effects. Of the total variance of change, only 1% could be assigned to specific technique. To the degree that models grow and thrive apart from the heart—the client's worldview and experience—they create disembodied therapeutic realities centered around therapists' theories and techniques. In so doing, model-focused approaches pass over the most potent player in therapy change, the client.

After a single session, Anna believed her therapist had heard her story (alliance) and she had hope that this therapy might help her (placebo). Anna decided to take her positive experience in the session into her own hands by initiating a concrete task for change (client factors). This early change was co-constructed through discussion of goals and steps in the first session (technique). Whatever else happened, the therapist had tapped into the gold mine of common factors by making room for Anna's ideas and energy to get things started on the right foot.

At first blush, tapping into client resources, ensuring the client's positive experience of the alliance, and accommodating therapy to the client's theory of change capitalizes on the two largest contributors to success. At the same time, closer examination makes clear that any concrete application across clients merely leads to the creation of another model. On this point, the research is clear: Whether client-directed or not, models matter little in terms of outcome.

To remedy the mere creation of yet another model and to give clients the voice in treatment that the research literature says they deserve, a client-directed approach can only be implemented one client at a time on the basis of that unique individual's perceptions of the progress and fit of therapy. To be client directed is to be outcome informed.

To be outcome informed begins with the recognition that the general trajectory of change in successful therapy is highly predictable, with most change occurring earlier rather than later in the treatment process (Brown, Dreis, & Nace, 1999). More specifically, the client's subjective experience of meaningful change in the first few visits strongly predicts whether a given pairing of client and therapist or treatment system will result in a successful outcome. Completing the outcome-informed one–two punch is to incorporate what researchers have already documented—that clients' early ratings of the alliance, like progress, are "significant predictors of final treatment outcome" (Bachelor & Horvath, 1999, p. 139).

Providing feedback to therapists regarding clients' experience of the alliance and progress in treatment has been shown to result in significant improvements in both client retention and outcome. Miller, Duncan, Brown, Sorrell, and Chalk (in press) found that clients of therapists who opted out of completing an alliance measure were twice as likely to drop out of treatment and 3 to 4 times more likely to have a negative or null outcome. In the same study, the average effect size of services at the agency where both outcome and alliance measures were used shifted from .5 to .8, a 60% increase.

As incredible as the results may appear, they are entirely consistent with findings from other researchers. In a meta-analysis of three studies, Lambert et al. (2003) reported that those therapeutic relationships at risk for a negative outcome that received formal feedback were, at the conclusion of therapy, better off than 65% of those without the benefit of information regarding progress. In another study, Whipple et al. (2003) found that clients whose therapists had access to outcome and alliance information were less likely to deteriorate, more likely to stay longer, and twice as likely to achieve a clinically significant change as clients of therapists without access to such information.

Client-based outcome and alliance feedback, therefore, is critical to clinical effectiveness. Therapists do not need to know in advance what approach to use for a given diagnosis as much as whether the current relationship is a good fit and, if not, to be able to adjust and accommodate early enough to maximize the chances of success. Anna's therapy is described to illustrate our approach. More important than theory, Anna's words give the best picture of an approach where the client is the essential integrative variable.

ANNA'S STORY
(DEMOGRAPHIC AND CLINICAL INFORMATION)

During Anna's first session, she spent much of the time discussing her reasons for her recent move and the dilemmas she now faced as "a stranger in a strange land." She described escaping to start a new life away from a former boyfriend who, at the break-up of their relationship, had begun a systematic campaign of harassment that included wiretapping her phone, hacking her computer, and terrorizing her with break-ins. Anna was convinced that this man had been spying on her through the use of remote microphones and cameras strategically placed throughout her private space. The result was an oppressive existence where she doubted her sanity and feared for her life. As a single parent, she had raised her son on her own by working as an "escort" for out-of-town businessmen. During the day, she attended a local nursing school, eventually earning her degree. Her nursing license had lapsed, however, because of the pressures of the abusive relationship, and she was now without means of support. She maintained herself through the financial gifts of her parents, who, Anna related, had physically and emotionally belittled her since she was a small child. Without friends and without a job, she felt compelled to swallow her pride and accept their help. Moving, as she had in her life, from one abusive situation to another, she came for therapy a demoralized and very sad person.

In between these stories of desperation, her eyes sparkled as she talked about her writing and the awards she had won at school for drama. She definitely had a way of telling a story, animating it with language and expression, now and then punctuated by a bright, musical laugh. She kept the therapist enthralled for the hour. Anna's therapist could not help communicating, both verbally and nonverbally, her fascination with Anna's tale of survival and her vibrant, artistic expression. Reflected back to Anna was an image of herself as a person who indeed had both the talent and the will to make a new life.

THE CLIENT'S THEORY OF CHANGE
(CASE FORMULATION AND THE THERAPEUTIC ALLIANCE)

Case formulation is a dynamic, ongoing endeavor of determining with the client how therapy is progressing, whether the alliance is on track, and how to enhance client engagement by exploring and incorporating the client's theory of change. Anna's story covered salient points related to her childhood, her determination to succeed as a single parent, and her present emotional and financial bankruptcy. Listening, a therapist might be seduced by various theories of psychopathology, including those having to do with paranoia, borderline personality, or codependency—any number of lenses through which her tale might be transcribed. Instead, a client-directed therapist values listening for those themes that recur and are focused on as relevant by the client. With appropriate therapist requests for more explanations of these points, Anna pinpointed what she believed to be key aspects of her dilemma, as shown by the following example:

> *Therapist:* Anna, you seemed to keep coming back to how you felt when you first realized your phone had been tapped. It must have been very horrifying when you learned that.

> *Anna:* My world changed from then on. Before, I had to deal with all the aftereffects of being hit and yelled at by my parents. But now, I felt like I didn't even own myself. It was like someone had sneaked into my soul.

From attentive listening and follow-up questions, the therapist learns the client's own meanings, her own interpretation of the effects of events in her life. From this absorbed tracking, the therapist can put one small toe into the client's world and see it as she sees it. What unfolds is the client's map of the problem—her ideas about how it came to be, what might help, and the role she would like the therapist to play in resolving it—in other words, the client's theory of change.

The client's theory of change is the quintessential element in formulating a congruent, workable problem definition and a viable plan for problem resolution. Within each client is a uniquely personal theory of change waiting for discovery, a framework for intervention to be unfolded and used for a successful outcome. To learn the client's theory, therapists may want to view themselves as aliens seeking a pristine understanding of a close encounter with the client's interpretations and cultural experiences. Clients' previous experiences with change and what they want from treatment and how those goals can be accomplished may be the most important pieces of information that can be obtained.

Using the client's theory occurs when a given therapeutic procedure fits or complements clients' preexisting beliefs about the change process. Therapists can simply listen and then amplify the stories, experiences, and interpretations that clients offer about their problems as well as their ideas about how those problems might be best addressed. The degree and intensity of our input vary and are driven by the client's expectations of our role. The client's theory of change is an "emergent reality" that unfolds from a conversation structured by the therapist's curiosity about the client's ideas, attitudes, and speculations about change. As the client's theory is uncovered, client-directed therapists implement the client's identified solutions or seek an approach that fits the client's theory and provides possibilities for change.

Anna believed that her experiences growing up in an abusive household had created a template that molded future events in her life. She wanted to step off the treadmill of abuse and resist the debilitating fear it had wrought in her life. The therapist, seeking to learn Anna's view of what kind of help she preferred, made a direct inquiry:

Therapist: How can I be of most help to you?

Anna: I would like you first to believe what I'm telling you. Without that, we can't go any further. Then, I'd like you to look for patterns in my life and point them out to me, so that I don't have to keep repeating them.

The therapist, valuing clients above theory, readily assured Anna that she believed her. In the past, those who had attempted to convince Anna that she did not see the world correctly (i.e., from their point of view) had alienated her and forfeited any chance of helping.

However, simply saying "I believe you" was not enough. The therapist conveyed her interest in Anna as a storyteller and her enjoyment of being with her. From this, the intangibles of a powerful relationship were born—empathy, trust, and an emotional bond. Quickly, the issue of believing or not believing in the story was put aside, so that more immediate and relevant issues, the client's goals and preferences for therapist intervention, could be clarified.

MONITORING THE ALLIANCE AND OUTCOME

Exploring the client's theory of change helps establish a working therapy alliance. Therapists, however, cannot assume that their evaluation of the quality of the therapy climate corresponds to their clients' perceptions. Clearly, then, it is critical for therapists to attend closely to the alliance developed with their clients and regularly monitor its quality. Although direct questions are useful, a formal alliance assessment can more accurately confirm and monitor this crucial predictor of therapy outcome. To make sure the alliance was on track, Anna's therapist used the Session Rating Scale (SRS; Duncan et al., 2003; see Appendix 17.1), a valid and reliable four-item analog alliance measure. This measure asks clients to rate the session according to the various aspects of the alliance. Taking less than a minute to integrate into the session, the SRS effortlessly elicits client disagreements about the therapeutic process so that the clinician may change to better fit client expectations.

Client-directed, outcome-informed therapy also includes ongoing use of the client's perception of progress in therapy, in real time and in every session. In Anna's case, the therapist used the Outcome Rating Scale (ORS; Miller, Duncan, Brown, Sparks, & Claud, 2003; see Appendix 17.2). Also a valid, reliable, and feasible four-item visual analog scale, the ORS taps into the three variables that researchers and practicing therapists consider relevant and strong predictors of client progress—symptoms, interpersonal relationship, and social role functioning (Ogles, Lambert, & Masters, 1996). Taken by the client at the beginning of each session, it provides a snapshot of how things are going from week to week. Information learned from this instrument is fed back into the therapy process, prompting the therapist and client to discuss whether they should proceed in the same manner or search for new ways of working. Also on the table is a dialogue about whether another type of support or different therapist might be of more benefit. Assessment no longer precedes and dictates intervention; rather, it weaves in and out of the therapeutic process as a pivotal component of change itself.

ANNA'S CHANGE (CHANGE MECHANISMS AND THE ROLE OF THE APPROACH IN GUIDING INTERVENTION)

In the first two sessions, Anna and her therapist explored Anna's theory of change. The therapist attempted to understand Anna's perceptions of her current problems and what she was expecting from her therapist and from therapy. She then followed Anna's lead with the flow and focus of interview questions, comments, and suggestions. Along with the intangible personal connection, that liking of each other, a positive working relationship flourished, confirmed by the early high SRS scores.

When asked, Anna identified what she felt would be starting points for regaining her life and dignity. These, rather than therapist- or theory-driven goals and objectives, became the traditional "service plan."

- Goal 1: Clean apartment
- Goal 2: Stop smoking
- Goal 3: Get a job

The therapist expressed her appreciation for these doable and concrete tasks. Together, they examined obstacles and strategies, formulating initial steps. The therapist encouraged Anna to proceed slowly and to realize that results might be fast or slow. At the same time, she commented that what mattered were Anna's apparent determination and the resourcefulness she had exhibited in surviving the adverse circumstances of her life.

Despite an auspicious beginning, Anna's scores on the ORS by Sessions 3 and 4 indicated a continued serious level of distress. Corresponding with an increasing isolation from her parents and from her son, Anna's scores were even lower by Session 5. Research not only points to early improvement as an indicator of eventual positive outcome, but also that early deterioration predicts the opposite (Lambert et al., 2003). Consequently, Anna's therapist became alarmed for Anna's well-being and for the implications of lack of early improvement on the eventual outcome of therapy. She brought these concerns into the conversation:

Therapist:	Anna, I know we seem to be doing fine with how we're talking and going over a lot of things in your life, but I'm worried that from what I see here [*showing Anna the graph of her ORS scores*], something is missing. What do we need to do to make sure that this line starts going up, and definitely not down any further?
Anna:	Yeah. I know what you mean. We don't want it to just sit there. It's great coming here, but I really want to get on with my life. I feel like I'm in this rut. I really hate being where there are so many people and cars. I miss going outside and walking in the woods and seeing hills. I feel like I'm in a prison in my apartment. The more I want to get things cleaned up, the more depressed I feel.
Therapist:	What ideas do you have about getting out of this rut?
Anna:	I don't really know. . . I know my friend Renée said I could come up and visit her any time. I think I need to get away for a few days—get some perspective.

Anna's therapist might have thought that "getting away" was just another name for "avoidance." Instead, she embraced this suggestion as one generated by a wisdom greater than her own: her client's insight into her situation and a possible solution.

When Anna returned 2 weeks later, her face glowed with a new tan from hiking outdoors and with an expression of peace her therapist had not seen before. During her trip away, Anna had reconnected with an old friend, reaffirming her view of herself as a valuable person. Her friend had been able to help Anna understand her son's developmental stage as troubling but not unusual. She also advised her to step back from her parents whenever possible, not letting them have free reign into every aspect of her life. Anna embraced these warnings as significant revelations. Anna called this a gift of understanding. Second, she met her friend's neighbor, Eileen, spending hours each day at her house chatting about life and love. Eileen described her own experience dealing with a wayward child and a series of damaging personal and family relationships. Still, this woman had maintained her pride and now was assisting others at a local women's shelter. Anna called this the gift of inspiration. Finally, on her return flight home, she struck up a conversation with a woman sitting next to her. This person described her rise from owning nothing and having no education to becoming a successful independent businesswoman, the owner of several local antique shops. This, according to Anna, was the gift of hope.

The therapist could have responded in several ways to Anna's newfound optimism. She could have welcomed the good news but cautioned a realistic appraisal of what this really meant for Anna's life dilemmas. She could have dismissed them altogether as distractions and steered the conversation back to the goals and problems at hand. She could even have felt a twinge of jealousy that such "breakthroughs" had happened outside of therapy and not within the confines of a trained clinician's office. Instead, Anna's therapist rejoiced with Anna and wondered in amazement that life had somehow conspired to have such events happen so serendipitously, just when she needed it. She speculated that perhaps there was more afoot than met the eye. Anna, as someone who had struggled in her life with issues of faith, mused as follows:

> Anna: You know, before I left, I really just felt like not going on. But now, I feel like God is speaking to me, like He isn't through with me. Now, I've got to figure out what He wants me to do.

> Therapist: Wow. That is amazing. And still, you had the eyes to see it, because, you know, it seems sometimes God may show things, but no one sees them.

Here, the therapist celebrated Anna's turn toward a new meaning for the events she had experienced. She did not need to have a particular pastoral counseling background, nor did she need to question Anna's explanations. She simply needed to capitalize on the sense Anna made of the diverse experiences along with the revitalized energy this instilled in her. At the same time, she noted that it was Anna who "saw" the connections where she may have simply overlooked them, unaware of their value in her life. Rather than persuade clients of insights more in line with the therapist's clinical training, client-directed therapists take their lead from the unique client-generated explanations for and solutions to life dilemmas.

Anna concluded at the end of the session that she needed to be part of a social situation where she could meet people and discuss issues of faith and the still nagging fallout from a life marred by abuse. Her therapist readily responded with a list of local groups that met informally and formally to talk about a variety of interests, including art, abuse survival, and religion. Several weeks later, Anna joined a woman's violence group and began to explore the churches in her area. It was not until she found a social and spiritual niche that she could bring herself to confront past memories, going through the boxes in her apartment and throwing away the pain, piece by piece. Gradually, her apartment became a home, with a small work of art here, a flower vase there, and books filling the shelves. Gradually, Anna's newfound sense of confidence began to shine forth, attracting friends and surprising those in her family who had long ago written her off.

AN ONGOING STORY (TERMINATION)

Anna's story, like our own, is yet unfolding. Her ORS score at the sixth "revelation session" jumped beyond the clinical cutoff, the total ORS score on all four dimensions where those scoring above tend not to seek therapy. Calling for a discussion of termination, over the next several sessions, her total score fluctuated but did not return to the desperately low level of before. Anna and her therapist discussed the scores at termination and concluded that Anna's higher scores on the individual and interpersonal scales signaled changes in her sense of herself and level of depression. They also concluded that there was a general improvement in how she was relating to significant people in her life. Her lower scores on social and overall domains indicated that she needed to become reemployed and to develop a core group of friends in her new environment.

Progress in client-directed, outcome-informed therapy is conceptualized as occurring within the framework of common factors. First, Anna and her therapist connected with one another in a genuine and appreciative relationship. It also speaks to the therapist's faith in clients, a faith grounded in her preferred view of human beings as capable of transforming their lives. This faith, then, became at least one source of hope for Anna. Experiencing how her therapist did not succumb, as others had, to a pessimistic view, her own belief in herself grew and became dominant in her quest for change. Second, Anna's therapist elicited in conversation Anna's views about her problem and the kind of help she desired. Her theory of change became the touchstone for collaboratively devising goals, interventions, and therapeutic directions. Anna took it from there. Primed to believe in herself and in the possibility of a different kind of life, she made use of situations occurring in her everyday world to fashion a new identity and a new possible future. The therapist amplified these new steps, facilitating the next. In this way, Anna, not theory, was the variable that determined the what, how, when, and where of therapy.

When Anna was not improving by Session 5, there was no guesswork or wait-and-see involved. The ORS provided the pivotal information needed to sound the alarm. Her therapist immediately voiced her concern, and both set to work to head off either a premature termination or some other kind of unsuccessful conclusion. Later ORS feedback gave clear indications of where progress was occurring, where more was needed, and when therapy could stop. Throughout therapy, Anna and her therapist had the reassurance provided by the SRS that their relationship was strong; the SRS provided a built-in way to correct it should it veer off course. This way of conducting therapy, grounded in the clients' preferences and immediate feedback, recommends modes of reimbursement based on outcome instead of diagnosis, transforms the role therapists play, and elevates clients to their rightful positions as leaders in their own change.

CONCLUSION

The history of psychotherapy can be characterized as the search for the specific processes that reliably produce change. Few would debate the success of this perspective in medicine, where the development of treatments containing specific therapeutic ingredients has led to the near extinction of a number of once fatal diseases. Unfortunately, for all the claims and thousands of research studies, psychotherapy in general and the integrative movement in particular can boast of no similar accomplishments. Theory, however elegant, does not matter much to the effectiveness of psychotherapy.

The love affair with theory relegates clients to insignificant roles in bringing about change. As theories proliferate, so do their specialized languages, categories, and arsenal of techniques. All such articulations take place outside the awareness of those most affected. When therapists' models, whether integrative or not, crowd our thinking, there is little room left for clients' models—their ideas about their predicaments and what it might take to fix them—to take shape.

The integration movement began as a goodwill effort to stem the tide of conceptual confusion long characteristic of the field of psychotherapy. Given the empirical evidence, we have come to believe that seeking integration in terms of therapeutic process is a mistake; indeed, it became simply more of the same kind of thinking that spawned the very rivalries the movement was supposed to address. In contrast, we believe that the best hope for integration lies in clients and their perspectives on the fit and benefit of the services they receive. Psychotherapy integration must occur at the individual client level. That can only happen by tailoring the combination or blend of approaches to client ideas using direct client feedback about the outcome of therapy, one client at a time.

APPENDIX 17.1
OUTCOME RATING SCALE (ORS)

Name _____ Age (Yrs):____ Sex: M / F
Session # ____ Date: _____
Who is filling out this form? Please check one: Self_____   Other_____
If other, what is your relationship to this person? _____

Looking back over the last week, including today, help us understand how you have been feeling by rating how well you have been doing in the following areas of your life, where marks to the left represent low levels and marks to the right indicate high levels. *If you are filling out this form for another person, please fill out according to how you think he or she is doing.*

Individually
(Personal well-being)

I--I

Interpersonally
(Family, close relationships)

I--I

Socially
(Work, school, friendships)

I--I

Overall
(General sense of well-being)

I--I

APPENDIX 17.2
SESSION RATING SCALE (SRS V.3.0)

Name _____ Age (Yrs):____
ID# _____ Sex: M / F
Session # ____ Date: _____

Please rate today's session by placing a hash mark on the line nearest to the description that
best fits your experience.

Relationship

I did not feel heard,
understood, and   I--I   I felt heard,
respected   understood, and
                                                                                                  respected

Goals and Topics

We did *not* work on or   We worked on and
talk about what I   I--I   talked about what I
wanted to work on and   wanted to work on and
talk about   talk about

Approach or Method

The therapist's   The therapist's
approach is a not a   I--I   approach is a good fit
good fit for me.   for me.

Overall

There was something   I--I   Overall, today's
missing in the session   session was right for
today   me

REFERENCES

Bachelor, A., & Horvath, A. (1999). The therapeutic relationship. In M. A. Hubble, B. L. Duncan, & S. D. Miller (Eds.), *The heart and soul of change: What works in therapy* (pp. 133–178). Washington DC: American Psychological Association.

Brown, J., Dreis, S., & Nace, D. K. (1999). What really makes a difference in psychotherapy outcome? Why does managed care want to know? In M. A. Hubble, B. L. Duncan, & S. D. Miller (Eds.), *The heart and soul of change: What works in therapy* (pp. 389–406). Washington DC: American Psychological Association.

Duncan, B. L., Miller, S. D., & Sparks, J. A. (2004). *The heroic client: A revolutionary way to improve effectiveness through client-directed, outcome-informed therapy.* San Francisco: Jossey Bass.

Duncan, B. L., Miller, S. D., Sparks, J. A., Claud, D. A., Reynolds, L. R., Brown, J., & Johnson, L. D. (2003). The Session Rating Scale: Preliminary psychometric properties of a "working" alliance measure. *Journal of Brief Therapy, 3,* 3–12.

Elkin, I., Yamaguchi, J., Arnkoff, D. B., Glass, C., Sotsky, S., & Krupnick, J. (1999). "Patient–treatment fit" and early engagement in therapy. *Psychotherapy Research, 9,* 437–451.

Frank, J. D. (1961). *Persuasion and healing: A comparative study of psychotherapy.* Baltimore: Johns Hopkins University Press.

Hubble, M. A., Duncan, B. L., & Miller, S. D. (Eds.). (1999). *The heart and soul of change: What works in therapy.* Washington, DC: American Psychological Association.

Lambert, M. J. (1992). Implications of outcome research for psychotherapy integration. In J. C. Norcross & M. R. Goldfried (Eds.), *Handbook of psychotherapy integration* (pp. 94–129). New York: Basic Books.

Lambert, M. J., Whipple, J. L., Hawkins, E. J., Vermeersch, D. A., Nielsen, S. L., & Smart, D. W. (2003). Is it time for clinicians routinely to track patient outcome? A meta-analysis. *Clinical Psychology, 10,* 228–301.

Miller, S. D., & Duncan, B. L. (2000). *The Outcome Rating Scale.* Available at http://www.talkingcure.com

Miller, S. D., Duncan, B. L., Brown, J., Sorrell, R., & Chalk, M. B. (in press). Using outcome to inform and improve treatment outcomes. *Journal of Brief Therapy.*

Miller, S. D., Duncan, B. L., Brown, J., Sparks, J. A., & Claud, D. A. (2003). The Outcome Rating Scale: A preliminary study of the reliability, validity, and feasibility of a brief visual analogue measure. *Journal of Brief Therapy, 2,* 91–100.

Miller, S. D., Duncan, B. L., & Johnson, L. D. (2000). *The Session Rating Scale.* Available at http://www.talkingcure.com

Ogles, B., Lambert, M. J., & Masters, K. S. (1996). *Assessing outcome in clinical practice.* Needham Heights, MA: Allyn & Bacon.

Orlinsky, D. E., Grawe, K., & Parks, B. K. (1994). Process and outcome in psychotherapy—Noch einmal. In A. E. Bergin & S. L. Garfield (Eds.), *Handbook of psychotherapy and behavior change* (4th ed., pp. 270–378). New York: Wiley.

Rosenzweig, S. (1936). Some implicit common factors in diverse methods of psychotherapy. *American Journal of Orthopsychiatry*, 6, 412–515.

Wampold, B. E. (2001). *The great psychotherapy debate: Models, methods, and findings.* Hillsdale, NJ: Erlbaum.

Whipple, J. L., Lambert, M. J., Vermeersch, D. A., Smart, D. W., Nielsen, S. L., & Hawkins, E. J. (2003). Improving the effects of psychotherapy: The use of early identification of treatment and problem-solving strategies in routine practice. *Journal of Counseling Psychology, 50,* 59–68.

18

THE CLIENT AS ACTIVE SELF-HEALER

ARTHUR C. BOHART

My integrative approach (Bohart, 2000; Bohart & Tallman, 1999; Tallman & Bohart, 1999) is based on the hypothesis that the client is the most important common factor in making therapy work. I briefly explain how I developed this hypothesis and what its implications are. The hypothesis resulted from an attempt to explain a variety of puzzling research findings, such as the dodo bird verdict (that all therapies work about the same for most problems; Wampold, 2001), that techniques do not appear to have unique outcome effects (Wampold, 2001), that therapist experience and training do not seem to make a substantial difference in outcome (see Bohart & Tallman, 1999), that self-help procedures appear to work nearly as well as professionally provided therapy (see Bohart & Tallman, 1999), that clients' perceptions of what is going on in therapy correlates more strongly with outcome than therapists' perceptions (Orlinsky, Grawe, & Parks, 1994), and that the therapist–patient relationship is more important than particular techniques (Wampold, 2001). This set of research findings makes sense if we postulate the client as the active agent who uses whatever positive structure is provided to solve problems.

In the typical medical model of therapy, the therapist is the expert who diagnoses the client's problem and then treats it with specific interventions. Most therapeutic theories describe change as resulting from the therapist's favorite interventions operating on dysfunctional client structures in order to modify them. For instance, interpretations in psychoanalysis "strengthen" the patient's ego, and cognitive–behavioral therapists "restructure" clients' dysfunctional cognitions, or, using exposure, modify clients' "fear structures." This approach to therapy can be modeled as follows:

Therapists → operate on clients' dysfunctional processes with various interventions → to effect change.

By contrast, Karen Tallman and I (Bohart & Tallman, 1999) have argued that it is clients who make therapy work by operating on therapists' interventions, from whatever school of practice their therapists come from, to make change. This model can be portrayed as follows:

Clients → operate on therapists' interventions → to produce change.

The hypothesis does not assume that clients can "make change" out of anything. Therapists must provide positive and useful learning structures. However, each of the major approaches to therapy does provide such structures. Most important is the provision of a relationship that supports, engages, and mobilizes clients' open involvement. Research has shown that client participation and involvement is the single most important factor in making therapy work (Orlinsky et al., 1994).

We construe therapy as education. Each of the major approaches to therapy provides different learning opportunities. The first and most basic learning opportunity is that of an empathic workspace, paralleling client-centered therapy. By *empathic workspace* I mean the provision of a safe, structured space within which the client can actively explore and think through problems. This may be akin to having a good dissertation mentor who helps a student think through the student's own ideas. The main thing the therapist contributes is sustained and focused empathic understanding.

The second learning opportunity is the provision of a relationship that fosters direct interactive learning. Clients learn (a) that they are worth listening to and worthy of respect; (b) that they, in collaboration with a therapist, can figure things out over time; and (c) that they can master things. This kind of learning is emphasized in modern psychodynamic, humanistic, and recent radical behavioral approaches.

The third learning opportunity is guiding, coconstructive dialogue. Here the therapist functions like a good teacher, who asks thought-provoking questions and provides new perspectives. One example is psychodynamic interpretation. Another is Socratic questioning in cognitive therapy.

The fourth learning opportunity is the use of structured exercises that promote the client's creativity. In school, this is akin to the use of improvisation exercises in acting classes. In therapy, examples include the use of "chair" techniques by experiential therapists and solution-focused procedures where clients are asked to imagine how their future might turn out (the "miracle question").

The fifth learning opportunity is direct tutoring. This is characteristic of cognitive–behavioral therapy. Cognitive–behavioral therapists tutor skills. Challenging dysfunctional cognitions is not only an example of coconstructive dialogue, it is also used by cognitive therapists as teaching a skill. Another example is the use of exposure, which is used to directly teach getting over and mastering fear.

Each of these five learning opportunities may be useful to different clients or to the same client at different times. In the case below, I focus on three: empathic workspace, coconstructive dialogue, and structured exercises for creativity. In all cases, what is most important is true collaboration. By true collaboration, I do not mean getting clients to comply with my agenda, but rather therapy as a genuine "meeting of minds"—two intelligences in dialogue.

CASE STUDY

Cynthia was a 32-year-old community college mathematics professor. Her presenting problem was anxiety, along with low-level depression. Cynthia had been experiencing an ongoing sense of anxiousness and worry for several months. Occasionally it interfered with her ability to concentrate. She also reported feeling a lack of energy.

Cynthia was involved with a solid, sensible, 35-year-old man named Fred. Fred wanted her to marry him, give up her job to be a housewife, and become a mother. Cynthia's relationship history had been spotty. During adolescence she had not dated extensively. Instead, she described herself as focused on her grades. She had had one serious boyfriend during college. She reported that she had kept delaying the issue of whether she wanted to get married and have a family. Her parents strongly wanted her to do just that; her mother had been a full-time housewife and her father a successful businessman. Her two brothers had followed the straight and narrow, one becoming a doctor, the other a lawyer. Both were married and had children. One recently had had another baby. On Christmas, Cynthia felt bad when they brought their kids home and she had none. She knew her mother in particular was disappointed.

Cynthia's anxiety had "just grown" over time, with no clear precipitating event, although Cynthia thought it was related to the birth of her brother's baby, getting involved with Fred and his expressing a desire to get married, and turning 32. Turning 32 had bothered her because it dawned on her that she was getting close to that magic age of 35, which she had heard from childhood was the upper limit for having babies. She knew objectively that

that was not true, that women were having babies past that age. However, the number 35 had become a kind of symbol of her need to make a choice.

There were two other complicating factors. First, Cynthia did not want to give up her career and be a mother. To the contrary, she was considering going back to school to get a doctorate in math. Getting married and having a child would make that more difficult. She was also not sure she actually wanted to have a child. She could not decide how much her desire to have a child was a personal "want" of her own or a "should" imposed on her by her family.

The second major conflict was that she was not sure of her sexuality. Prior to her relationship with Fred, she had been involved with a woman, Marta. She had never thought of herself as a lesbian. Marta was a fellow instructor in English at the community college that Cynthia worked at, and they had gotten involved and had carried on an affair for 6 months. Marta had been the one to break it off when Marta had gotten involved with someone else. This had caused Cynthia a good deal of despair, and it was clear she was not over Marta yet. It was not long after the end of the affair with Marta that she had gotten involved with Fred.

Cynthia's conflicts then were as follows: Should I marry Fred and have a family? Or should I go back to graduate school? Am I gay, am I heterosexual, am I bisexual? What do I want in terms of my personal life?

My integrative approach is a "meta-model," which can be used with a variety of theoretical approaches. My particular approach is grounded in client-centered therapy. As is typical of that orientation, I did not formally formulate Cynthia's case. Had I done that, I could have formulated Cynthia as (a) suffering from a failure to mourn the loss of her relationship with Marta, (b) having unresolved conflicts from childhood with her parents, (c) having internalized "shoulds" that were causing her problems (dysfunctional cognitions: I must be normal, have a family, please my parents), or (d) experiencing an anxiety disorder requiring the use of a manualized treatment program for anxiety, or medication.

However, I believe that the client is the expert on his or her life and that the meaning of symptoms will become apparent through exploration. I do not automatically assume that generalized anxiety disorder, for instance, is a conditioning disorder needing a behavioral protocol. On the contrary, I stay open to the possibility that some kinds of generalized anxiety represent problems in meaning, either problems in deciding on a meaningful direction in life or problems in personal meaning based in unresolved childhood issues (as in a psychodynamic formulation). Because I did not decide, assuming that the meaning of Cynthia's symptoms would be revealed through our interaction, it could have turned out that a behavioral conditioning approach or a psychodynamic might fit the best, in which case we would have discussed switching to one of those (or I could have referred her elsewhere for help).

In fact, Cynthia's focus was not so much on her anxiety and depression as it was on her conflicts. Cynthia herself was inclined to see the problems as centering around difficult fundamental life choices she needed to make and the conflicts involved. She also did believe that an important component had to do with her family, her parents, and their approval and disapproval. Furthermore, although we discussed medication, she was not interested in that approach.

I also did not formulate her problems using a theory of psychopathology because I do not believe that the theory of psychopathology matters. Psychopathology could be any number of things: biological, cognitive, psychodynamic, systemic, or humanistic. My theory is not about what causes pathology; it is about what helps people get over it. There is a difference between mechanisms that cause problems and those that facilitate recovery. What helps people get over problems, no matter what their causes, is helping them mobilize their capacities for self-healing and self-righting.

There were three factors that emerged as interfering with Cynthia's productive problem-solving capacities. One was self-criticism. Self-criticism is a part of some theories of psychopathology. As far as I am concerned, independent of whether it contributes to psychopathology, the problem with self-criticism is that it gets in the way of positive problem-solving processes. Cynthia's self-doubt took the form of wondering if there was something "fundamentally wrong" with her. Such "entity-oriented" thinking has been found by Carol Dweck and others (Dweck & Leggett, 1988; Tallman, 1996) to interfere with the ability to productively cope with difficult learning challenges. When something is not going right, individuals thinking in this way are more likely to focus on what the problems mean about them than on what can be done to proactively solve them (a productive "task focus"). Cynthia was so concerned with deciding whether she was okay that she was getting in the way of her productive problem-solving capacity.

A second interfering factor was thinking in an "either–or" categorical way about herself and her problems: I cannot do anything until I decide whether I am heterosexual, bisexual, or lesbian; I must categorically decide either to get married and have a child or go back to school. Categorical thinking is also part of some theories of psychopathology. From my perspective, the problem with either–or thinking is that it makes it difficult to change when life challenges outstrip one's belief system. Such thinking is not psychopathology, however; there are plenty of people who think in an either–or fashion who get along well in life.

A third factor that was getting in the way of Cynthia's productive problem-solving capacities was feeling frightened and threatened. When one is frightened and feeling unsafe, one may function in a defensive mode rather than feel free to engage in the cognitive, emotional, and behavioral risk taking needed for productive problem solving.

I believe that the most fundamental change mechanism in therapy is clients using their intelligence to sort out their problems. What I offer as a therapist is first a supportive, empathic relationship in which the client can feel safe enough to move out of a defensive, frightened stance. Second, in collaboration with the client as agent, I offer different types of learning opportunities that the client decides might be useful.

Empathic Workspace

Following our integrative model, my "default" position is to offer an "empathic workspace," à la client-centered therapy, where the client can think, explore, and reflect. Clients have the opportunity to "spread out their problems on a table," so to speak. Often they are then able to see patterns and relationships and figure things out themselves.

Cynthia was not quite sure where to start, so we started with what was uppermost on her mind: the loss of her relationship with Marta. Through the first few sessions, I primarily tried to empathically understand what Cynthia was expressing and experiencing. A recent qualitative study by Bohart and Byock (2003) found that clients may use empathic understanding responses for at least three different possible purposes: to feel supported and validated, for information-processing purposes (gaining insight, accessing feelings, differentiating information), and for an interpersonal function of establishing and building common ground. Cynthia used empathic understanding responses in all three of these ways.

The first thing Cynthia seemed to be looking for was a response to this question: "Do I make sense?" It was clear that my ability to understand in an appreciative and validating way helped her feel supported, validated, and less "crazy." Clients have a hard time productively evaluating their problems when they worry that they do not make sense. Having an empathic listener demonstrate through understanding that the client and the conflicts are sensible is reassuring, and clients can use this to free up their capacity for intelligent evaluation and solution finding. This happened with Cynthia, who spontaneously began to reduce self-doubting and began to generate reevaluations of her relationship with Marta on her own.

Clients use empathic responses in a second way, as an aid to their thinking and experiencing process. Here clients use the therapist's responses informationally to "test" their understandings, as "tools" for digging out further implications, and as a kind of mirroring prosthetic device for gaining a different perspective on their thoughts, problems, and experience. As has been pointed out elsewhere (Bohart & Byock, 2003), the "mirror" analogy can be misleading. When people look in mirrors, they do not do so motionlessly. Instead they move, creating variation so that they can see themselves from different angles. Analogously, good empathic understanding responses are not simply still reflections but come through another's experience and perceptions so that they always "come back" in a slightly different form. Clients see their experience as reflected through another's eyes, thereby gaining a slightly different angle on it.

Using these two functions of empathic responses, Cynthia did clarify and discover components of her experience of loss with Marta. One thing she explored was the issue of her attractiveness. Did Marta leave her for another because she was not sufficiently physically attractive? Marta had wanted a "pretty" girl friend, and although Cynthia was nice looking, she worried that perhaps she had not been nice looking enough. As she explored this, she realized that Marta was a bit of an adventurer, not given to fidelity, and that it probably was not Cynthia's attractiveness that was the issue but rather Marta's chance for a new conquest. This was disappointing to Cynthia, because Cynthia was a faithful type and had been thinking that she might form a commitment to Marta. This realization about Marta helped her let go of the relationship.

A third function of empathic understanding responses is that of establishing a common ground, where therapists and clients mutually come to understand one another better. Clients understand therapists better through therapists' attempts to understand them, and vice versa. This leads to a shared coexperiencing and cothinking, where each participant "feeds off" the other's thinking and experiencing in an upward spiral of discovery and creative problem-solving. The analogy is to jazz musicians, who build off of one another's improvisations. When this happens in therapy, it is not accurate to say that the client is "internally reflecting" while the therapist accompanies the client. Instead, thinking is being shared and carried forward through the "dance" of the two participants together. This also includes an educative function whereby the therapist (in this case me) who was not familiar with lesbian experience was educated by Cynthia about that experience.

It was through this kind of coparticipation that Cynthia and I both began to understand that Marta would not have met her needs, and Cynthia was able to continue the process of letting her go. Cynthia came to make some peace with losing Marta. She still was not sure what she wanted to do in terms of her major life choices, so we moved on to them next.

Guiding Coconstructive Dialogue

There was a natural, organic evolution in Cynthia's concern from the issue of Marta to the more entangled issues of (a) am I lesbian or bisexual; (b) do I want to marry a man, in this case Fred, and have a family; (c) do I want to pursue a doctorate or give that up; (d) how does all of this interface with my feelings about my family and their acceptance or nonacceptance of me; and (e) how would I feel if I adopted a lifestyle that was "not normal" in the mainstream's eyes?

These issues were complexly interrelated, and Cynthia would cycle from one to another as she explored them. The logic of connection was an associative logic, based both on semantic and emotional linkages. Talking about her mother would bring up issues having to do with career choice, relationship choice, or children, and she might side-track off on those for a while. Those issues would then lead her back to issues with her family, and so on. Thus, the course of therapy was not one of single-minded pursuit of a given topic, as in writing, where one forms a topic sentence and then develops everything from that. Instead, her path of exploration meant cycling and recycling through the various connections that formed the net of these topics.

At any given moment, I would try to participate in the exploration activity through my empathic understanding responses as well as through both sharing my own thoughts and hypotheses and suggesting exercises when they struck me as possibly useful. As a teacher, I share my perspective, experiences, and interpretations with my students. Ideally they do not swallow them whole, but chew on them and integrate them in with their own thinking, either by partially accepting them, by rejecting them but coming up with their own alternatives, or by creatively responding to them and developing their own ideas based on them. I hope that the same thing happens in therapy.

As an example, as someone who had felt "different" myself as a teenager, I wondered if Cynthia had felt "different" as a teenager and perhaps earlier, and if that had bothered her. Cynthia readily acknowledged this and used it to explore and identify some of the bad feelings she had had as a teenager for being different from her family and other teens—more interested in intellectual matters, less traditionally achievement oriented, and not actively interested in heterosexual relationships. Subsequently, I also wondered if she might have felt some pride in feeling different at the same time. Cynthia particularly felt recognized by this speculation, saying "Yes!" Cynthia used these speculations to help her evaluate how much "feeling different" was okay with her. She came to feel that in some sense, she had courageously chosen a different path from her siblings and parents. Her achieving the sense that she had courageously chosen to be different rather than seeing herself as defective for not fitting in helped her feel better.

I also speculated that her self-criticism might be getting in her way of making a choice. She was able to empathically recognize her self-criticism (instead of criticizing herself for being self-critical). She spontaneously discovered that self-criticism had been a proactive attempt on her part to try to figure out what was best. This helped her to feel more in control if it. She was then able to take seriously the "voices" within her that were calling her to pursue her math career. This issue emerged as the most central one over time, with the issue of relationship becoming second. As she was able to "listen" to this voice, she began to be more able to critically weigh and evaluate the pros and cons of choosing a career path that might conflict (a) with her relationship with Fred, (b) with her parents' wishes, and (c) with possibly having children.

Structured Exercises for Exploration

A third kind of learning opportunity that therapy provides is structured opportunities for the client to explore problems. Several times, I used the Gestalt empty chair and two-chair techniques with Cynthia (Elliott, Watson, Goldman, & Greenberg, 2004). The two-chair technique was used to help her explore the split between her desire to pursue a doctorate in math and her critical side that said she should be choosing to pursue having a family. What came out of this was greater clarity that she did indeed want to pursue a doctoral degree. However, it also turned out that this was a genuine split. It was not merely between a want (I want to pursue my degree) and a should (I should want marriage and children). Rather, it was between two wants: she truly did want to go on for a doctorate in math, but it turned out that she also did want to have children. Then she had to go through a bit of a mourning process of letting go of having children, if she was to go on for a doctorate, or at least she had to realize that that was a risk.

The empty chair procedure was used to give her a tool for working through issues with her parents, Marta, and Fred. Role-playing dialogues with Marta helped her complete the process of letting go of that relationship. Role plays with Fred helped her clarify her feelings about that relationship. Role plays with her mother and father helped her further differentiate her wants from theirs while realizing that she cherished her connections with them as well and would work to maintain them as best she could while also choosing what was best for her.

The final example of this kind of learning opportunity, and the one that seemed to help Cynthia cement her choice, was when I used the miracle question from solution-focused therapy: "If you went to sleep tonight, and during the night a miracle occurred, and when you woke up, your problem was solved, but you didn't know it had been solved, what would be the first clue that something had occurred during the night to solve your problem?" Cynthia's answer was that she would have a clear sense that it was the right thing for her to go on for a doctorate. This seemed to ring true for her, and Cynthia decided that that was what she was going to do.

Her career choice had been the focal point of the exploration for most of the sessions after our early work on the relationship with Marta. During this time, we also explored her sexual orientation. As she explored it, she came to think that she was not sure "what she was," and she began to distrust labels and began to wonder if she had to be "one thing or another." The affair with Marta had been passionate, and for a time she had thought she wanted to have Marta as her partner, but she now thought that she might just as well fall in love with a man. She liked Fred, but she also had the sense that Fred was perhaps a bit of a rebound choice after Marta. What she realized was that she did not want to marry him, at least now. She also realized that she wanted to stay in the relationship and see how it went. So, as of termination, she was still not entirely clear where she stood on sexual orientation and relationships.

It was at this point that Cynthia decided to terminate therapy. Her anxiety and depression had considerably diminished. She had decided to pursue her doctorate. She was willing to accept the possibility that she might not have children. She had stopped comparing herself with her siblings in order to judge her worth. She had recognized that she truly did care about her family and wished she could fit in with them and do what they wanted but that it might not be fully possible. She had been able to let go of Marta. And she had decided to stay with Fred for the time being, if he was willing, although she was not ready to get married. She imagined some of her choices for the future: If I like Fred enough, perhaps he will live with my finishing my PhD. We can see about children later. Or, perhaps I will come to want to have a child, and then we can work out how I have a child while getting my PhD. Alternatively, if Fred is not willing to do these things, then I will deal with that at the time. Or I may decide that I don't like Fred enough and seek out someone else. Or I may decide I don't like Fred, and than perhaps I really am more interested in a relationship with a woman. Cynthia decided to live in a process-oriented way, to take these things and to explore them rather than to decide that she had to be one way or the other.

In conclusion, she felt less anxious and depressed because she felt more sure of her decision to pursue her doctoral degree. More important, she felt more confident that she could find solutions to her problems, even the ones that were not yet solved.

CONCLUSION

The work with Cynthia demonstrates the active collaborative process of working with a client from the stance that the client is the active self-healer in therapy. Ultimately, it was Cynthia who discovered and thought through the challenges facing her. Some of this occurred simply through my empathically accompanying her, some through our engaging in coconstructive dialogue, and some through her use of tools such as the empty chair. In our interactions, the most important part of the process for me was to stay continually aware that I was in dialogue with another intelligent human being rather than that I was working "on" her with my interventions. It is this fundamental difference in mind-set that I believe is the most important part of working with clients as active self-healers. It provides one integrative basis for doing psychotherapy.

REFERENCES

Bohart, A. C. (2000). The client is the most important common factor. *Journal of Psychotherapy Integration, 10*, 127–149.

Bohart, A., & Byock, G. (2003, July). *How does empathy facilitate?* Paper presented at the World Conference for Person-Centered and Experiential Psychotherapy and Counseling, Egmond aan Zee, the Netherlands.

Bohart, A., & Tallman, K. (1999). *How clients make therapy work: The process of active self-healing.* Washington, DC: American Psychological Association.

Dweck, C. S., & Leggett, E. L. (1988). A social–cognitive approach to motivation and personality. *Psychological Review, 95*, 644–656.

Elliott, R., Watson, J. C., Goldman, R. N., & Greenberg, L. S. (2004). *Learning emotion-focused therapy: The process-experiential approach to change.* Washington, DC: American Psychological Association.

Orlinsky, D. E., Grawe, K., & Parks, B. K. (1994). Process and outcomes in psychotherapy—Noch einmal. In A. E. Bergin & S. L. Garfield (Eds.), *Handbook of psychotherapy and behavior change* (4th ed., pp. 270–376). New York: Wiley.

Tallman, K. (1996). *The state of mind theory: Goal orientation concepts applied to clinical psychology.* Unpublished master's thesis, California State University, Dominguez Hills.

Tallman, K., & Bohart, A. (1999). The client as common factor: Clients as self-healers. In M. A. Hubble, B. L. Duncan, & S. D. Miller (Eds.), *The heart and soul of change: What works in therapy* (pp. 91–131). Washington, DC: American Psychological Association.

Wampold, B. E. (2001). *The great psychotherapy debate: Models, methods, and findings.* Mahwah, NJ: Erlbaum.

19

PATIENT-INITIATED INTEGRATION

JERRY GOLD

This particular example of psychotherapy integration is unique in that the integrative shifts from one technique to another, or from a first theoretical perspective to a second, are signaled, inquired into, requested, or demanded by the patient. This form of psychotherapy integration has been influenced by those integrative writers who put great stress on the patient's activity (Bohart & Tallman, 1999; Hubble, Duncan, & Miller, 1999). The emphasis in this therapy is the discovery (Gold, 1994) that changes in technique often arise from the patient's intellectual and emotional appraisal of his or her psychological needs; the status of the therapy and its immediate and long-term applicability to the patient's own goals, desires, and fears; and the patient's conclusions about the necessity and desirability of change in therapeutic focus, intervention, and direction. The patient may or may not have the specific knowledge to request a particular technique. Many patients come to therapy after educating themselves about the variety of therapeutic schools that currently are available or become interested in literature about psychotherapy while they are in therapy. They may make use of the self-help literature, read the many articles in the popular press about psychotherapy, or turn to professional books or journals. Such patients may then take control of the therapy by suggesting or insisting on a new therapeutic approach. At other times the patient may make use of an additional alternative intervention outside of the therapy sessions or may initiate integration by consulting a second therapist concurrently, or at a later point, in a type of sequential integration (Gold, 1994).

Other patient-initiated integration can occur when the patient lacks this type of specific information but knows and can describe a set of events or experiences that he or she thinks would be helpful and that may approximate a particular intervention. It is the therapist's responsibility to find a way to match the patient's interest in a new experience with a technique familiar to the therapist.

Patient-initiated integration places unusual and powerful demands on the therapist as a person and as a professional. It significantly influences the patient–therapist relationship in ways both subtle and overt, with ramifications that may not be fully understood for long periods of time, if ever. This form of integration, more than any other, and perhaps more than any single form of psychotherapy, challenges the therapist's stance as an authority or "expert" and confronts and undermines his or her need to be in charge of the therapy. Unlike any form of therapy that may have been learned in one's training, this form of integration cannot proceed on a predetermined path; therefore, it can be enormously anxiety-provoking for the therapist. When the patient initiates integration, there is a unique and ironic role-reversal in the therapeutic relationship. Many therapists may resist or avoid this change out of personal and professional anxieties.

The therapist who participates successfully in this type of therapy must respect the patient's healthy and competent ability to recognize what he or she needs and the corresponding ability on the part of the patient to take action to realize those needs. Therapists who are insecure about their professional status, who lack respect for the patient's ability to make decisions about therapy, and who need to be in control of the process are likely to miss the patient's more subtle or incompletely articulated interest in changing direction. These therapists may send signals that discourage patient's exploration of other possibilities for intervention, and when met with frank, direct requests for such change by the patient, they are likely to label these discussions as "resistance" or as counterproductive attempts to take control of the therapy. Some instances of integration that are suggested by patients may indeed represent resistance, veiled expressions of a challenge to the therapist, or some other transferential issue. However, this cannot be ascertained without careful, patient, and open-minded inquiry. A patient's efforts at integrating often have positive and healthful underpinnings: A newly emergent confidence in her or his own ability to think through problems, or a newly acquired comfort with autonomy and independence, to name just two factors, are as likely to motivate these efforts as are resistance or negative transference.

The therapist's task is to explore the patient's interest in changing direction with respect, curiosity, and an open-minded attitude about the potential merits and risks of a new approach. Sometimes, just as therapists can be too quickly discouraging, therapists can be too quick to agree to the patient's idea in a well-meaning effort to create an egalitarian relationship. The therapist's intention here must be to work with the patient and to explore the meaning, intentions, sources of information, applicability of technique, status of the therapeutic relationship, and any other relevant issues until the patient can make an informed and potentially advantageous decision about the proposed integration. When a decision is made, the therapist may teach the patient the particular technique; help the patient to decide where, when, and how to apply a technique that the patient has learned in or outside of the therapy; or simply observe and help the patient to evaluate, modify, continue, or discard the newly integrated technique. Typically, after each of these events, patient and therapist explore the meanings and ramifications of the integrative event. Together they explore the impact of the new technique on the patient's symptoms or problems; its actual effectiveness compared with its desired effect; and the impact of the integration, the patient's efforts, and the therapist's participation on the patient's perception of self, the therapist, and the relationship. Often, this post hoc debriefing and exploration is as or more important than the integration itself, because it opens up many new facets of the patient's psychology and of the therapeutic encounter for discussion.

CASE STUDY

Richard was a White single man in his mid-20s who sought therapy for what he described as mild but chronic depression, a variety of anxiety symptoms that he did not initially specify, and difficulties in sustaining intimate relationships with women.

He was employed as a schoolteacher in a middle-class suburban area close to where he had grown up, and he had a number of close friends and an "acceptable relationship" with his parents and siblings who lived in the area. Richard had recently become engaged to Patricia. He mentioned that it was this engagement that had prompted him to seek therapy. Patricia had told him that she was concerned about his depression and its effect on their relationship. Richard indicated that he was concerned about this issue as well and that he had found himself unaccountably moody, distant, and guarded with Patricia without any evident reason for this behavior.

Richard had completed several psychology courses in college and had read a good deal about psychotherapy. He had asked the psychologist in his school for a referral to a psychodynamically oriented therapist and stated his wish to come to therapy twice weekly. Psychotherapy of this type and frequency was begun and for several months proceeded in a reasonably successful and unremarkable way. As Richard gained insight into himself, his depression improved and his relationship with Patricia improved. The issues connected with his depression receded into the background of the discussions, which came to be dominated by a more detailed description of Richard's anxiety symptoms and their effect on his life.

Richard described a number of situations in which he experienced intense anxiety that bordered on panic. These situations included flying, elevators, ascending to the higher floors of tall buildings, driving over bridges and through tunnels, and driving in the passing lane to overtake another car. He also indicated that there were a number of situations in which he experienced intense performance anxiety. These included sexual relations, in which he became overly focused on his ability to obtain or maintain an erection, and occasions when he had to speak in public. In the former he often experienced bouts of impotence or premature ejaculation; when addressing an audience he often began to stammer and stutter.

As Richard began to focus more exclusively on his anxiety symptoms, the atmosphere of the therapy began to shift and darken. Until this point, a relatively positive and consistent therapeutic alliance had existed. Now, Richard often came late to sessions; was silent for long periods of time in a glowering, vaguely angry way; and seemed more detached. After several instances in which I pointed out this attitudinal change, he announced that he did not find the exploration of the psychodynamic origins of his anxieties helpful in overcoming these anxieties. He mentioned, in a sheepish and uncomfortable way, that he had been reading a number of books and articles about cognitive–behavioral therapy and that he had been trying, without success, to apply these techniques to his fears. He also said that he felt that his anger and avoidance were caused by guilt and fear: He felt that his interest might be seen as disloyalty to me, the therapist who had been helpful in lessening his depression, and he anticipated some sort of attack or rebuff for this new interest and confidence in nonpsychoanalytic methods.

These fears seemed to have a strong transference component to them, and Richard had alluded to his awareness of these issues as well. His father had been a rigid, demanding autocrat who needed to believe that his perspective and his word were law. At the same time, it seemed important to acknowledge the plausibility of Richard's anxiety. Did I not feel a twinge of resentment and some bristling of anger when he owned up to his "sneaking around," even though I often read about and use cognitive–behavioral ideas and methods in my work? I am not immune to feeling resentment when my authority is challenged and am not always free of the need to be in charge of the therapy. So I chose to postpone the exploration of the transference and instead to work with his attempt to heal himself and to create an integrative period in the therapy. I responded along these lines:

> I'm glad we cleared this up, and it makes sense that you might be afraid
> to try a new approach for fear it would upset me. It's actually a brave and

creative thing to do. I'm also a fan of those methods. What have you been trying to do?

Over the next several sessions we discussed the cognitive techniques (thought stopping, calming imagery, and soothing self-statements) that Richard had been trying to learn on his own. We looked into his rationale for choosing these techniques, the times at which he applied them, and the possible reasons why they had not yet worked for him. We concluded together that he had not been able to get the most out of these techniques because he had not practiced them sufficiently when he was relatively free of anxiety. He tried to "turn them on all at once" at moments of heightened anxiety, such as during the approach to a bridge, or when Patricia made a sexual overture to him. I suggested that he might add to these techniques the use of diaphragmatic breathing, which would give him physiological relief from the anxiety as well.

This discussion led to several very positive changes in the therapy. The atmosphere lightened, and positive therapeutic alliance was reestablished on a more solid footing than previously. The transference meanings of this interaction emerged, and we worked through them spontaneously; Richard identified the source of his guilty fear in his relationship with his father and was able to discuss in a very emotional way the impact of my acceptance of his use of these techniques. He finally made very successful use of these cognitive–behavioral methods, which led to a steady improvement in his anxiety symptoms and to deepened exploration of their psychodynamic contributions.

After this episode, the therapy was marked by extended periods of psychodynamic exploration that were interrupted at several points by therapeutic shifts and integrations, all of which were initiated by the patient and that were addressed in a manner similar to that just described. Perhaps the most telling and important of these episodes was prompted by a period of inquiry into Richard's feelings of grief and disappointment about his compromised relationship with his father. He talked about feeling "stuck" with these feelings and began a session by announcing that his recent reading in the psychotherapy literature had suggested to him that some gestalt work, perhaps the empty chair or two chair techniques, might help him come to terms with this "unfinished business." He then went on, in a manner that conveyed anger and anxiety, to berate me for not having suggested this integrative shift first! He expressed his disappointment and bitterness that I, as the professional, had not made use of this literature. He also expressed hurt about another discovery: "When I was reading about this, I found out that you write about this integrative way of working, and that you have written about using this technique for prolonged grief!"

I was floored by his confrontation. As we talked about these issues, it became clear to us both that not only had his efforts at redirecting his therapy led to the selection of an extremely appropriate intervention but that this integrative shift was his way of bringing my countertransference enactment to my attention. I do write about psychotherapy integration, and I practice an integrative version of psychodynamic psychotherapy in which I often comfortably introduce experiential techniques, including those that he had suggested. How had I missed this opportunity for such a suggestion? How many others had I missed? It seemed that I had become his father, caught rigidly within the assumption that my narrow way of looking at things was the best, indeed the only, way to see them.

After this discussion, Richard was able, with my guidance, to effectively use an empty chair dialogue with his imagined father to gradually free himself of his grief. Equally important, my ability to recognize my failings in the therapy, my acceptance of and willingness to explore Richard's reactions to my failure and to my attempts to correct it, and our collaboration in the experiential integration that he had introduced, all contributed to the processes of resolving his grief. We talked at great length about his strength and courage and about his new optimism that other people in the world would and could come around to seeing the validity of his ways of understanding things.

This episode in the therapy was followed by relatively long periods of exploratory work that were punctuated by an occasional integrative shift, which I now introduced more frequently than did Richard. He suggested a final integrative effort that is instructive in that it was abandoned as unsuccessful, having been attempted only after a difficult and painful exploration of his intentions and goals in making this suggestion.

Late in the therapy, our focus shifted to Richard's sexual difficulties. His performance anxiety and bouts of impotence had almost disappeared, but he was still troubled by episodes of premature ejaculation. We explored these experiences, and it seemed clear to me that his sexual woes were connected to disavowed feelings of anger toward Patricia. I offered this interpretation to Richard and suggested that we find a way to monitor his emotional state and to test this hypothesis. He seemed less than enthused about this idea, though he had little to say about his feelings or thoughts at that time. However, soon afterward, he mentioned that he had again delved into the psychotherapy literature and had found some behavioral techniques that had proved successful in treating premature ejaculation. He asked if I would see Patricia and him together to assist them in learning these techniques. If not, he wondered, could I refer them to a sex therapist? My lack of enthusiasm for these ideas mirrored his earlier lack of interest in my interpretative hypothesis about the underlying dynamics of his now infrequent sexual dysfunction. I mentioned that most sex therapists probably would want to assess the emotional climate of the couple's relationship before teaching techniques and ask if this new interest in an adjunctive therapy might have some defensive meaning: Was it a way of avoiding exploring and accepting his anger toward Patricia? He assured me, in an irritated and impatient way, that I was incorrect, and he asked again for a referral, which I supplied. We turned to other issues, but the climate of the sessions was frosty and distant for several weeks.

Things warmed up again when Richard informed me that he and Patricia had seen the sex therapist a couple of times. This therapist had interviewed them in depth before introducing any interventions and had suggested that his simmering but barely acknowledged anger was interfering with his performance. With an embarrassed, "I guess I've heard that before, and I could see in our discussions with her where you and she could see anger operating," from him, we began to investigate the reasons that he found anger, especially at Patricia, to be such a sensitive and uncomfortable topic. Although this integrative shift did not yield the immediate results for which the patient had hoped, it too, ultimately, was an important and highly useful event in the therapy. Richard and I did not create a stalemate or a crisis over our different perceptions of his sexual problems and his proposed solution, as he and his father might have done in the past. We did not get into a power struggle in which I tried to convince him that he was resisting the awareness of a painful conflict in his relationship with Patricia, though I did believe that to be the case. Instead, we agreed to disagree, endured the temporary tension and irritation that eventuated (which helped him to tolerate and to be more aware of anger outside of therapy), and continued our work on this issue after his experiment with sex therapy made him aware of his defensiveness.

CONCLUSION

Richard's integrative efforts led to the introduction of cognitive–behavioral and experiential interventions into a primarily psychodynamic therapy. These patient-initiated integrations were invaluable not only for their immediate impact on his thoughts, feelings, and symptoms, but because of their consequences for the therapeutic relationship and for his ways of construing and structurally organizing his self-perceptions and perceptions of others. Each instance of patient-initiated integration led to a strengthened therapeutic alliance, to insight into transference or countertransference, and to a corrective emotional experience in which his problematic internal representations of self and of others were modified or revised in more positive, loving, and hopeful ways. The multiplicity of meanings and of the kinds of impact that eventuated from these changes in technique are identical to those described by Stricker (chap. 5, this volume) in his description of assimilative psychodynamic psychotherapy, and by Gold and Wachtel (chap. 7, this volume) in their presentation of cyclical psychodynamic psychotherapy. The crucial difference here is that the patient started and guided the process.

Few patients are as eager or as skilled as Richard was in using the psychotherapeutic literature to address his sense of needing more from his therapy. These activities were consistent with his intellectual gifts and his scholarly, academic style. However, many patients signal their interest in changing the orientation and manner of their therapy. They use information from magazines, television, and the Internet. When their requests are less sophisticated or more incompletely articulated than Richard's highly specific suggestions, it is the therapist's job to work with them to identify those possibilities. Often, the signal to the therapist consists of the familiar question, "What do you think of . . . " followed by a reference to a particular technique that was mentioned in a news report, a Web site, or a magazine article. Only then can therapist and patient together evaluate the benefits and drawbacks of any integrative shift. The therapist's failure to help the patient articulate an incompletely formed interest in integration may lead not only to a missed technical opportunity but also to profound and negative issues in the therapeutic relationship. Such a failure may be construed by the patient as a test failed by the therapist (Weiss & Sampson, 1986) and lead to the reinforcement of the patient's negative transference perceptions and beliefs, because the therapist is experienced as yet another person who cannot recognize, accept, or encourage the patient's initiative, intelligence, and competence. On the other hand, the therapist's acceptance of the patient's integrative attempts often results in important corrective emotional experiences (Alexander & French, 1946). These experiences can be the source of new internalizations of a parental figure who is approving and accepting of the patient's viewpoint, competence, and ability to explore the world.

REFERENCES

Alexander, F., & French, T. (1946). *Psychoanalytic therapy*. New York: Ronald Press.

Bohart, A. C., & Tallman, K. (1999). *How clients make therapy work*. Washington, DC: American Psychological Association.

Gold, J. (1994). When the patient does the integrating: Lessons for theory and practice. *Journal of Psychotherapy Integration*, 4, 133–154.

Hubble, M., Duncan, B., & Miller, S. (1999). *The heart and soul of change*. Washington, DC: American Psychological Association.

Weiss, J., & Sampson, H. (1986). *The psychoanalytic process*. New York: Guilford Press.

20

A HERMENEUTICALLY INFORMED APPROACH TO PSYCHOTHERAPY INTEGRATION

JACK C. ANCHIN

In this chapter, I present an approach to psychotherapy integration infused with key assumptions and perspectives of hermeneutics, a tradition-rich paradigm of inquiry carrying enlightening implications for clinical science and practice. An art and a science backed by 5 centuries of evolution (Palmer, 1969), hermeneutics devotes itself to the profoundly important challenge of cultivating an understanding of "the life and history of human beings" (Polkinghorne, 1983, p. xi) through, most fundamentally, the interpretation of meanings. Indeed, beating at the ontological, epistemological, and moral heart of hermeneutics is the assumption that in understanding all that is specifically human, "the question of meaning is primary" (Thompson, 1981, p. 21).

THE TRIANGLE AS A METAPHOR FOR HERMENEUTIC PROCESSES

Originating as a "set of techniques for interpreting written texts" (Packer, 1985, p. 1082), hermeneutics first emerged as a formal discipline during the

I dedicate this chapter to the memory of my mother, Ida Anita Anchin. Her innumerable meanings to me, and their beauty, are everlasting.

Reformation to guide accurate interpretation of Scripture. Over ensuing centuries it was secularized into methods of textual interpretation in law, literature, and the arts, and then over the 19th and 20th centuries proved pivotal to development of the "modern interpretive approach" (Martin & McIntyre, 1994, p. 159). This flourishing movement was carved out by such notable philosophers as Friedrich Schleiermacher, Wilhelm Dilthey, Martin Heidegger, Hans-Georg Gadamer, Jürgen Habermas, Jacques Derrida, Paul Ricoeur, and Charles Taylor through groundbreaking and invariably illuminating applications of hermeneutic theory and methods to the social and human sciences. Crucial to their transformational formulations was extending the concept of text to include human action (cf. Packer, 1985; Thompson, 1981), creating a highly fertile meeting ground for hermeneutics, psychology, and psychotherapy.

The hermeneutic approach to inquiry is positioned within the liberating perspective of postmodernism (Anchin, 2005a), a worldview in which reality, human experience, and knowledge are understood to be socially constructed and intersubjective, pluralistic and complex, contextual, perspectival, and relativistic (see Moran, 2001; Neimeyer & Mahoney, 1995; Young, 1997). The core of "interpretationism" (Young, 1997, p. 37) implicit in these themes is evident not only in hermeneutics but also in other branches of postmodern thinking (e.g., narrativism, semiotics, dialecticism). Postmodern thinking thus provides a host of complementary perspectives that enable penetrating insights into the interpretive processes that pervade both the science and the practice of psychotherapy.

Within these postmodern schools, metaphor is a valued explanatory tool, and in this vein the triangle offers a valuable geometric metaphor for crystallizing key dimensions of the hermeneutic approach to understanding. The hermeneutic triangle (see Figure 20.1) underscores that "understanding" in the hermeneutic sense is a subsuming concept that develops out of the interplay among three constitutive components: one's being-in-the-world, interpretations of that being, and meanings thereby educed and elaborated.

Understanding in Relation to Events, Situations, Actions, and Subjective Experience

Taylor (1971/1994) articulated a fundamental component of the dimensional structure of experiential meaning: "Meaning is of something; that is, we can distinguish between a given element—situation, action, or whatever—and its meaning" (p. 185). This distinction is vital to sharpening the quest for meaning in therapy, where phenomena that we seek to render intelligible are so multifaceted and intertwined. However, discerning order amid this complexity, patients' narratives emphasize domains of phenomena that significantly overlap with primary targets of hermeneutic understanding. Depicted in Figure 20.1 as domains composing being-in-the-world, these

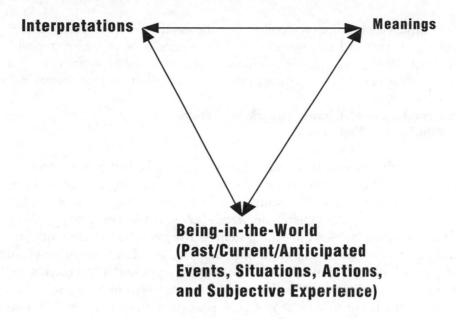

Interpretations ⟷ **Meanings**

**Being-in-the-World
(Past/Current/Anticipated
Events, Situations, Actions,
and Subjective Experience)**

Figure 20.1. The hermeneutic triangle of understanding.

encompass specific events and situations in one's life; actions by self and others relative to those contexts; and the intertwined elements of subjective experience relative to events, situations, and actions (Anchin, 2003a; Polkinghorne, 1988). Any of these domains, located at any point on the temporal continuum, may be the focus of efforts at understanding, and the therapeutic process is moved forward as significant meanings embedded in any given such domain are comprehended and addressed.

Meanings of Events, Situations, Actions, and Subjective Experience

Meaning goes beyond the manifest level of events, situations, actions, and elements of experience by imbuing these domains with intelligibility. In experiencing meaning, we make sense of our actions, experiences, or their contextualizing circumstances through comprehending their relationships to other elements and processes composing our being-in-the-world (cf. Polkinghorne, 1988). Two major types of meaning in hermeneutic inquiry are strikingly pertinent for therapy: "The meaning of acts or their products can refer either to what the agents intended by them or to their significance for those who feel their effects" (Fay, 1996, p. 151). I also note that intentions emerge within a cognitive–affective matrix; hence, in therapy, fully discerning the meaning of actions entails understanding not only the patient's motives and purposes but also grasping the related network of thoughts and feelings being expressed through those actions. The dimension of meaning entailing significance asserts the importance of consequences, alerting us to the clinical importance of apprehending the significance of not only actions but also events and situations. Thus, "meaning may be of different kinds" (Palmer, 1969, p. 120), but it is a hermeneutic maxim that meaning itself is never absolute or final, pointing to the vast generativity of interpretation.

Interpretations of Events, Situations, Actions, and Subjective Experience

Meaning's capacity to expand and deepen is driven by the recursive capacities of the interpretive process. In hermeneutic inquiry, one returns "to the object of inquiry again and again, each time with an increased understanding and a more complete interpretive account" (Packer, 1985, p. 1091). The changeable nature of meaning stems partly from the fact that interpretive perspectives are strongly shaped by language and historicity, which "run like dual leitmotifs throughout hermeneutical literature" (Wachterhauser, 1986, p. 6). Historicity holds that at any given moment in time one is inescapably situated in specific geopolitical, sociocultural, and personal circumstances and that the temporally bound—and therefore changing—nature of these intertwined contexts cause one's perspectives to be different at different times; as a consequence, meanings change with time (Palmer, 1969). Language influences interpretive constructions through its pervasive effects on thought (Anchin, 2003a), and this is particularly so in therapy, because a given theory is couched in a specialized language that powerfully mediates a therapist's interpretations of meaning. Hermeneutically, then, psychotherapy theory is double-edged: essential in organizing and making sense of patients' productions in ways that have vital mutative implications yet, being something of a preformed meaning system, intrinsically predisposing meanings to be interpreted in certain directions—especially if theory becomes doctrine.

Fortunately, as a pervasively dyadic system (Anchin, 2002), psychotherapy has a built-in counteracting influence against the risk of dogma: the process of dialogue. Gadamer (1989) instilled into hermeneutics the centrality of dialogue and conversation, explicating that "meaning only emerges out of the relation between two subjects" (Fay, 1996, p. 142). In a therapeutic process permeated by dialogical properties conceived by Gadamer as essential to hermeneutical understanding, interpretations of meaning are thoroughly intersubjective and collaborative. Dialogue also enables another process integral to interpreting meanings embedded in another's being-in-the-world. Initially described by Dilthey as the method of Verstehen and more contemporaneously likened to empathy (Wakefield, 1988), the latter cultivates a form of knowledge that assists sensitive discernment of personal meanings that may be embedded in the patient's experience. Articulating these sensed meanings subjects them to the patient's experiential and interpretive scrutiny and to dialogical processing, thus collaboratively advancing the process of understanding.

IMPLICATIONS FOR PSYCHOTHERAPY INTEGRATION: THE THEORETICAL FRAMEWORK

The integrative theory contextualizing my therapeutic work fuses traditional theoretical approaches with significant hermeneutic features. At the level of traditional theories of psychotherapy, the approach synthesizes elements from systemic, interpersonal–psychodynamic, humanistic–experiential, and cognitive–behavioral perspectives (Anchin, 1982, 1987, 2002, 2003a). I conceptualize the patient most broadly as a biopsychosocial system whose being-in-the-world at any given moment is constituted by a constellation of heterogeneous yet interdependent domains bound together through reciprocal influences (Anchin, 2005b, in press). Defining more substantively this holistic structure at the outset of treatment, the patient is invariably experiencing affective pain, conceptualized as complexly rooted in and emerging out of a way of being-in-the-world dominated by recurring patterns of interpersonal dysfunction most fundamentally tied to problematic issues and processes pertaining to self. These entwined difficulties in relation to self and others are themselves integrally related to dynamic matrices of beliefs, feelings, and motivations most formatively developed in the family of origin and that continue to give rise to actions whose multiple consequences for self and others perpetuate the patient's problems and subjective pain. In this circular process conception, the patient remains stuck in painful ways of being-in-the-world because of mutually reinforcing feedback loops among different self-relational, interpersonal, and affective processes. In line with systems principles of equifinality and positive feedback loops, therapeutic changes evolving in a given domain (e.g., the self-relational) affect structures and processes in other domains (e.g., the interpersonal and affective).

This integrative model is multiply enhanced through intersecting with the hermeneutic paradigm. Theoretical frameworks are viewed as interpretive systems for bringing ever-greater meaning to the patient's affective states, maladaptive self-relational and interpersonal patterns, and processes in those domains serving the patient well. That meaning is never absolute or final encourages interplay among different theories, because each deepens understanding of different dimensions of those self-relational, interpersonal, and affective processes. Furthermore, openness to different interpretive frameworks allows nontraditional perspectives to contribute to therapeutic interpretations of meaning. Thus, as one element of a process for fostering dialogue that advances understanding, interpreting meanings is among my major forms of intervention. With new and different meanings and understandings, the patient has potent fulcrum points (Magnavita, 2005) with which to work on change, for example translating new understandings of self into healthier modes of self-reaction. The patient and I also actively promote these changes by explicitly drawing out change implications of new understandings and translating these into both covert and overt action-oriented interventions.

Hermeneuticism contributes to my process in additional ways. Historicity's centrality to interpretation is harnessed through recognizing that understanding meanings maintained over the long haul by the patient relative to past events, situations, actions, and experiences requires grasping the historical circumstances operating when those meanings were undergoing formation. Yet, the patient and I also bring new or revised meanings to past circumstances through the lens of the patient's present historical situation. My awareness of the influential effects of language encourages acute mindfulness of words that I use to express interpretations and other interventions, and I also strongly rely on the language of metaphor (cf. Anchin, 2003a, 2005b). Furthermore, empathic attunement is fundamental to my process: Whatever the material serving as context for dialogue and intervention, I attempt to grasp and appreciate the patient's subjective experience and personal meanings and to respond in part from within those understandings.

CASE STUDY

Gary was a 49-year-old internist practicing hospital medicine at a teaching hospital in upstate New York. He was separated and living with his elderly mother and was in the midst of divorce proceedings from his wife of 23 years; the couple had three daughters, ages 20, 17, and 13. After a 3-year period of abstinence from all substances, Gary had relapsed to use of cocaine, prompting his referral to me by the Committee for Physicians' Health (CPH) of the Medical Society of the State of New York. When referred, he had been in treatment with another psychologist over the previous 4 years and was also participating in the 12-step self-help group Alcoholics Anonymous (AA); weekly group therapy at an outpatient chemical dependency program; and Caduceus, a peer support group for impaired physicians.

Prior to the onset of cocaine dependence at age 43, Gary had had a 25-year history of substance abuse, beginning at age 18 with alcohol and marijuana, and although he eventually eliminated alcohol, he had continued to use marijuana until age 43. He had first snorted cocaine at age 26 but developed no particular fondness for it at that time. However, at age 43 he had been introduced to crack cocaine and quickly developed difficulties with this drug; before the year was out, he was arrested for cocaine possession. Charges were dismissed, he entered the CPH program, and then spent 1 month in an inpatient treatment program, followed by transfer to another inpatient facility for 2 months of treatment. However, he relapsed shortly after discharge and 2 months later spent 30 days in his third inpatient chemical dependency facility. Over the next 3 years, he was in recovery and substance-free. However, as mentioned above, he had a relapse in which he snorted cocaine and 3 days later smoked crack cocaine, with CPH detecting this relapse through a urine screening.

Gary's Relapse Narrative and the Case Formulation

Aware that I would likely be seeing Gary on a long-term basis, I never-theless started giving shape to my formulation as of the first session, with the narrative of his relapse, as articulated in this first session, acting as a major springboard. Rapidly developing a formulation was rooted in a brief-therapy attitude (Anchin, 2003b), which encourages rapid assessment and formula-tion of the patient's problems in order to establish therapeutic foci and in turn initiate intervention as promptly as possible, thereby quickly giving shape and direction to the therapeutic process.

The immediate context of his first usage was his wife's birthday party; amid relational strain, he was living at times with his wife and at times with his mother. His wife's brother had come into town for the day and threw the party for her at another friend's house, and Gary, "wrapped up in myself," was "envious" and "sad" about not having been able to orchestrate this event. Having arrived late, he felt "out of place . . . very uncomfortable," as well as "filled with self-pity and . . . [feeling] bad for myself." Feelings of resentment and loneliness, as well as being "angry . . . hungry and tired," were also expressed. He believed that had he been experiencing these feel-ings 6 months earlier, he'd have gone to an AA meeting or called colleagues in recovery. Instead, he "took advantage" of an offer to snort cocaine at the party, even though in the past this mode of intake had done nothing for him. Still, "I wasn't thinking. I was so caught up in the emotions . . . maybe I was hoping it would brighten my spirits," yet once again "it did nothing for me." However,

> 3 days later I got hold of crack cocaine, and that is my drug of choice. It was like a sexual orgasm in the past. . . . It was a day off, I was lonely, not seeing my wife or anyone. So I went out and made contact with a guy I know who had crack cocaine. I had that blast, and the prolonged sexual orgasm didn't happen. It didn't give me the expected high, rush, or at-tendant thrill. . . . Instead, I got sweaty, fearful, scared, and . . . instead of . . . thoughts of having sex, women, were thoughts of [the judge who oversaw his case before his third inpatient admission]. She decided to give me one last try there. But she was pissed.

He was angry immediately after this second usage, but it was at feeling "betrayed" by the drug's negative effects. "I realized this was 'nowhere,'" he reported. Thoughts of the judge recurred, and 2 days later he attended a Nar-cotics Anonymous meeting, "a steppingstone back." Indicating that Narcot-ics Anonymous was "good for addiction stuff" but that AA was "good for me, for *life* . . . being with professionals leading a life of recovery," he then re-turned to his Saturday morning men's AA group. Shortly thereafter, his CPH case worker informed him of the positive testing for cocaine.

These circumstances depicted the immediate context and aftermath of his relapse, but additional antecedents contributed. In fact, he dated the on-set of the "slippery slope" to the previous October, almost a year earlier, when surgery had ignited fears of relapse because of the pain medications he would need to take. However, doubling recovery efforts prevented relapse, but with his worries having proved unfounded, "I started to believe I could handle it [on my own]." Additionally, a few months after the surgery, the Department of Health (DOH) Office of Professional Medical Conduct (OPMC) held a hearing following his disclosure to the State Education Department when he renewed his registration that he had been arrested for cocaine possession. Nevertheless, having received treatment and being in recovery, he was al-lowed to continue to practice, retrospectively the "tour de force" in fostering complacency in working recovery. Then, through the late spring of the fol-lowing year, as he got caught up in the medical aspects of a life-threatening medical crisis involving his mother, he let go of "daily prayer and faith" de-spite feeling "very scared." The "death of my spiritual program" ensued as he cut back on AA, and by early summer he was no longer attending Caduceus or his valuable Saturday morning AA meeting.

Using this relapse narrative as the principal basis for my formulation reflected two overarching considerations. Most pragmatically, if Gary suf-fered another relapse at this particular juncture, its effects on his life, profes-sionally and otherwise, would likely be ruinous. Considerable clinical expe-rience with chemically dependent patients had also validated for me the axiom that there can be no meaningful growth or change in this population without total abstinence and sobriety. Therefore, instituting from the very outset a primary focus on promoting changes in relapse processes could reduce risk of a recurrence, enhance his capacities to maintain abstinence and sobriety, and create conditions necessary to pursue significant characterological and functional advancements.

Interpreting the relapse as an interactive chain of factors—a process—that coalesced over time, I was especially focused on his difficulty coping with and regulating negative affectivity. I viewed his addictive process as partly activated by this pain and his return to cocaine as motivated by his desire to terminate that pain and replace it with the intense pleasure he experienced when high. Painful affective states just prior to his drug use (e.g., resentment, loneliness, self-pity) were interpreted as most fundamentally emanating from self-pathology, but it took certain interpersonal contexts and experiences to activate these issues. When activated, those issues and their attendant pain dominated his subjectivity and heightened vulnerabil-ity to dysfunction. My formulation also recognized *inactions*—not reaching out to his recovery-based support system—and the preventative role such connecting could have played. Thus, relapse prevention also necessitated engagement with others who supported abstinence and who could assist him in constructive handling of his pain.

Details of the Therapy

On the basis of this formulation, the first 8 months of treatment consistently focused on several highly interrelated domains: (a) relapse and recovery, (b) negative affective states, (c) self-relational processes and dynamics, and (d) interpersonal processes and dynamics. Three and a half months into treatment, Gary also learned that because of his relapse, an administrative hearing with OPMC was to be held, with his license to practice clearly at stake. This highly significant development gave rise to additional therapeutic foci, samplings of which—along with aspects of our work following the state's decisions—are also touched on in the following treatment discussion.

Relapse and Recovery

Work in this domain was two-pronged: (a) jointly understanding the relapse in ways that could turn this event into a springboard for constructive change, particularly in directions that could reduce his risk of relapse as well as foster meaningful characterological growth, and (b) strongly reinforcing and enhancing positive effects of Gary's involvement in his program of recovery.

Gary's insight into his relapse as a process that "began many months ago" was accompanied by assuming total responsibility for his role in different relapse factors, interpreted as an expression of having reassumed the mindset of recovery and his constructive attitude toward working on self. In addition to targeting distal relapse factors, we highlighted as proximal his emotional state just prior to snorting cocaine, homing in on his self-pity. He alluded to the AA aphorism "poor me, poor me, pour me a drink" to convey the flavor of how this operated, and in other contexts he linked self-pity to experiencing himself as a victim, describing the experiential sequence as "poor me, I'm a victim, nobody cares, it doesn't make a difference: fuck it," with substance use at risk for ensuing. The anger and resentment infused within his self-pity were also illuminated.

We also accented how drifting away from his recovery program had been central to his relapse. Interpreting unhealthy processes that had been at play, for example inaccurately believing that he could just "tread water" and be alone with his emotional pain (cf. Fosha, 2000), we culled a vital change implication: When in pain, it was crucial that he openly share those feelings with trusted others. This pointed to reengaging with his program, which provided pathways to what emerged as the core of his recovery: reembracing and deeply integrating spirituality. As in religion, the sense of transcendence is fundamental to spirituality, but unlike religion, spirituality "connotes a direct, personal experience of the sacred unmediated by particular belief systems prescribed by dogma or by hierarchical structures of priests, ministers, rabbis, or gurus" (Berenson, cited by Sperry, 2001, p. 4).

Integrating spiritual elements is characteristically not a facet of my therapeutic approach. However, adhering to a solution-focused attitude that emphasizes capitalizing on change processes already in motion (Anchin, 2003a), the positive meanings given by Gary to his recovery work and spirituality and his desire to "reinvigorate" them carried clear meanings for a key dimension of therapeutic stance and intervention: it was essential to actively support, reinforce, and build on his participation in recovery while also synthesizing the "language of recovery" (Kurtz & Ketcham, 1992, p. 160) with work undertaken in the other major domains.

Negative Affective States

Diminishing negative affective states was partly pursued through self-relational and interpersonal work. However, the significant role of ineffective handling of negative affective states during his relapse also necessitated development of tools for effectively self-regulating those states while also cultivating processes that could foster more frequent experiencing of positive affective states.

For example, to short-circuit negative affectivity—especially anger and resentment, pathways to self-pity—I provided the systemically based perspective that in addition to their subjectively felt quality, his feeling states could be interpreted as valuable feedback (Anchin, 2003a) to which he could constructively respond. Within that framework, he was taught the cognitive–behavioral method of using his affective state as a cue to step back, appraise his construal of the other, and revise his interpretation in a direction that dissipated negative affectivity and facilitated more constructive overt responding. Applications of this procedure at work enabled him to be less reactive, to adopt a more patient and understanding attitude, and to move into dialogue with colleagues and patients' families.

Constructive affective change was also significantly advanced through spiritually based procedures. He practiced mindfulness meditation (as taught by Zen Buddhist teacher Thich Nhat Hanh; Hanh, 1987), breeding both moment-to-moment awareness of thoughts, feelings, and physical sensations and deep acceptance of whatever he thus experienced. Using the meditative methods of Eckart Tolle (1999), Gary also worked at being more focused and grounded in the present moment. He also turned to prayer when entering fearful situations, asking his Higher Power to "take away everything I think I know." These practices induced peacefulness and relaxation; facilitated clearing his mind and in turn approaching situations in a way that felt fresh and open; reduced the threatening nature of his emotions, thereby enabling him to experience emotion more fully; and improved his energy and efficiency.

Self-Relational Processes and Dynamics

The self-absorption hinted at in Gary's relapse narrative gave me an early sense that narcissistic dynamics were a significant facet of his personality structure and functioning, an assessment reinforced by ensuing data. The centrality that I ascribe to the relationship between the relative health of self-relational processes and the felt quality of affective states deemed intervention in his narcissistic self-relational dynamics essential; intervention would be aimed at understanding the nature and sources of key issues and promoting distinct changes in problems so identified and understood.

Early in treatment, he captured the core of his self-relational difficulties, depicting himself as an "egomaniac with an inferiority complex," a duality we jointly unpacked to achieve keener understanding that he harbored deep-seated feelings of inadequacy, shame, of being "damaged goods," and at rock bottom that something was fundamentally wrong with him, yet he also experienced self-feelings saturated with grandiosity, superiority, and entitlement. Resonating to interpretations that the latter were powerful compensatory mechanisms fueled by an inflated sense of self designed to defend against his painful feelings of inadequacy, we drew out salient meanings from historical experiences as to their role in development of this bifurcated experience of self. Emerging as a major source of insight and an intervention catalyst in different contexts, he recalled as a child repeatedly going to his room feeling hurt, demeaned, and humiliated, and in the context of these painful self-feelings, having thoughts and feelings that he would "get back," "get the last laugh," and "be the survivor." When older, humiliating actions with peers fueled by wanting to be liked intensified his shame. Now, in adulthood, his substance abuse and its emotionally damaging effects on his family reinforced feelings of inadequacy, guilt, and shame. In contrast, his high intelligence and numerous academic achievements throughout high school, college, graduate school, and medical school provided fodder for a markedly divergent, inflated experience of self. His status and power as a physician only served to further feed his arrogance and grandiosity.

Among key interventions to cultivate healthier self-relational processes was intrapsychic work aimed at healing the painful, "injured" self spawned during his earliest years. For example, I offered a perspective for thinking about the hurt "young boy" within, suggesting that although he could not change past events, he could change emotional reactions toward and self-meanings resulting from those events. This suggestion resonated with him, and blending traditional and spirituality-based methods, I suggested that in one of his meditation sessions he "go back" to that young boy and embrace him with love and compassion. In the next session, he reported positive effects in doing this meditation, also indicating that it was "a new idea" that he could "meditate and call back past experiences and change my reaction to them." After that, he productively applied this mutative process in other contexts.

Self-relational work was complemented by Gary's deepening spirituality, framed as providing "antidotes" to his narcissistic self-processes. As a salient example, vital to effectively making the critical shift from self-centeredness to focusing on others (a major intervention strategy in treating narcissistic pathology; Millon, 1999), was recitation of a prayer in which he directed himself to "seek to comfort rather than to be comforted, seek to love rather than to be loved, seek to understand rather than to be understood." Greater sensitivity and more selflessly responding to others' needs and feelings were among positive consequences flowing from this invocation.

Interpersonal Processes and Dynamics

Affective and self-relational work contributed significantly to changes in the interpersonal sphere, but the latter was also a direct treatment focus. We sharpened awareness of maladaptive patterns of interaction, increased understanding of salient intentions to which these patterns gave expression, heightened cognizance of their negative consequences for others and so for self, and translated this growing knowledge into meaningful change.

Collaborative interpretations of relational narratives illuminated frequent enactment of a dominant and controlling interpersonal style laced with arrogance and haughtiness, consistent with theoretical and empirical translations of narcissism at the level of overt action (e.g., Millon, 1999). Developing insight into underlying motives, we saw that the young boy within could be hooked—in essence, activated and drawn out—by feeling demeaned, hurt, scared, challenged, dominated, or otherwise threatened, precipitating intense defensively based actions intended to get the upper hand. Significantly, in gaining these insights, he experienced strong echoes of the young boy who had vowed to "get back," "win," "have the last laugh," and be "the survivor." Seeing that he was still reflexively operating on the basis of childhood motives impelled him to catch shifts toward domination and to attempt more collaborative interaction, efforts that progressively bore fruit, as in his newly found "mutuality" at work.

Still other processes associated with his proclivity to dominate and control were illuminated. Thus, we saw how hypersensitivity, activated by perceived criticism, led to shame, anger, and then defiance. Moreover, we clarified the rigidity of his expectations and his being prone to react with condescension, rudeness, and sarcasm when others countered his expectations. Helped to empathically understand the aversive interpersonal impacts of these actions, he related his felt sense of these impacts to others' tendencies to react to him negatively, and in turn he connected their negative behavioral reactions to his own feelings of isolation, victimization, and self-pity. Understanding how these relapse potentiating states thus derived from his narcissism heightened his motivation to work at implicated changes, such as modifying expectations and accepting others' rights to have their own perspectives.

Gary's recovery work also contributed to interpersonal change efforts. For example, the 12-step concept of "defects of character" provided a spiritual framework for accepting and undertaking concerted work on his narcissism and its relational facets, and the important recovery-based concept of "dealing with life on life's terms," encouraging acceptance, patience, and serenity in dealing with others, powerfully counteracted his tendency to create expectations of others.

The Administrative Hearing

In the midst of these clinical developments (approximately 3 months after treatment began), Gary and his attorney met with OPMC to discuss his relapse. Despite positive feelings about how that meeting went, 2 weeks later DOH informed Gary's attorney that they wanted to revoke Gary's license. Shortly thereafter, OPMC granted his request for a hearing to address the state's revocation, initially scheduling this for February of the following year and then rescheduling it for April.

Fear spawned by this event, including the very real possibility of losing his license, became another primary therapeutic focus. Meditative practices were valuable in facilitating staying grounded in the present, underpinned by awareness that thinking about the hearing only stirred up anxiety. Enhancing present centeredness, I also suggested that he maintain "a strong emotional presence" in the life of his family and thereby continue to strengthen those bonds. Following through, he stated, "I will not lose sight of my family or my integrity, nor do I want to play 'pity-pot' stuff." We also drew positive meanings implicit in colleagues' support, both in recovery and at work.

The day before the hearing, we processed his thoughts and feelings about this event, undertook planning around using prayer and meditation to stay centered and manage his reactions, and reflected on his significant progress since relapsing. The next day, I had an opportunity to be a participant–observer through providing testimony on Gary's behalf; others testifying were Gary's chemical dependency counselor and an expert witness. I was struck by Gary's seeming centeredness and self-composure, especially noteworthy given the state attorney's clear efforts to cast him in an extremely negative light in arguing for revocation of his license.

An additional day for the hearing was scheduled for 1 month later to enable him to provide his own testimony. Processing the first day, positive feelings about having remained centered during a "tumultuous" process and about witnesses' testimony were offset by fear regarding the final outcome, which he interpreted as signifying a "lack of faith" and not having ultimate control in this situation. Thus, we discussed intensifying efforts at harnessing his spiritual tools to induce the faith, regarding both his own testimony and the final outcome, that fostered greater peace.

Following his testimony, Gary, although pleased that he had been genuine and able to remain nondefensive in the face of extremely difficult questioning, was unable to shake his fear and sadness about the possibility of losing his license. He managed his anxiousness chiefly through tools of recovery while staying focused on his job and working productively in treatment on a painful situation involving one of his daughters. During the summer, a 2-month hiatus from therapy ensued while he dealt with a series of serious medical problems.

During this time, OPMC also issued its decision. The Hearing Committee voted to suspend his license for 5 years but also voted to stay the suspension and place him on probation for 5 years, thus permitting him to continue practicing medicine but under a formal set of conditions. Tempering Gary's relief about this decision was his attorney's anticipation that DOH would appeal the decision, which indeed it did, 2 weeks after the state rendered its decision. He returned to treatment in August, and during the next month an OPMC Administrative Review Board reviewed all hearing-related materials and rendered a modified decision: They voted to revoke his license, voted to stay the revocation, and upheld 5 years of probation with slightly modified conditions, thus still allowing him to continue to practice.

Therapeutic Emphases Following the State's Decisions

As treatment unfolded pursuant to the state's eventful decisions, marital and work-related circumstances especially warranted attention while providing contexts for consolidating affective, self-relational, and interpersonal gains. Central within the marital realm was the couple's legal separation and plan to divorce. Different situations sparked intense negative affectivity, at times triggering strong temptations to become entangled in verbal conflict and thoughts of resuming drug use. Insight-oriented work helped Gary get a better handle on his anger by surfacing the dynamic of the "defiant little boy" thinking "I'll have the last laugh" or "ultimately, I'll win," yet also sensing that "little boy's" fear. Healthier reactions sprang from his realization that "it's time to grow up, to not be the 'little boy' who goes into his room, closes the door, and thinks 'I'll have the last laugh.'" To self-regulate affective and behavioral responding, he cultivated a recovery-based approach toward his wife, drawing on prayer to understand, comfort, and love to enhance mindfulness of *her* pain, at times joined to "the practice of restraint" through saying nothing inflammatory. He reduced his level of fear by not getting bogged down in excessive thinking about finances and maintaining spiritually based faith about the outcome. He addressed thoughts of drug use through self-regulatory processes (e.g., discussing them with trusted others) and extracting meanings embedded in those thoughts, notably motives (e.g., his retaliatory intention of financially foiling his wife and her attorney, because another relapse would almost certainly lead to revocation of his license, thereby greatly lowering income) and self-destructive consequences were he to act on them.

As an example of facets of treatment relative to his job, he experienced intense disappointment when his practice group, having decided to privatize and develop a contract relationship with the hospital, selected a member other than him to handle negotiations. Disappointment turned to resentment, but over several weeks he came to accept their selection. I facilitated his acceptance by interpreting beneficial meanings in the group's choice (e.g., not having to deal with the politics and negative affectivity of negotiation; freeing up time to help out with his daughters). Rethinking the situation from this angle helped to transform the group's selection into "a blessing in disguise." Furthermore, exploring meanings of his initial reactions, he realized he was acting "like a spoiled brat," again likened to the pouting child who vowed "I'll show them!" and fostering recognition that "I have to let it go." To "clear the air," he also talked with the colleague that the group had chosen over him.

We also continue to draw on all aforementioned areas of recovery work to fortify abstinence and sobriety and to strengthen integration of spirituality into his interpretive perspectives, coping and problem solving processes, and self-relational and interpersonal dynamics. Opportunities to expand on previous insights also emerged. For example, as he voiced appreciation about AA cohorts essential to his growth, I offered the metaphor that it was as if the "young boy" had come out of his room and joined others and allowed them to join him, and that ironically, this had strengthened him. He concurred, adding "It was immaturity. It's time to give up that immaturity." We also revisited his hearing in ways that demonstrated how meanings of a key event expand and deepen with time. Growing acceptance of his imperfection was another major spiritually related focus, and being of greater service to others in recovery was reflected in his becoming a sponsor in AA.

These transformative processes greatly improved Gary's quality of life, but he was realistic that his chemical dependence rendered relapse an ever-present risk. In this regard, having engaged his recovery program even more intensively because of increasing acrimony associated with the divorce and emerging uncertainties at work, he offered a concise statement of the overarching mind-set vital to his continued sobriety and personal growth: "I'm committed to the spiritual journey." In his 3rd year of abstinence and sobriety since relapsing, his constructive actions on numerous fronts were expressions of this profoundly important commitment.

The Therapeutic Relationship and Alliance

The type of therapeutic relationship that I seek to develop, cultivate, and utilize has evolved out of clinical experience interacting with my own personality factors, theory, and empirical findings. It can be characterized as a synthesis of language and conceptions associated with humanistic, hermeneutic, interpersonal–psychodynamic, and systemic perspectives, though during the live interactional process these elements operate holistically and interactively.

Fundamental attitudes that I have expressed transactionally in this relationship have been authenticity, respect, genuine caring, acceptance, warmth, deep interest, and empathic understanding, which are all traditionally associated with a humanistic perspective. These relational processes have deepened as treatment has unfolded and as my understanding of Gary's challenges and struggles and my appreciation of his intense commitment to working on himself have grown. All such attitudes and their relational meanings are ultimately expressed and conveyed through verbal and nonverbal communicative processes, themselves continuously expressed within a therapeutic process firmly anchored in the foundational hermeneutic principle of open dialogue and conversation.

Fostering an alliance imbued with these qualities is also strongly anchored in a systems perspective on dyadic relationships, particularly its emphasis on the irreducibility of bidirectional influence processes (Anchin & Kiesler, 1982; Magnavita, 2005). This systemic conception of the therapeutic relationship translates into a highly participative mode of engagement (see Anchin, 2002), solidifying my rationale for maintaining a high level of openness and receptivity to, and empathic understanding of, the patient's perspectives while also actively responding to those perspectives in ways that advance and deepen the patient's understanding and change efforts. Embracing the ineluctability of therapist influence also opens the way for me to proactively cultivate, based on my growing understanding of the patient's clinical issues and needs, a type of relationship and interpersonal process that is itself intended to have therapeutic impact (cf. Anchin, 2003a).

Using Fosha's (2004) interpretation in the language of the analytic concept of the corrective emotional experience, my mode of interaction has entailed "*leading* with the corrective emotional experience" (p. 85, italics added), contrasting with the traditional corrective strategy of responding to in-session enactments of maladaptive self–other processes through withholding reactions that one is feeling pulled to provide (cf. Anchin, 2002). Thus, from the very outset, in the treatment under discussion, I sought to develop a deeply accepting and affirming relationship, providing salutary interpersonal experiences that complemented mutative effects stemming from Gary's profitable experiences in recovery and from interventions encased within our therapeutic process. In this relational approach, "the therapist's unwaveringly affirmative stance earns the patient's deep trust and short circuits his resistance" (Fosha, 2004, p. 78), which may partially explain why, in working with this patient, noncompliance and resistance have indeed been virtually nil. The affective–interpersonal climate created by deep acceptance and affirmation and the safety this creates lessened Gary's in-session need for defenses, thereby undercutting resistance and countercontrol (Fosha, 2000). To this relational climate, Gary brought his own fervent motivation, stemming from his intense desire to grow and mature, awareness of the enormous costs to be incurred were he to slide back into patterns that could eventuate in relapse, and the benefits experienced from numerous changes over the course of therapy and recovery. His relational capacities, high level of intelligence and verbal facility, and notable openness to therapeutic input were additional patient variables, synergistically interacting with therapist contributions, that were vital to development and solidification of our strong alliance.

Essential Change Mechanisms

The essential mechanisms accounting for change were Gary's heightened awareness and deepening understanding of the nature, interrelatedness, and costly consequences of problematic interpersonal, self-relational, and affective patterns and his ongoing translation of those insights into modifications in key structures and processes composing those domains. Thus, as treatment unfolded, expanding and deepening understanding reciprocally and iteratively interacted with new, more adaptive covert and overt processes and their consequences to advance therapeutic change.

In the case described in this chapter, Gary's chemical dependence introduced another crucial dimension to the clinical situation. Given the nature of chemical dependence generally and Gary's addiction to crack cocaine specifically, change mechanisms could not eliminate dependence; more realistically, they could facilitate relapse prevention and maintenance of sobriety. At one level, those mechanisms lay within the multiple components of his recovery program, but overarchingly they stimulated the potent change mechanism of spirituality, which interacted with mutative insights, actions, and relationship processes tied to traditional therapeutic approaches to engender change across domains.

Specifically, spirituality provided Gary with "teleological meaning" (Anchin, 2003a), an overarching purpose and direction for his life crisply captured here by the metaphor of the "spiritual journey." Values centered on being more attuned, sensitive, and responsive to others infused interpersonal expectations, construals, and actions with far more salutary consequences. Meanings given to his experience of different facets of self were also spiritually affected: Imperfections were more often accepted as inevitable expressions of his humanness and as bases for self-improvement, whereas strengths and talents were increasingly viewed as assets and gifts to be appreciated but used in the service of helping others. Affectively, spirituality's distinct experiential quality colored in positive tones the subjectively felt character of his psychic interior.

These self–other changes fused with decisive transmutations—catalyzed by insight- and action-oriented interventions blending hermeneutics with traditional perspectives—in principal structural and process aspects of both the self-relational and interpersonal dimensions of his narcissism. Indeed, underscoring the meaningfulness of his multiple self-relational and interpersonal changes is the fact that they constitute opposites of narcissistic patterns. Traditional approaches also fostered Gary's understanding of the crucial importance of remaining attuned to and regulating his affective states, and he acquired a body of methods for doing so, enhanced by his use of recovery and psychotherapy as safe and trusted contexts in which to process feelings. Through these internal and interpersonal processes around his affectivity, subjective affect itself took on new meanings—for example, that feelings are safe, even when painful; that aversive feelings can be managed; that those regulatory processes are vital to maintaining abstinence; and that all of his feelings warranted being fully experienced and brought rich meaning to his life.

CONCLUSION

Though not always readily apparent, all approaches to psychotherapy are driven by interpretive processes. Different theoretical terminologies describing and explaining personality development and functioning; the nature of psychological health and disorder; and psychotherapeutic principles, procedures, and processes demarcate therapeutic approaches. However, a significant commonality is that each of these components of an approach's theoretical structure and language provides a basis for imparting significant meanings to different facets of the patient's past, present, and anticipated being-in-the-world. Furthermore, the conversational nature of the therapeutic process creates between patient and therapist a continuous dialectical and intersubjective process of sharing interpretations of meaning, resulting in ongoing coconstructions of new and expanded understandings. Psychotherapy is thus fundamentally a hermeneutic endeavor, but with the crucial corollary that the process and content of understandings so derived be harnessed to intervene in the service of promoting meaningful changes in the patient's life.

Infusing my integrative work with hermeneutic principles is itself underpinned by a strong pragmatic dimension, in that given the characteristic complexities of an individual and her or his relationships throughout life, in my view virtually any interpretive scheme that offers ways of understanding events, situations, actions, and experience that can facilitate constructive change warrants consideration. Thus, although from the standpoint of traditional therapeutic paradigms my integrative approach can be most accurately characterized as assimilative integration, entailing an integrated systemic and interpersonal–psychodynamic core that incorporates humanistic–experiential and cognitive–behavioral elements, I remain open to and deeply respectful of other meaning systems that can contribute to beneficial interpretations of meaning and their therapeutic translations. In the present case, this is reflected in substantial assimilation of the powerful spiritual perspectives brought into treatment by virtue of Gary's immersion in recovery. Thus, the tradition-rich hermeneutic paradigm, in prizing the open-ended nature of understanding and in offering substantive principles and fertile pathways for advancing the collaborative interpretation of meaning, can invaluably enhance the flexibility of multiple therapeutic processes, the sine qua non of psychotherapy integration.

REFERENCES

Anchin, J. C. (1982). Sequence, pattern, and style: Integration and treatment implications of some interpersonal concepts. In J. C. Anchin & D. J. Kiesler (Eds.), *Handbook of interpersonal psychotherapy* (pp. 95–131). New York: Pergamon Press.

Anchin, J. C. (1987). Functional analysis and the social–interactional perspective: Towards an integration in the behavior change enterprise. *Journal of Integrative and Eclectic Psychotherapy, 6,* 387–399.

Anchin, J. C. (2002). Relational psychoanalytic enactments and psychotherapy integration: Dualities, dialectics, and directions: Comment on Frank (2002). *Journal of Psychotherapy Integration, 12,* 302–346.

Anchin, J. C. (2003a). Cybernetic systems, existential phenomenology, and solution-focused narrative: Therapeutic transformation of negative affective states through integratively oriented brief psychotherapy. *Journal of Psychotherapy Integration, 13,* 334–442.

Anchin, J. C. (2003b). Integratively oriented brief psychotherapy: Historical perspective and contemporary approaches. *Journal of Psychotherapy Integration, 13,* 219–240.

Anchin, J. C. (2005a). Introduction to the special series on philosophy and psychotherapy integration and to the inaugural focus on moral philosophy. *Journal of Psychotherapy Integration, 15,* 284–298.

Anchin, J. C. (2005b, May). Using a nonlinear dynamical biopsychosocial systems paradigm to individually tailor the process of psychotherapy. In J. J. Magnavita & J. C. Anchin (Co-chairs), *Unified psychotherapy: Implications for differential treatment strategies and interventions.* Symposium presented at the 21st Annual Conference of the Society for the Exploration of Psychotherapy Integration, Toronto, Ontario, Canada.

Anchin, J. C. (in press). Pursuing a unifying paradigm for psychotherapy: Tasks, dialectical considerations, and biopsychosocial systems metatheory. *Journal of Psychotherapy Integration.*

Anchin, J. C., & Kiesler, D. J. (Eds.). (1982). *Handbook of interpersonal psychotherapy.* New York: Pergamon Press.

Fay, B. (1996). *Contemporary philosophy of social science.* Cambridge, MA: Blackwell.

Fosha, D. (2000). *The transforming power of affect.* New York: Basic Books.

Fosha, D. (2004). Brief integrative therapy comes of age: A commentary. *Journal of Psychotherapy Integration, 14,* 66–92.

Gadamer, H. (1989). *Truth and method* (2nd ed., rev.). New York: Continuum.

Hanh, T. N. (1987). *The miracle of mindfulness: An introduction to the practice of meditation.* Boston: Beacon Press.

Kurtz, E., & Ketcham, K. (1992). *The spirituality of imperfection.* New York: Bantam Books.

Magnavita, J. J. (2005). *Personality-guided relational psychotherapy: A unified approach.* Washington, DC: American Psychological Association.

Martin, M., & McIntyre, L. C. (1994). Introduction to Part III. In M. Martin & L. C. McIntyre (Eds.), *Readings in the philosophy of social science* (pp. 159–162). Cambridge, MA: MIT Press.

Millon, T. (1999). *Personality-guided therapy.* New York: Wiley.

Moran, J. C. (2001). An introduction: Contemporary constructions and contexts. In J. C. Moran (Ed.), *Self-relations in the psychotherapy process* (pp. 3–44). Washington, DC: American Psychological Association.

Neimeyer, R. A., & Mahoney, M. J. (1995). *Constructivism in psychotherapy.* Washington, DC: American Psychological Association.

Packer, M. J. (1985). Hermeneutic inquiry in the study of human conduct. *American Psychologist, 40,* 1081–1093.

Palmer, R. E. (1969). *Hermeneutics.* Evanston, IL: Northwestern University Press.

Polkinghorne, D. (1983). *Methodology for the human sciences.* Albany: SUNY Press.

Polkinghorne, D. E. (1988). *Narrative knowing and the human sciences.* Albany: SUNY Press.

Sperry, L. (2001). *Spirituality in clinical practice.* Philadelphia: Brunner-Routledge.

Taylor, C. (1994). Interpretation and the sciences of man. In M. Martin & L. C. McIntyre (Eds.), *Readings in the philosophy of social science* (pp. 181–211). Cambridge, MA: MIT Press. (Original work published 1971)

Thompson, J. B. (1981). Editor's introduction. In P. Ricoeur (Ed.), *Hermeneutics and the human sciences* (pp. 1–26). New York: Cambridge University Press.

Tolle, E. (1999). *The power of now: A guide to spiritual enlightenment.* Novato, CA: New World Library.

Wachterhauser, B. (1986). History and language in understanding. In B. Wachterhauser (Ed.), *Hermeneutics and modern philosophy* (pp. 5–61). Albany: SUNY Press.

Wakefield, J. (1988). Hermeneutics and empiricism: Commentary on Donald Meichenbaum. In S. B. Messer, L. A. Sass, & R. L. Woolfolk (Eds.), *Hermeneutics and psychological theory* (pp. 131–148). New Brunswick, NJ: Rutgers University Press.

Young, G. (1997). *Adult development, therapy, and culture.* New York: Plenum Press.

21

PSYCHOTHERAPY INTEGRATION USING CONTRASTING VISIONS OF REALITY

STANLEY B. MESSER

A different kind of psychotherapy integration is described in this chapter, one that is based neither on common factors nor on the blending of different theories or techniques. Rather, it emphasizes four contrasting "visions of life," each of which directs the therapist's attention to different aspects of clients' problems and personality. In a series of articles and chapters, Messer and Winokur (1980, 1984, 1986) applied these perspectives on reality to three major schools of therapy, namely, psychoanalytic, behavioral, and humanistic. The visions include the tragic, comic, romantic, and ironic, which also have been used to describe different genres of literature (Frye, 1957, 1965) and psychoanalysis (Schafer, 1976). The Messer and Winokur works sounded a cautionary note regarding the prospects for integration. However, they also discerned a trend on the part of proponents of these three schools of therapy to incorporate elements from each other's predominant vision (Messer, 1986; Messer & Winokur, 1986), a tendency that has increased over time.

This chapter aims to demonstrate that it is both possible and desirable to keep in mind each of the visions in treating the same client in order to appreciate fully his or her complexity. They can usefully be brought to bear in therapy either to highlight the many dimensions of an individual's experience or to consider how each vision may best apply to different clients or specific circumstances. The visions can also help guide the nature of the outcomes sought in an integrative therapy because they point in different directions. This approach has the potential to opening up new vistas for the integratively inclined psychotherapist.

In what follows, I very briefly review the four visions of reality followed by a case presentation. (For a fuller exposition of the visions, see the Messer & Winokur references above. For their application to a case of brief psychodynamic therapy, see Messer, 2000.) The visions are applied to the case and highlight how different features of the client's issues and personality are most readily captured by one vision or another. In addition, I refer to the effect of each vision on the process or technique of therapy and the outcomes most consonant with it.

THE TRAGIC VISION

Within the tragic vision, the limitations of life are accepted: Not all is possible, not all is redeemable, not all potentialities are realizable. The clock cannot be turned back, death cannot be avoided, human nature cannot be radically perfected. As in the ironic posture, these sensibilities favor reflection and contemplation on the part of both client and therapist, whereas the romantic and comic views predispose them toward action. Unlike irony, however, tragedy involves commitment. In a tragic drama, the hero has acted with purpose and in so doing, has committed, at least in his or her mind, an act causing shame or guilt. He or she suffers by virtue of the conflict between impulse and duty and, after considerable inner struggle, arrives at a state of greater self-knowledge. Many aspects of traditional psychoanalysis fall within the tragic vision. The outcome of psychoanalytic treatment is not unalloyed joy and happiness or all obstacles overcome as in the comic vision, but rather the client's fuller recognition of what one's struggles are about and a more complete understanding of the conditions and limitations of life.

THE COMIC VISION

Whereas tragedy emphasizes the dark side of human nature and existence and a tendency for things to go downhill, in comedy the direction of events is typically from problematic to better. There is always light at the end of the tunnel. Although there are obstacles and struggles in a comedy, these ultimately are overcome, and there is reconciliation between hero and antagonist, between the person and his or her social world. Joy, harmony, and unity prevail. The conflicts portrayed in a comedy are ones between people and the difficult situations in which they find themselves and not the kind of inner struggles or implacable oppositions encountered in dramatic tragedy. Cognitive behavior therapy is a good example of this outlook: Conflict is ascribed to external situations or internal forces that can be mastered through application of correct therapeutic technique or technology (e.g., Fishman & Franks, 1997).

THE ROMANTIC VISION

From the romantic viewpoint, life is an adventure or quest in which each person is a hero. "It is a drama of the triumph of good over evil, of virtue over vice, of light over darkness" (White, 1973, p. 9). The romantic vision idealizes individuality and what is "natural." It encompasses the creative spark, which is said to reside in everyone. This vision advocates free, uninhibited, and authentic self-expression: "The fully developed individual is characterized by true spontaneity, by the richness of his subjective experience" (Strenger, 1989, p. 595). The romantic vision is often manifested by people seeing life through rose-colored glasses, in the way lovers idealize each other. For example, romance is said to flourish in the dark, where blemishes and imperfections are obscured. This perspective is fundamental to humanistic psychotherapy (Perls, 1969; Rogers, 1961), which emphasizes such romantic goals as risk taking, the pursuit of a unique lifestyle, and the continuous search for self-realization.

THE IRONIC VISION

The tragic and ironic visions are linked insofar as they both include a distrust of romantic illusions and happy (comic) endings. The ironic attitude is antithetical to the romantic view. It is an attitude of detachment, of keeping things in perspective, of recognizing the fundamental ambiguity of every issue that life presents. Each aspect of a person's behavior may represent something else, be it a dream (latent vs. manifest content), a symptom (a displaced or distorted wish), or an interpersonal interaction (hostility disguised by excessive smiling or kindness). In common with the tragic vision, the ironic viewpoint underscores the inherent difficulties in human existence, that life cannot be fully mastered, nor its mysteries truly understood.

Irony suggests that human behavior can be quite at odds with conscious intention. Gold and Wachtel (1993), for example, emphasized the irony in patients' seeking out others who will not require them to change. The ironic result is the continuation of the anxiety they have been trying to avoid, which is the opposite of what they presumably intended.

The following case illustrates how the visions of reality might be integratively applied in an actual clinical situation.

CASE STUDY

Tara was a 42-year-old woman who was married with two teenage sons and one preteen daughter. She was of European background and grew up abroad. On September 11, 2001, Tara witnessed the second plane crash into the World Trade Center while knowing that several of her close associates were in the building for a meeting. At that time she had a human relations position in a corporation where she did the hiring. In this capacity, she arranged the funeral services for two of the employees and served as the liaison for their families, taking care of matters such as insurance and death certificates. She was also an emotional support for the bereaved families.

From a few months after that time and the subsequent loss of her managerial job, she had frequent crying spells, anxiety attacks, and a sense of despondency. She found that her thoughts were disconnected, making her unable to focus on any task for very long. Beset by physical problems (high blood pressure, a severe facial rash), Tara experienced chest pains and heart palpitations, making her feel as if she were having a heart attack. She also had diabetes, for which she had been treated for several years. Complaining of diminished libido, she had less interest in being intimate with her husband. Since not long after 9/11, Tara had been less involved in social activities, preferring to be alone. Her feelings, except for grief, sadness, and irritability, had been numbed.

Tara came to see me in a distraught, tearful state 1 year after the attack. Referring to her experience at that time, she told me that she had learned that one of her associates was on fire when she left the building and died shortly afterward. She still imagined herself in conversation with the deceased employees who were also her friends. The 9/11 events were replayed in her mind both in the waking state and in her disturbing nightmares. Tara believed that she was responsible in some fashion for her associates' deaths, which became one important focus of therapy.

Because of the business downturn in New York City after 9/11, her firm decided not to do any more hiring and Tara was let go. The loss of her high-paying, challenging position was a big blow to her self-esteem. She was unable to find other employment and soon stopped trying because of her increasingly debilitating symptoms. Her financial situation deteriorated, made worse when her husband lost his job as well. She first sought treatment with a psychologist a few months after 9/11, which was helpful, but she had to terminate when she no longer had insurance coverage. She had also been seen by a psychiatrist who prescribed antidepressant and antianxiety medications.

Tara was the younger of two children of older parents. Her father had died when she was 13, leaving her and her mother in poor financial circumstances. She had worked her way through college in part by playing the violin in orchestras and bands. She was an occasional writer and had had articles published in magazines. At the time of writing this chapter, Tara was not fully recovered, but she was much less subject to anxiety and mood swings, was working part time, and was functioning better on a day-to-day basis.

Tragic Vision in Tara's Therapy

How might the visions of reality influence the therapist's perspective at different points along the way in therapy? In terms of the content of therapy, the tragic vision would highlight the irreversible features of Tara's life. She was unfortunate enough to witness the shocking events of 9/11 and to experience the sudden and tragic loss of people to whom she was close. The effect of the current losses was exacerbated by the succession of losses she had experienced as an adolescent, including, most importantly, her father whom she had adored. Nothing could undo these facts of her life. As it happens, it was she who had argued, not long before 9/11, to keep on one of these employees (the one who was on fire when she left the building) when her boss wanted to let her go. She agonized over and felt guilty about the fact that had she not been so effective in getting the boss to relent, this employee–friend would not have been attending a meeting at the World Trade Center on behalf of the corporation and would be still alive today.

Tara had a variety of medical conditions, such as high blood pressure and diabetes, that were not directly related to the effects of 9/11. She could not wish these away in the spirit of the romantic vision, nor could she avoid the daily reminders of her symptoms. In terms of her functioning at the time she sought treatment, she no longer felt she could handle the responsibilities of high-level managerial work because she did not want to risk being the cause of others' distress.

From the point of view of process and technique, the tragic view calls for the therapist to aid the client's expression of feelings and thoughts around terrible events. I encouraged Tara to relate the experience in some detail and to allow herself to be in touch with the feelings it brought back. The therapist's job in this instance was to reflect empathically and expand on what she said, which is most typical of psychoanalytic and humanistic approaches. She came to understand that a central feature of her personality, namely, her unusually caring attitude toward her employees, made things worse for her following their loss. There is considerable irony as well as tragedy in the fact that they were indirectly "killed by her kindness."

Within the tragic vision, the therapist identifies with the client's problems in a similar manner to an audience's identification with the hero in a tragic drama. Just as the audience responds with pity and terror to the hero's dilemma, therapists respond empathically to clients by virtue of their ability to resonate to tragic themes in their own lives. We have all experienced losses and thus can appreciate the suffering Tara was enduring. Understanding and treating the sequelae of life's blows within the tragic vision call for an introspective and subjective stance on the client's part, with the therapist encouraging a thoroughgoing internal focus as just described.

In terms of expected outcomes, the tragic vision stresses limits to human possibility. In Freud's view (see Breuer & Freud, 1895/1955), one at best exchanges neurotic misery for everyday unhappiness. Even the successfully treated person will be subject to occasional reversals that can range from mild to severe, depending on how chance and fate play themselves out. There may continue to be an ongoing struggle with the same issues, although it is hoped at a diminished level. From the angle of the tragic vision, both the therapist and Tara came to realize that the best she could do was accept her losses and medical conditions with a certain degree of equanimity—a calm acceptance combined with an understandable measure of despair.

The tragic view, in isolation from the leavening provided by the other visions of reality, can lead to an overly gloomy and pessimistic therapeutic stance. The danger is in subtly encouraging the client to remain mired in her suffering, leading to passivity, which would allow opportunities for action to pass her by. The therapist, simultaneously keeping in mind the comic vision to which we now turn, provides some of this leavening.

Comic Vision in Tara's Therapy

In comic drama, one might view the content of Tara's problems as obstacles to be overcome through direct action. Tara needed help finding a job or needed retraining for a different one. The dramatic comic character is typically presented as dominated by a habit (or *humor* in Shakespearean terms) rather than by shameful acts, mixed motives, or tragic flaws. In this connection, one might say that there were irrational cognitions at play in Tara's assumption that it was she who was to blame for her associates' demise.

Within the comic vision, one would approach Tara's therapy with a sense of optimism and can-do spirit. True, she was depressed and life was not easy for her, but mental health practitioners have tools and techniques to make things better. Her irrational assumptions could be challenged in the style of rational–emotive therapy. Her depression and anxiety could be alleviated with the appropriate medications, which in fact helped somewhat to lift her mood and quell her anxiety. (It was also true, however, that her medications had to be monitored carefully because she suffered from considerable side effects.) Although this is not exactly what I did, she could be administered an "empirically supported treatment" for depression such as cognitive or interpersonal therapy (Task Force on Promotion and Dissemination of Psychological Procedures, 1995).

Acting within the comic mode, I encouraged Tara to consider employment that she could more readily handle, at least for now. I encouraged her to engage in daily exercise, which has been shown to have antidepressant effects. She started to walk every day, which at least got her out of the house and helped to control her tendency to gain weight. I suggested meditation and relaxation exercises that have anxiety-relieving properties. Even while exploring the tension between her and her husband that was contributing to her decreased libido, I encouraged them to seek marital or sex therapy to deal with this issue directly.

Outcomes within the comic vision are decidedly more optimistic than within the tragic view. There is an increased pragmatic capacity to perform social roles more adequately—in this case, Tara's role as wife and mother. Happy endings are anticipated, including improvement in coping skills, such as Tara's way of handling her illnesses, an increased ability to get her needs met regarding her husband, and to find a suitable job.

The limitations or danger in the action-oriented comic approach is "in the assumption that the therapist knows best and that the client merely has to follow advice in order to lead a satisfying life" (Andrews, 1989, p. 808). This can remove too much responsibility from clients for charting their own course and destiny. The comic vision can also induce expectations for cure in the client that are unrealistic, leading to disappointment.

Romantic Vision in Tara's Therapy

The content of therapy within the romantic vision highlights the creative, fulfilling, and adventurous aspects of life, even if there are temporary setbacks. In Tara's case, she had musical interests that could be capitalized on to help her live a more satisfying life. I encouraged her to rediscover her interest in the violin, which she had not been playing in recent years, and to develop her artistic talents as an important source of gratification. We explored her repressed wishes, fantasies, and daydreams with the view of encouraging her to see herself as a complex, striving individual who was not defined solely by her current life conditions or her symptoms and illnesses. Following her relating and reexperiencing the trauma, I tried to help her live her life more in the moment than in the past.

An important aspect of any therapy is the nature of the relationship established between therapist and client. Tara quickly formed an idealizing transference to me. By this, I mean that she admired me, imputed special healing powers to me, and made particular note of my professional and academic credentials. In general, she went out of her way to choose health professionals who had university positions, were heads of departments, or were otherwise distinguished by their accomplishments. She devalued those professionals whom she regarded as mediocre, especially a lawyer who was representing her interests in gaining compensation for her posttraumatic stress disorder. My initial and deliberate response was to allow the idealization to occur because I felt that it gave her strength to persevere under very difficult circumstances and increased my ability to help her. As therapy progressed, she discovered (alas) that I was not perfect and that she could be, at times, disappointed in me. This enabled her to explore her need to see herself and others associated with her as special and how this view had affected her relationships with me and others. (For an elaboration of how her sense of specialness contributed to the posttraumatic stress disorder, see the next section.) An idealizing relationship falls within the purview of the romantic vision because it is unrealistic, existing largely as a wish fulfillment.

With respect to outcomes within the romantic vision, Tara's drama was one of the opposing forces of light and darkness, which, consonant with this vision, could be settled favorably. That is, she could again be the vibrant, socially engaged, and artistic person she once was. My unwavering acceptance of her along with her sense of enhanced agency helped to bring her back to a better place emotionally and in terms of self-fulfillment. However, the danger in a one-sided emphasis on the romantic vision is of overplaying the creative possibilities and ignoring the client's and life's realistic limitations. Clearly, not all wishes can be realized nor all aspirations fulfilled.

Ironic Vision in Tara's Therapy

The ironic vision provides a corrective to the romantic vision in particular. The process or technique of therapy within the ironic perspective calls for therapists to be skeptical of all that they hear from clients. It encourages a questioning, challenging, even confrontational attitude toward what the client says and does. The ironic vision also predisposes the therapist to keep the three visions in balance. Things may not be as bad as they appear for Tara, but they are not infinitely malleable.

What might seem at first blush, then, like a clear-cut case of fate having conspired against Tara (as viewed from the tragic perspective) may be complicated by the attributes or unconscious attitudes that she brought to the situation (*content*). The following primary question arose in my mind: Why had her symptoms persisted so long and with such virulence? Was there something more to it than a natural human response to disaster? Why did she feel so very responsible for the fate of her employees who were simply going about their business in a usual way? She did not, after all, deliberately send them to their deaths and was only "responsible" to the extent that she had hired them and made the case for keeping one of them on when the boss wanted to let her go.

When I asked my client to tell me what came to mind about her feeling responsible for the employees' demise, she said that she had long believed that she possessed magical powers—that she was, in her words, "a small deity." I asked her for examples of what she meant. In response, she told me how she was able to locate objects even years after others had lost them simply by holding something of theirs in her hand. In another instance, she knew where a friend would find her lost passport, namely, in a taxi under the seat near the door. She also saw herself as clairvoyant. As an example, she told me how on three separate occasions she had heard a knock on the door, although no one was there, and knew instantly who in the family had died.

It became clear to both of us that her sense of specialness (or grandiosity) had played an important role in her slow recovery from the trauma. After all, if she could foresee the future, why had she not prevented her associates from going into the World Trade Center on that fateful day? When I pointed out to her that her excessive guilt over their deaths was closely linked to her belief in her special powers, she responded ruefully that if she were more humble she might not be suffering so much. This dynamic also helped her to understand that her sadness was not related only to the 9/11 losses but also to the loss of her secret sense of being extremely powerful and special. At first, she experienced this revelation as a considerable narcissistic blow (to use the language of self psychology).

With respect to outcomes, one goal of irony is honest self-perception and freedom from illusion. At first, Tara tried to explain the lapse in her clairvoyance as happening because 9/11 had been her 1-year anniversary at the company, which put her in a celebratory mood. In this way, a possible intuition about the coming disaster was masked. Clearly, she was trying mightily to hold on to this source of self-esteem, however unrealistic. With further exploration and reflection about this unusual feature of her personality, her narcissism diminished somewhat as she became more accepting of herself as just an ordinary mortal.

Another goal within the ironic vision would be to reduce the discrepancy between the ideal (e.g., complete harmony between Tara and her husband, a full recovery from her illnesses, the attainment of a concert career or that of a CEO) and what is possible by recognizing the exaggerated nature of the ideal and then working to modify it. (To modify one's behavior to approximate the ideal would be a comic rather than ironic goal.) That is, irony, like tragedy, is characterized by a certain degree of resignation, not action. For example, Tara came to recognize her own role in her strong reaction to 9/11. Although it caused her grief, it also led to relief at its exposure in a safe therapeutic setting. The liability of the ironic stance is that the therapist's unremitting skepticism can lead to accusatory interpretations (Wile, 1984), to which the client may react with an intensification of her self-criticism.

Focusing alternately and integratively on the different visions contributed, I believe, to Tara's improvement. She had the cathartic opportunity to face the tragic elements of her existence and to come to terms with them, at least in some measure. Her grandiosity was somewhat tamed (ironic vision) through attaining insight into her romantic ideas of possessing special powers and struggling with their loss. Especially helpful was her recognition of how these served as a filter through which she viewed me in the transference and others as well. Insofar as her grandiosity led to some idealization of me, this also helped early on to give me leverage to encourage certain behaviors, as dictated by the comic vision. and getting her to follow through on them. These included her becoming more active in dealing with health issues and pursuing less stressful job opportunities. My being less than ideal while still supporting her may have provided a model that allowed her to relax her own demands on herself. In this manner, she could come to terms with such events as her failure to rescue her employees–friends. In addition, being guided by the romantic vision helped me to see her as a uniquely creative person with talents that had lain dormant. Returning to these satisfying activities enhanced her sense of self, thereby hastening her recovery.

CONCLUSION

Each of the four visions can exert an influence on how therapy is conducted. The treatment can assume an integrative character according to the mix of visions that therapists prefer and according to their degree of attachment to a particular theoretical or therapeutic framework. The emphasis on different visions clearly should also depend on the specific features of the case and how receptive the client is to working within one or another vision.

REFERENCES

Andrews, J. D. W. (1989). Integrating visions of reality: Interpersonal diagnosis and the existential vision. *American Psychologist, 44*, 803–817.

Breuer, J., & Freud, S. (1955). *Studies on hysteria.* London: Hogarth Press. (Original work published 1895)

Fishman, D. B., & Franks, C. M. (1997). The conceptual evolution of behavior therapy. In P. L. Wachtel & S. B. Messer (Eds.), *Theories of psychotherapy: Origins and evolution* (pp. 131–180). Washington, DC: American Psychological Association.

Frye, N. (1957). *Anatomy of criticism.* New York: Athenaeum.

Frye, N. (1965). *A natural perspective: The development of Shakespearean comedy and romance.* New York: Columbia University Press.

Gold, J. R., & Wachtel, P. L. (1993). Cyclical psychodynamics. In G. Stricker & J. R. Gold (Eds.), *Comprehensive handbook of psychotherapy integration* (pp. 59–72). New York: Plenum Press.

Messer, S. B. (1986). Behavioral and psychoanalytic perspectives at therapeutic choice points. *American Psychologist, 41*, 1261–1272.

Messer, S. B. (2000). Applying the visions of reality to a case of brief therapy. *Journal of Psychotherapy Integration, 10,* 55–70.

Messer, S. B., & Winokur, M. (1980). Some limits to the integration of psychoanalytic and behavior therapy. *American Psychologist, 35,* 818–827.

Messer, S. B., & Winokur, M. (1984). Ways of knowing and visions of reality in psychoanalytic therapy and behavior therapy. In S. B. Messer & H. Arkowitz (Eds.), *Psychoanalytic therapy and behavior therapy: Is integration possible?* (pp. 63–100). New York: Plenum Press.

Messer, S. B., & Winokur, M. (1986). Eclecticism and the shifting visions of reality in three systems of psychotherapy. *International Journal of Eclectic Psychotherapy, 5,* 115–124.

Perls, F. S. (1969). *Gestalt therapy verbatim.* Lafayette, CA: Real People Press.

Rogers, C. (1961). *On becoming a person.* Boston: Houghton Mifflin.

Schafer, R. (1976). *A new language for psychoanalysis.* New Haven, CT: Yale University Press.

Strenger, C. (1989). The classic and the romantic vision in psychoanalysis. *International Journal of Psychoanalysis, 70,* 593–610.

Task Force on Promotion and Dissemination of Psychological Procedures. (1995). Training in and dissemination of empirically validated psychological treatments. *The Clinical Psychologist, 48,* 3–23.

White, H. (1973). *Metahistory.* Baltimore: Johns Hopkins University Press.

Wile, D. B. (1984). Kohut, Kernberg, and accusatory interpretations. *Psychotherapy, 22,* 793–802.

22

OVERVIEW: AN ATTEMPT AT A META-INTEGRATION

GEORGE STRICKER AND JERRY GOLD

When this book was first designed, the outline was clear to us. The book would be organized along the lines of the four major approaches to psychotherapy integration: technical integration, common factors, theoretical integration, and assimilative integration. This would be followed by some material taken from family therapy because all of the other cases in the book concerned individual therapy; by a recognition of an exciting new development, the patient-directed approach; and by some philosophical positions that are central to the psychotherapy integration movement. A funny thing happened on the way to the casebook.

We were successful in having our chosen authors agree to participate and are pleased that the work presented in this volume represents psychotherapy integration at its best. The authors are all well-known and describe approaches that they have made famous. As the chapters came in, we were excited to see how closely our guidelines were followed and how each of the chapters is an exemplar of the system it was chosen to represent. We were less excited to note that the chapters did not fall so neatly into the assigned categories, not because the authors were not doing their job but because the demarcation lines are not as neat as we had presumed.

We reached the following conclusions, which are elaborated further as we review the cases:

- *Technical eclecticism* appears to embrace two different approaches. The first, widely practiced, is a clinically determined approach that cannot easily be systematized because it depends so much on the intuition of the clinician and the needs of the patient. The second approach is highly systematized and may not properly be called *eclectic* because of its reliance on a theoretical framework, whether the theory is of personality or of change.
- *Common factors* is a ubiquitous approach, seen in every variant of psychotherapy integration. However, it does not easily lend itself to implementation as a stand-alone method of doing psychotherapy. If *common factors* refers to principles of change, which it usually does not, it is much more easily implemented and has a great deal of promise.
- The boundary between theoretical integration and assimilative integration is not easy to draw. It depends on the extent to which a primary theory is maintained or is blended, and that is not readily discerned from the presentations.
- Just about every approach emphasizes the therapeutic relationship and places specific interventions in a secondary position. That is consistent with the literature, which also emphasizes the centrality of the relationship and other common factors rather than the technique as the critical change agent (Norcross, 2005). This does lead us to question why the scientific community is so taken with assessing the impact of specific interventions (Chambless & Ollendick, 2001) rather than relationship factors (Norcross, 2002). However, that is a question for another time and place.
- There is no reason to question the oft-repeated finding that there is little difference between the various pure schools of treatment (Wampold, 2001). If this is coupled with the general feeling that what we do does make a difference, the resolution must lie in the further development of psychotherapy integration, taking the best from each orientation and applying these approaches, whether they be common or specific, in a manner dictated by the needs of the patient. This can be seen in current approaches to psychotherapy integration varying as widely as Beutler's prescriptive matching efforts and the new developments in patient-centered treatment.
- There is great value in looking to psychology for basic research in developing models of psychotherapy. Contributions from developmental psychology, such as attachment theory, from the

study of emotion, and from the study of cognition all have yielded important insights to the practice of psychotherapy.

REVIEW OF CASES

The first two cases were contributed by Lazarus and by Beutler, Harwood, Bertoni, and Thomann. They were intended to represent technical eclecticism. Earlier, we noted that technical integration bears a close resemblance to what is loosely called *eclecticism*, and its distinguishing characteristic is its minimization of theory as a basis for choosing interventions. The two outstanding systematic exemplars of technical eclecticism can be found in the work of Lazarus (multimodal psychotherapy; Lazarus, 1981) and Beutler (prescriptive psychotherapy; Beutler & Harwood, 2000). Each of them contributed an example of their approach to this book. Both are so systematic that it is hard to avoid the conclusion that they are only presenting an "eclectic" approach (as they prefer to refer to their work) because they have an organizing principle that is based not on a theory of personality but rather on a theory of organizing data. For Lazarus, that theory consists of his BASIC ID, a comprehensive form of assessment that encompasses many dimensions of human functioning. However, the underlying role of social learning theory in this presentation would provide a good argument for calling this a form of assimilative integration, with social learning theory being the home theory and techniques from cognitive, experiential, and behavioral approaches being readily assimilated. For Beutler et al., the organizing principle is not truly a personality theory but rather a set of research findings such that the choice of intervention can be guided by established knowledge where it exists. Rather than developing a set of technical interventions, Beutler et al. seem to be presenting a set of psychological principles that can be applied within the therapeutic setting, thus leading to a systematic approach to behavior change. However, if this is a fair characterization, how different is this from a set of common factors? Beutler et al.'s approach is an outstanding example of how common factors, when the factor is a principle of change, can be implemented and form a school of integration, but this is not "eclecticism" in the standard usage of the term. These conclusions are not meant to disparage either Lazarus or Beutler et al., clinician–researchers who have made early, repeated, and important contributions to psychotherapy integration, but rather to point out the convergence that may be occurring on a more meta-integrative level. It may be the case that eclecticism is restricted to an undisciplined combination of techniques without a clear rationale other than the preference of the therapist and that the more elegant systems of technical integration draw their elegance from their systematization, an approach that elevates them above the merely eclectic.

The common factors approach was represented in this volume by Beitman, Soth, and Good. *Common factors* was defined in our introduction as those effective ingredients of therapy that occur in almost all approaches, regardless of the theoretical position taken by the therapist. There have been several systematic compilations of potential common factors, beginning with the early work of Rosenzweig (1936), followed by the seminal work of Frank (1973), a compilation and categorization of the common factors (Grencavage & Norcross, 1990), and an analysis of how the common factors may lead to change (Weinberger, 1993). However, there have not been many attempts to use the common factors in a systematic approach to change, as opposed to understanding such efforts in terms of the common factors that cut across orientations. One notable exception is the work of the late Sol Garfield (1992), but we were unable to ask him for a contribution. A reinterpretation of Beutler et al. provides another approach that can be classified under common factors. Beitman et al. represent another exception; they too present a clear and systematic approach based on a common factor, the future orientation of the therapeutic process. They develop a four-stage process to underline the teleological nature of change, drawing techniques from many orientations in doing so.

The similarities between the work of Beutler et al. and of Beitman et al. are striking, although they would ordinarily be categorized differently. Both Beutler, the technical eclectic, and Beitman, the common factors theorist, have an underlying theory of change (albeit a different one) rather than a personality theory. They systematically apply that conceptualization to their approach to psychotherapy. Should we describe Beutler as a common factors theorist, or Beitman as a technical eclectic, or does it matter what we call them as long as we recognize the similarity in what they do and the clear conception each has of the human change process? The critical point is the convergence of methods across apparent divides, a convergence that was initially noted in psychotherapy integration in general and now seems present in particular applications of psychotherapy integration.

The next group of contributions concerned assimilative integration. Assimilative integration occurs when a central theoretical position is maintained and techniques from other orientations are introduced as appropriate and helpful within the treatment. There were two exemplars of this approach. In the first, Stricker presented a case using the assimilative psychodynamic psychotherapy integration approach, an approach we have presented in greater detail elsewhere (Gold & Stricker, 2001; Stricker & Gold, 1996). In this approach, a relational psychodynamic approach is central, but techniques derived from cognitive–behavioral and experiential orientations were incorporated. The second example was Wolfe's approach, which is based on a theoretical conception of the anxiety disorders that is rooted in experiential theory but incorporates psychodynamic, cognitive–behavioral, behavioral, and biomedical techniques. This too has been presented in detail elsewhere (Wolfe, 2005).

There are striking ways in which assimilative integration can resemble sequential integration, in which one model is adopted and then followed by another. In assimilative integration, the home theoretical model is adopted, and it is followed by another model as treatment progresses, with the difference being that the second model is incorporated in the home treatment within assimilative integration, rather than practiced as such. The difference here is the variation in the meaning of the intervention depending on the context in which it is offered. The question of which sequential model might be best may depend on the relative advantages of sequencing. Researchers (see Shapiro & Firth, 1987; Shapiro & Firth-Cozens, 1990) may favor the sequence in which expressive models are followed by more behavioral ones, but this depends on whether the target is a symptom or a personality constellation. For personality, the expressive model, with other techniques incorporated, such as in assimilative psychodynamic psychotherapy integration, is helpful. However, for a symptom such as anxiety, Wolfe's approach, beginning with a systematic experiential formulation of the origin of that symptom, may be superior. As is consistently true within psychotherapy integration, no single approach can claim pride of place. These two assimilative approaches do not attempt to blend the theories, just the techniques, of the alternative orientations, and so the term *assimilative integration* seems well placed.

Most contributions represent several approaches to theoretical integration. In the first of these, Gold and Wachtel presented cyclical psychodynamics, the approach to integration that heralded the beginning of the current wave of the psychotherapy integration movement (Wachtel, 1977). In this approach, interpersonal and relational psychodynamic concepts are integrated with ideas drawn from social learning theory, experiential theory, and family systems theory. Watson then presented process-experiential psychotherapy, an emotion-focused approach that combines experiential ideas with those of attachment theory, interpersonal theory, and emotion theory. Allen has referred to his system as *unified therapy* (Allen, 2003). It is an approach designed for personality disordered adults and is an integration of family systems, cognitive–behavioral, and psychodynamic theories. Ryle and McCutcheon presented cognitive–analytic therapy, an approach (Ryle, 1990) that, as may be guessed from the title, integrates cognitive and psychodynamic theories. McCullough has an elaborate and well-defined model, cognitive behavioral analysis system of psychotherapy, designed for the integrated treatment of depression. This elegant approach (McCullough, 2000), which began here with a clear statement about the nature of depression, is rooted in social learning theory combined with interpersonal theory. Goldfried, who has referred to his approach as *cognitive–affective–relational–behavior therapy*, begins with a behavioral orientation but incorporates principles of change as a source of understanding and intervention in his clinical work. Fosha and Yeung described accelerated experiential–dynamic psychotherapy, an approach (Fosha, 2002) that combines attachment theory, emotion theory, short-term psychodynamic theory, and experiential and emotion-focused theories. Finally, Consoli and Chope presented contextual integrative therapy, an approach that seeks a synthesis through an emphasis on change processes and common factors.

All of these disparate types of therapy rely on more than one approach, drawing variously from psychodynamic, cognitive–behavioral, humanistic, systems, attachment, emotion, and change principle theory, among others. It is clear that the differences lie in the choices of which of the approaches to combine. However, there are also similarities that are not as obvious. Many of these theoretically integrated approaches might as easily be seen as assimilatively integrated, because one theory seems dominant in the integration. For example, cyclical psychodynamics clearly and explicitly is rooted in psychoanalysis. Others, such as cognitive–affective–relational–behavior therapy, may be seen as based on a common factors model, with the emphasis on change processes common to all treatment rather than on any orientation to psychotherapy. A good argument can be made that change processes should be the focus of psychotherapy integration, because there are no clear differences in outcome among orientations. Is there a clear rationale that would place McCullough's approach to depression in one category of psychotherapy integration and Wolfe's to anxiety in another? Does the work of Consoli and Chope differ categorically from that of Beutler? Most important, does it matter what category these approaches are placed in as long as it is clear that each of the authors is imaginatively cutting across narrow boundaries in order to provide a more effective means of treatment to the patient? The artificial nature of some of the categorization becomes clear as we study these fine exemplars of psychotherapy integration, differently categorized but similarly conceptualized.

It is at this point that we move to an examination of the presence of psychotherapy integration in family therapy. Nichols has combined psychodynamic theory, behavioral theory, and systems theory, and he has looked to research about the family life cycle to inform his approach to the treatment of families (Nichols, 1996). Looking at the theories being combined, there is some resemblance between this blend and cyclical psychodynamics, although the resulting combination differs. The use of information from general psychology is interesting and resembles the use of emotion and attachment theory by other contributors. This is a praiseworthy development, because it can place psychotherapy integration within the broader knowledge base of the discipline of psychology.

Lebow has referred to his approach as *integrative couple therapy*. He also began within the corpus of psychology, drawing on a multilevel understanding of human functioning. He has seen his major debt as being owed to other integrative theorists rather than to any pure form theorist, and if this is a development of a second generation of psychotherapy integration, it is an auspicious one. The field may be entering into a period of cumulative knowledge rather than relying solely on creative individuals working in a vacuum.

Patient-directed approaches might be classified within the common factors approach, with the critical factor being the therapeutic relationship. Rather than beginning with the therapist, who determines the needs of the patient and provides interventions accordingly, it begins with the needs of the patient, who then influences the therapist's choice of interventions. If the therapist is responsive, a good relationship (the critical common factor) will result, as will therapeutic progress. If the therapist insists on acting in a Procrustean manner, fitting the patient to the intervention, it is unlikely that much progress will be made. It should be noted that eclectic therapists long have advocated being responsive to the patient rather than being guided by a theory. Duncan, Sparks, and Miller have presented one such patient-directed approach, noting that by definition, this cannot be a system of therapy but rather an approach to it. Each patient, then, will be the recipient of a carefully crafted treatment geared toward his or her needs, and the only commonality is that the patient rather than a theory drives the treatment.

Bohart adopted a similar position in valuing the input and direction of the patient. The critical therapeutic factor is the relationship, and the critical change process is the active collaboration between the therapist and the patient. Although this approach seems linked to a client-centered system, that only is the case because of the emphasis on the empathic relationship. The primary conceptualization is in terms of learning opportunities rather than therapist interventions.

Gold's approach, on the surface, represents a familiar integrative psychodynamic approach. However, the difference is in the explicit value placed on the ability of the patient to suggest alterations in technique and the willingness of the therapist to follow that lead. The issue here, as with the other patient-centered approaches, is whether these represent a new approach to psychotherapy or a more standard approach with weight being given to the needs of the patient, a conception that certainly should not be revolutionary. Perhaps it is the imposition by some therapists of a preset system on the patient that makes it so important to attend to these theorists who remind us of the importance of listening to, and following the direction of, the patient we are trying to serve.

The concluding two chapters emphasized a philosophical approach to the psychotherapy endeavor. Anchin described his approach as being hermeneutically informed. Hermeneutics is a postmodern approach to knowledge that is in contrast to a more familiar scientific epistemology. It is rooted in the experience of the observer, with meaning related to the narrative truths that the patient tells. Anchin's approach does not reject science but rather expands on it as a way of knowing, also allowing information from less traditional sources. The body of psychological knowledge is respected and drawn on, but the patient also dictates the meaning of much that transpires, as is true of the patient-informed approaches.

Messer's presentation of contrasting visions of reality is an older and important one that already has exercised much influence on psychotherapy integration (Messer, 1992). The critical issue is not that these different visions make integration impossible but that different visions characterize different approaches, and the vision may make one orientation better suited for work with a particular patient than another. A clear understanding of these visions and their relationship to the different orientations is essential before attempting to integrate them.

CONCLUSION

Psychotherapy integration initially grew out of the recognition that the pure form approaches were only pure on paper and that practitioners were inclined to integrate in ways that were not described in the literature of the pure approach. It is ironic that the most significant conclusion that this book leads to is that psychotherapy integration itself may be undergoing an integrative process and that the four categories of approach may exist more clearly on paper than in the consulting room. This parallelism with schools of psychotherapy is striking, and it may be that psychotherapy is moving toward a position where practitioners are not at all bound by the confines of a taught system, whether that system be a pure form or an integrative form. The great success of the psychotherapy integration movement may be the disintegration of orientation barriers, whether that orientation is theoretical or technical.

The empirical findings about the role of experience in psychotherapy (Fiedler, 1950) are relevant to our observations about the unreliability of categorization within psychotherapy integration. This research about experience has demonstrated that as therapists gain in experience, they tend to move away from the purer theories and methods in which they were trained and toward more individualized models that are difficult to assign to any school of pure-form psychotherapy. Thus, experienced therapists have been found to resemble each other more than they resemble novices of the school in which the more seasoned person was originally trained. All of the contributing therapists in this volume are highly experienced, and despite their allegiances to their integrative models, have been shaped by clinical necessity and experience. Perhaps the blurring of the integrative boundaries that exists in these cases reflects these same blending processes.

We close with some words about the nature of categorization. In studying psychotherapy, it is unlikely that we can carve nature at its joints, because the categories do not exist in nature but are imposed by our linguistic systems. The linguistic system we choose may emphasize difference, thus producing more than 400 schools of psychotherapy and allowing for the categorization of many different approaches to psychotherapy integration. However, it also may emphasize sameness, in which case common factors, or basic principles of change, can underlie all attempts at psychotherapy. This is reminiscent of the conflict in biology between lumpers and splitters (Hey, 2001), a distinction based on the approach taken to recognizing differences or commonalities between organisms. Lumping has the problem of creating unwieldy definitions with categories having little in common. Splitting may lead to a large number of small categories, with a disregard of underlying similarities. Whether we choose to lump or split seems irrelevant to the task at hand; psychotherapy integration is a burgeoning and creative field, and the various contributors have demonstrated a wide variety of approaches that regardless of their similarities and differences bode well for the development of the field.

REFERENCES

Allen, D. M. (2003). *Psychotherapy of borderline personality disorder: An integrated approach.* Mahwah, NJ: Erlbaum.

Beutler, L. E., & Harwood, T. M. (2000). *Prescriptive psychotherapy: A practical guide to systematic treatment selection.* New York: Oxford University Press.

Chambless, D. C., & Ollendick, T. H. (2001). Empirically supported psychological interventions: Controversies and evidence. *Annual Review of Psychology, 52,* 685–716.

Fiedler, F. E. (1950). The concept of an ideal therapeutic relationship. *Journal of Consulting Psychology, 14,* 239–245.

Fosha, D. (2002). *The transforming power of affect: A model for accelerated change.* New York: Basic Books.

Frank, J. D. (1973). *Persuasion and healing* (2nd ed.). Baltimore: Johns Hopkins University Press.

Garfield, S. L. (1992). Eclectic psychotherapy: A common factors approach. In J. C. Norcross & M. R. Goldfried (Eds.), *Handbook of psychotherapy integration* (pp. 169–201). New York: Basic Books.

Gold, J., & Stricker, G. (2001). Relational psychoanalysis as a foundation of assimilative integration. *Journal of Psychotherapy Integration, 11,* 43–58.

Grencavage, L. M., & Norcross, J. C. (1990). Where are the commonalities among the therapeutic common factors? *Professional Psychology: Research and Practice, 21,* 372–378.

Hey, J. (2001). *Genes, categories, and species: The evolutionary and cognitive causes of the species problem.* New York: Oxford University Press.

Lazarus, A. A. (1981). *The practice of multimodal therapy.* New York: McGraw-Hill.

McCullough, J. P. (2000). *Treatment for chronic depression: Cognitive behavioral analysis system of psychotherapy (CBASP).* New York: Guilford Press.

Messer, S. B. (1992). A critical examination of belief structures in interpretive and eclectic psychotherapy. In J. C. Norcross & M. R. Goldfried (Eds.), *Handbook of psychotherapy integration* (pp. 130–165). New York: Basic Books.

Nichols, W. C. (1996). *Treating people in families: An integrative framework*. New York: Guilford Press.

Norcross, J. C. (Ed.). (2002). *Psychotherapy relationships that work: Therapist contributions and responsiveness to patients*. New York: Oxford University Press.

Norcross, J. C. (2005). A primer on psychotherapy integration. In J. C. Norcross & M. R. Goldfried (Eds.), *Handbook of psychotherapy integration* (2nd ed., pp. 3–23). New York: Oxford University Press.

Rosenzweig, S. (1936). Some implicit common factors in diverse methods of psychotherapy. *American Journal of Orthopsychiatry, 6,* 412–415.

Ryle, A. (1990). *Cognitive–analytic therapy: Active participation in change*. Chichester, England: Wiley.

Shapiro, D., & Firth, J. (1987). Prescriptive vs. exploratory psychotherapy: Outcomes of the Sheffield Psychotherapy Project. *British Journal of Psychiatry, 151,* 790–799.

Shapiro, D., & Firth-Cozens, J. (1990). Two-year follow-up of the Sheffield Psychotherapy Project. *British Journal of Psychiatry, 157,* 389–391.

Stricker, G., & Gold, J. R. (1996). Psychotherapy integration: An assimilative, psychodynamic approach. *Clinical Psychology: Science and Practice, 3,* 47–58.

Wachtel, P. L. (1977). *Psychoanalysis and behavior therapy: Toward an integration*. New York: Basic Books.

Wampold, B. E. (2001). *The great psychotherapy debate: Models, methods and findings*. Mahwah, NJ: Erlbaum.

Weinberger, J. (1993). Common factors in psychotherapy. In G. Stricker & J. R. Gold (Eds.), *Comprehensive handbook of psychotherapy integration* (pp. 43–56). New York: Plenum Press.

Wolfe, B. E. (2005). *Healing the wounds to the self: An integrative theory and therapy for complex anxiety disorders*. Washington, DC: American Psychological Association.

AUTHOR INDEX

Numbers in italics refer to listings in the references.

Lietaer, G., 90, *105*
London, P., 18, *28*
Low, J., 61, *63*
Luborsky, L., 4, *15*
Lushene, R., 37, *41*
Lyons, J., 29, *41*
Lyons-Ruth, K., *184*

Madsen, W. C., 45, *54*
Magnavita, J. J., 265, 276, *280*
Mahoney, M. J., 262, *280*
Mahrer, A. R., 91, *106*
Main, M., 172, *183*
Malik, M. L., 29, 33, 40, *41*
Manber, R. M., 139, *150*
Marks, I. M., 7, *15*
Martin, M., 262, *280*
Masters, K. S., 232, *239*
McCullough, J. P., Jr., 137–142, *150–151,*
      297, 301
McCullough, L., 165, 174, *183*
McCullough Vaillant, L., 165, *183*
McIntyre, L. C., 262, *280*
McKinney, M. K., 199, *210*
Mendelson, N. J., 156, *164*
Messer, S. B., 11, *14–15,* 55, *63,* 81, *87,* 212,
      222, 281–282, 290–291, 300, *302*
Miller, N. E., 6, *14*
Miller, S. D., 14, *15,* 212, 219, 222, 226–
      228, 231, 237–238, *239,* 253, *260*
Miller, W. R., 47, *54,* 165, 179, *183*
Millon, T., 271, 272, *280*
Milne, C. R., 36, *40*
Mintz, L. B., 44, *54*
Mishne, J. M., 205, *209*
Moleiro, C., 9, *14, 40*
Moran, J. C., 262, *280*
Morgan, A. C., *184*
Muran, J. C., 148, *151*

Nace, D. K., 228, *239*
Naham, J. P., *184*
Napier, A. Y., 201, *210*
Neimeyer, R. A., 262, *280*
Nemeroff, C. B., 138, *151*
Newman, C., 4, *15*
Nichols, W. C., 200–201, 203–207, *209–*
      210, 298, 302
Nielsen, S. L., *239–240*
Norcross, J. C., 4, 8, *15–16,* 188, *197,* 212,
      221–222, 294, 296, *301–302*

Ogles, B., 232, *239*
O'Hanlon, B., 45, *54*
Ollendick, T. H., 294, *301*
Orlinsky, D. E., 68, *77,* 212, 223, 227, *239,*
      241–242, *251*
Osimo, F., 165, *183*

Pace-Nichols, M. A., 201, *210*
Packer, M. J., 261–262, 264, *280*
Padawer, W., 153, *164*
Page, A. C., 162, *164*
Paivio, S. C., 165, *183*
Palmer, R. E., 261, 264, *280*
Panksepp, J., 165, *183*
Parks, B. K., 227, *239,* 241, *251*
Pedersen, P., 187, *197*
Penfold, K., 162, *164*
Perls, F. S., 90–92, *106,* 283, *291*
Person, E. S., 165, *183*
Piaget, J., 137–138, *151*
Pinsof, W. M., 212, *223*
Polkinghorne, D. E., 261, 263, *280*
Prochaska, J. O., 188, *197,* 207–208, *210*

Reese, E. P., 107, *120*
Reid, J. J. J. R., 187, *197*
Remer, P., 44, *54*
Rennie, D. L., 14, *16*
Reynolds, L. R., *239*
Rhodes, J. W., 7, *15*
Rice, J., 138, *150*
Rice, L. N., 89, 91, *105–106*
Rich, M., 192, *197*
Rogers, C. R., 44, *54,* 90, 283, *106, 291*
Rollnick, S., 47, *54*
Romanelli, R., 9, *14, 40*
Rosen, G., 186, *197*
Rosenthal, R., *15*
Rosenzweig, S., 6, 9, *16,* 186, *197,* 226, *240,*
      296, *302*
Rotter, J. B., 18, *28*
Rush, A. J., *151*
Ryle, A., 11, *16,* 61, *63,* 121, 123, 132, *136,*
      297, 302

Safran, J. D., 90, *105,* 148, *151*
Sager, C. J., 214, 220–221, *223*
Samoilov, A., 161, *164*
Sampson, H., 260, *260*
Sander, L. W., *184*
Santoro, S. O., 4, *16*
Schafer, R., 281, *291*

Schatzberg, A. F., *151*
Schmidt, J. A., 138, 140, 148, *150*
Schore, A. N., 166–167, *183*
Seligman, D. A., *15*
Sexton, T. L., 212, *221*
Shapiro, D., 57, 63, 297, *302*
Shapiro, R. W., 139, *150*
Siegel, D. J., 167, 172, *184*
Skinner, B. F., 138, *151*
Slipp, S., 113, *120*
Slowiaczek, M. L., 167, *183*
Smart, D. W., 239, *240*
Sorrell, R., 228, *239*
Soth, A. M., 45–46, *53*
Sotsky, S., *239*
Sparks, J. A., 226, 231, *239*
Sperry, L., 269, *280*
Spielberger, C. D., 37, *41*
Steer, R. A., 31, *40*
Stern, D. N., 165, *184*
Strenger, C., 283, *291*
Stricker, G., 4, 8, 11–14, *15–16*, 55–56, *63*,
    296, *301–302*
Stroebel, C., 195, *197*
Sullivan, H. S., 200, *210*

Tallman, K., 14, *14*, 241–242, 245, *251*, 253,
    260
Task Force on Promotion and Dissemination
    of Psychological Procedures, 286,
    291
Taylor, C., 262, *280*
Tellegen, A. M., 31, *40*
Teyber, E., 44, *54*
Thase, M. E., *151*
Thompson, J. B., 261–262, *280*
Thompson, L., 29, *40–41*
Tolle, E., 270, *280*
Tomkins, S. S., 165, *184*

Trevarthen, C., 167, *184*
Tronick, E. Z., 165, 166, *184*

Vagg, P. R., 37, *41*
van der Kolk, B. A., 168, *184*
Van Sant, G., 192, *197*
Vermeersch, D. A., *239–240*
Vivian, D., *150*

Wachtel, P. L., 6, 8, 11, *16*, 79–81, 87, 199,
    210, 212, 223, 283, 290, 297, *302*
Wachterhauser, B., 264, *280*
Wakefield, J., 264, *280*
Walsh, F., 212, *223*
Wampold, B. E., 186, *197*, 222, 226–227,
    240, 241, *251*, 294, *302*
Ward, C., 156, *164*
Watson, J. C., 89–92, *105–106*, 158, *164*,
    249, *251*
Weinberg, K., 166, *184*
Weinberger, J., 296, *302*
Weiss, J., 260, *260*
Whipple, J. L., 228, *239–240*
White, H., 283, *291*
Wile, D. B., 289, *291*
Williams, O. B., 31, 38, *41*
Williams, R. E., 186, *197*
Wilson, E. O., 108, *120*
Winokur, M., 281, *291*
Wise, S. L., 36, *40*
Wolfe, B. E., 65–66, 68, 72, *77*, 296, *302*
Worell, J., 44, *54*
Wyden, P., 217, *221*

Yamaguchi, J., *239*
Young, G., 262, *280*

Zur, O., 19, *28*

SUBJECT INDEX

Attention retraining, for social phobias, 74
Attunement (AEDP), 166
Avoidance, and anxiety disorders, 67

Bandura, Albert, 137
Bandura's self-efficacy theory, 195–196
BASIC ID, 295
    applicability of, to MMT, 20–26
    and multimodal therapy, 18–19
Beck Depression Inventory
    in cognitive–affective–relational–
      behavior therapy case study, 156
    STS case study use of, 31
Beck Depression Inventory—II, 148–149
Behavioral theory, 200
Behavior patterns, self-defeating/destructive,
    107
Behavior–psychodynamic sequence, 57
Behavior therapy, psychodynamic, 7
Betz's self-efficacy theory, 195–196
Blood phobia, 158, 162
Bodily experiences of affect, 175
Borderline personality disorder, patients with
    and multiple self states model, 124–125
    parental roles contributing to, 116
    and reciprocal role patterns, 124–125
    unified therapy case study for, 110–
      118
Breathing anxiety, 52
Breathing, diaphragmatic (DB), 72

Caretaker–child interactions. *See also* Par-
    ent–child relationships; Reciprocal
    role procedures
    in AEDP case example, 173
    dyadic experiences and regulation in,
      167–168
Case example(s)
    for accelerated experiential–dynamic
      psychotherapy, 172–181
    for assimilative integration, 68–75
    for assimilative psychodynamic psycho-
      therapy integration, 57–62
    for client-directed, outcome-informed
      approach, 229 238
    for cognitive–affective–relational–be-
      havior therapy, 154–163
    for cognitive analytic theory, 126–136
    for cognitive behavioral analysis system
      of psychotherapy, 139–149
    for contextual integrative psycho-
      therapy, 188–196

    for contrasting visions of reality, 284–
      290
    for cyclical psychodynamic psycho-
      therapy, 81–87
    for future-oriented psychotherapy inte-
      gration, 48–53
    for multimodal therapy, 20–26
    for patient-initiated integration, 255–
      260
    for process-experiential therapy, 91–103
    review of, 295–300
    for systematic treatment selection, 31–
      40
    for unified therapy, 110–118
CAT. *See* Cognitive analytic therapy
Categorical thinking, 245, 300–301
Central cognition, 22
Change. *See also* Client's theory of change
    "intentional change," 207
    mechanisms for, in assimilative integra-
      tion case study, 76
    mechanisms for, in hermeneutic ap-
      proach case study, 277
    mechanisms for, in integrative family
      therapy, 206–207
    mechanisms for, in unified therapy case
      study, 118
    patient responsibility for, 207
Characteristic style markers, 92
Child abuse, in process-experiential therapy
    case study, 98–99
Childhood experiences, and cyclical psycho-
    dynamic therapy, 81
Child sexual abuse, unified therapy for, 111
Chronic depression, cognitive behavioral
    analysis case study of client with,
    138–139
Classical conditioning, 6
Client
    as active self-healer, 241–251
    as integrative variable, 228
Client-based outcome and alliance feedback,
    228
Client-centered integrative therapy, 225–
    238. *See also* Patient-initiated inte-
    gration
    case example for, 243–251
    client-directed, outcome-informed ap-
      proach, 226–228
    coconstructive dialogue, in case ex-
      ample, 247–249
    empathic workspace, 242

empathic workspace, in case example, 246–247
and self-criticism, 238
and structured exercises for exploration, 249–250
Client-directed, outcome-informed approach, 226–228
case example, 229–238
progress in, 235
Client's theory of change, 227, 229–231
Clinical interactions, in MMT case study, 21–26
Clinician rating form, STS, 31
Cluster B personality disorder, case study of client with, 107–119
Cluster C personality disorders, 108
Coconstructive dialogue, 247–249
Codes of engagement markers, 92
Cogitation, obsessive, 67
Cognitive–affective–relational–behavior therapy, 153–163, 297
clinical case, 154–163
empty chair exercise, in case study, 158
relaxation training, in case study, 162–163
role-playing, in case study, 161
therapeutic alliance, 156
therapeutic relationships in, 153–154
two-chair dialogue, in case study, 161–162
Cognitive analytic theory
case example for, 126–136
developments of, 123
diagnosis of, 124–125
and goodbye letters, 61
referral, assessment, and case formulation in, 126–129
and reformulation letter, 123
and self processes, 125
Cognitive analytic therapy (CAT), 121–136
Cognitive behavioral analysis system of psychotherapy (CBASP), 137–149
case example for, 139–149
interpersonal discrimination exercise, 142, 146–148
situational analysis exercise, 142–146
treatment goal of, 138
Cognitive–behavioral intervention, 208
Cognitive–behavioral techniques
role-playing, 56
used in future-oriented psychotherapy case study, 50, 51

Cognitive–behavioral therapy
and direct tutoring, 243
and future-oriented psychotherapy integration, 44
in integrative family therapy case example, 208
Cognitive–emotive development, 137
Cognitive interventions, in three-tier approach to assimilative psychodynamic psychotherapy integration, 61–62
Cognitive–perceptual reorientation, 85
Cognitive therapy, dyadic, 219
Comic vision, 282–283, 286–287
Commission, errors of, 175
Committee for Physicians' Health (CPH), 266–267
Common factors integration, 9–10, 294, 296
approach to psychotherapy integration, 6
and future-oriented psychotherapy, 43–53
hypothesis formulation for, 6
Communication process, in integrative couple therapy, 217
Communication, sign-mediated, 124
Conflict, triangle of, 168–169
Contextual integrative psychotherapy, 185–196, 298
case example for, 188–196
and shared worldviews, 192–193
treatment plan for, in case study, 193–194
and treatment with family members, 194
and working alliance, 192–193
Contrasting visions of reality, 281–290, 300
case study for, 284–290
comic vision, 282–283, 286–287
ironic vision, 283–284, 288–290
romantic vision, 283, 287–288
tragic vision, 282, 285–286
Conversational therapy, 19
Coping style assessment, 34–35
Core affective experiences, 172, 178
Core state experiences, 172, 179–181
Corrective emotional experiences, 7, 154
in assimilative psychodynamic psychotherapy integration, 56
in assimilative psychodynamic psychotherapy integration case study, 59, 62
in cognitive–affective–relational–behavior therapy case study, 162

in hermeneutic approach to psychotherapy, 276
Countertransference and transference. *See*
Transference–countertransference
interaction
Couple therapy. *See* Integrative couple
therapy
CPH (Committee for Physicians' Health),
266–267
Cultural revolution, effect on family relationships, 109
Cyclical psychodynamic psychotherapy
and active interventions, 81
and anxiety, 80
case example, 81–87
and inferred unconscious processes,
80
Cyclical psychodynamics, 8, 79
Cyclical psychodynamic theory
defined, 79
Wachtel's, 11

DB. *See* Diaphragmatic breathing
Depression. *See also under* Chronic depres-
sion; Major depression
assimilative psychodynamic psycho-
therapy integration case study of cli-
ent with, 57–62
Beck Depression Inventory, 31, 156
Beck Depression Inventory—II, 148–
149
DSM–IV "double depression," in
CBASP case study, 139–149
Treatment of Depression Collaborative
Research Project, 227
Desensitization techniques, systematic, 47
Dialogic sequence analysis, 124
Diaphragmatic breathing (DB)
used in cyclical psychodynamic therapy
case study, 85
used in public-speaking phobia treat-
ment, case study, 72
Dilemmas, in pre- and posttherapy grids, 122
Direct behavioral intervention, 62
Direct tutoring, and cognitive behavior
therapy, 243
Discrimination tasks, 147–148
Disruption (AEDP), 166
Distress levels, and systematic treatment se-
lection, 37–39
Dollard, John, 6
"Double depression," patient with, 139–149

Dowd Trait Reactance Scale, STS case study
use of, 36
DSM–IV "double depression," patient with,
139–149
Dyadic affect regulation, 167–170
Dyadic cognitive therapy, 219
Dyadic experiences, in caretaker–child interactions, 167–168
Dynamic psychotherapy, 121
Dysfunctional behavior, by family members,
109
Dysthymia, patients with
in cognitive behavioral analysis system
of psychotherapy case study, 139–
149
unified therapy case study for, 110–118

Early attachment histories, in EFT, 91
Early experiences
internalization of, 123
reciprocal role patterns affecting, 124–
125
Eclecticism, 295. *See also* Technical eclecticism
Eclectic psychotherapy, technically. *See*
Technically eclectic psychotherapy
EFT. *See* Emotion-focused therapy
Ego-dystonic defenses, 175
Either–or thinking, 245
Elicitation phase, 142–144
Emotional arousal, dyadic regulation of, 166–
172
Emotional experiences, corrective. *See* Corrective emotional experiences
Emotion-focused therapy (EFT), 89, 91. *See
also* Process-experiential therapy
and early attachment histories, 91
and empathic attunement, 90
exploratory response style for, 91
and marker-guided interventions, 91
task principles of, 90–91
and the therapeutic relationship, 90, 91
treatment principles of, 90–92
Empathic attunement
in EFT, 90
in EFT case study, 90
Empathic workspace, 242, 246–247
Empathy, experiential. *See* Experiential empathy
Empty chair technique

in cognitive–affective–relational–behavior therapy case study, 158
in patient-initiated integration case study, 258
in process-experiential therapy case study, 94–96, 104
used in future-oriented psychotherapy case study, 50
Environmental disconnection, in CBASP case study, 140
Errors of commission, 175
Etiological theory, 65
Events, situations, actions, and subjective experience
interpretations of, 264
meanings of, 263–264
understanding in relation to, 262–263
Expectation videos, 45
identifying problematic, 46–47, 50–51
modifying/constructing, 47–48, 51–53
systematic desensitization techniques for, 47
Experiential empathy, 104
Experiential meaning, 262
Experiential therapy. See Emotion-focused therapy; Process-experiential therapy
Exploratory response style, 91
Extratherapy interventions, 129

Fairbarn's object relations theory, 200
"False self," in therapeutic relationship, 118
Family dysfunction, and unified therapy, 107
Family members, treatment with, 194
Family relationships. See also Parent–child relationships
in cognitive analytic theory case example, 126
dysfunctional behavior within, 109
effected by cultural revolution, 109
metacommunicative discussions of, 118
uncovering emotional experience in, case study, 175–178
and unified therapy, 107, 109
Family systems-based intervention, 208
Family systems theory, 200–201
Family therapy model, 201, 298
Feedback, contributing to therapeutic relationships, 228
Felt-in-the-body affective experience, 173–174

Feminism, psychotherapists oriented toward, 44
Focusing technique, Wolfe's, 68
Frank's State–Trait Anxiety Inventory State score, 36
French, Thomas, 6, 7
Functional impairments assessment, 33–34
Future, faulty images of, 46
Future-oriented psychotherapy integration model, 45–48
activating the observing self in, 46, 49–50
applied to clients with major depression, 49–53
applied to clients with panic disorders, 49–53
case example, 48–53
and problematic expectation videos, 46–48, 50–53
Future-oriented videos, 45. See also Expectation videos

Gender roles, in unified therapy case study, 108–109
Generalized anxiety disorder, 244
General learning theory, 208
Good-Bye Letter, Ryle's, 61
Good-bye letters
in cognitive analytic theory case study, 135–136
of patient to therapist, 136
of therapist to patient, 135–136
Grid techniques. See Pre- and posttherapy grids
Grief, clients exhibiting, 44

Healing affects, 171
Helplessness, feelings of, 140
Here-and-now-processing, 44
Hermeneutic approach to inquiry, 262
Hermeneutic approach to psychotherapy, 266
case example for, 266–279
corrective emotional experiences in, 276
therapeutic relationships in, 275–277
Hermeneutic process, 261–264
Hermeneutics approach, 299
Hopelessness, feelings of, 140
Hypermasculinity, in assimilative integration case study, 70

IDE. *See* Interpersonal discrimination exercise
"I" language, in process-experiential therapy case study, 103
Impact Message Inventory (IMI), in CBASP case study, 140
Impression management
    and anxiety disorders, 67
    as interpersonal strategy for social phobias, 70–71
    for social phobias, 74
Inadequacy, feelings of
    in anxiety disorders, 66
    and masculinity, in unified therapy case study, 70
    self-acceptance strategy for, 74
Individualism, cultural effect on familial roles, 108
Inferred unconscious processes, 80
Inquiry, hermeneutic approach to, 262
Integration. *See specific types, e.g.:* Assimilative integration
Integrative approach
    effect of, on patient's psychopathology, 206
    growth perspective embodied in, 208
Integrative couple therapy, 213–221, 298–299
    case example, 214–221
    dyadic cognitive therapy in, 219
    therapeutic alliance in, 214–215
Integrative family therapy, 199–208
    case example for, 201–208
    mechanisms for change in, 206–207
    transference in, 207–208
Integrative psychotherapy, for treatment of anxiety disorders, 67–68
Integrative psychotherapy model, 67–68
Integrative therapy, 12, 293–301
Integrative therapy model, 133
Intellectual competence, conflict with masculinity, in case study, 70
"Intentional change," 207
Interaction cycles, 84
Interactions, clinical, 21–26
Interactive learning, 242
Interpersonal discrimination exercise (IDE)
    in CBASP case study, 142, 146–148
    discrimination task, 147–148
Interpersonal strategies, for social phobias, 70–71
Interpersonal theory, 200
Interpersonal therapists, use of here-and-now-processing by, 44

Interpretationism, 262
Interpretations of events, situations, actions, and subjective experience, 264
Interventions, 212–213
    family systems-based, 208
    in MMT case study, 21–26
    selection of, in integrative family therapy, 208
    selection of, in unified therapy case study, 118
    sequencing of, in assimilative integration case study, 75
Ironic vision, 283–284, 288–290

Kelly's personal construct theory, 121
Kiesler Impact Message Inventory (IMI), 140
Kin selection, 108

Learning, interactive, 242
Levels of resistance. *See* Resistance level, and systematic treatment selection

Major depression, future-oriented psychotherapy integration model applied to clients with, 49–53
"Marital contract," 221
Marker-guided interventions, 91
Markers
    of characteristic style, 92
    defined, 91
    micro markers, 91
    modes of engagement, 92
    task markers, 92
Masculinity
    conflict with intellectual competence, in case study, 70
    and inadequacy, in unified therapy case study, 70
Meanings
    of events, situations, actions, and subjective experience, 263–264
    experiential, 262
Memory, procedural. *See* Procedural memory
Metacommunicative strategy
    for family relationship discussions, 118
    in unified therapy case study, 118
Meta-integration, 293–301
Meta-model, 244
Micro markers, 91
Miller, Neal, 6
Minnesota Multiphasic Personality Inventory—2 (MMPI–2), 31, 36

MMT. *See* Multimodal therapy
Motivation/subjective distress, 37, 38
Multicultural orientations, psychotherapists oriented towards, 44
Multimodal Life History Interview, used in MMT case example, 20–21
Multimodal therapy (MMT), 9, 17–27
    and BASIC ID, 18–19
    case example, 20–26
    conversational therapy vs., 19
    and technical eclecticism, 9
    and technically eclectic psychotherapy, 9
    trimodal, 18
Multiple self states model, 124–125

Negative affective states, 270
"Next day imagining," 47

Object relations ideas, 123
Object relations theory, 200
Observing self, in future-oriented psycho- therapy, 46, 49–50
Obsessive cogitation, 67
Outcome Rating Scale (ORS), 231–232, 235, 237

Panic attacks, fear of, 68–75
Panic disorders, clients with
    in contextual integrative psychotherapy case study, 189–196
    future-oriented psychotherapy applied to, 49–53
Panic, redefining for patient, 75
Parent–child relationships. *See also* Family relationships; Reciprocal role proce- dures
    and adoption, 158–160
    in CBASP case study, 141
    in cognitive–affective–relational–be- havior therapy case study, 158–160
    role relationships effect within, 108–109
    sexual abuse in, 111
Parental roles
    and ambivalence, 116
    and borderline personality disorder, 116
    conflicted, 109
Patient-directed approaches, 299
Patient-initiated integration, 253–260. *See also* Client-centered integrative therapy
    case example for, 255–260

empty chair dialogue, in case study, 258
    therapeutic relationships in, 254
    and transference, 256
Patient Performance Rating Form, 146
Patient's letter, in cognitive analytic theory case example, 136
Pavlov, Ivan, 6
Perceived functionality, 139
Perceptual reorientation. *See* Cognitive– perceptual reorientation
Personal construct theory, 121
Personal data questionnaire, 156–157
Personality disorders
    Cluster B, 107–108
    Cluster C, 108
    cognitive analytic theory case study for adolescent with, 126–129
Personality theory, 8
Person-centered therapy, 44
PET. *See* Process-experiential therapy
Philosophical approaches, 299
Phobias. *See specific types, e.g.:* Blood pho- bia
Physical relaxation strategies, used in con- textual integrative psychotherapy case study, 195
Piaget, Jean, 137
Positive expectations, 153
Postmodern thinking, 262
Posttherapy grids. *See* Pre- and posttherapy grids
Pre- and posttherapy grids, 121–122
    and dilemmas, 122
    procedural sequence in, 122
    and snags, 122
    and traps, 122
Prescriptive psychotherapy, 9
Prizing (term), 7
Problem complexity, 194–196
Problem severity, 194–196
Procedural memory, 45, 47
Procedural sequence, in grid techniques, 122
Process-experiential therapy (PET), 89. *See also* Emotion-focused therapy
    case example, 91–103
    and intense feelings, 96
    and the therapeutic process, 94–103
Process-guiding relational stance, for EFT, 91
Psychoanalysis and Behavior Therapy: Toward Integration, 8
Psychodynamic–behavioral sequence, 57

Self-at-best, 168–169
Self-at-worst, 168–170
Self-criticism, clients exhibiting
    client-centered integrative therapy for,
        238, 245
    in PET case study, 95
Self-destructive behavior patterns, unified
        therapy for, 107
Self-efficacy theories, 195–196
Self-endangerment, and anxiety disorders,
        66–67
Self-experiencing, and assimilative integra-
        tion case study, 69–70
Self-fulfilling prophesy, 60
Self-management, and reciprocal role proce-
        dures, 123
Self-preoccupation, 67
Self processes, and cognitive analytic theory,
        125
Self-relational processes, 270–271
Self-views, and assimilative integration case
        study, 73
Self-wounds, 76
    in assimilative integration case study,
        69
    eliciting, in assimilative integration case
        study, 72–73
    healing, in assimilative integration case
        study, 73–75
Sequence analysis, dialogic, 124
Sequential integration, 297
Session Rating Scale (SRS), 231–232, 235,
        238
Severe anxiety, 66
Sexual abuse, in unified therapy case study,
        111
Shared worldviews, 192–193
Short-circuit negative affectivity, 270
Sign-mediated communication, 124
Situational analysis (SA)
    action interpretation in exercise for, 145
    and CBASP, 142–146
    and cognitive behavioral analysis system
        of psychotherapy, 138–139
    elicitation phase of, 142–144
    remediation phase of, 144–146
Snags, in pre- and posttherapy grids, 122
Social and cognitive learning theory, 18
Social learning theory, 137
Social phobias. See also specific types, e.g.:
        Public speaking disorders
    and anxiety disorders, 67

assimilative integration case example of,
        68–75
attention retraining for, 74
impression management for, 74
and self-wounds, 66
The Society for the Exploration of Psycho-
        therapy Integration, 8
"Speaker–listener technique," 216
SRS. See Session Rating Scale
State–Trait Anxiety Inventory State score.
        See Frank's State–Trait Anxiety In-
        ventory State score
Structured exercises for exploration, 249–250
STS. See Systematic treatment selection
STS Clinician rating form, 31
Subjective distress, 37, 38
Substance abuse, hermeneutics approach case
        study for client with, 266–279
Sullivan's interpersonal theory, 200
Symptoms, treatment of vs. underlying de-
        terminants, 76
Systematic desensitization techniques, for
        expectation videos, 47
Systematic evocative unfolding, 97
Systematic treatment selection (STS), 29–40
    case example of, 31–40
    coping style assessment, 34–35
    distress levels, 37–39
    four-step process for, 30
    functional impairments assessment, 33–
        34
    motivation/subjective distress, 37, 38
    and resistance levels, 36–37, 39
    for technical eclecticism, 29–40
    treatment intensity level, 38–39

"Task focus," 245
Task markers, 92
Technical eclecticism, 9, 294, 296
    and MMT, 9, 17–27
    and prescriptive psychotherapy, 9
    STS, 29–40
    theoretical integration vs., 18
Technical integration, 167
Technically eclectic psychotherapy, 9
Tension, MMT strategy used for, 21
Theoretical integration, 8, 10–11
    and assimilative integration, 294
    and cognitive analytic therapy, 121–136
    and cyclical psychodynamics, 79–87
    and process-experiential therapy, 89–
        105

Verstehen, 264
Videos. *See* Expectation videos
Visions of life, 281
Visions of reality. *See* Contrasting visions of reality

Wachtel's cyclical psychodynamic theory, 11
Wolf's focusing technique, 68

Working alliance, 192–193. *See also* Therapeutic relationships/alliances
Worry, clients exhibiting, 101

Yeung, Danny, 173

ABOUT THE EDITORS

George Stricker, PhD, has been professor of psychology at Argosy University/Washington, DC, since 2004. He taught at Adelphi University from 1963 to 2004, where he was dean of the Derner Institute and served as Distinguished Research Professor of Psychology. He received a PhD in clinical psychology from the University of Rochester in 1960 and an honorary PsyD from the Illinois School of Professional Psychology, Meadows Campus, in 1997. Dr. Stricker is a diplomate in clinical psychology and was elected Distinguished Practitioner in Psychology. He received the American Psychological Association (APA) Award for Distinguished Contribution to Applied Psychology in 1990, the APA Award for Distinguished Career Contributions to Education and Training in Psychology in 1995, the National Council of Schools and Programs of Professional Psychology Award for Distinguished Contribution to Education and Professional Psychology in 1998, the Allen V. Williams Memorial Award from the New York State Psychological Association in 1999, the Florence Halpern Award for Distinguished Professional Contributions in Clinical Psychology from the Society of Clinical Psychology (Division 12) in 2002, and the Bruno Klopfer Lifetime Achievement Award from the Society for Personality Assessment in 2005. He has been president of the Society of Clinical Psychology of the APA, the Society for Personality Assessment, the New York State Psychological Association, and the National Council of Schools of Professional Psychology. Dr. Stricker's most recent books are *Comprehensive Handbook of Psychotherapy Integration*, with Jerry Gold, and *The Scientific Practice of Professional Psychology*, with Steven Trierweiler.

Jerry Gold, PhD, is the author of *Key Concepts in Psychotherapy Integration*; coeditor, with George Stricker, of the *Comprehensive Handbook of Psychotherapy Integration*; and editor of the *Journal of Psychotherapy Integration*. He was associate editor of the *Journal of Integrative and Eclectic Psychotherapy*, and he is a member of the editorial board of PsycCRITIQUES/*Contemporary Psychology*. He received his PhD in clinical psychology from the Institute of Advanced Psychological Studies, where he is professor of psychology and chair of the undergraduate program in psychology. He completed psychoanalytic training at Adelphi University's postdoctoral program in psychoanalysis, and he is a faculty member and supervisor in the program and in the postdoctoral program in couples and family therapy.